HISTORIC PHOTOS OF
OREGON

TEXT AND CAPTIONS BY WILLIAM C. STACK

TURNER
PUBLISHING COMPANY

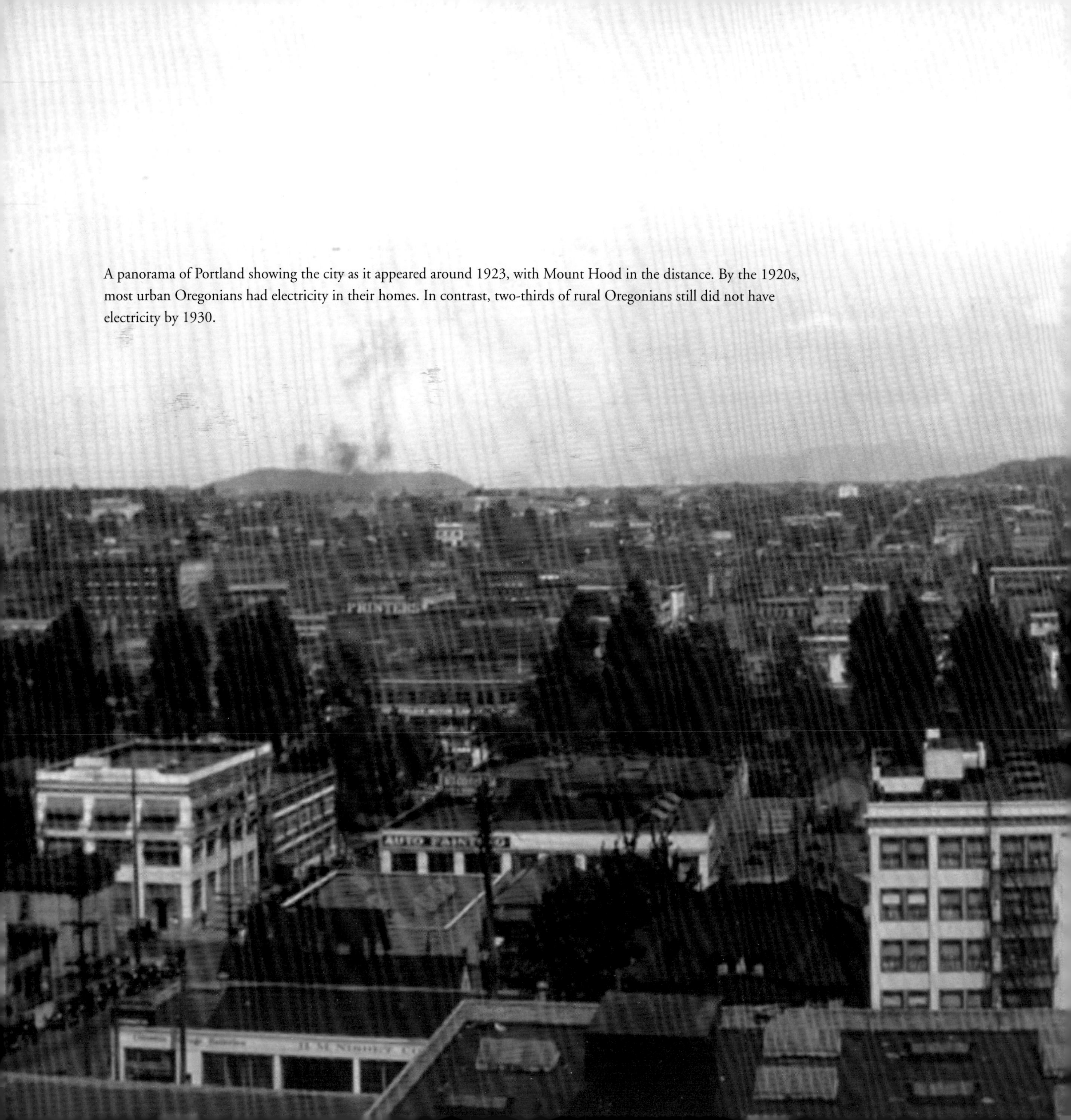

A panorama of Portland showing the city as it appeared around 1923, with Mount Hood in the distance. By the 1920s, most urban Oregonians had electricity in their homes. In contrast, two-thirds of rural Oregonians still did not have electricity by 1930.

HISTORIC PHOTOS OF
OREGON

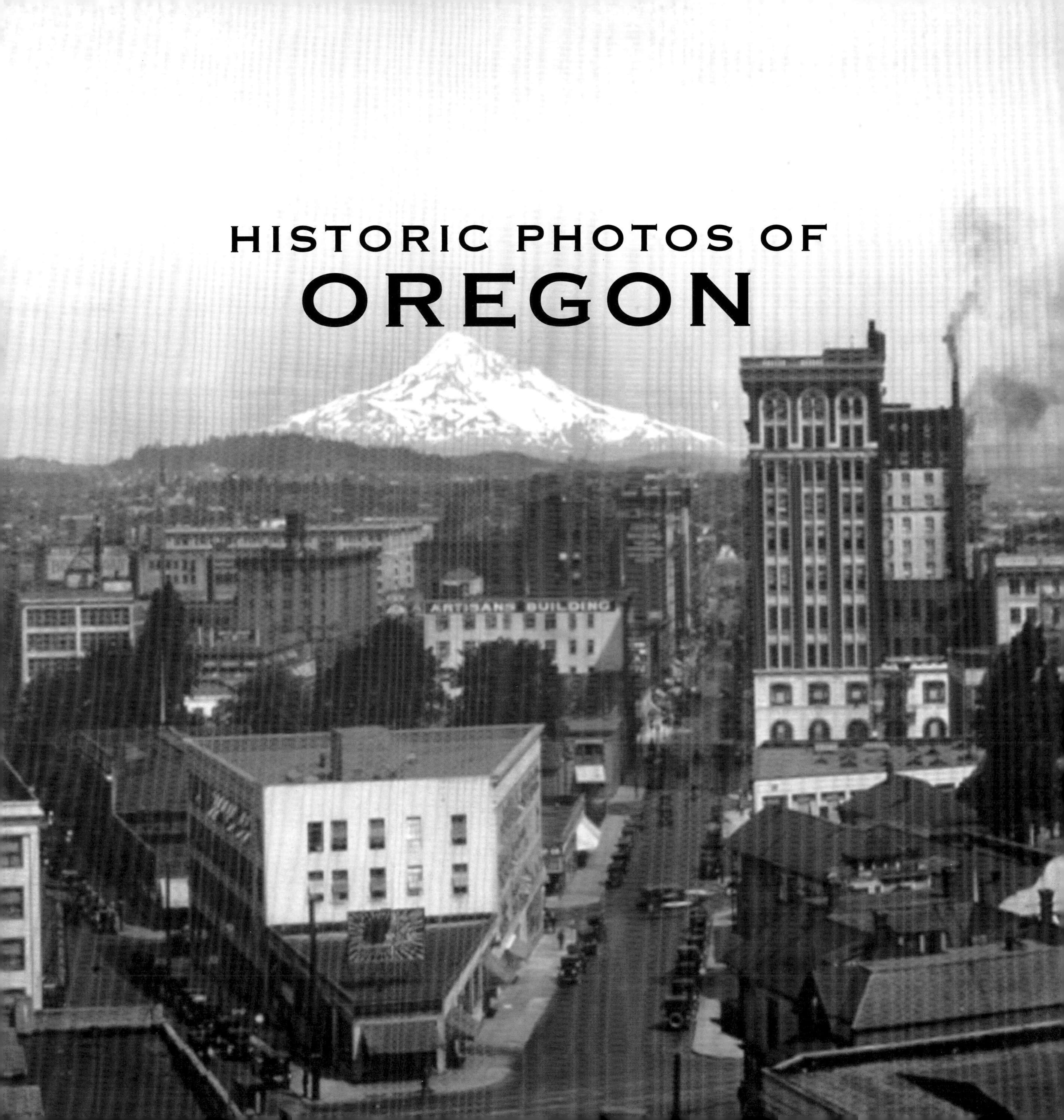

Turner Publishing Company
200 4th Avenue North • Suite 950
Nashville, Tennessee 37219
(615) 255-2665

www.turnerpublishing.com

Historic Photos of Oregon

Library of Congress Control Number: 2009933007

ISBN: 978-1-59652-556-6

Printed in China

10 11 12 13 14 15 16—0 9 8 7 6 5 4 3 2 1

Contents

Acknowledgments vii

Preface viii

Early Inhabitants and Newcomers (1860–1899) 1

Challenges and Opportunities (1900–1919) 31

Between the Wars (1920–1940) 103

The War Years (1941–1945) 155

Vignettes of Modern Times (1946–1971) 187

Notes on the Photographs 199

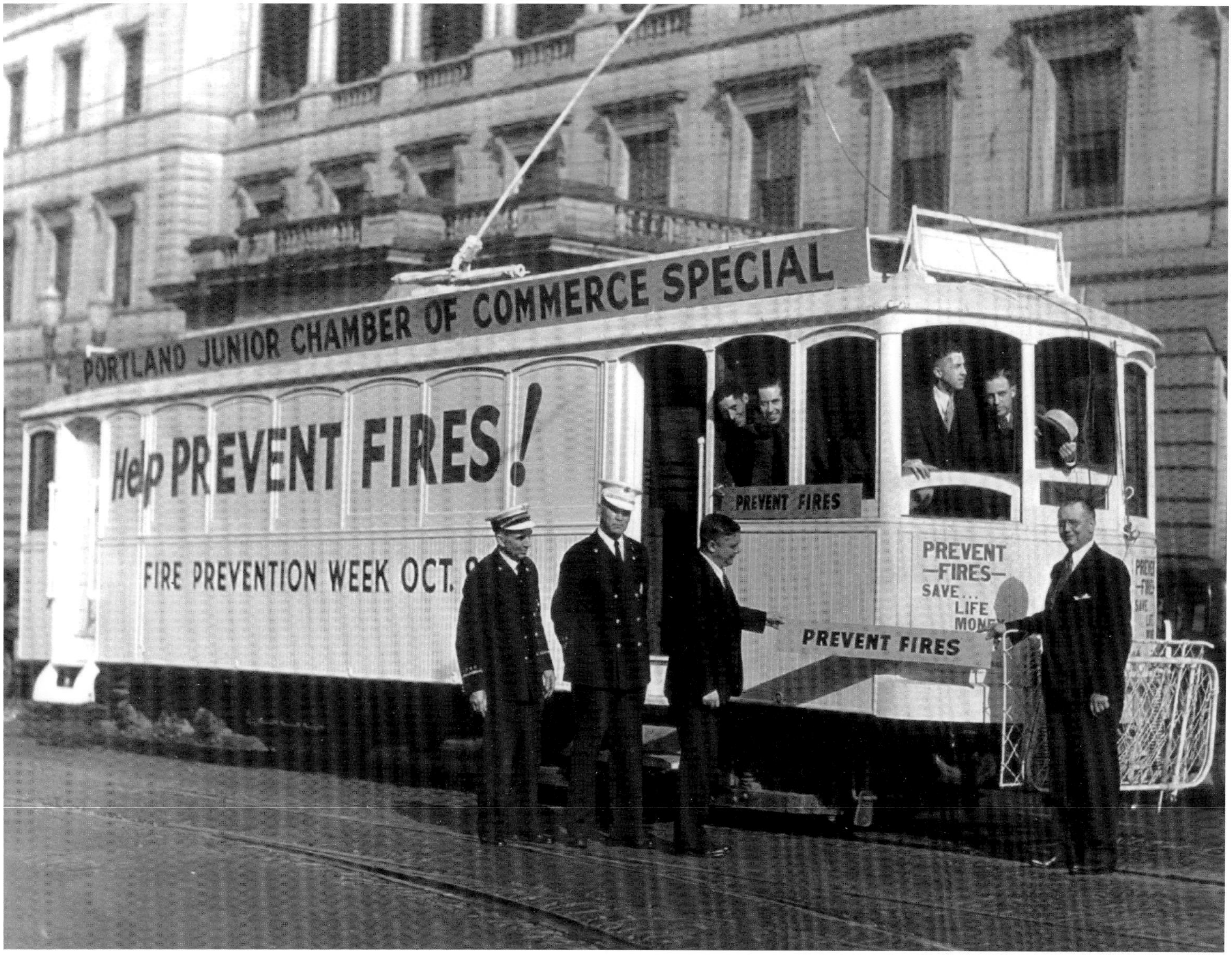

A Junior Chamber of Commerce streetcar advertises Fire Prevention Week in Portland.

Acknowledgments

This volume, *Historic Photographs of Oregon,* is the result of the cooperation and efforts of many individuals and organizations. It is with great thanks that we acknowledge the valuable contribution of the following for their generous support:

Library of Congress
University of Oregon Library

The writer would also like to thank these individuals for their assistance in making this book possible:

Mary A. Lindsley
Rebecca V. Shoemaker
Madeleine J. Stack

Preface

The state of Oregon presents a compelling story, and the effort to tell that story in 200 photographs and captions poses a challenging task. This pictorial history of Oregon is an attempt to present the main political, cultural, and economic themes in the state from the 1860s to the 1970s, chronicling the efforts of individuals, both well known and obscure, who have made Oregon what it is today. Early on, the region was home to the Nez Perce, Kalapuya, Umpqua, Klamath, and Chinook. After settlers arrived, Oregon became known for its economic opportunities, most notably in farming, mining, fishing, canning, ranching, and logging. Oregon achieved statehood in 1859, and from that year forward, the history of the state was marked by the coming of the railroads, an abundance of natural resources, Bonneville Dam, entrepreneurs, immigrants, labor difficulties, and a panoply of fascinating characters and events that together would begin to shape its colorful portrait as one of today's fifty states in the union.

The nearly 200 images presented here include several photographs by two of America's most famous photographers, Edward S. Curtis and Dorothea Lange. Curtis's photographs of the Chinook, Klamath, Umatilla, and Cayuse tribes in southern and eastern Oregon illustrate their dress and lifestyle with the haunting images of Crater Lake, the forest, and Klamath Basin and give a keen view of the area. Dorothea Lange's images of southern and eastern Oregon during the Great Depression give the viewer a glimpse of the hardscrabble lives and poor living conditions common among Americans living through the era. Lange's photographs also convey a brighter side to the era, depicting the daily lives of average rural and urban Americans in a way that shows their inner strength, pride, and joy.

The photographs in this book are organized into five chronological eras. The first section covers the period from the 1860s to 1899. Encounters between early Americans and the settlers moving into their ancestral lands are chronicled in these images. The second section spans the period from 1900 to 1919 and focuses on the development of river, railroad, fishing, timber, and agricultural commerce, which helped Oregon's population to expand in the twentieth century. During this era, Oregon was attempting to deliver a message of its importance to the rest of the United States. The third section concentrates on the period between the world wars, from 1920 to 1940. New rail transportation, New Deal building projects, and highways are shown as the state pursued growth during the twentieth century. The fourth section focuses on the World War II era, from 1941 to 1945. This section shows the growth of the Pacific Northwest and its connections to the popular culture of the western United States of that day. Oregon retained its rural flavor through such events as Fourth of July parades and carnivals. In contrast, the war effort required Oregonians to sacrifice, contributing to the defense of the nation through building ordnance depots, ships at the Kaiser Shipyards, and other work. The final section of the book samples the postwar era from 1946 to 1971. The images in this section illustrate subjects like the destruction of Celilo Falls on the Columbia River, and the social, cultural, economic, and technological changes of the era that affected the state.

With the exception of touching up imperfections that have accrued with the passage of time and cropping where necessary, no changes to the photographs have been made. The focus and clarity of many images is limited by the technology and the ability of the photographer at the time they were taken.

It is hoped that this collection of photographs will give the reader the rare opportunity to see the natural beauty of remarkable and unique Oregon, and how it fits into the overall history and culture of the United States.

—William C. Stack

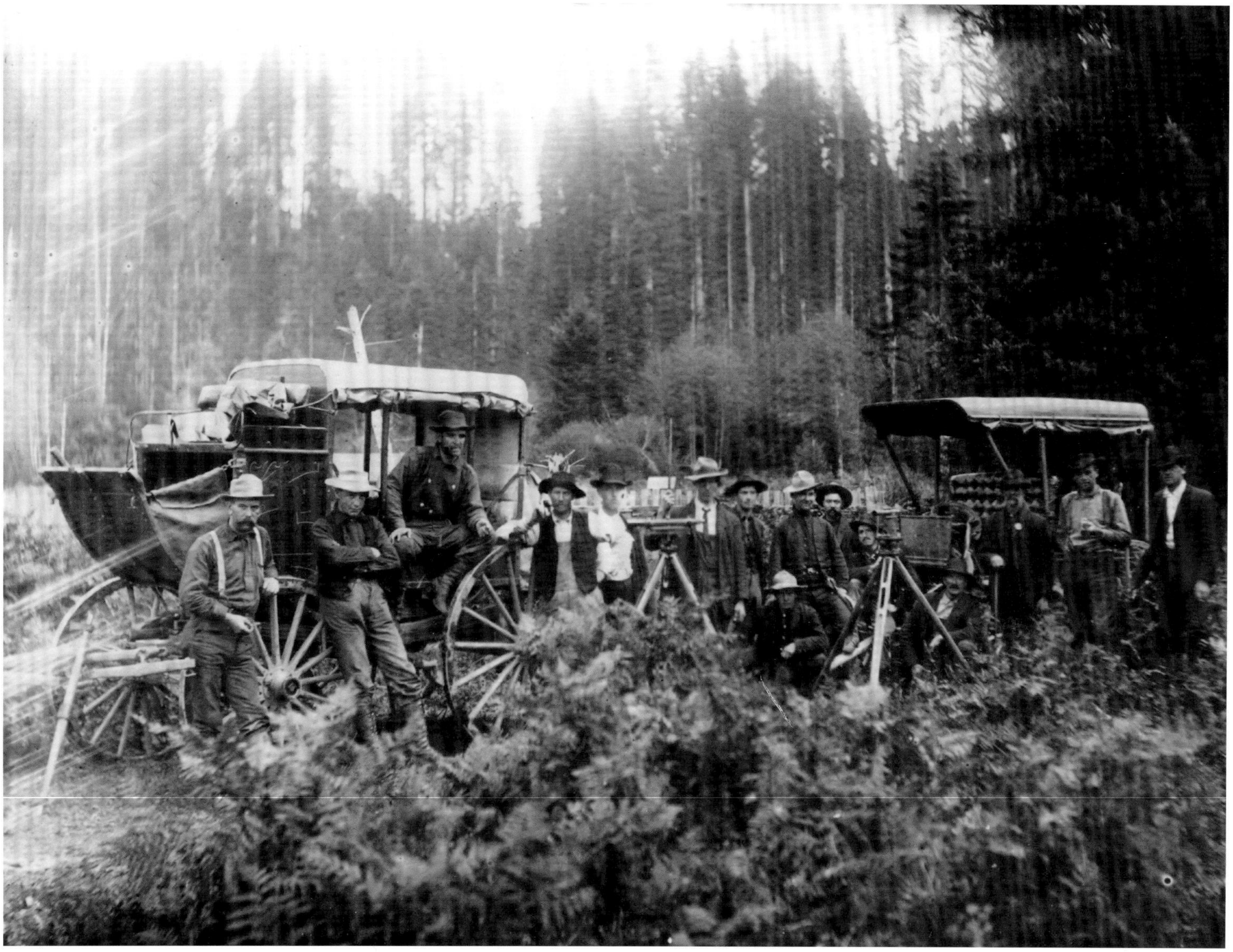

Surveying crews helped determine the routes railroad lines would follow. Posing for a group shot beside their vehicles and equipment, this crew is at work surveying a route between Grants Pass, Oregon, and Crescent City, California.

Early Inhabitants and Newcomers

(1860–1899)

The historical origins of the land that became the state of Oregon begin with the early Americans who populated the region for 10,000 years prior to the coming of other peoples. Early European explorations began with rumored sightings by the Spanish and English from sailing ships during the sixteenth century. A little more than two hundred years later, the Lewis and Clark Expedition would make its way from St. Louis to the Pacific Ocean on behalf of a fledgling nation and President Jefferson.

During the early part of the nineteenth century, it appeared that the Oregon Territory might become part of the British Empire. Fort Vancouver, on the Washington side of the Columbia, was the headquarters of Britain's Hudson's Bay Company, until 1846, when it moved to Victoria, British Columbia. Soon afterward, the 49th parallel was designated the boundary between Canada and the United States.

By the 1840s, thousands of pioneers were coming to the area on the Oregon Trail. A decade later, discord between settlers and the indigenous inhabitants they encountered would result in a series of wars that reached into the 1870s, culminating in the federal government's removal of Chinook, Klamath, and other groups to reservations. The photographs in this first section chronicle the early inhabitants of Oregon and settlement by immigrating pioneers, focusing on contact between peoples, economic development, and everyday life during the era. The images in this chapter also detail the role that the lumber industry, agriculture, fishing and salmon canning, the railroad, steamships, and the river began to play in the development of the state. Of paramount importance, the building of the railroad by Ben Holladay, Henry Villard, and others opened the region to commerce with the rest of the United States.

During the nineteenth century, Chinese, Japanese, and Latino immigrants as well as Europeans settled in the state, working in lumber mills and mines, building railroads, and pursuing fishing and agriculture. African-Americans who came to Oregon during the era often worked as Pullman porters and laborers for the railroad. All settlers, and these groups in particular, faced many challenges as they assimilated into the culture and forged the road to prosperity for the generations of Oregonians to follow in the twentieth century.

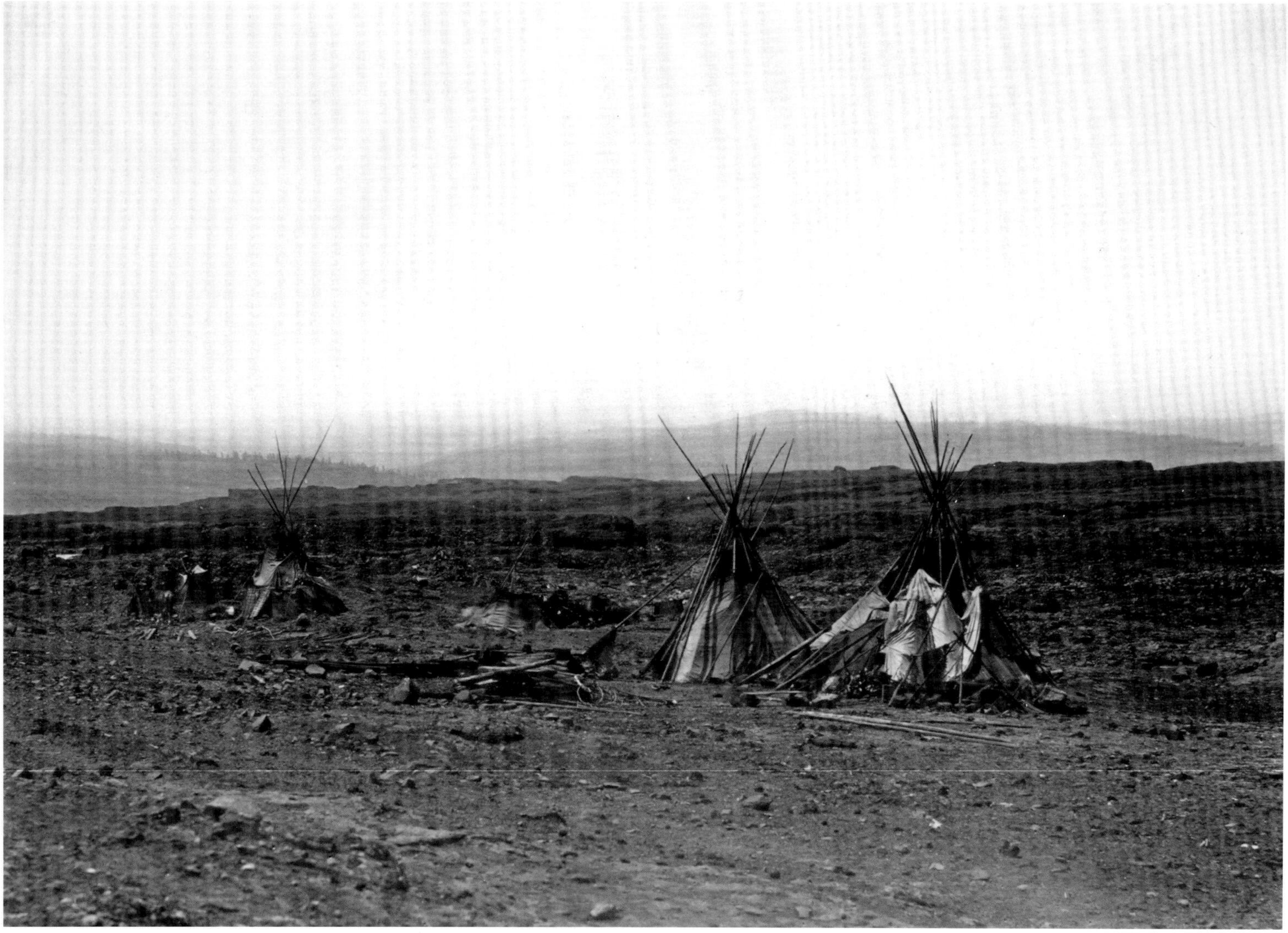

Encampment on the Columbia River, near the Dalles, 1860. Native Americans believed that the influence of nature was paramount in their lives, giving them food, clothing, shelter, implements, and weapons.

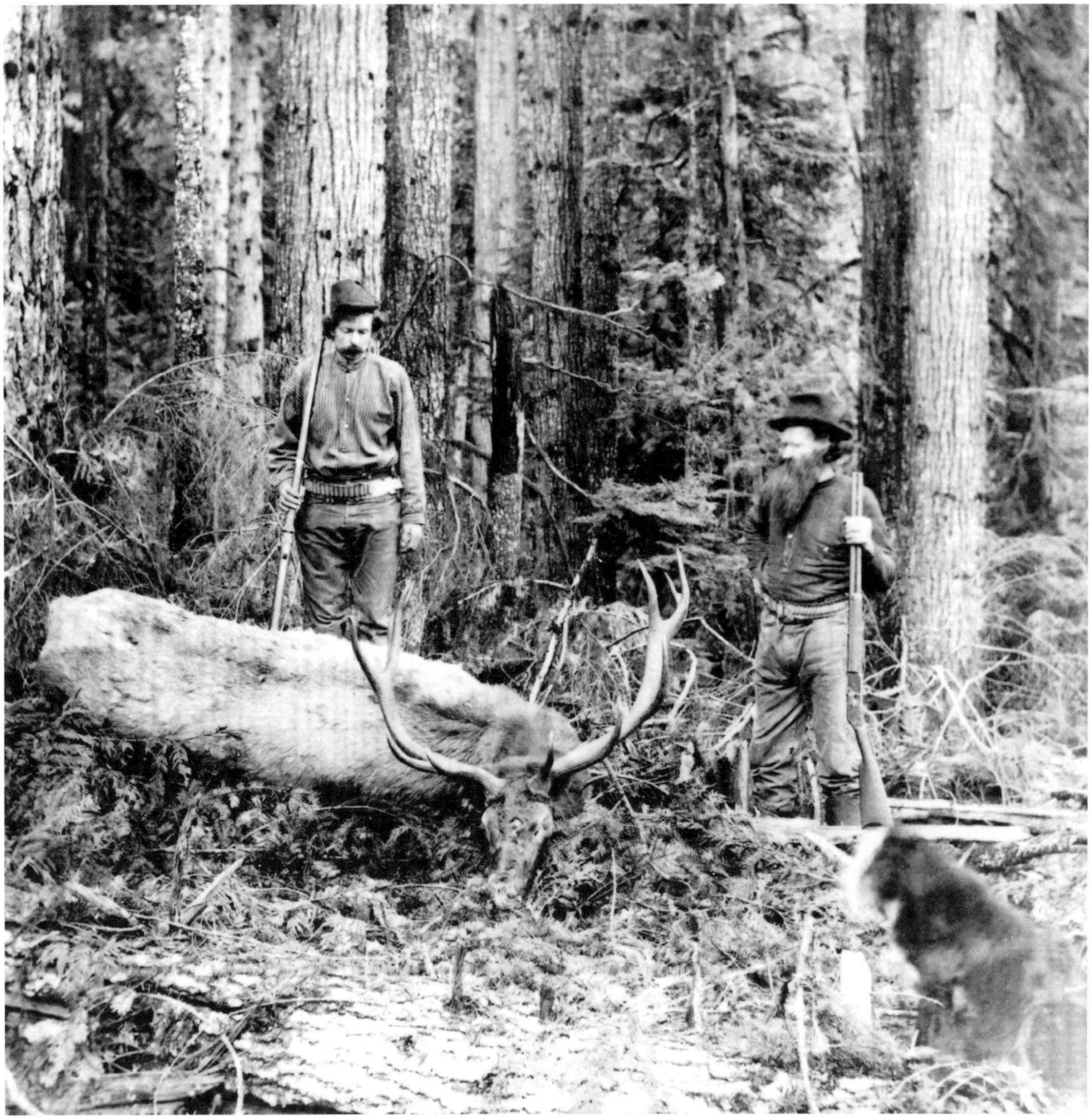

Two hunters with dead elk in the Coast Range Mountains. Wildlife was plentiful and hunters killed for food as well as sport. The Coast Range runs parallel to the Oregon coast and extends from the Columbia River south into Coos County. The Klamath Mountains run to the south of the Coast Range. The average elevation of the Coast Range is 1,500 feet above sea level, and the tallest peaks are Saddle Mountain (3,283 feet) and Mary's Peak (4,097 feet).

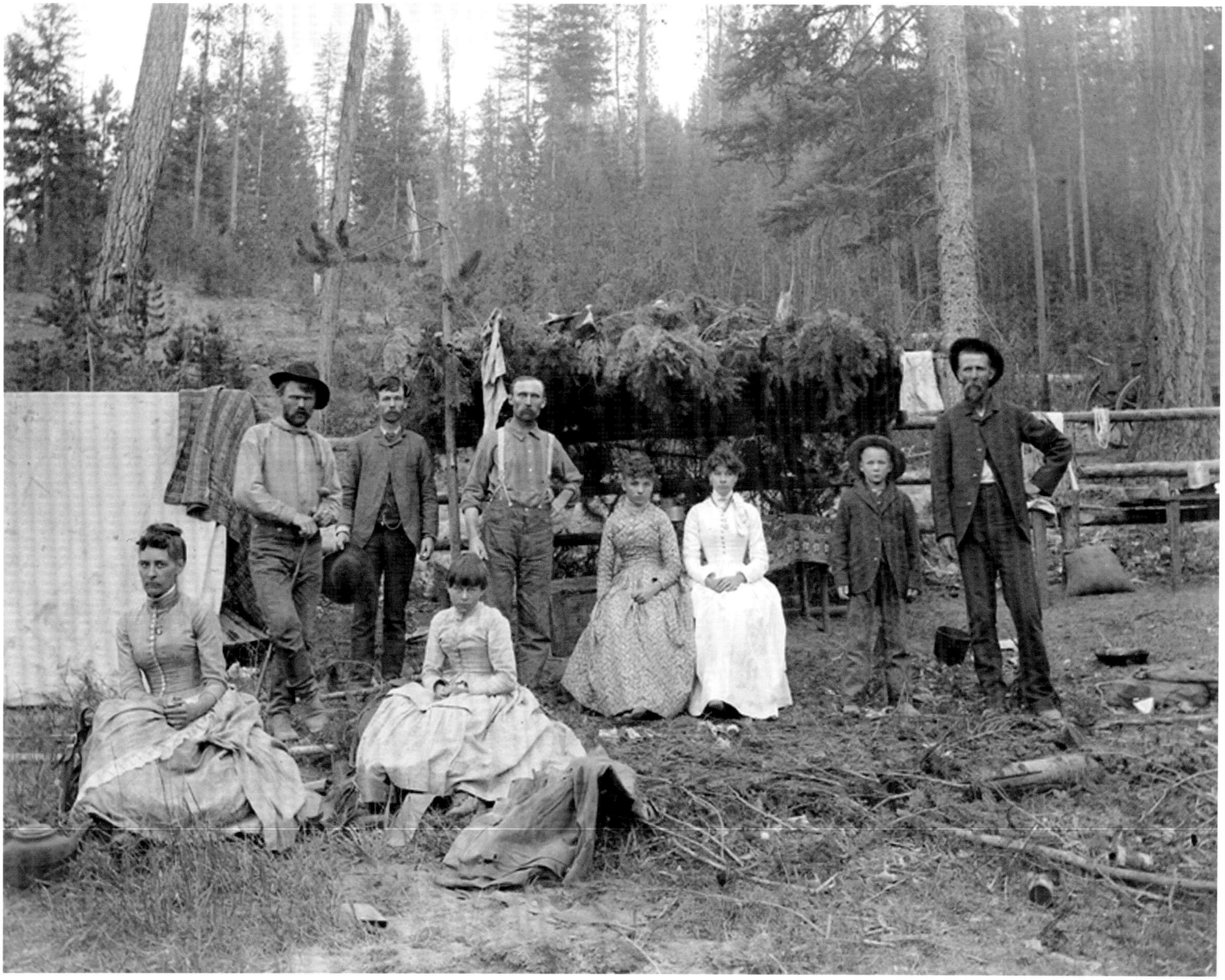

A family camping trip reportedly near the town of Heppner. The great majority of settlers to Oregon came with large extended families and kept these ties once they arrived. Farm families did not travel much, and people usually wed others who lived in the same area.

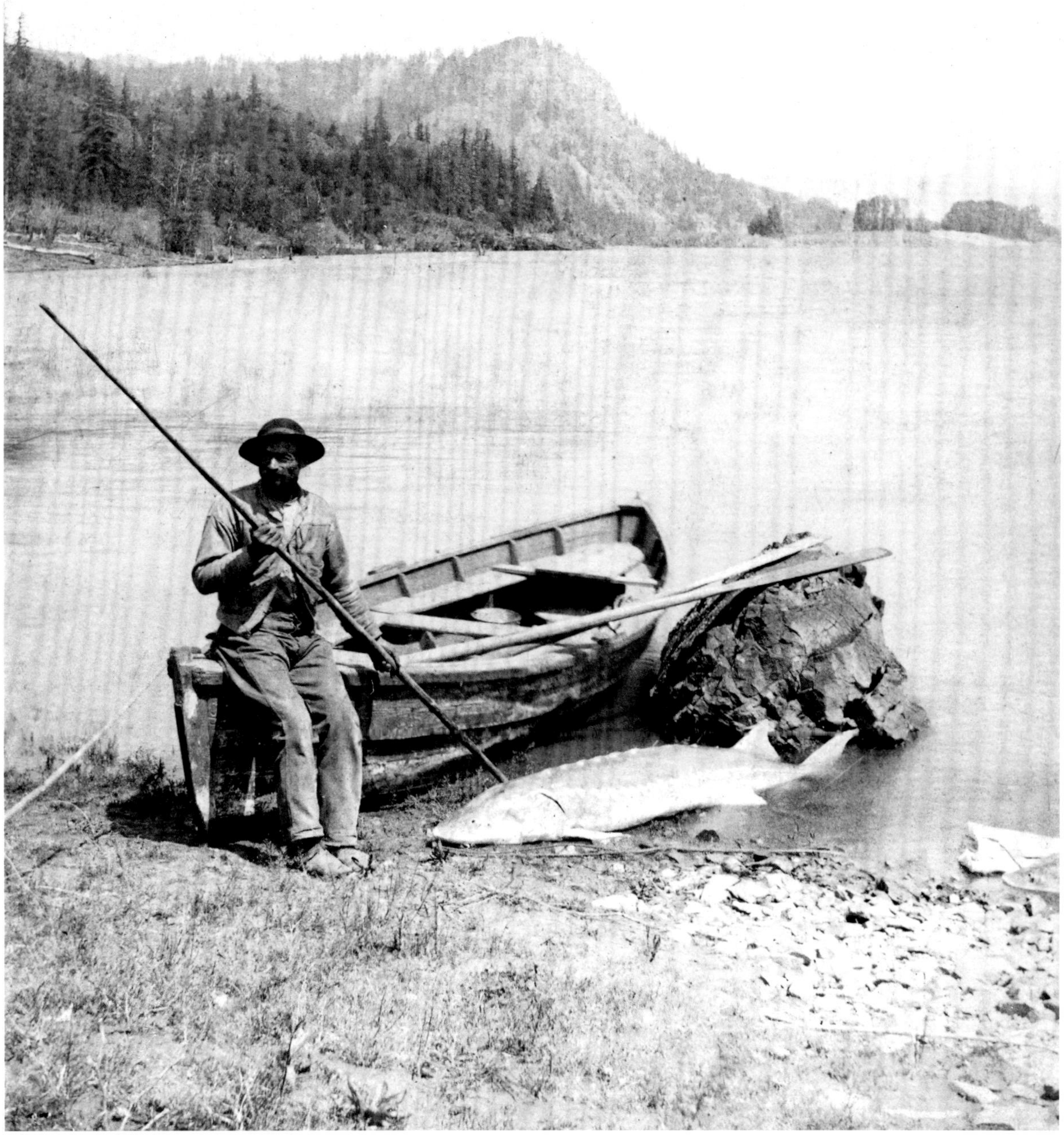

Fishing was a popular recreational activity on the Columbia River. By the 1880s, recreational, gill-netters, and commercial fishermen were experiencing a decline in catches brought on by overfishing.

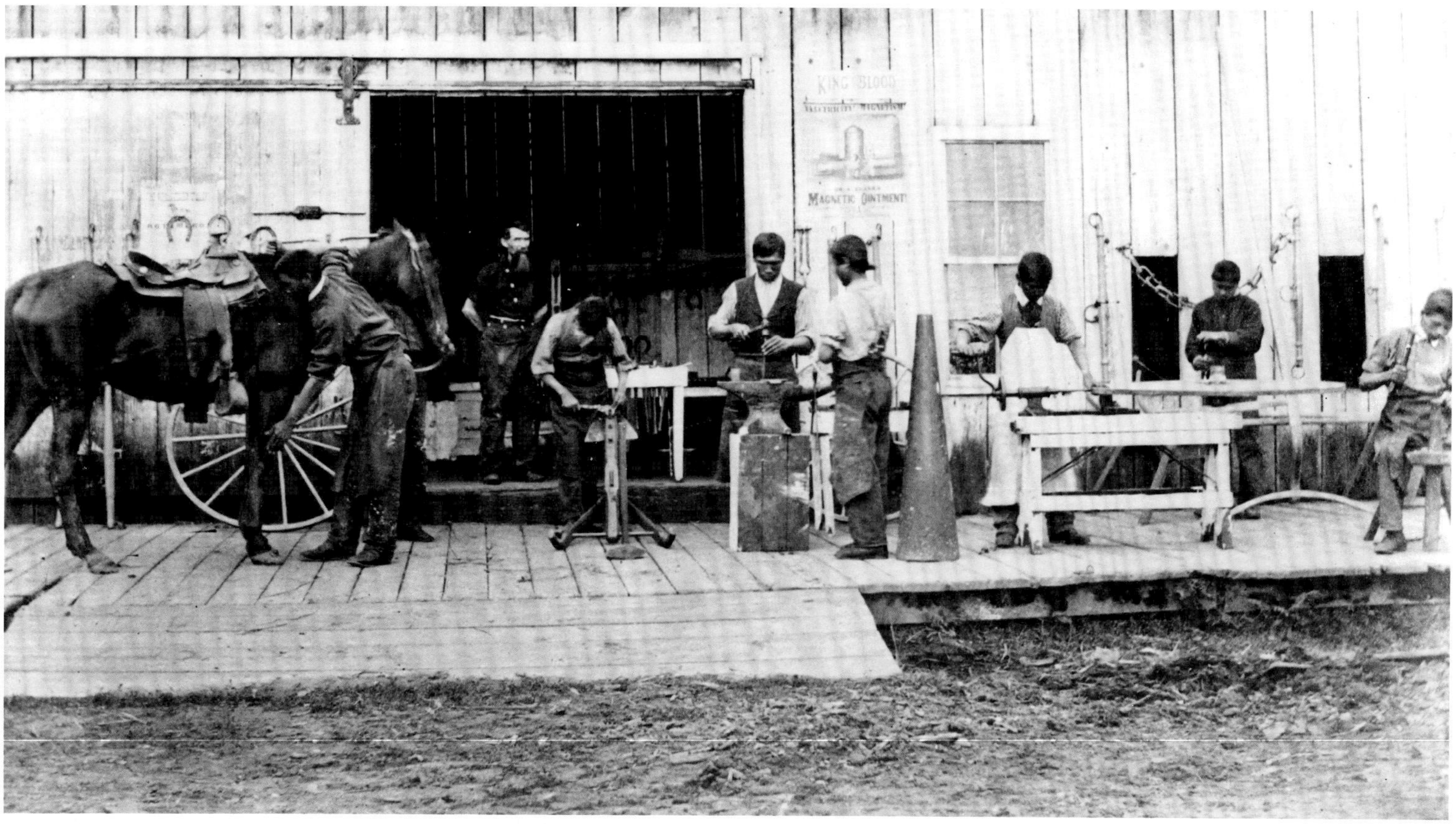

The various tribes of Native Americans were concentrated on reservations and taught various skills focused on farming and trades. Here a group of students learn blacksmithing.

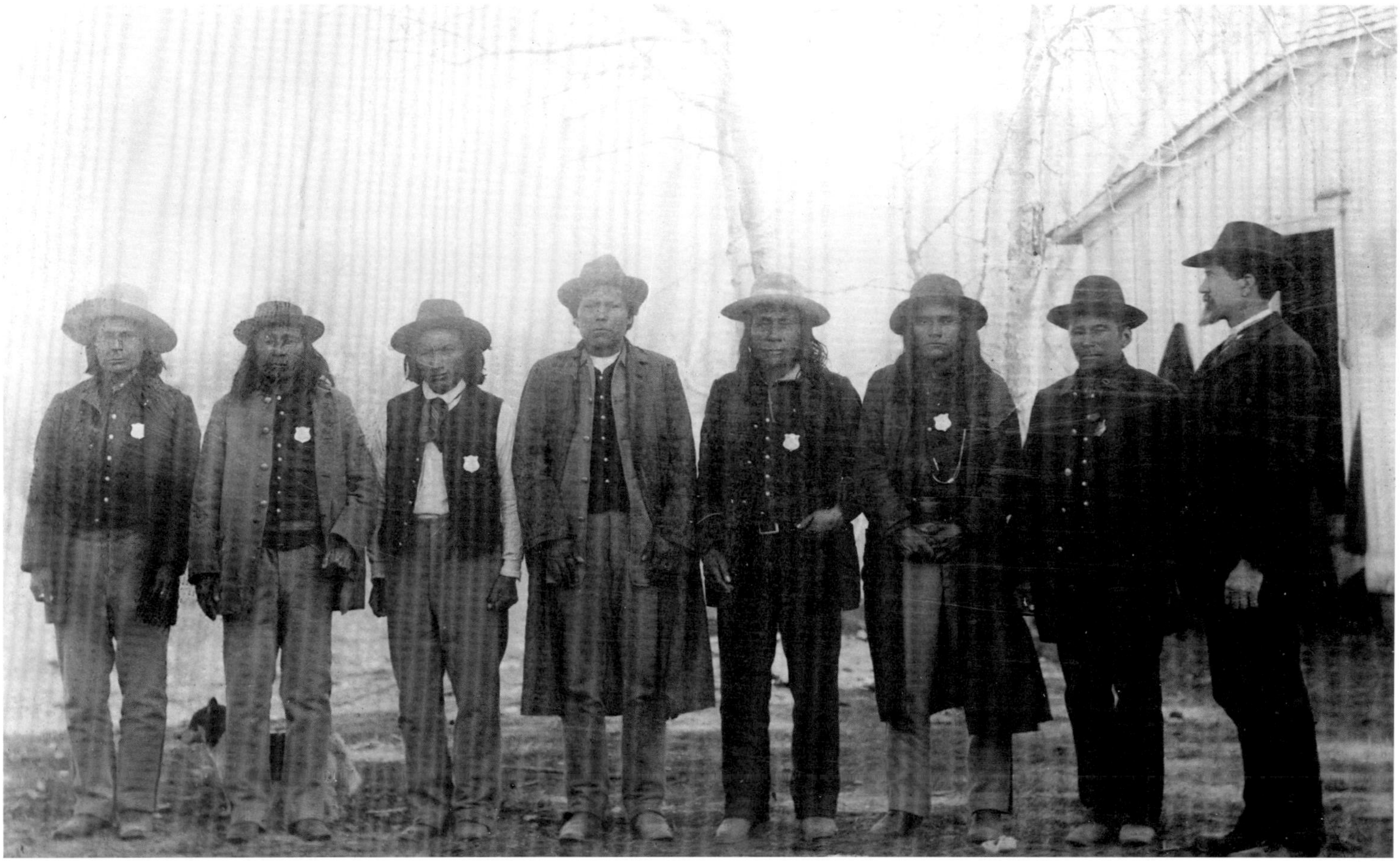

This photograph taken in 1880 shows a police force on the Umatilla reservation. The Indian agent and his staff were responsible for assimilating Native Americans into the surrounding culture. The agent's tactics consisted of force, persuasion, example, and cajolery. Resistance among tribes was widespread.

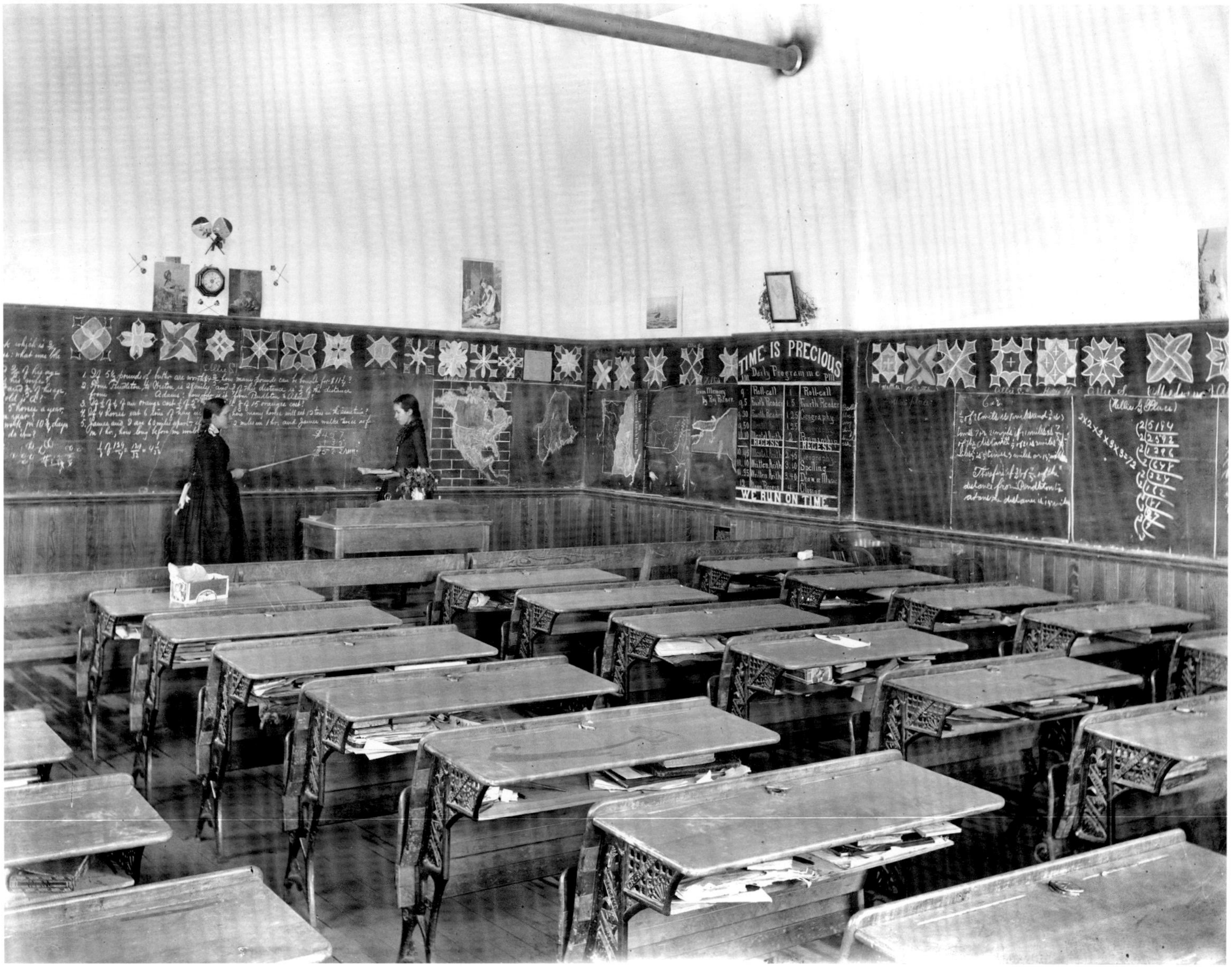

In 1851, the first elementary public school, and in 1869, the first public high school opened, both in Portland. The blackboard in this classroom is evidence of diligent efforts to teach reading, writing, and arithmetic. One student, who signed his work "Roy Ritner," has drawn a map of the state of New York "from memory."

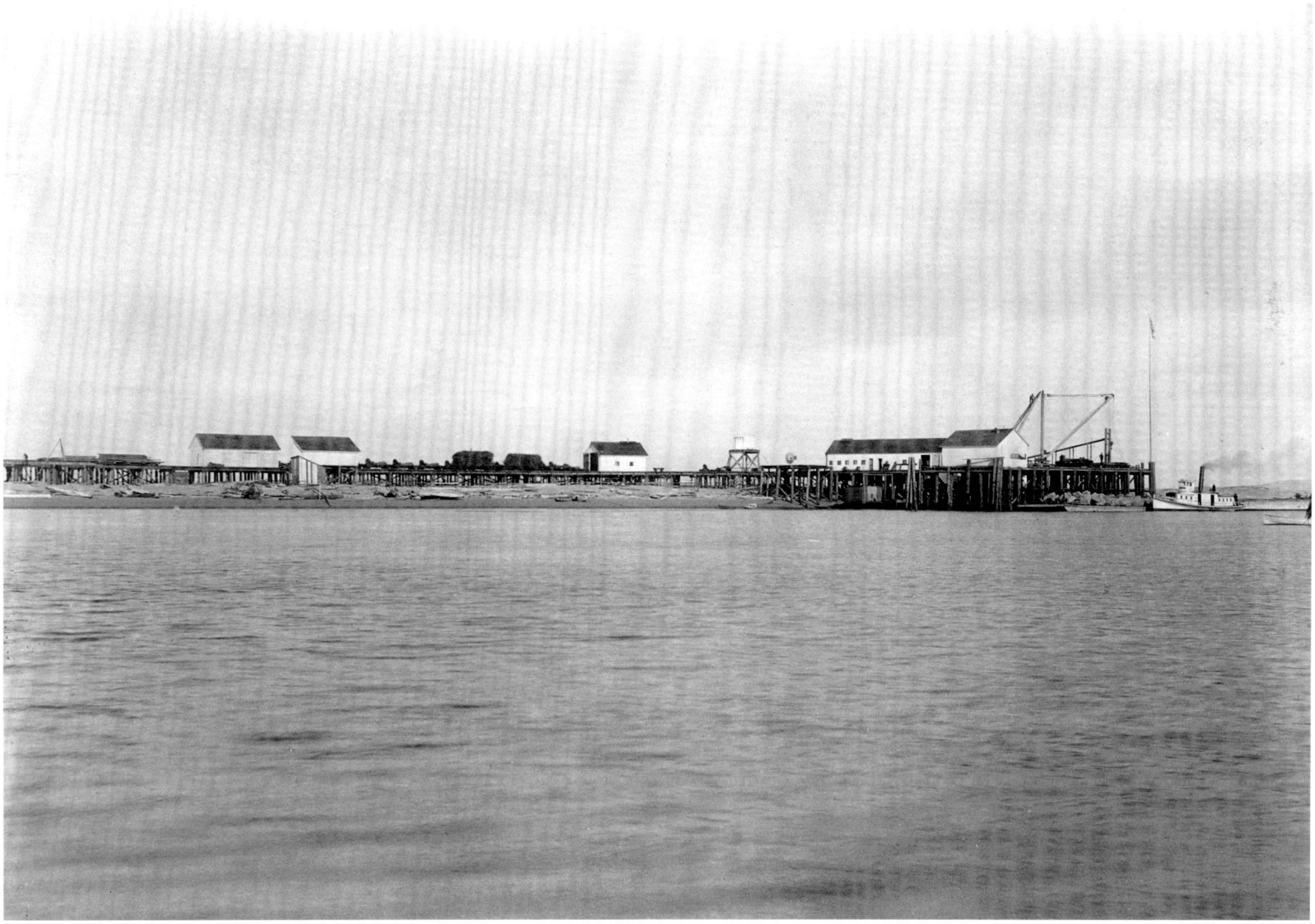

The town of Marshfield was founded in 1854. In 1944, the name of the town was officially changed to Coos Bay. Timber and shipping were the largest industries in Coos Bay into the 1980s but had faded by the 1990s.

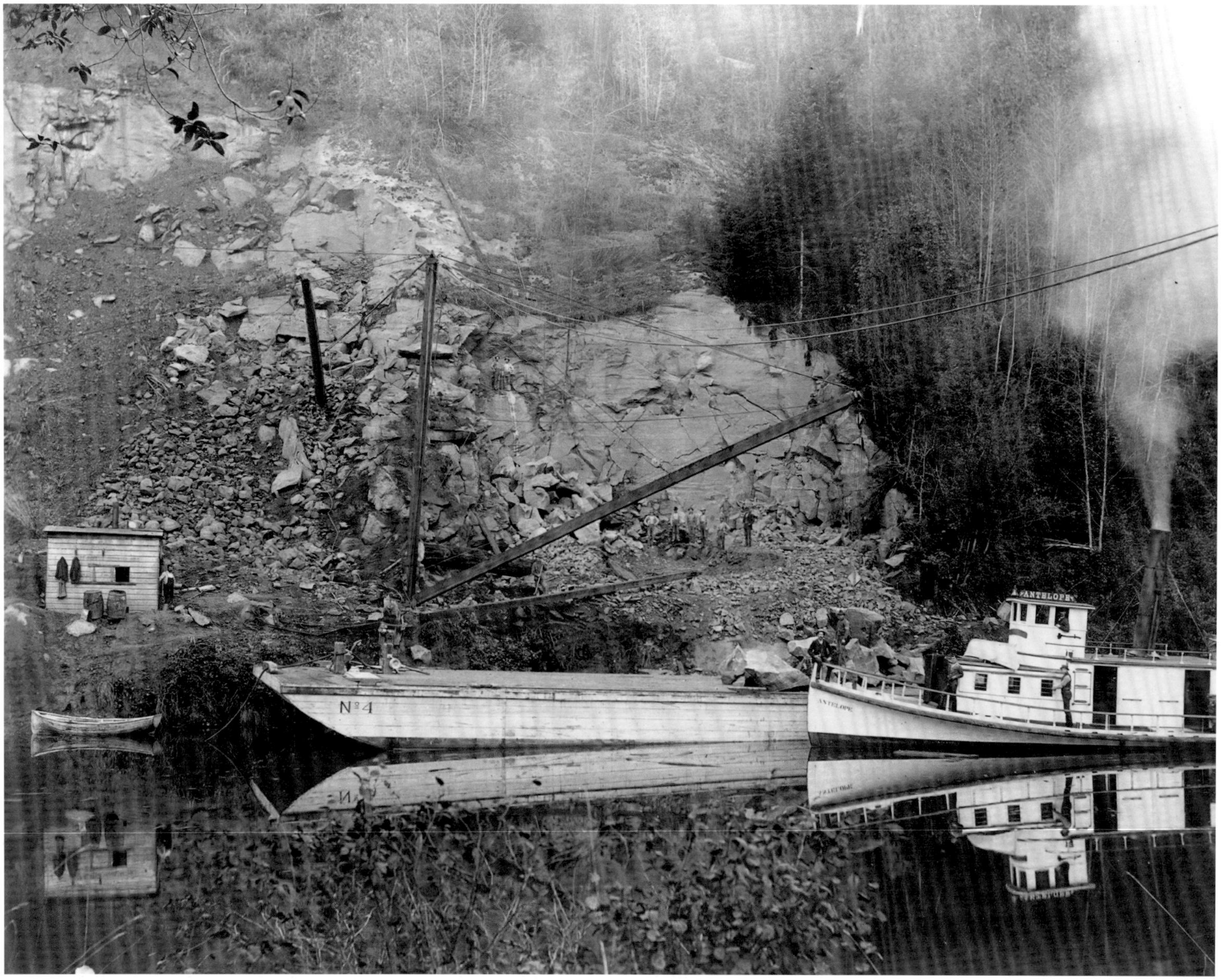

In the 1850s, gold was discovered near Coos Bay. Its gold and its good port brought logging and lumber milling, coal mining, and shipping to the area. The gold and coal were eventually depleted, and lumber milling had declined rapidly by the end of the twentieth century.

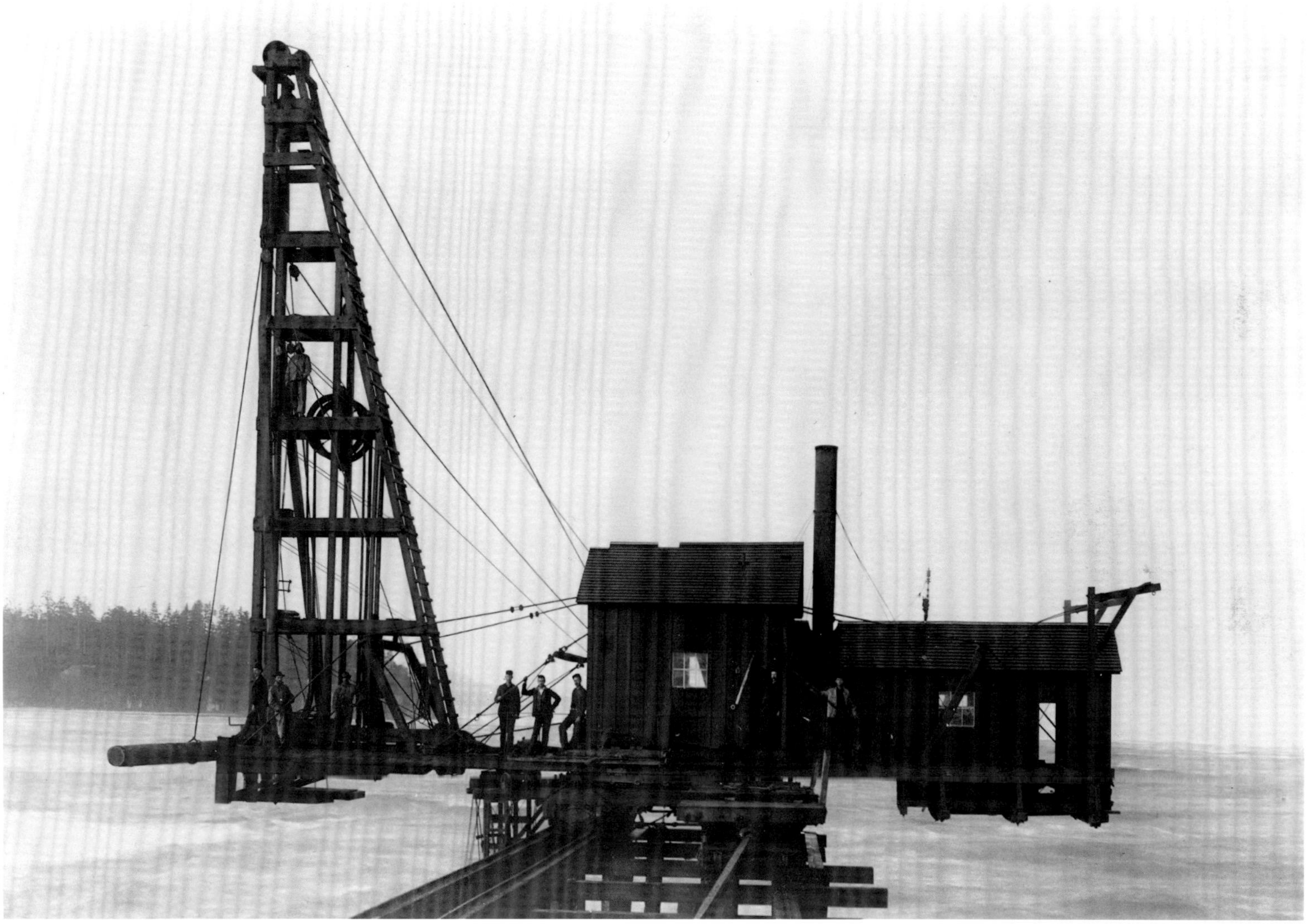

Workers at Coos Bay pose for a photograph standing atop a mobile pile driver around 1892. The revolving pile driver was used for maritime engineering projects, including the jetty on which the pile driver sits.

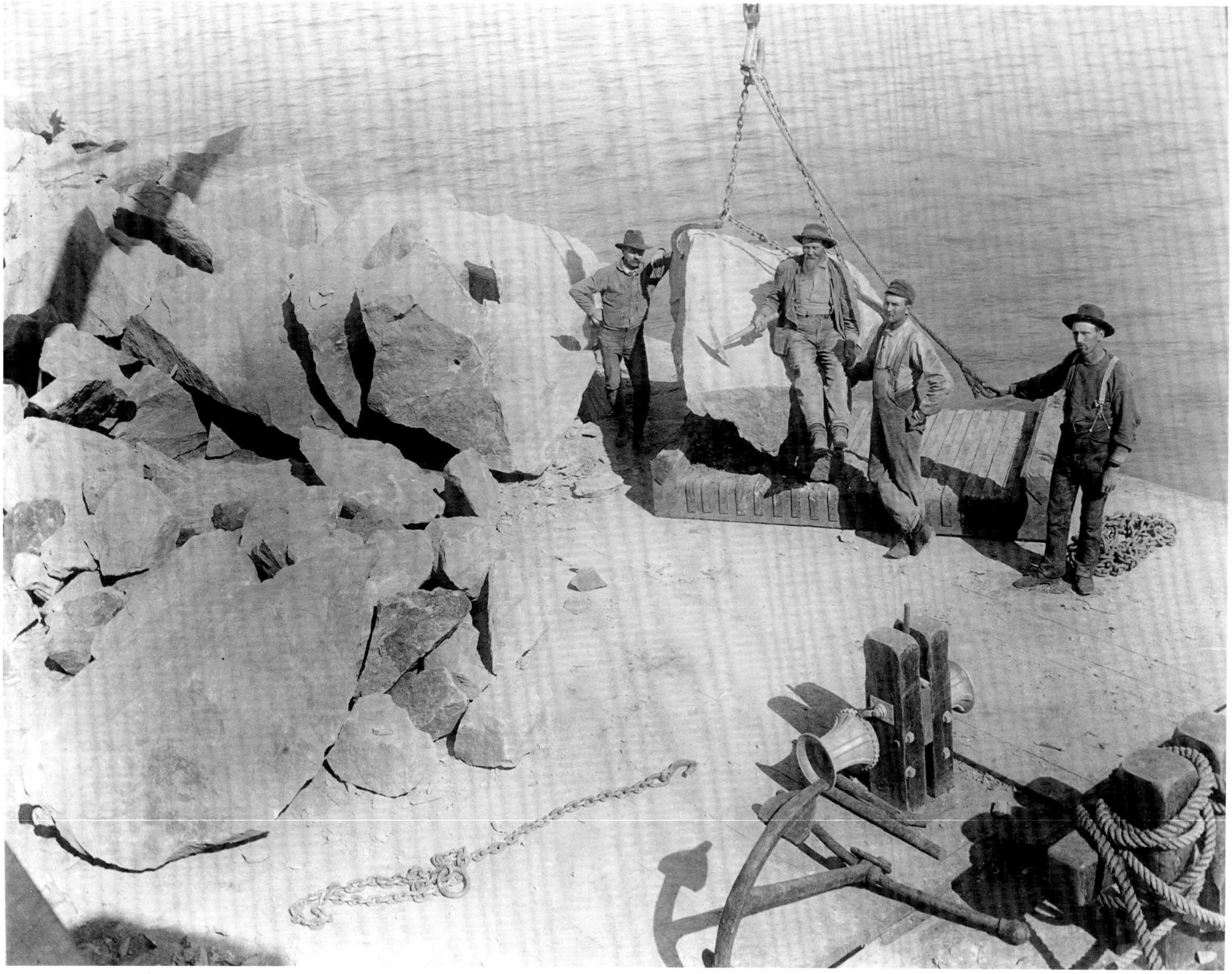

Crews unload rock from scows in the harbor at Coos Bay, for use in building the Coos Bay jetty. The U.S. Army Corps of Engineers was chiefly responsible for creating Oregon's water transportation infrastructure, playing a strong role in the state's economic growth through projects like this one.

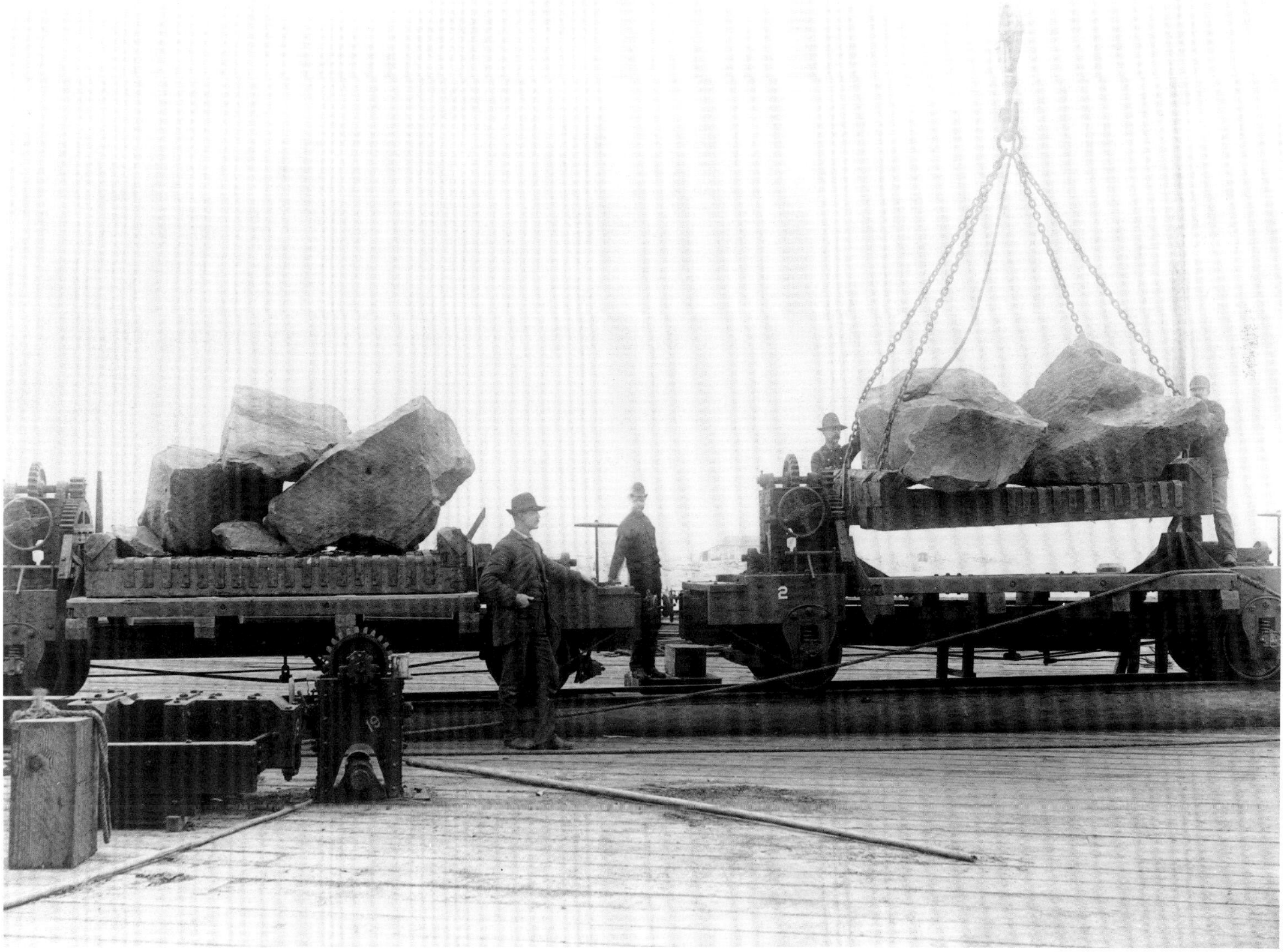

This image shows the self-righting rail cars used in transporting rock for construction projects, including construction of the jetty to deepen and stabilize the channel at Coos Bay, at the time the most important lumber port on the coast.

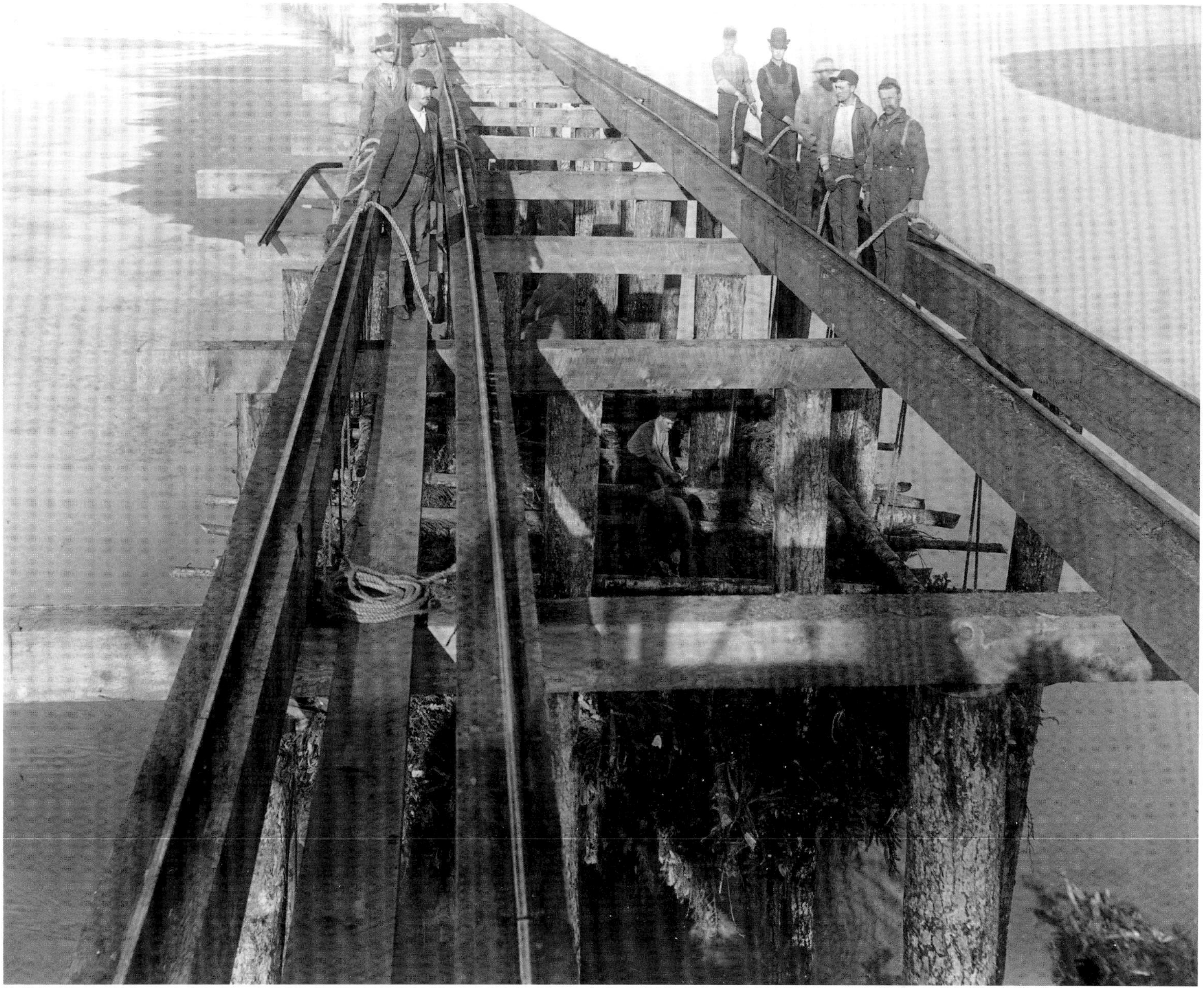

Workers at the Coos Bay jetty are shown working to complete the project.

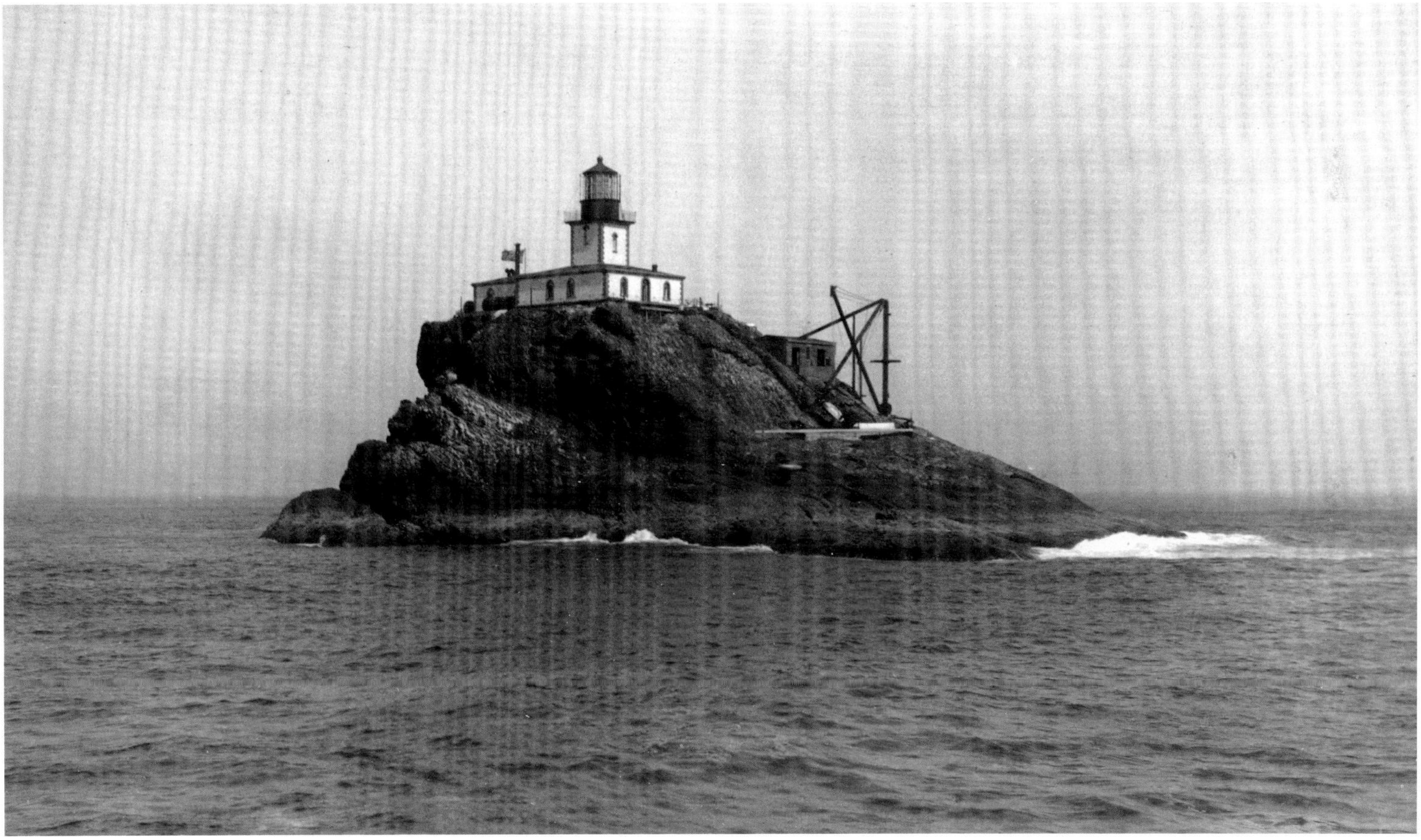

Tillamook Rock, located off the shore of Tillamook Head in Clatsop County, was one of Oregon's most powerful lighthouses. The lighthouse was decommissioned in 1957 and would serve as a columbarium from 1980 to 1999.

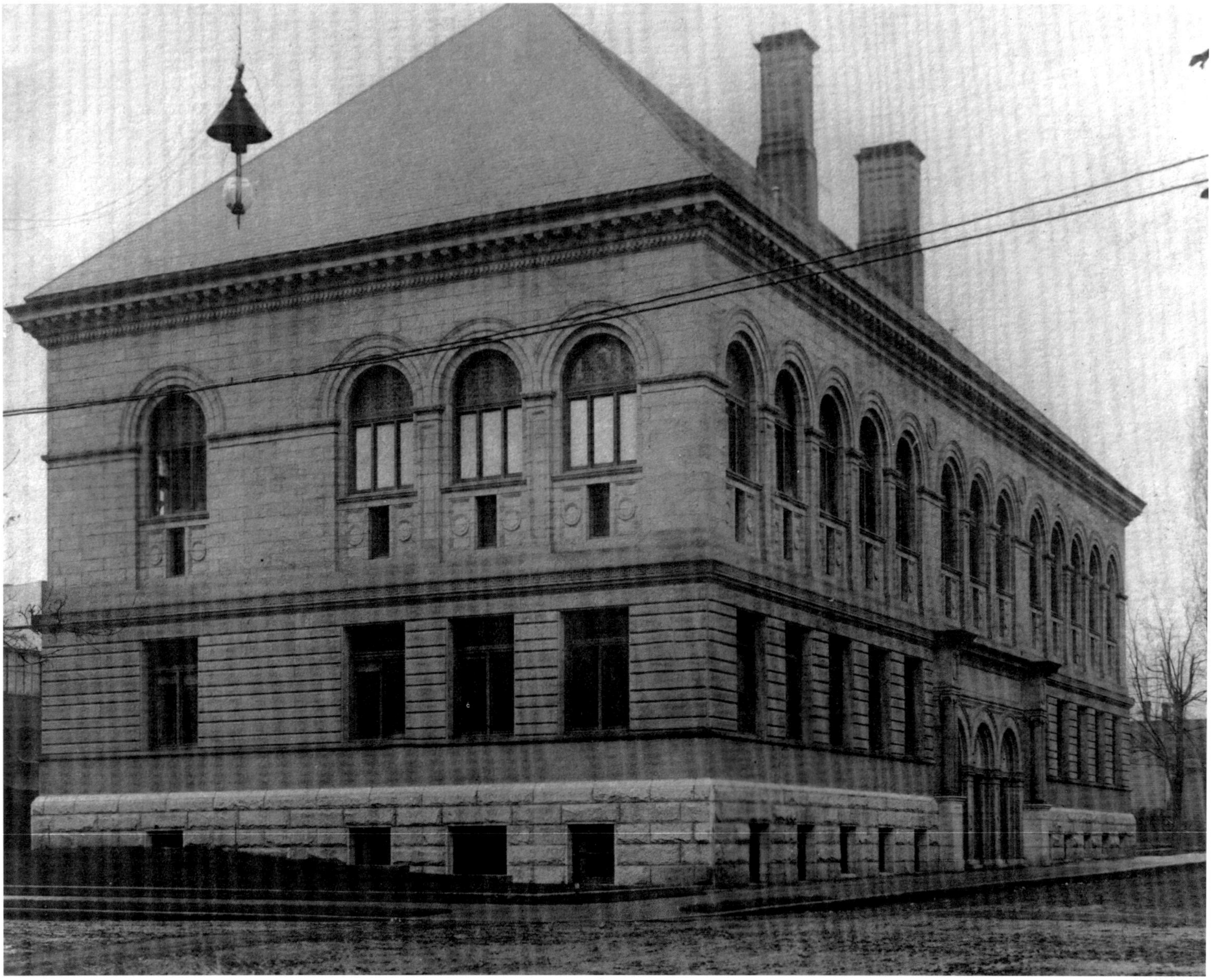

The Portland Library Association once received a bequest from a merchant named John Wilson, who left 8,000 volumes and $2,500 in gold coin to the association. The state legislature decided to support this beneficence by passing a law in 1901 that authorized a property tax for library purposes. The City of Portland and the library entered into a contract where the privately owned library continued to own its collection but the city provided services, in effect creating a publicly supported library. On March 10, 1902, the first library in the state made available through taxing property owners came into existence.

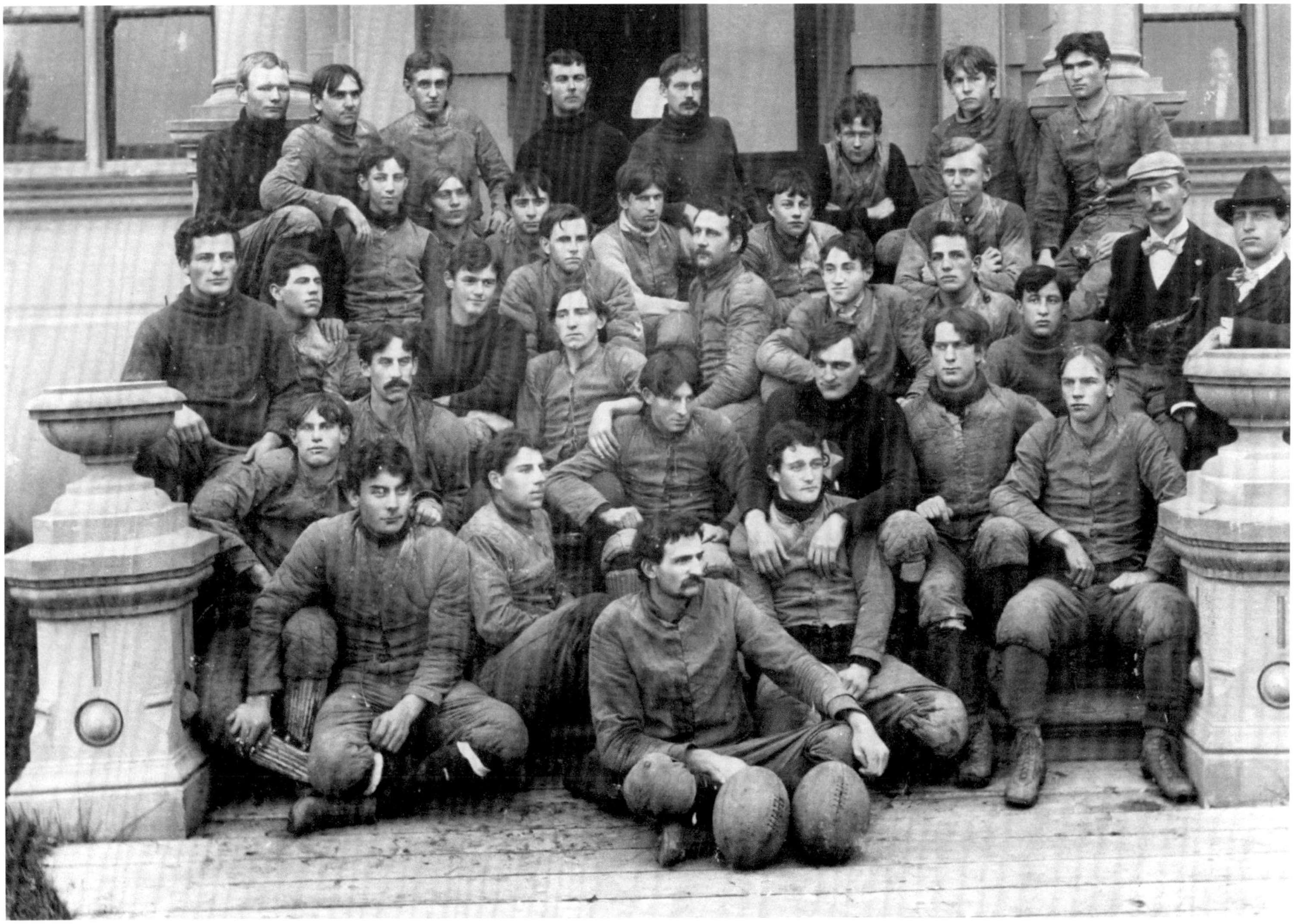

This 1896 photograph shows the University of Oregon football team in front of Villard Hall, which opened in 1886. Railroad magnate and philanthropist Henry Villard became the University of Oregon's first benefactor with significant financial contributions to the school. Early football uniforms offered little protection to the players by comparison with the uniforms of today.

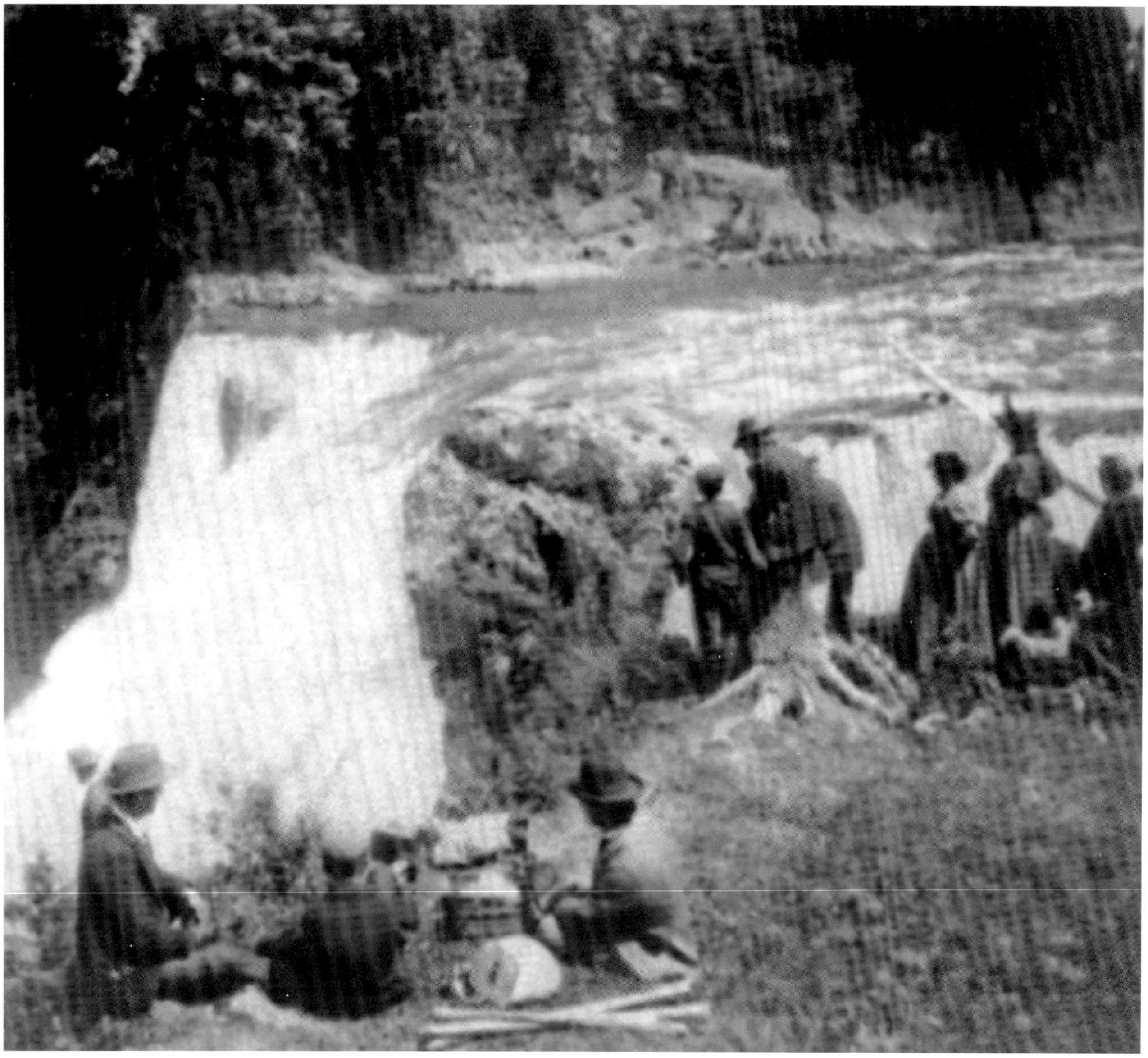

Americans have always found time to engage in recreational pursuits, such as this picnic on the Columbia River at Snoqualmie Falls around 1898.

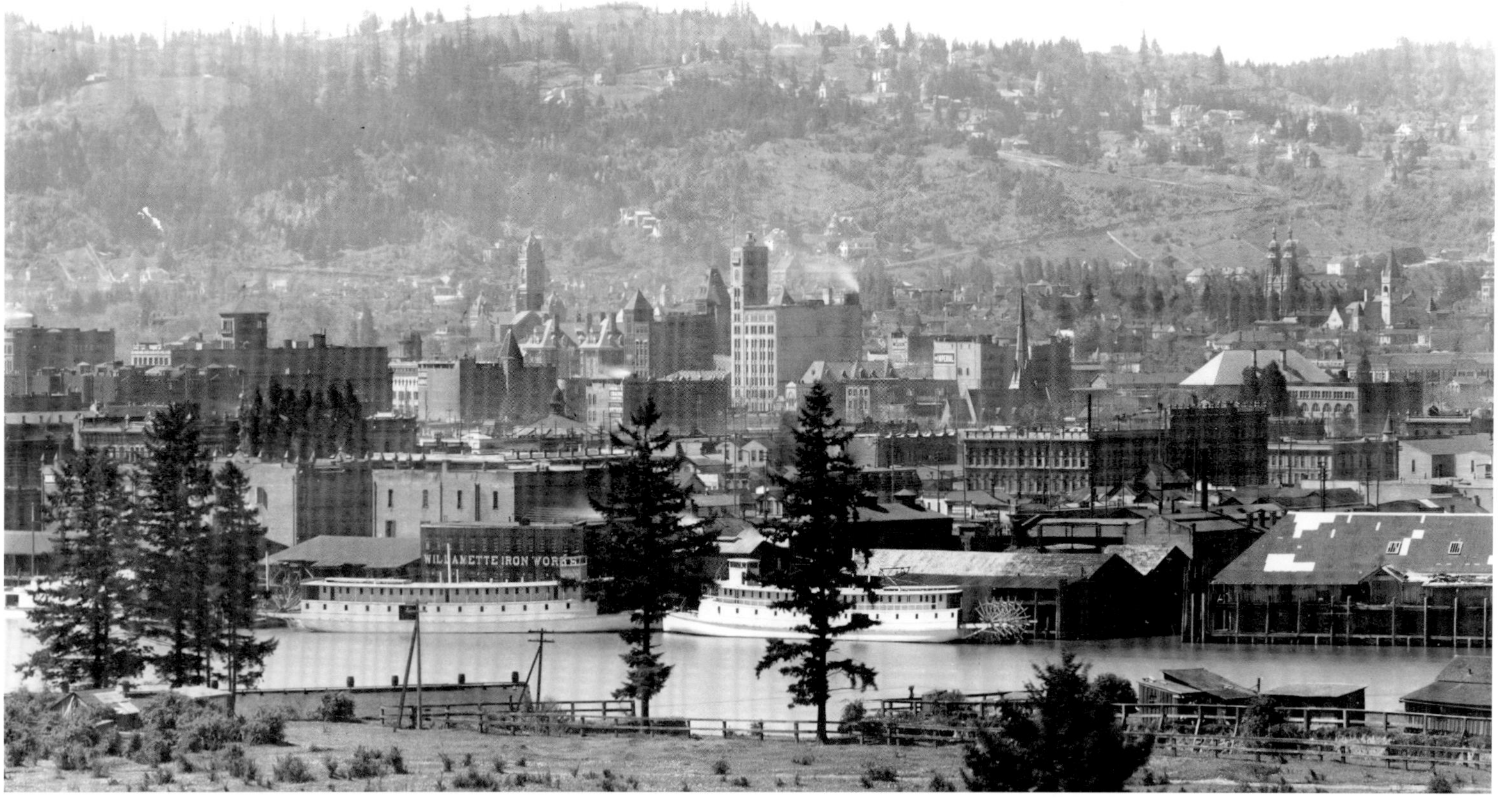

Americans who first settled in Oregon were often from the Midwest and had an agricultural background. The next wave of immigrants preferred settling in urban areas, and the city of Portland developed early on as the only real metropolitan area of the state. The growth of its population and the development of the electric streetcar allowed Portland to expand geographically and annex small towns nearby.

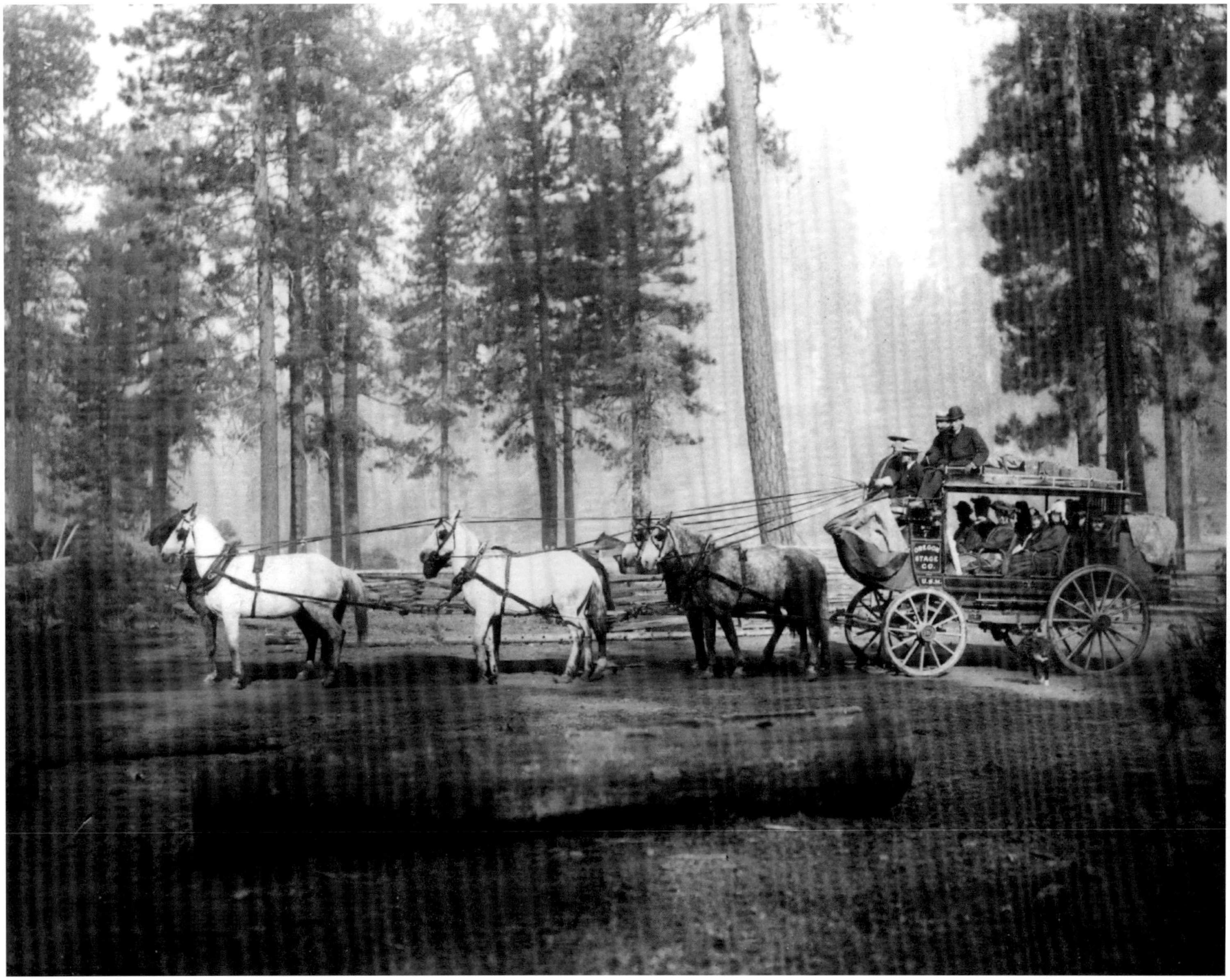

A stagecoach carrying 13 sightseers and pulled by 6 horses has come to a halt at Spencer's, on the road to Crater Lake.

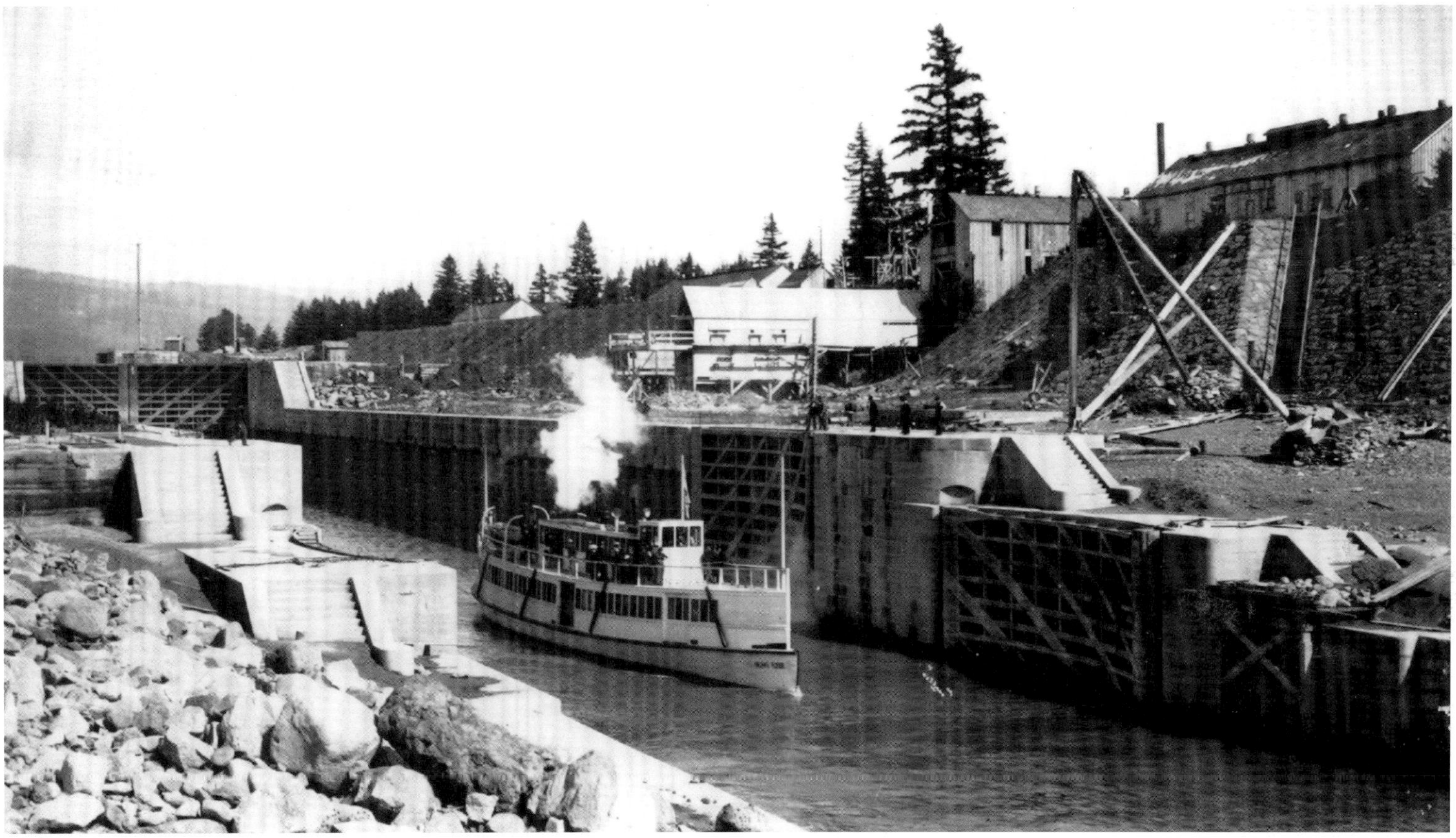

The Oregon Steam Navigation Company was formed in 1860 for the purpose of gaining access to the interior of the state, where mining operations were located. The OSNC earned enormous profits and was instrumental in improving Portland's fortunes as well as the cultural life of the city.

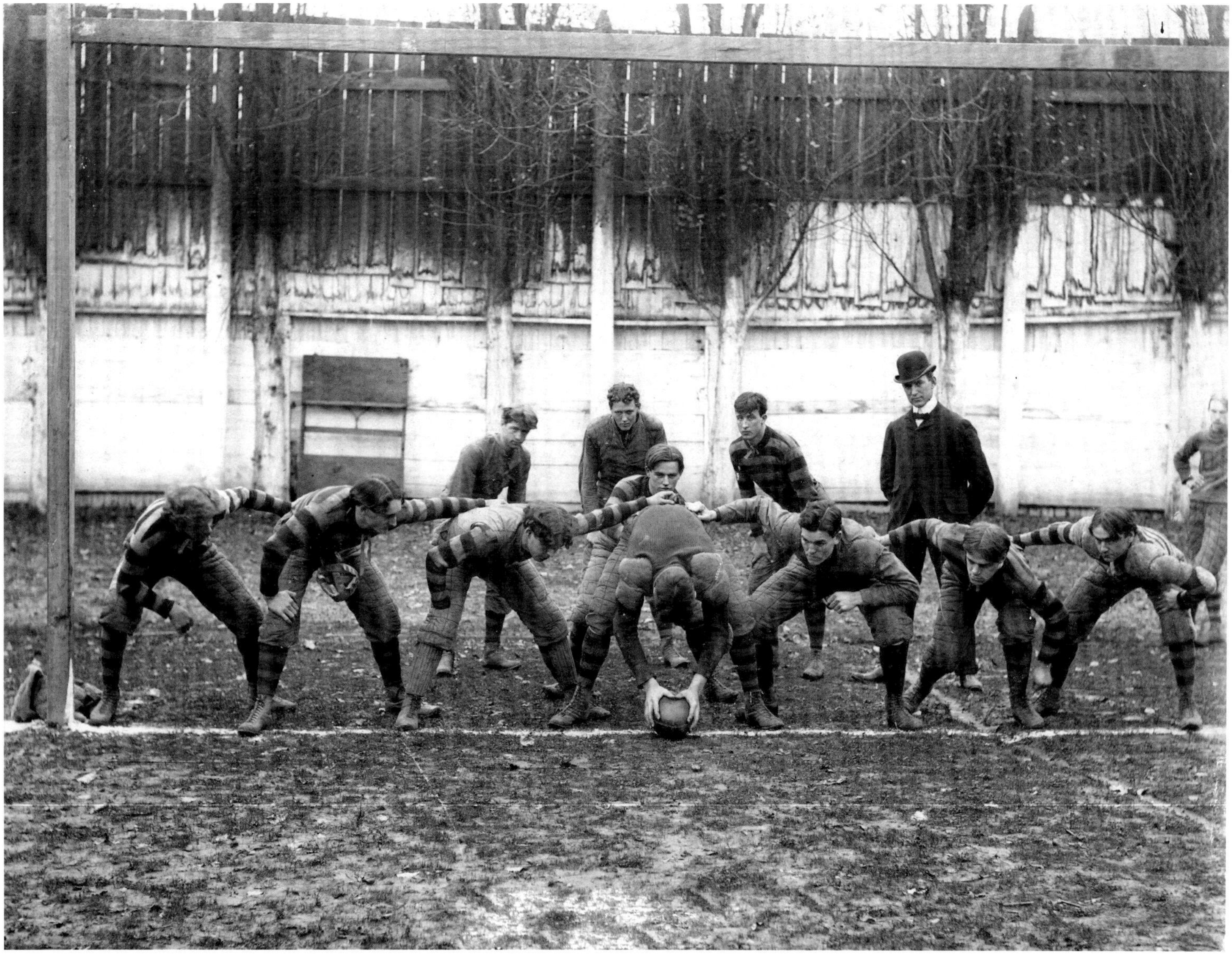

These football players pose for a group shot on land that had held a tannery and earlier, in the 1880s, vegetable gardens operated by Chinese farmers. In 1893, the land became a possession of the Multnomah Athletic Club and subsequently the venue for many public events, including football games, presidential visits, and religious revivals. In 1966, the club sold the field to the City of Portland and it became known as Civic Stadium (now PGE Park).

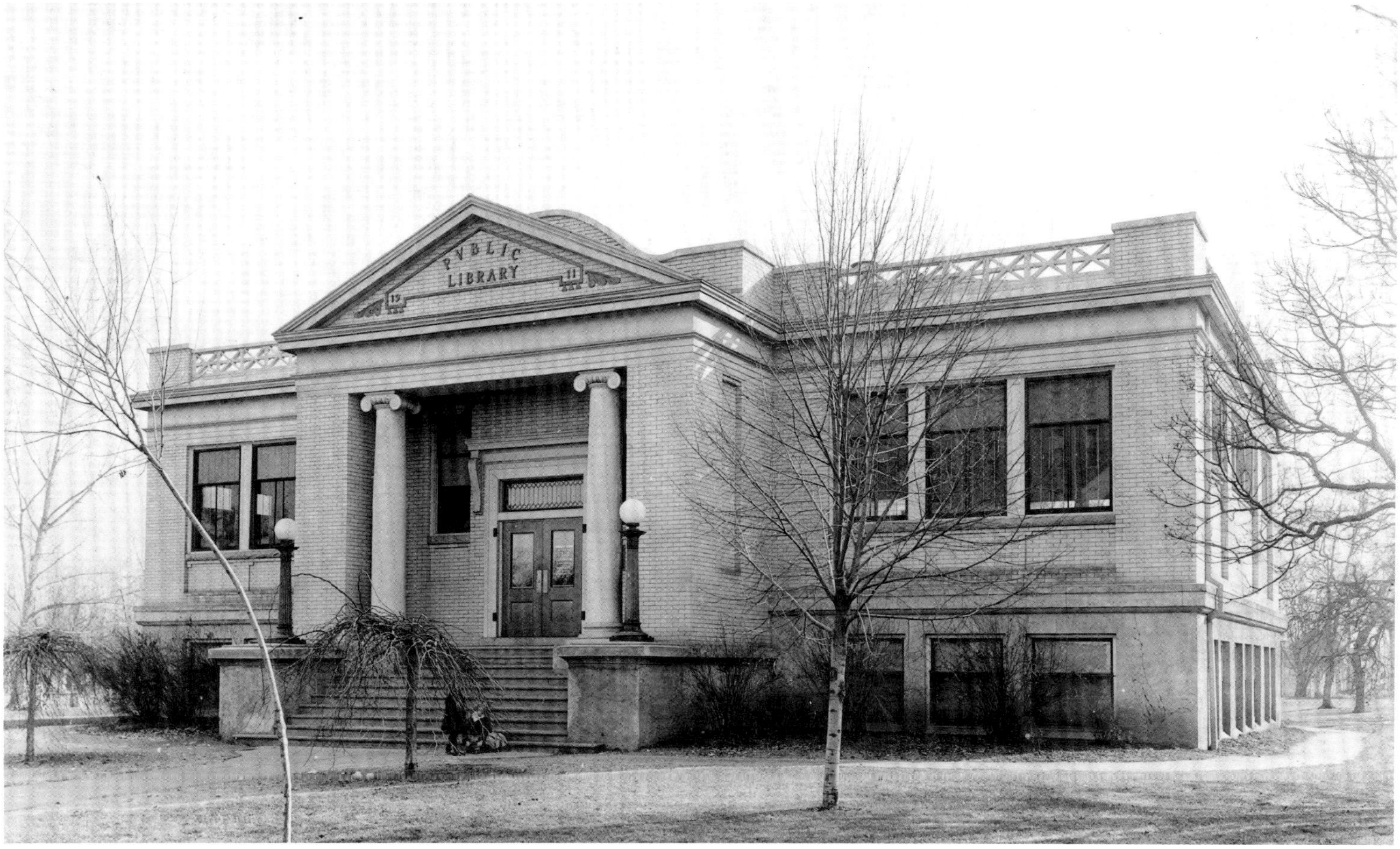

The county seat of Jackson County in southern Oregon, Medford was platted by surveyors in 1883 after the Oregon and California Railroad staked a route through the area. It soon became the chief trading center for the region. By 1900 there were 1,791 individuals residing in Medford, and its economy was prospering as a result of fruit packing, mining, and farming. The Medford Library was a direct result of this robust economy.

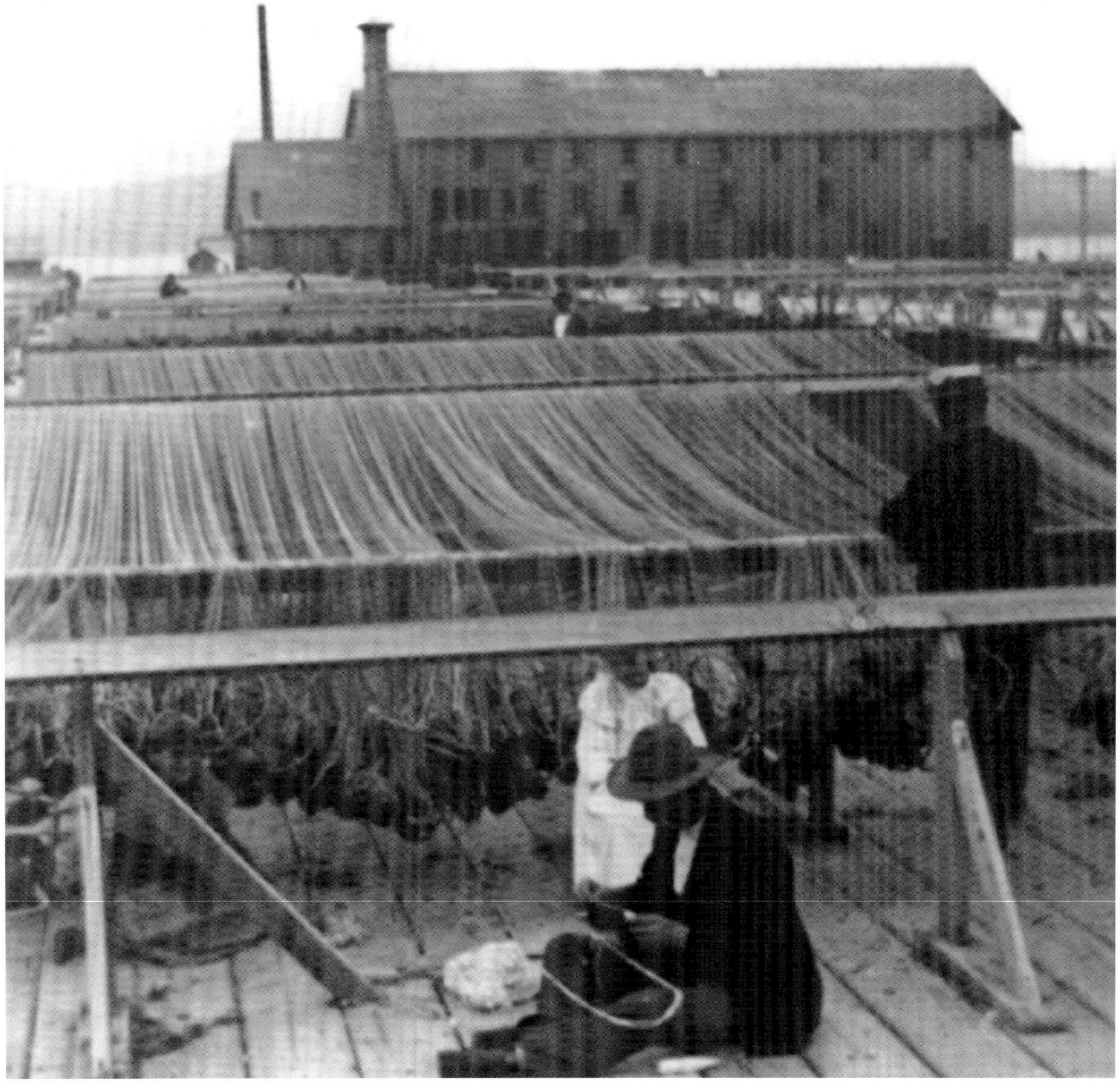

The Columbia River Gorge is the source of some of Oregon's extraordinary beauty. Historically, the Columbia River was important for transportation, fishing, salmon canning, and lumber milling. Fishing nets and Oregonians engaged in the industry are shown here around 1899.

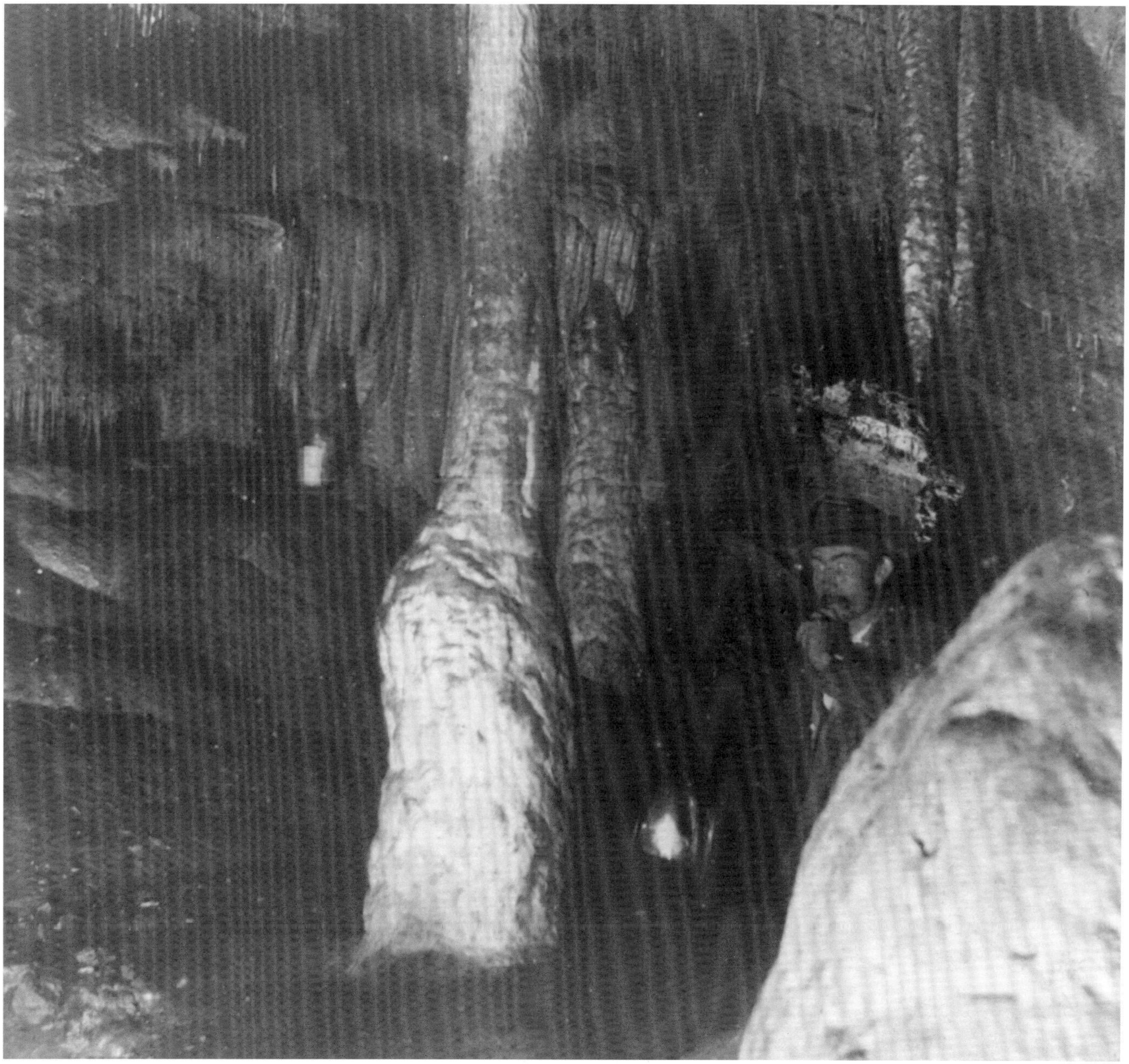

This image, from around 1899, shows the Oregon Caves located in the Siskiyou Mountains of Jackson County. The caves were discovered by Elijah Davidson in 1874 and were designated a National Monument in 1909 by President Theodore Roosevelt.

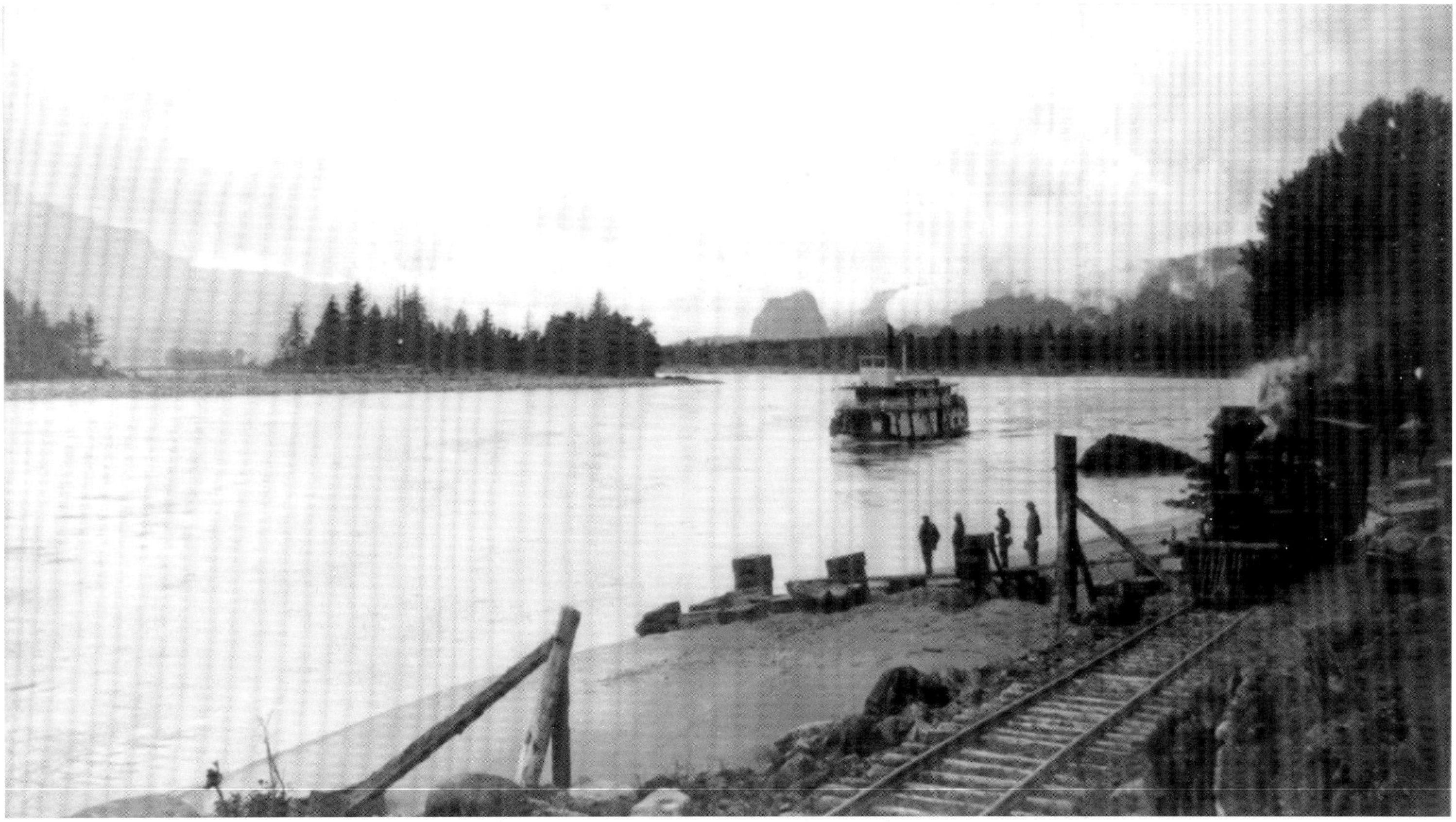

In 1811, British explorer David Thompson became the first European to journey the entire length of the Columbia River. Sternwheel steamboats plied the river from the 1850s until the 1920s, but local river traffic declined after the railroad reached the area in the 1880s and again when highways were built in the 1920s. Passenger traffic on the Columbia River had come to a complete end by the 1930s.

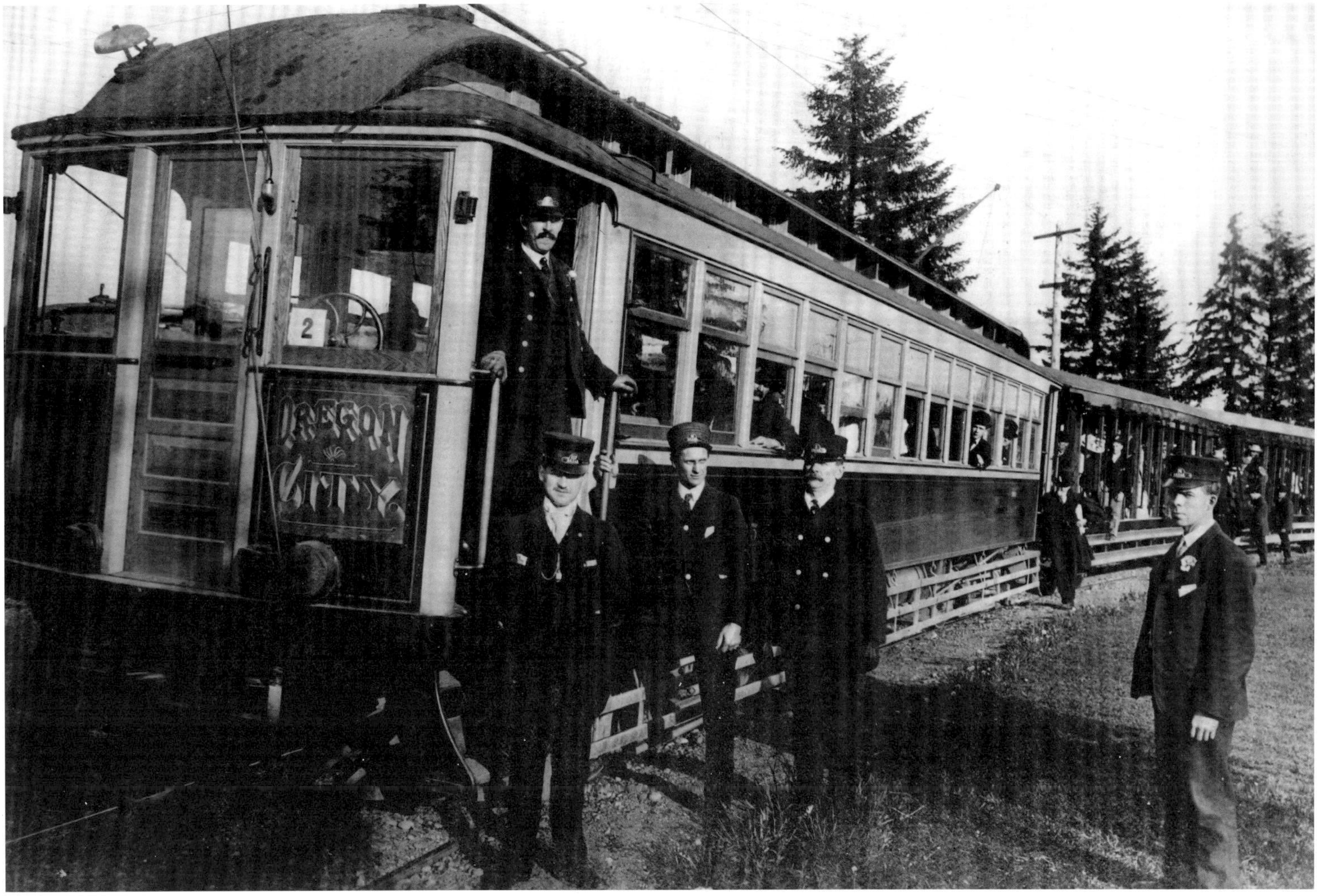

By 1893, an electric interurban railway connected Oregon City and Portland, one of the first in the nation to link cities. Oregon City's population grew as a result, from 1,263 in 1880 to 3,494 by 1900.

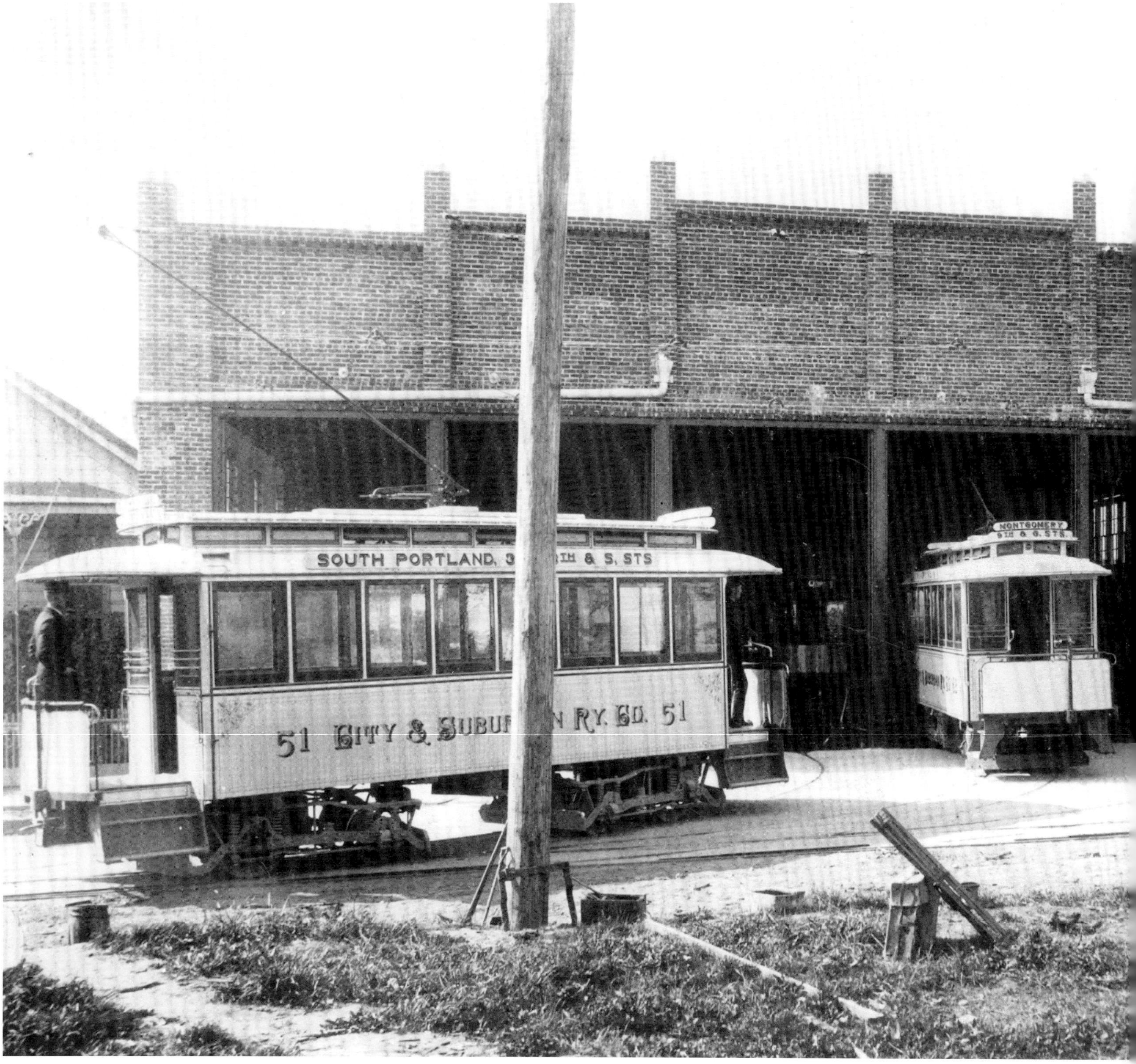
SOUTH PORTLAND, 3
TH & S. STS
51 CITY & SUBUR N RY. CO. 51
MONTGOMERY
9TH & G. STS.

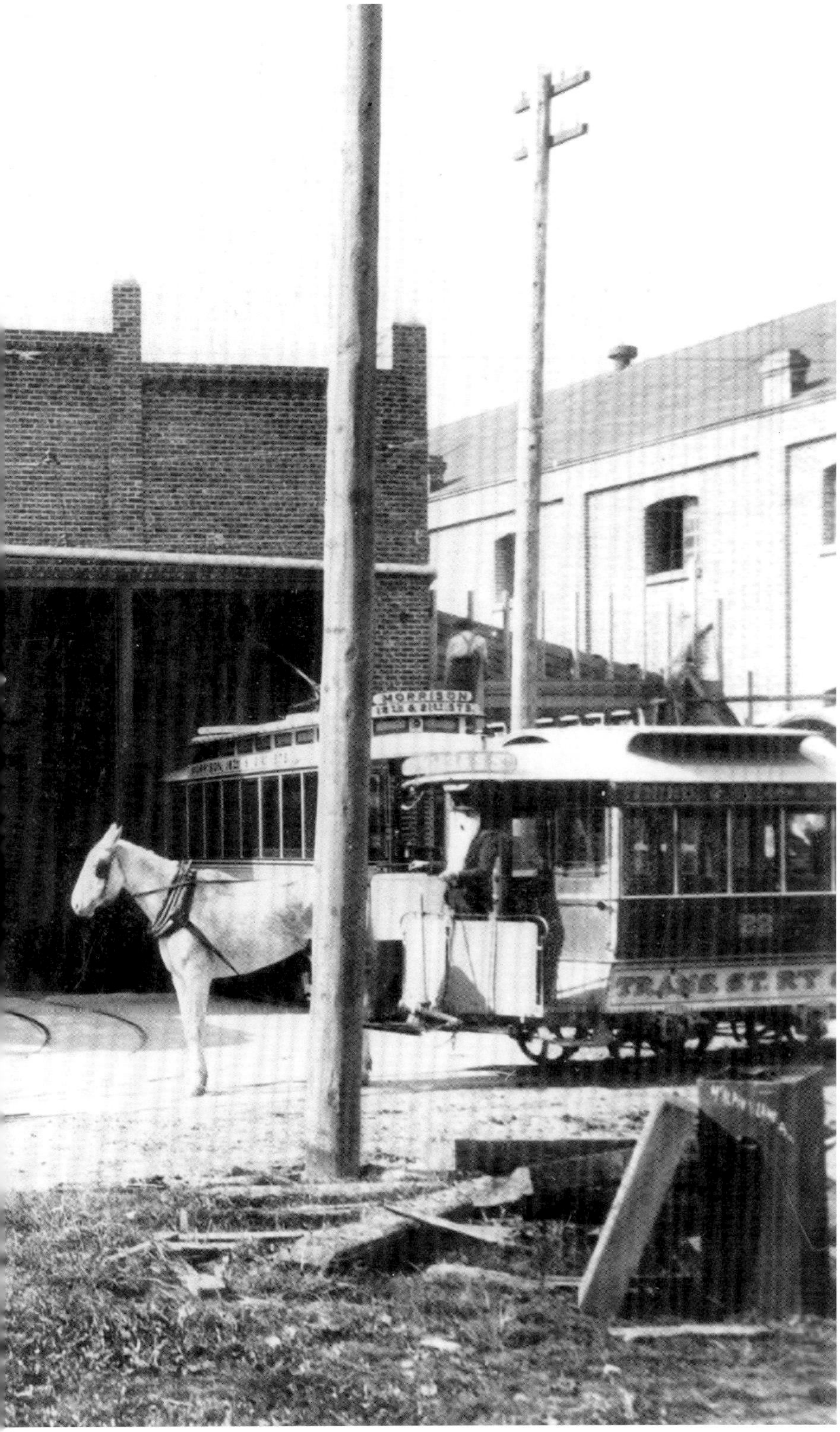

Streetcars operated on rails laid along public streets. The earliest cars were pulled by horses or mules. By the 1890s, most systems across the United States had switched to electric power. Examples of both kinds of vehicles are shown here. Streetcars operated in many Oregon towns, including Astoria, Forest Grove, Albany, Salem, Eugene, Springfield, West Linn, Baker City, Medford, Klamath Falls, and Portland.

Immense log rafts such as the one shown here in 1902 were visual proof of the abundance of timber in Oregon and its extensive lumber industry. Transporting logs in rafts would soon give way to transport by rail, which was more efficient. By 1929, Oregon had approximately 608 lumber mills; by 1947, there were 1,537. Timber production fell into decline by 1980 and many mills in the state have since closed.

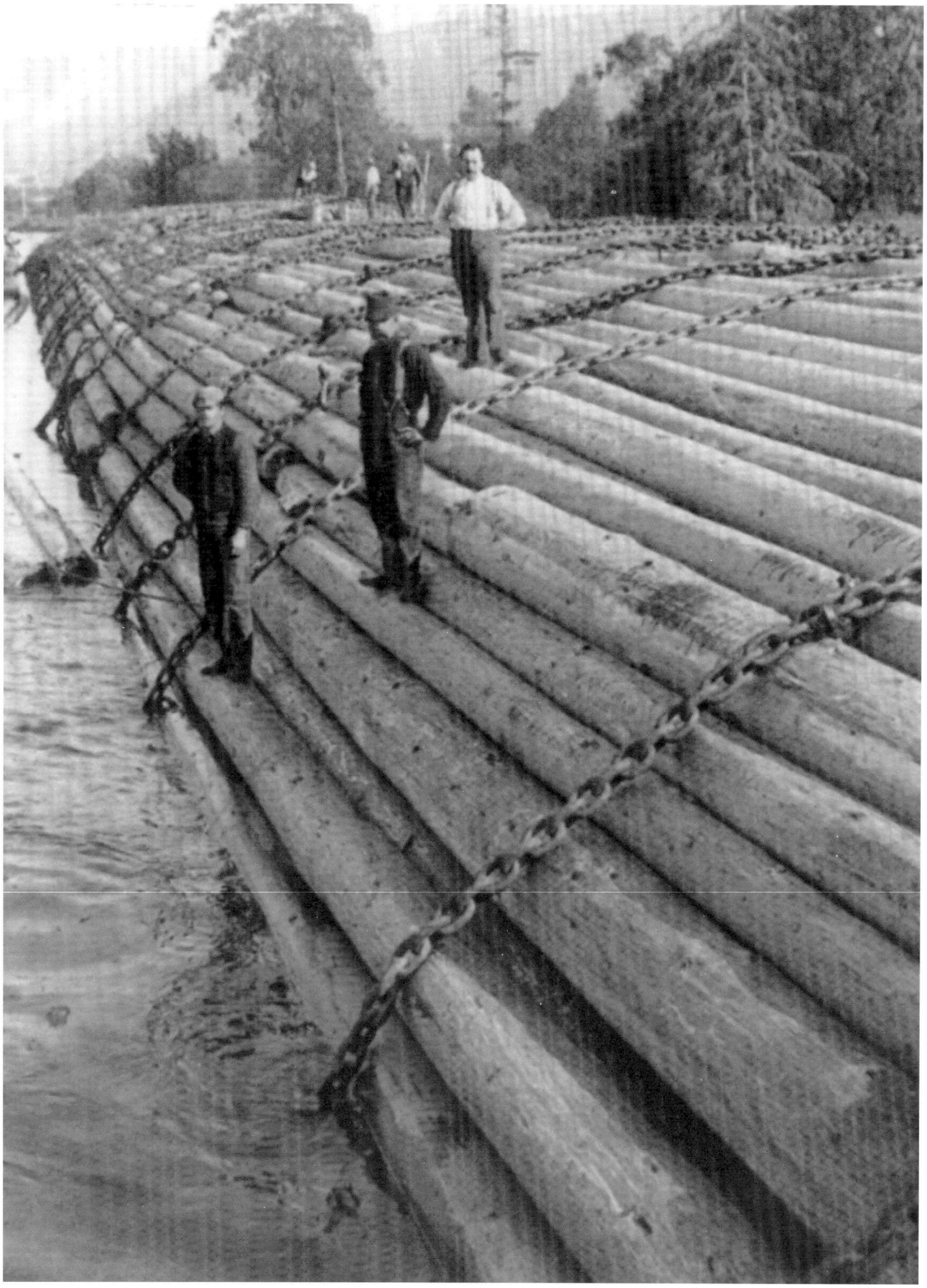

Challenges and Opportunities

(1900–1919)

As Oregon entered the twentieth century, it was apparent that change was in the air for the state economically, politically, socially, and culturally. The Progressive era was under way nationwide, and politics in Oregon, which went from conservative to progressive, was no different. Instrumental in this shift was state senator William U'Ren, whose efforts in the legislature were successful in passing the initiative and referendum, the ability to recall officials, the presidential primary election, and the popular election of U.S. senators. These efforts were collectively called "the Oregon System." The progressive era also saw a movement by workers in rural and urban areas throughout the state (the Populists) to improve their working conditions. A more extreme labor group, the International Workers of the World (known as "Wobblies"), pushed for radical changes in labor and government in the United States. Women's suffrage also gained a foothold under the leadership of Abigail Scott Duniway, resulting in the passage of the Women's Suffrage Act in Oregon in 1912.

Immigrants from Europe and Asia continued to arrive, working mostly at construction, fishing, and salmon canning, for the railroads and lumber mills, and in service industries. Portland grew economically during the era, largely owing to the increase in population, job opportunities, and the Lewis and Clark Exposition of 1905. The fair, which celebrated the centennial of the Lewis and Clark Expedition, attracted 1.6 million visitors, some of whom stayed.

World War I would end 20 months after the United States joined the conflict in April 1917, removing all doubt that the U.S. had entered the world stage as a world power able to shape nations when threatened. More than 24,000 Oregonians volunteered to fight the war, and of the more than 44,000 who participated, 1,030 gave their lives in defense of the nation. Those who had left insular communities for the war returned home with global experiences and changed perspectives.

Victory in war was followed by economic prosperity. Oregon was enthusiastic about its economic and population growth, and citizens looked forward to the promise of future opportunity, evidenced by images showing the state's prosperity in transportation, shipping, lumber milling, and agriculture. Oregonians, like most people in the United States, would by and large enjoy a strong economy throughout the 1920s.

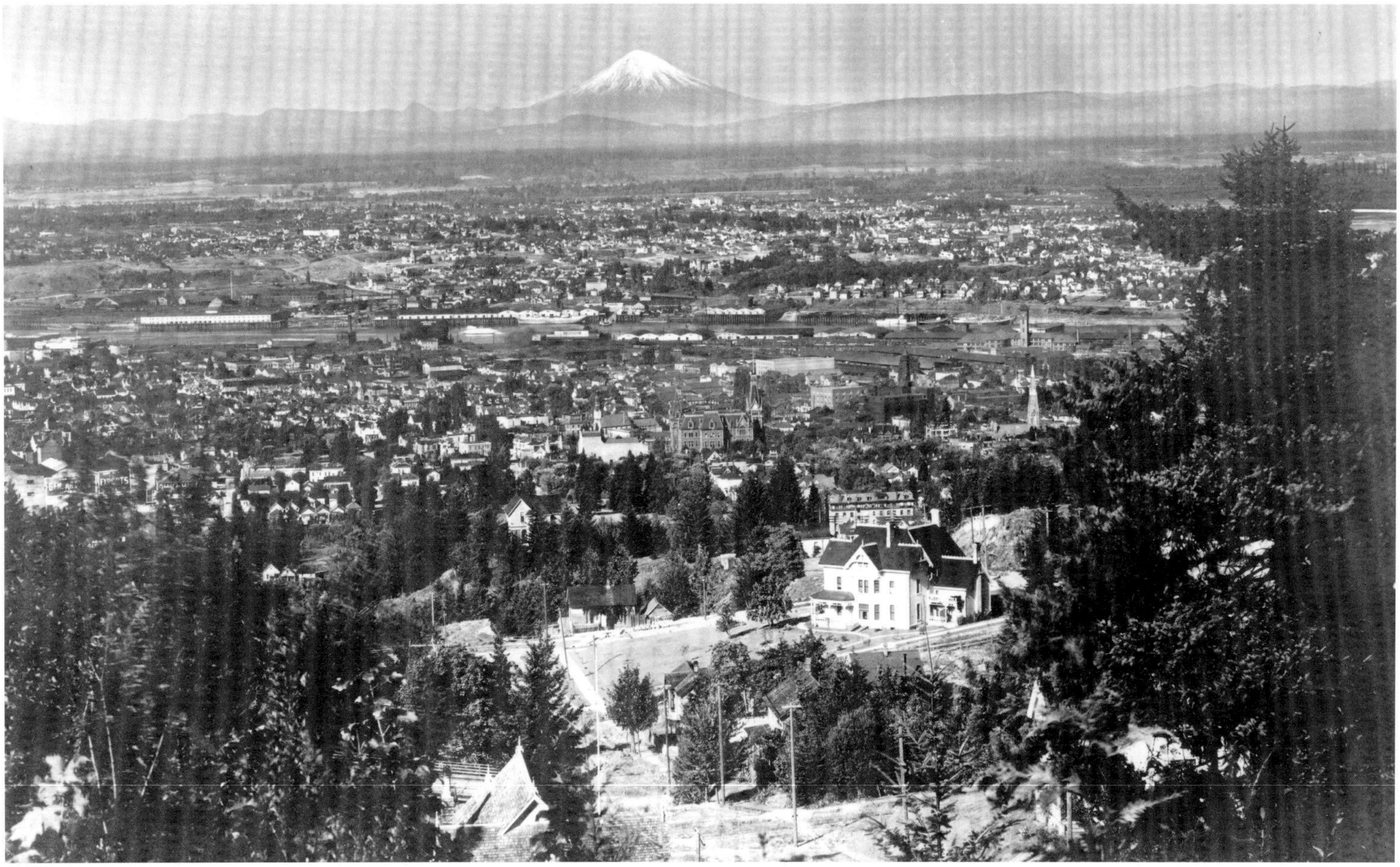

Volcanic Mount Hood, the tallest mountain peak in Oregon, rises in the background above Portland in 1903. New buildings reflect the prosperity of the city following completion of the railroad and the trade that it brought to the city.

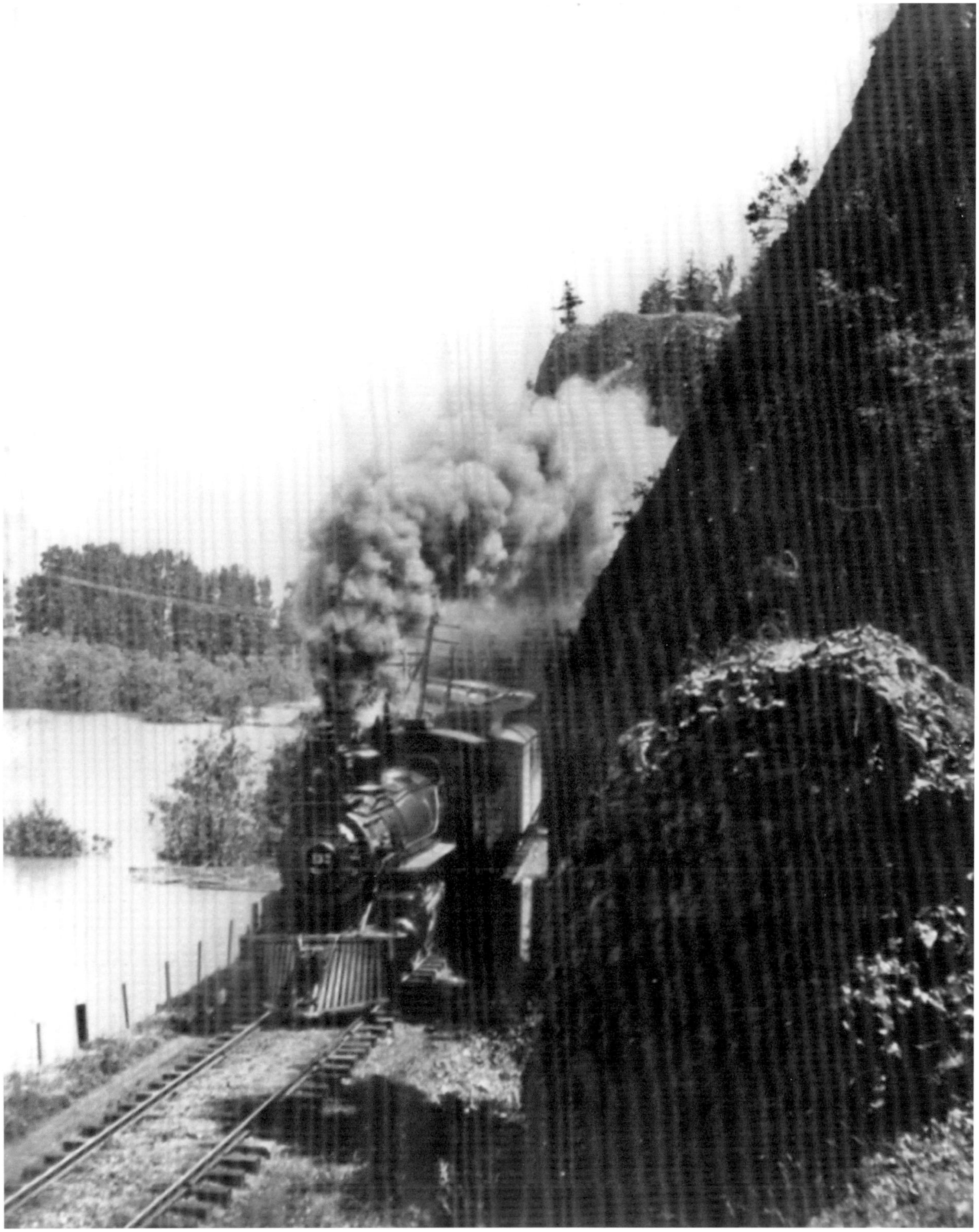

The Oregon and California Railroad had opened the state to commerce in 1887. Pictured here is the Oregon "Short Line" on the Columbia River in 1903. The Northern Pacific Railroad and the Union Pacific Railroad would also connect the state to points east. Other railroads of the era were the Spokane, Portland and Seattle Railway, the Oregon Electric Railway, and the Oregon Trunk Railway.

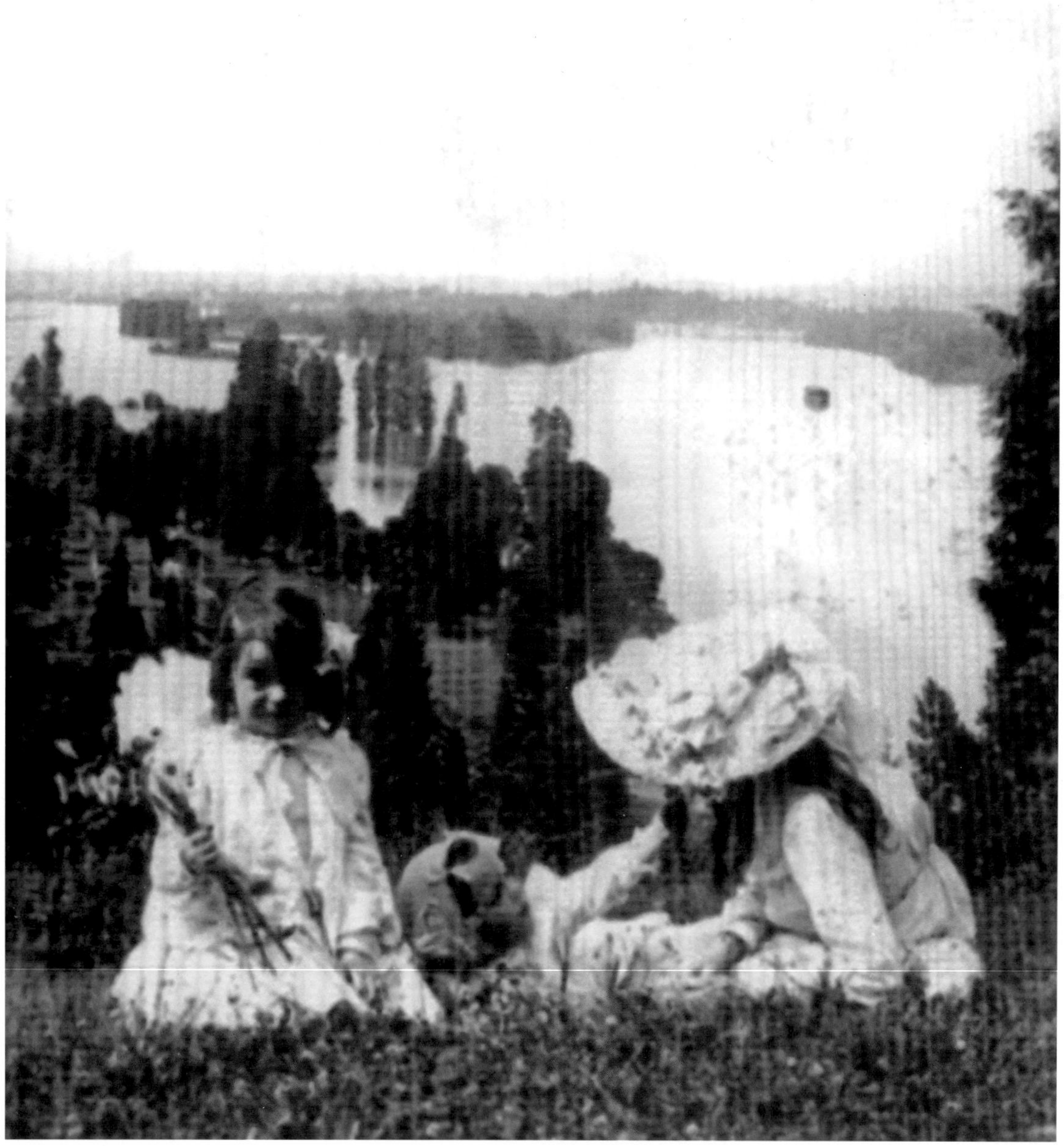

Three young girls are having a picnic on a hill overlooking the Columbia River early in the new century. The Columbia River has at various times been a leading travel artery, with transportation ranging from canoes to diesel-powered barges, and a source of hydroelectric power for the region, beginning in the 1930s.

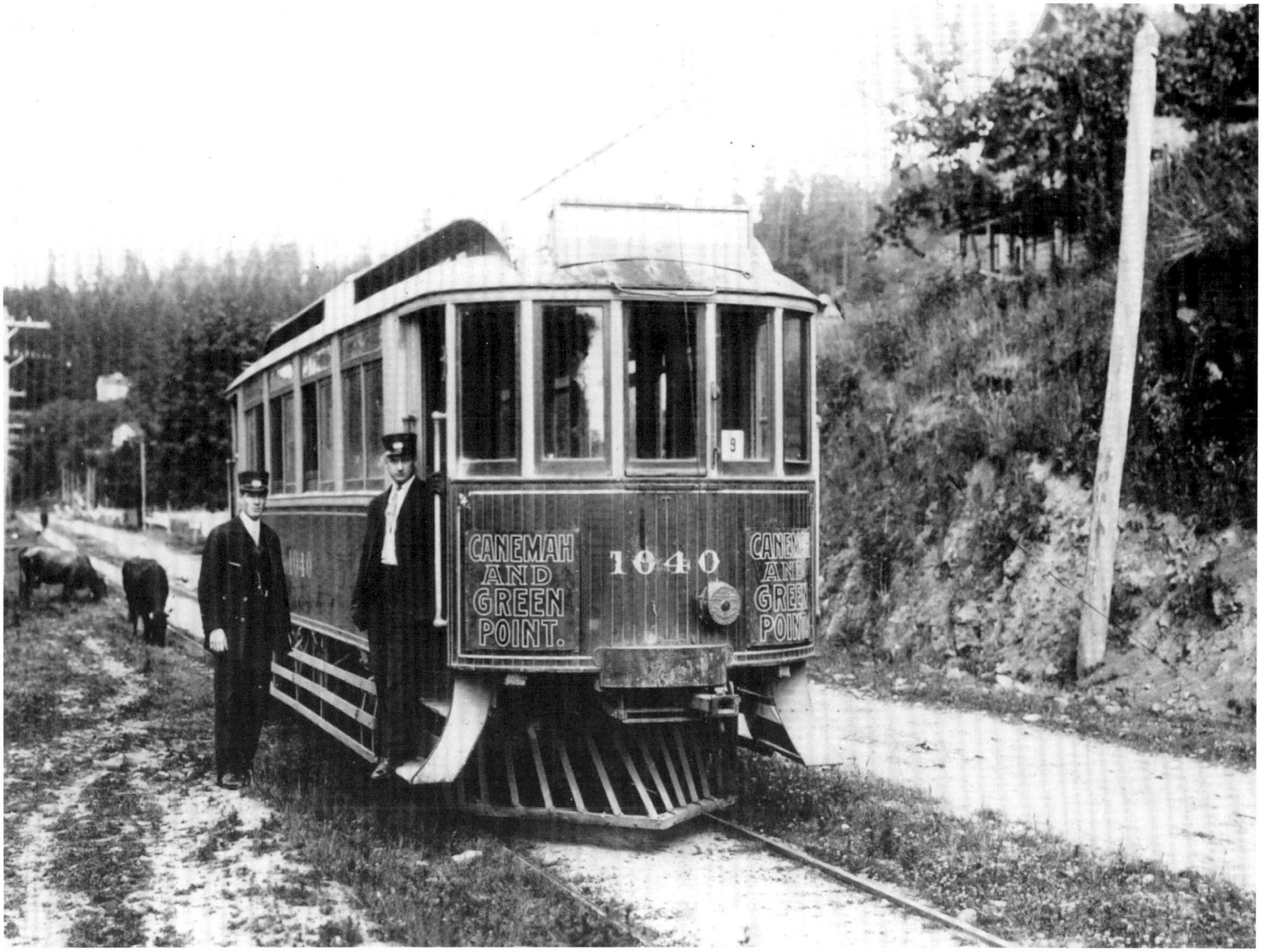

Canemah (now part of Oregon City) was the terminus of the East Side Railway, the interurban railway that extended to Portland when it opened in 1893. The picnic area and baseball field in Canemah made it a favorite destination for Sunday excursions from Portland.

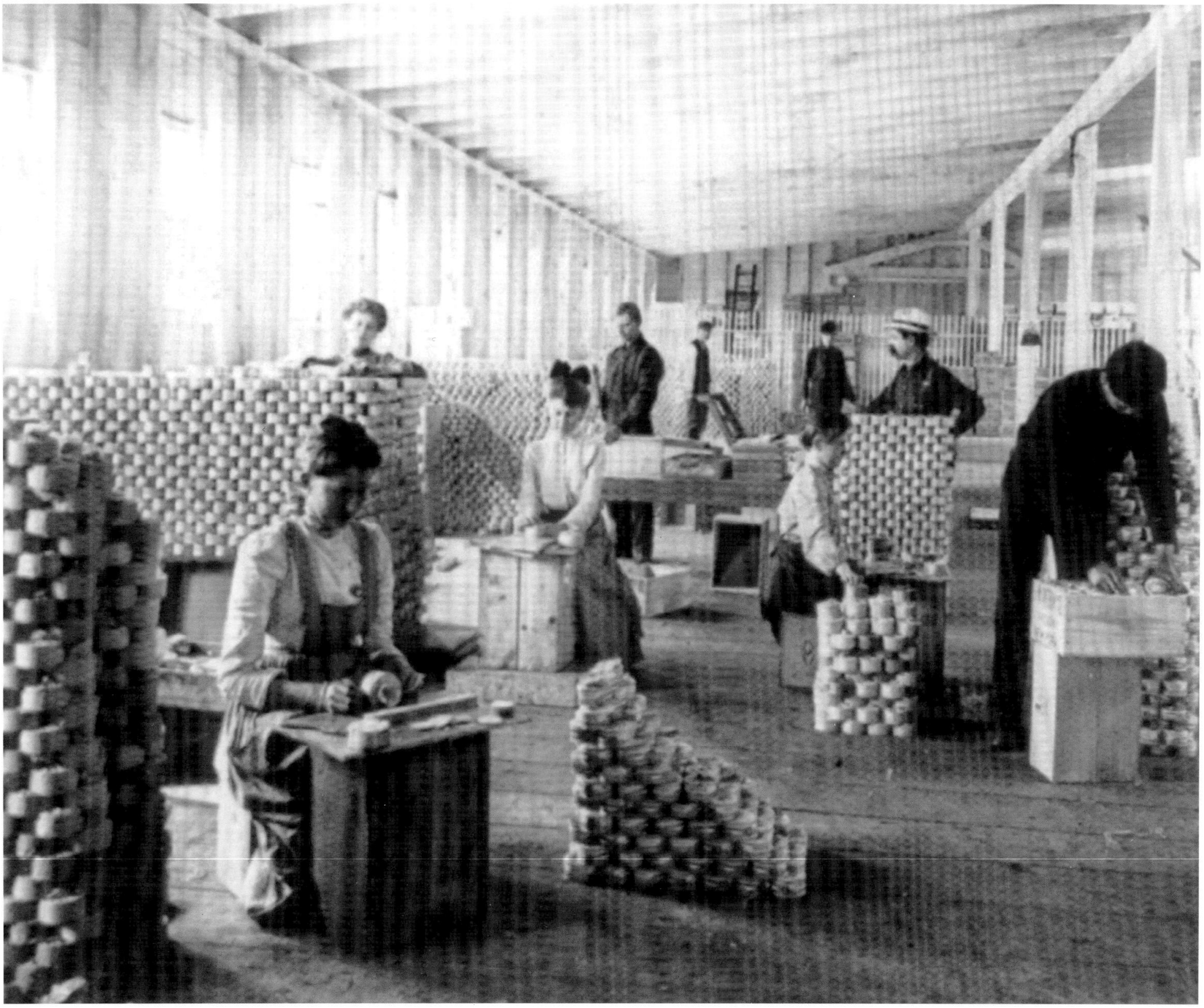

Huge salmon runs up the Columbia River propelled the growth of commercial fishing and canning operations in Astoria on the northern Oregon coast. Chinese, Finns, Swedes, and other immigrants came to Astoria to work in the fishing and logging industries during the early part of the twentieth century.

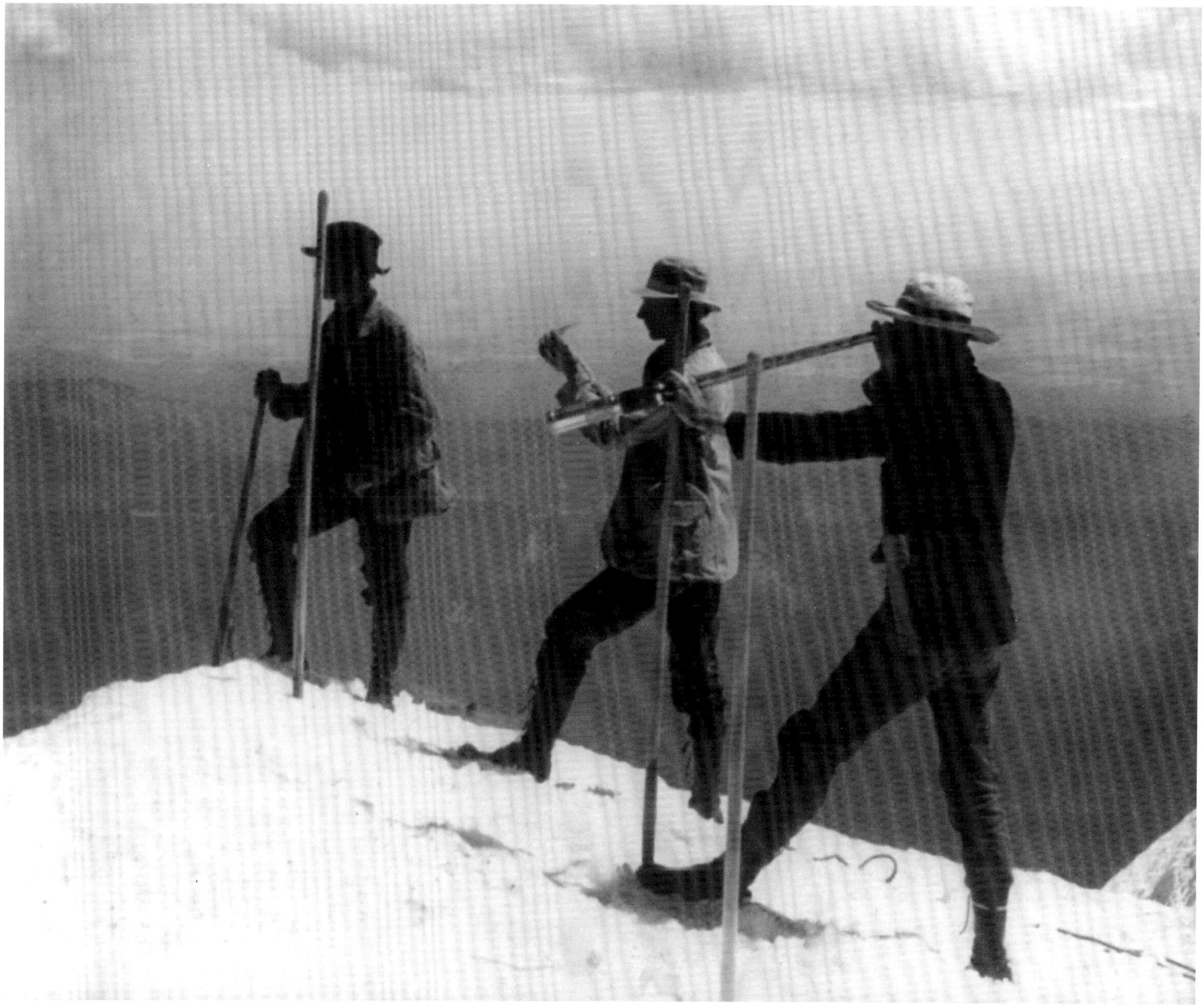

Three mountain climbers have reached the summit of Mount Hood, 11,249 feet above sea level, around 1904. The first recorded successful climb of Mount Hood had taken place some decades earlier, on August 6, 1857.

Vacations to the ocean were once reserved for those who could afford a journey to the coast. In the late nineteenth century this began to change as families of average income began riding the rails to beaches like this one. When the Oregon Coast Highway was completed in the early 1930s, Oregonians could at last visit the coast by automobile.

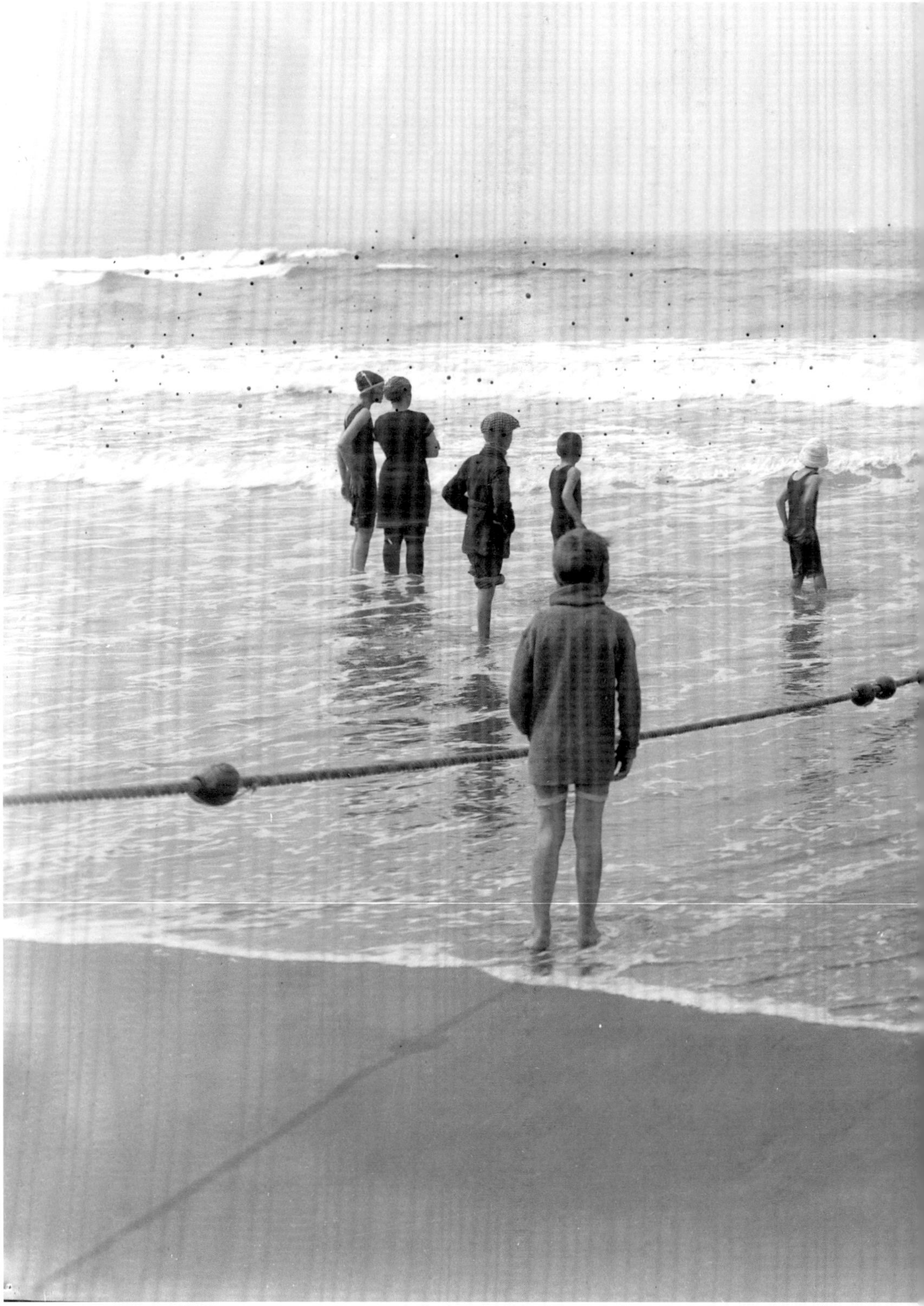

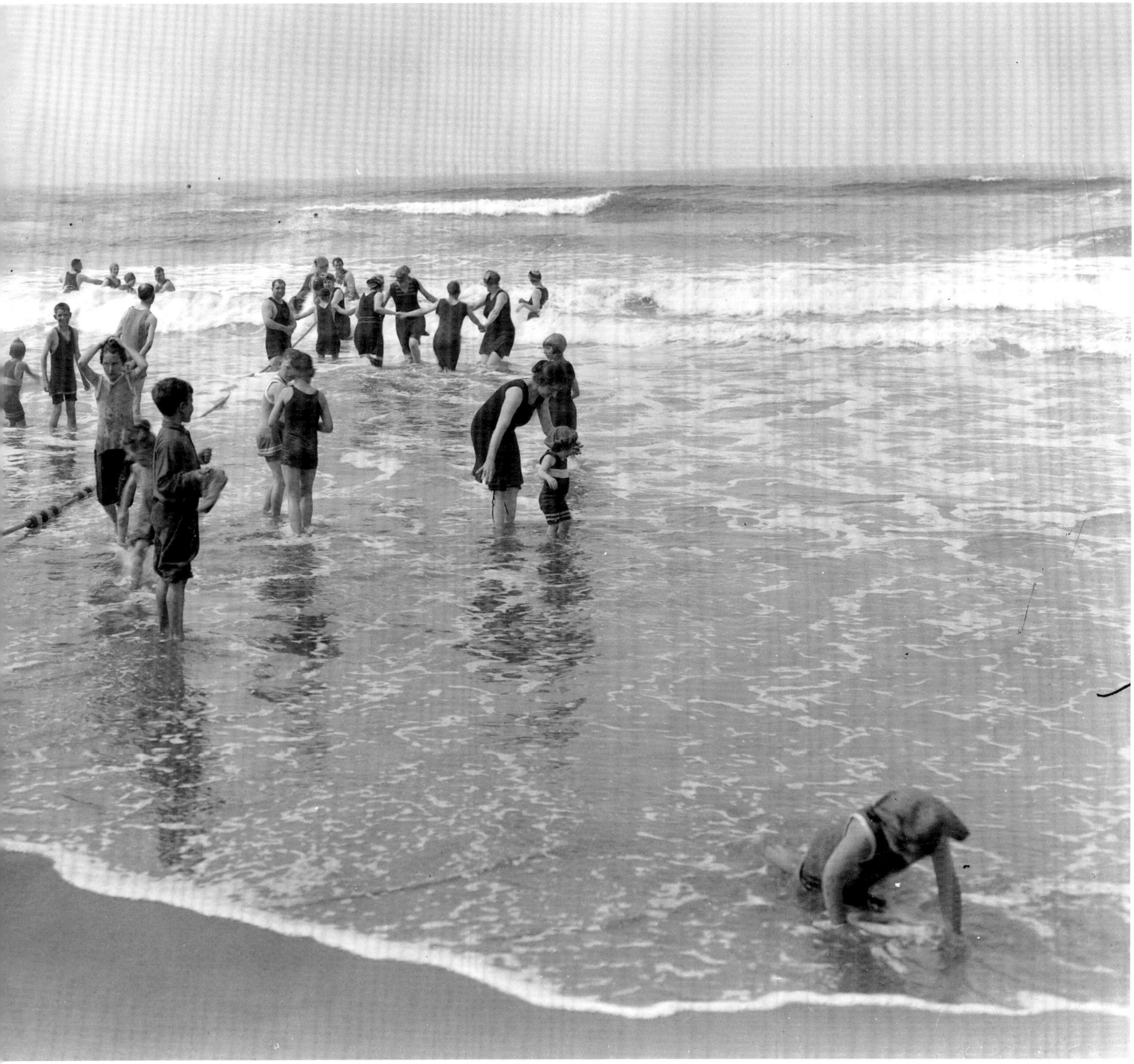

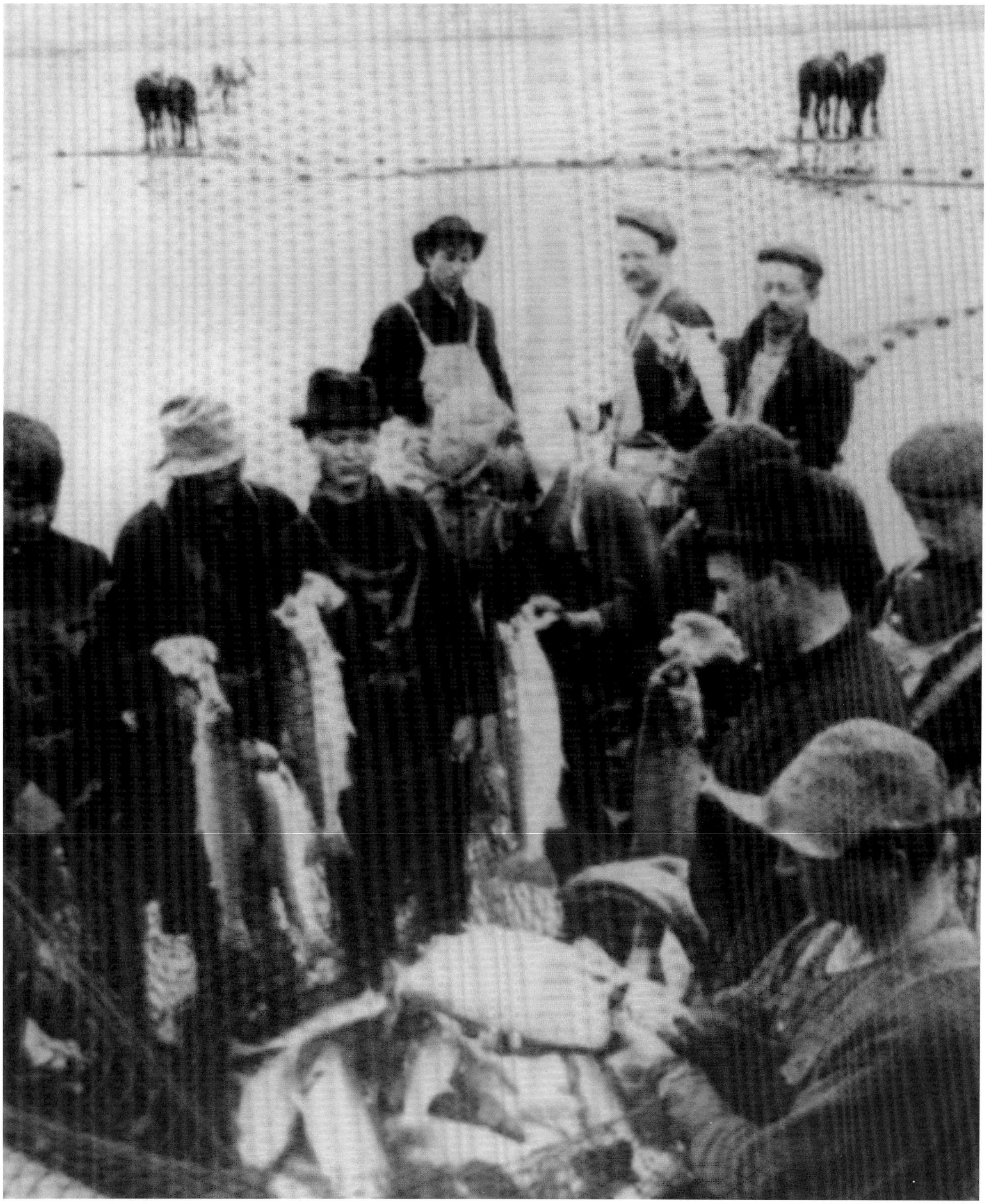

Chinook salmon was the main target of commercial fishing beginning in the 1870s, but overfishing led to a drop in fish populations by the late nineteenth century. The salmon fishing industry in Oregon would eventually fall into decline.

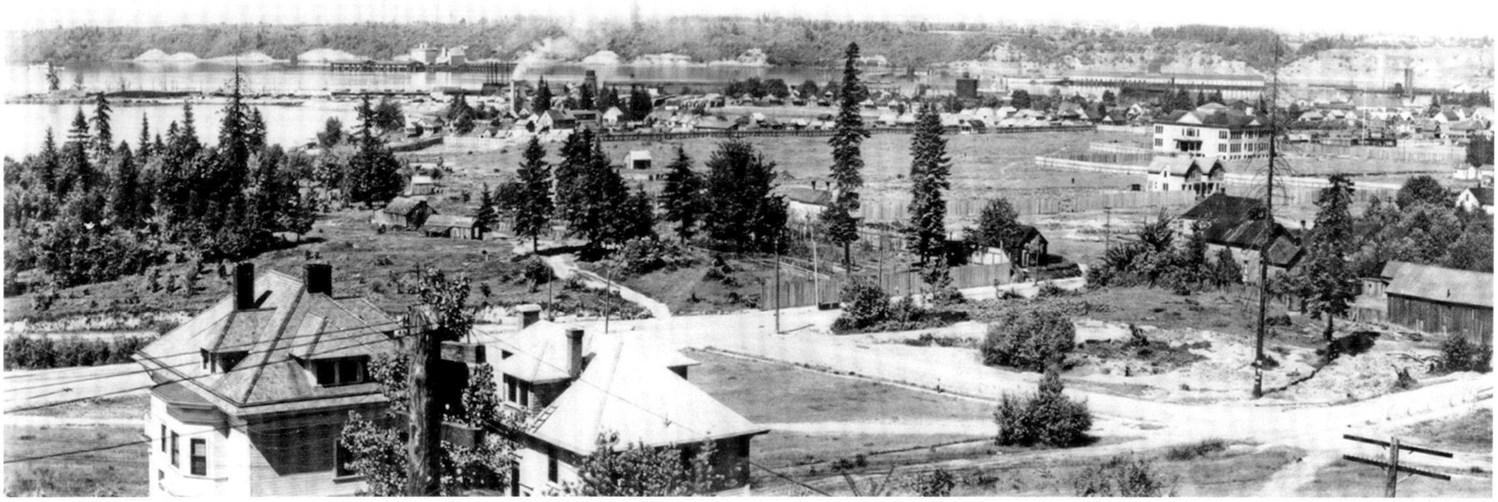

The Lewis and Clark Centennial Exposition of 1905 was built in the Guild's Lake area of northwest Portland. Prior to the exposition, the area was mostly pasture land and stagnant water. Oregon added 110,000 residents in the five years that followed the exposition, a profitable venture often credited for the new arrivals.

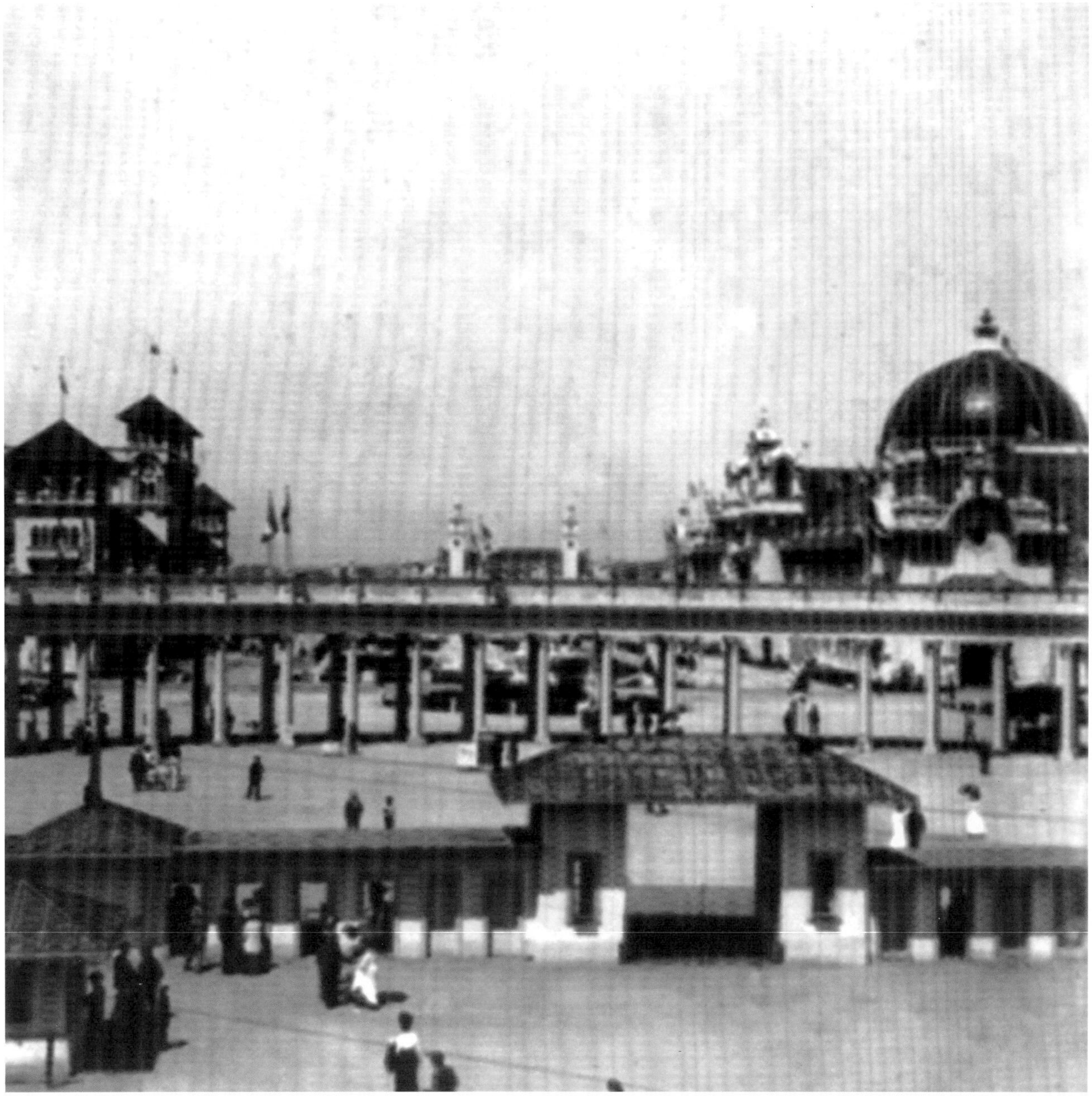

Portland's civic leaders had decided to host the Lewis and Clark Exposition to commemorate the centennial of the 1805 Lewis and Clark Expedition, which charted the Louisiana Purchase frontier from St. Louis to the Pacific Ocean. This image shows the main entrance to the exposition.

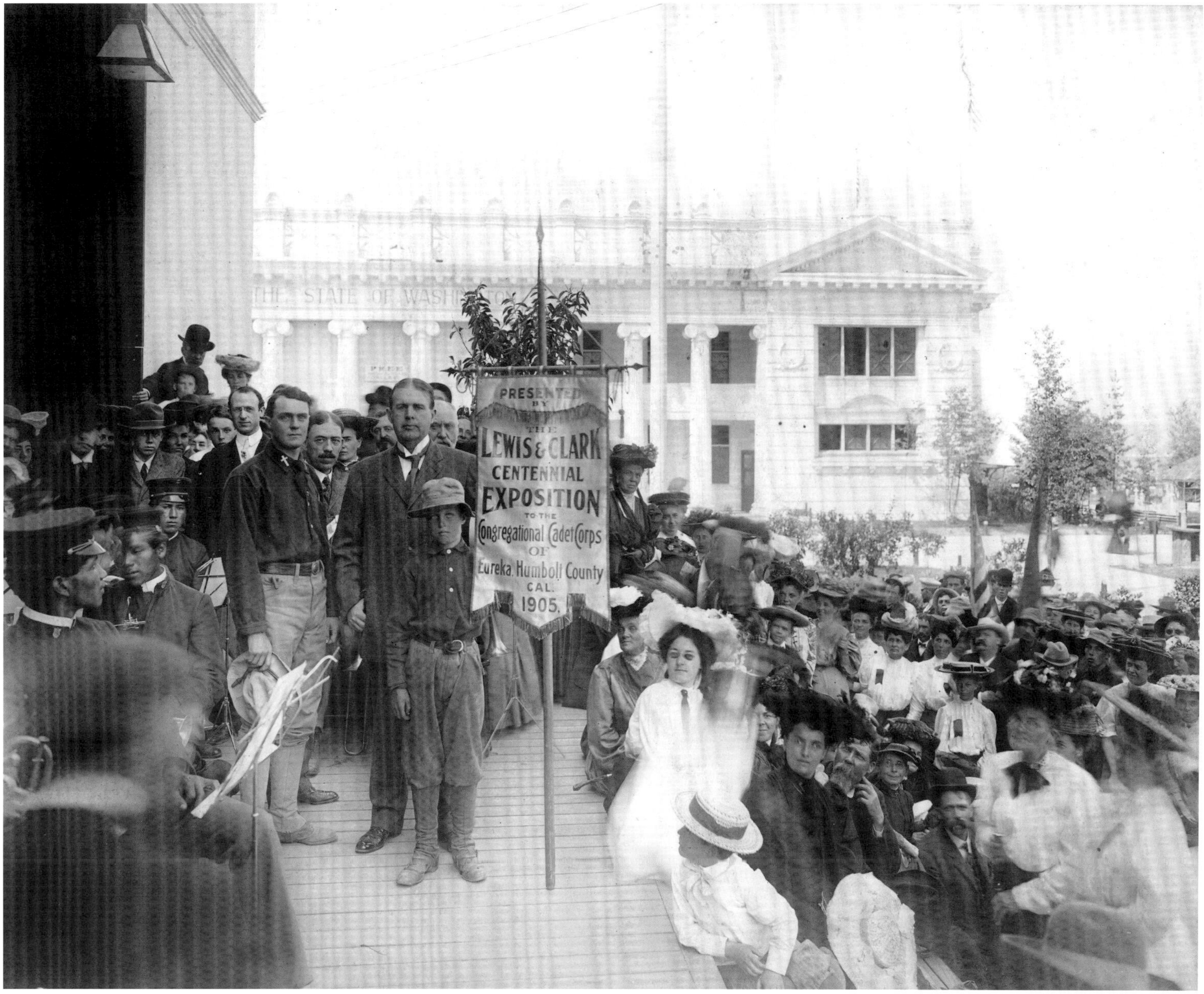

Attendees gather on the stage at the Lewis and Clark Exposition in Portland in 1905. Over its four-and-a-half month run, the fair would draw 1.6 million visitors, 400,000 of them from areas outside the Pacific Northwest. Portland was competing with other cities in the West for investment and immigration, and expositions like this one were seen nationwide as an excellent way to advertise.

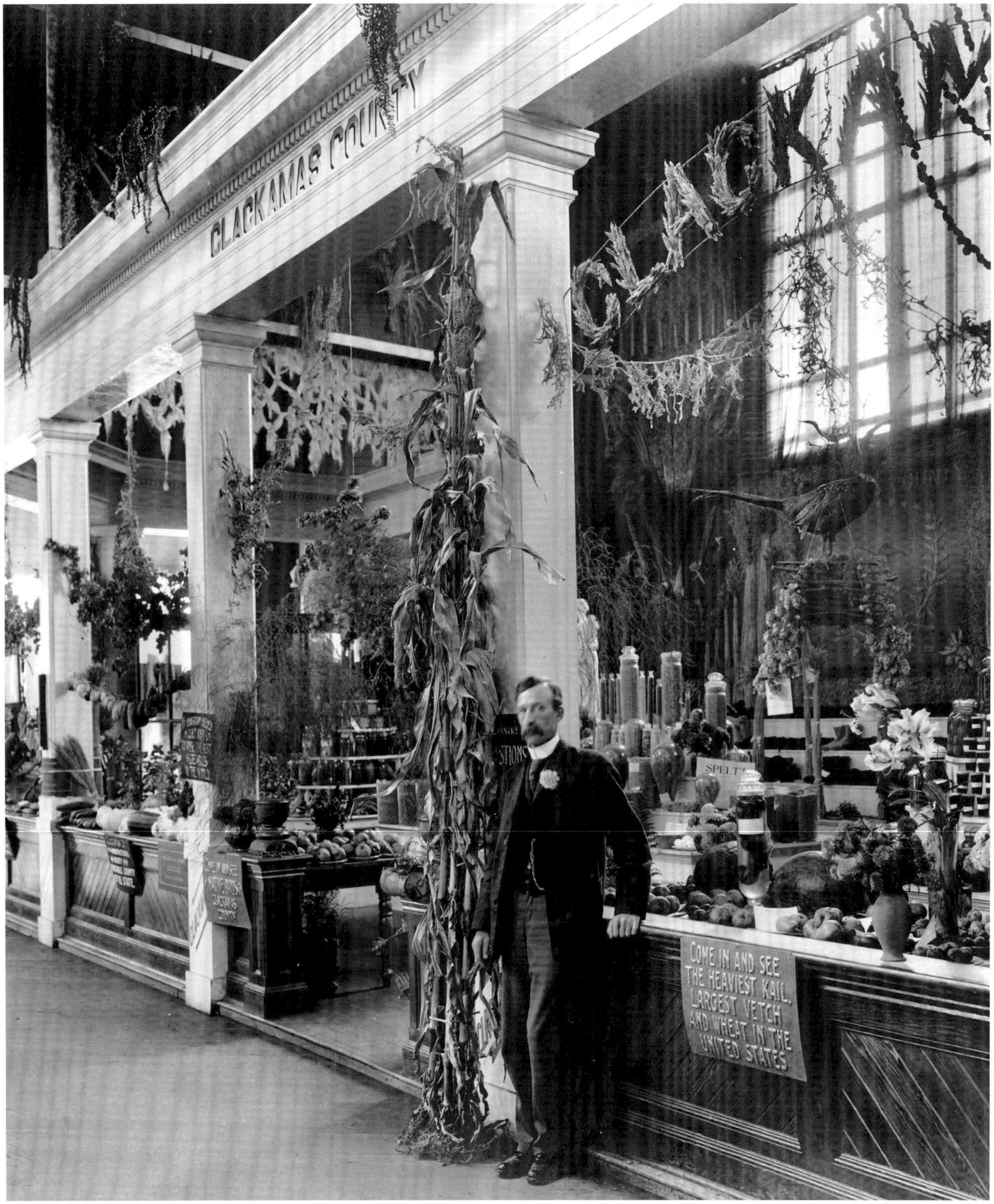

An official stands in front of the Clackamas County exhibit at the Lewis and Clark Centennial Exposition. The sign at lower-right says, "Come in and see the heaviest kail, largest vetch and wheat in the United States."

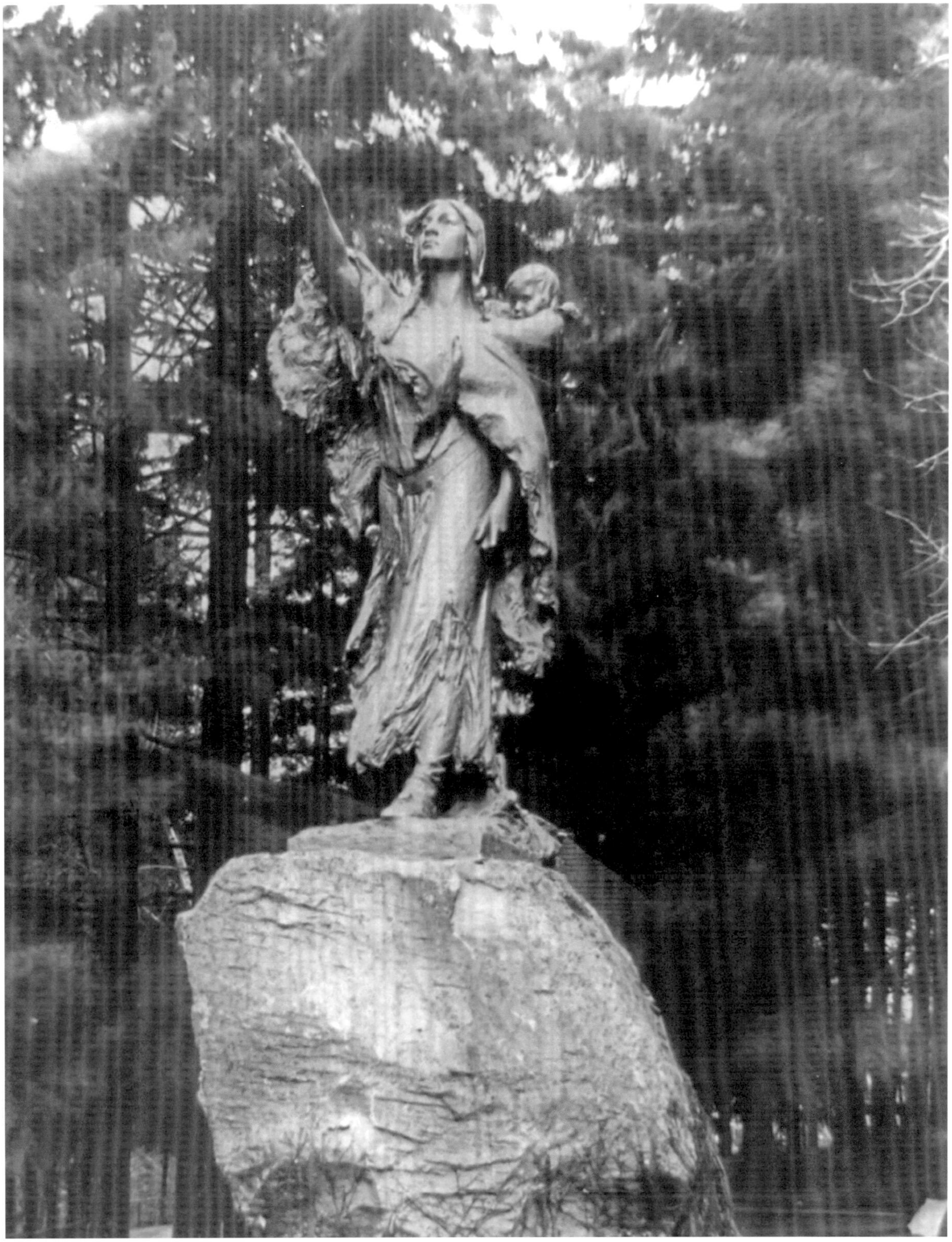

The statue of Sacajawea honored the Native American woman who served as a guide for the Lewis and Clark Expedition. It was unveiled at the Lewis and Clark Exposition in 1905. Today the statue is on display in Washington Park in Portland.

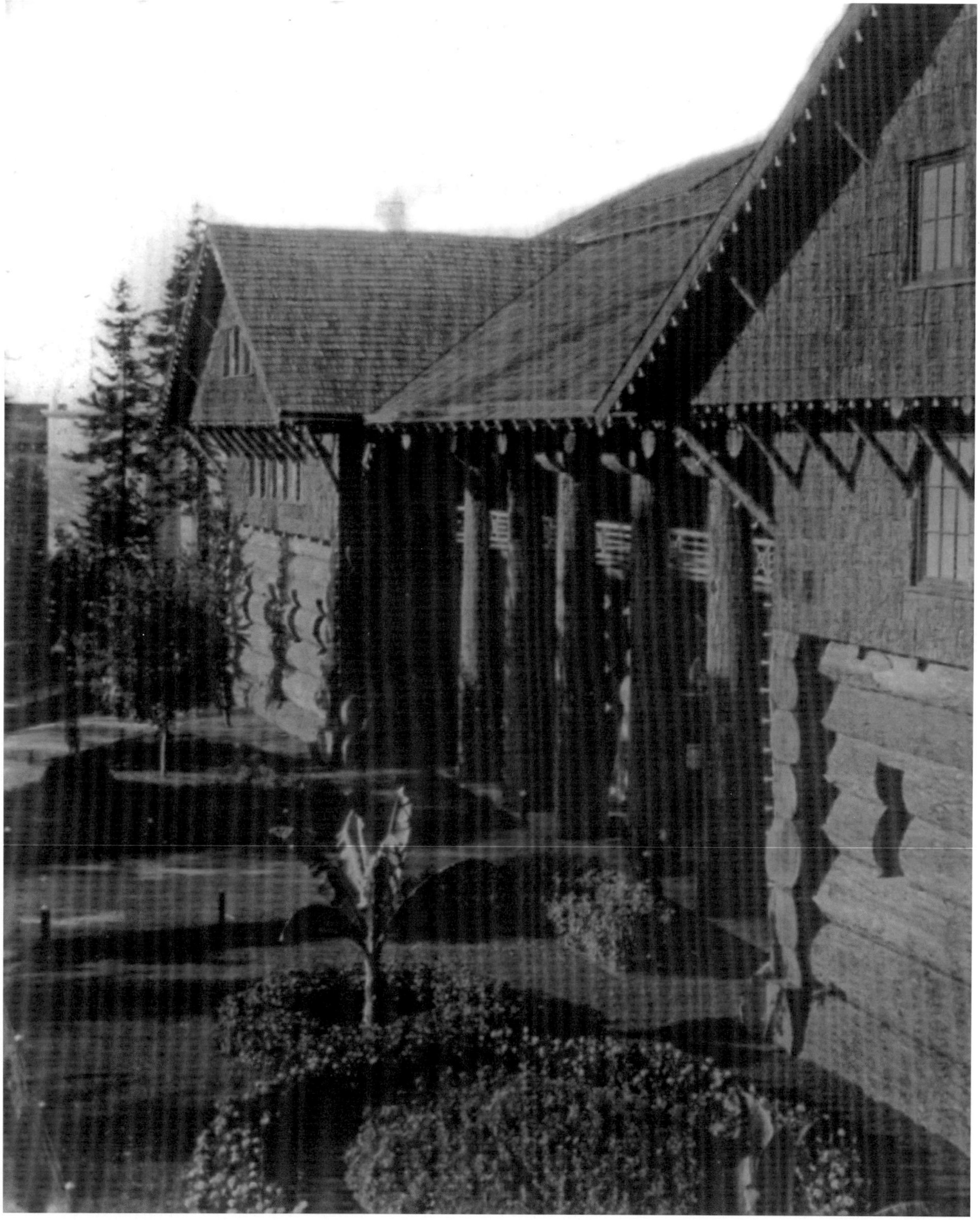

Constructed of enormous Douglas fir logs 48 feet tall and 4 to 5 feet in diameter, the Forestry Building was the pride of the Lewis and Clark Exposition. Shown here around 1906, it was considered to be the largest "log cabin" in the world. Efforts to maintain and protect the venerated building would come to naught when it burned to the ground in 1964.

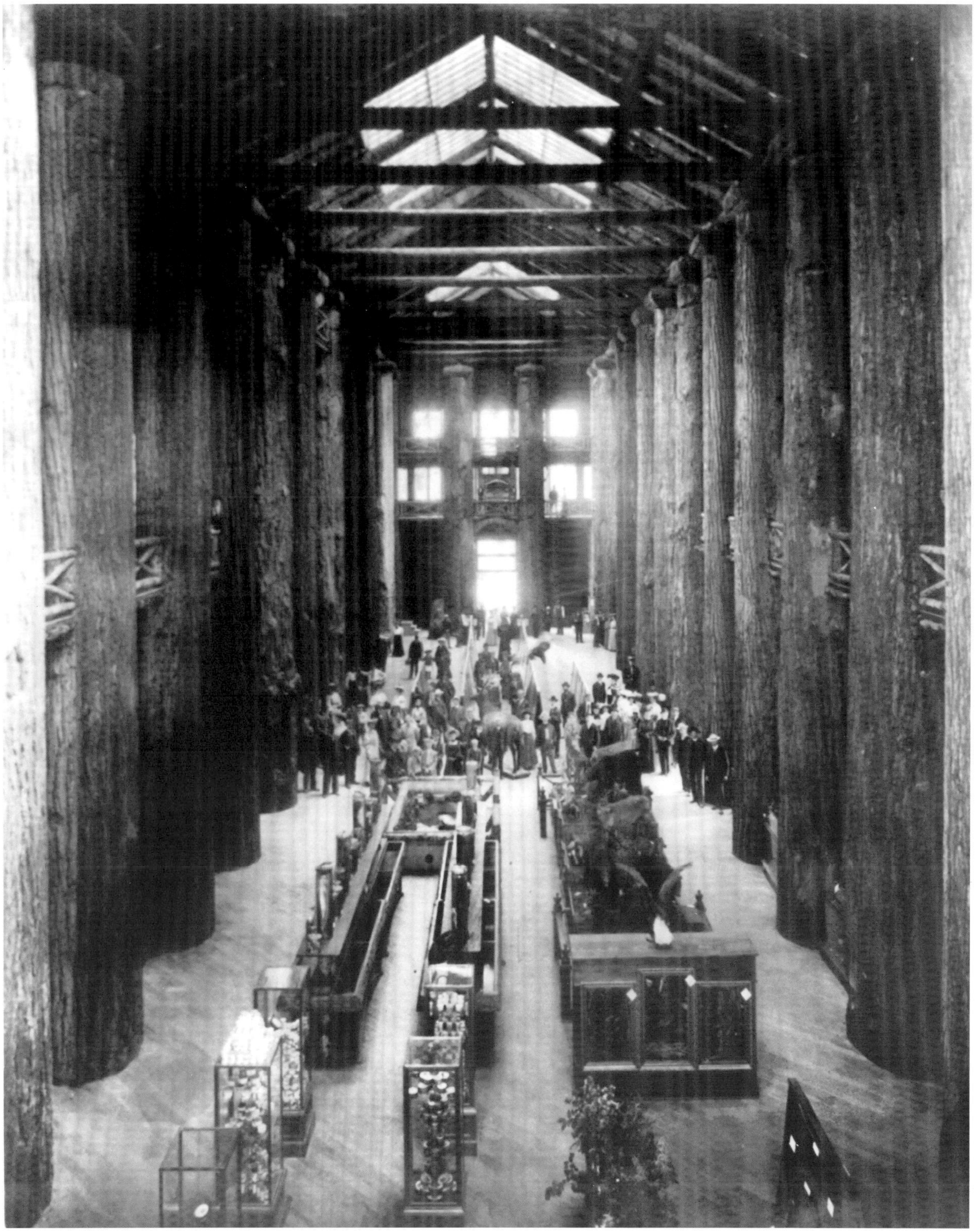

Interior of the Forestry Building at the Lewis and Clark Exposition during the fair. As the most popular attraction of the exposition, the enormous structure made news that reached New Yorkers, a group of whom offered $200,000 to dismantle it and ship it to Coney Island for reassembly. Portland turned down the offer.

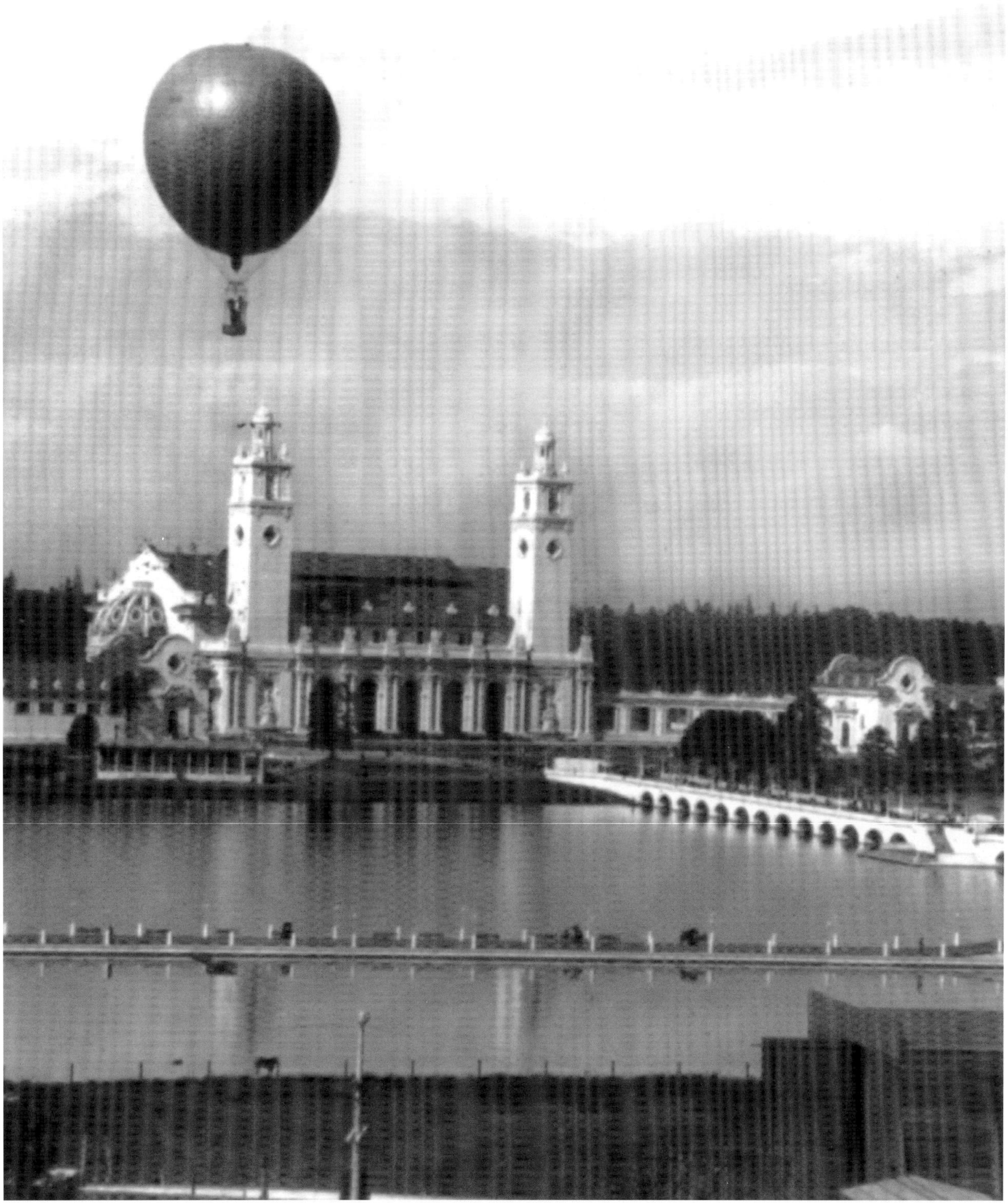

A balloon glides over Guild's Lake at the Lewis and Clark Exposition in Portland. The fair featured exhibits from other states and 21 foreign nations, offered amusements including motion pictures, and was the finish line for the first transcontinental automobile race from New York City to Portland.

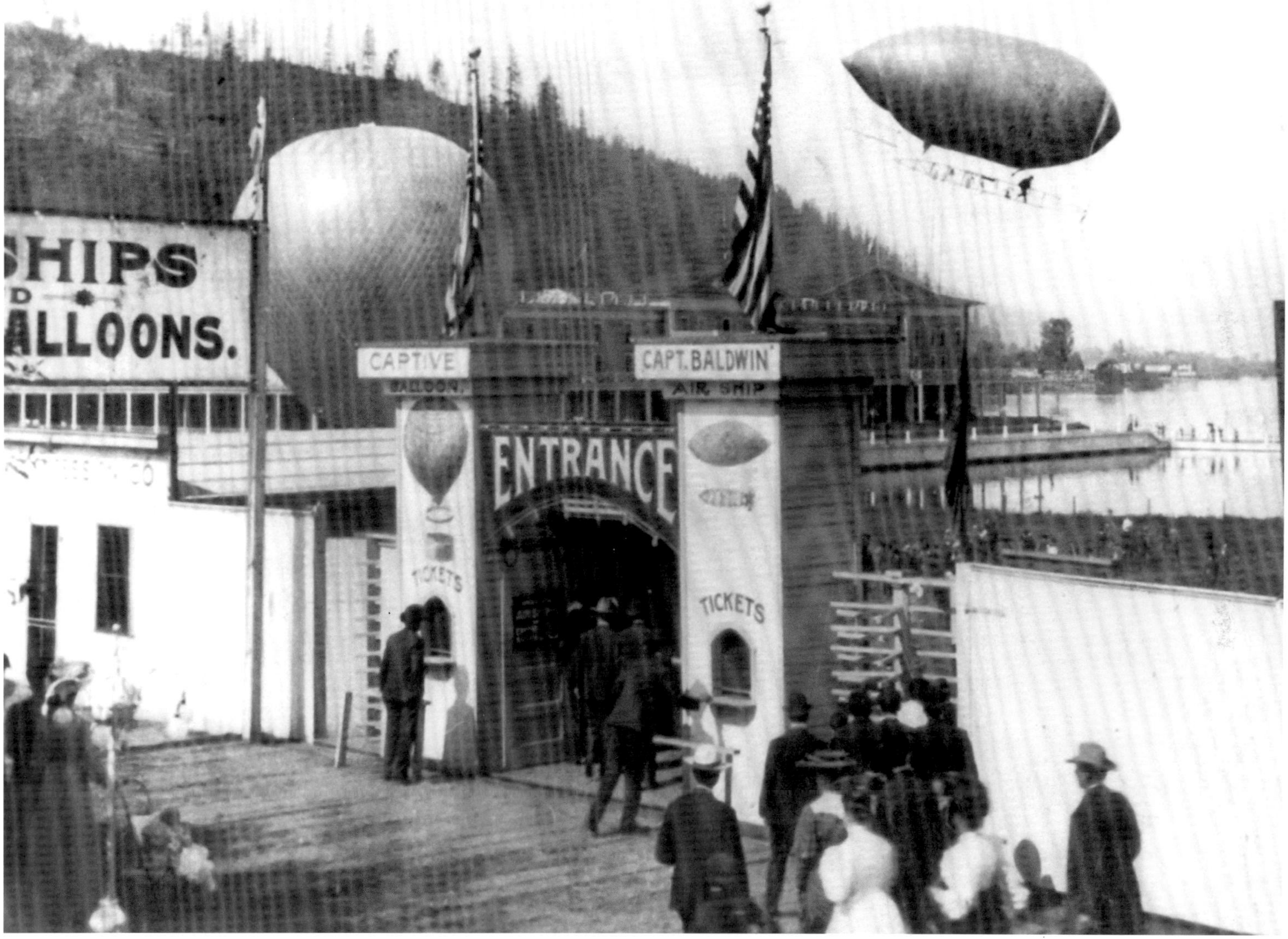

Lewis and Clark Exposition crowds flocked to see airships like the *Gelatine,* shown in flight here. Balloon pioneer Captain Thomas Baldwin built several powered airships to be flown at the fair. One of his designs, the *Angelus,* was piloted by aviation legend Lincoln Beachey, who steered the ship by walking to the rear of its gondola, which caused the ship to tilt upward and ascend, and by walking to the prow, which shifted the center of gravity forward, causing the ship to descend.

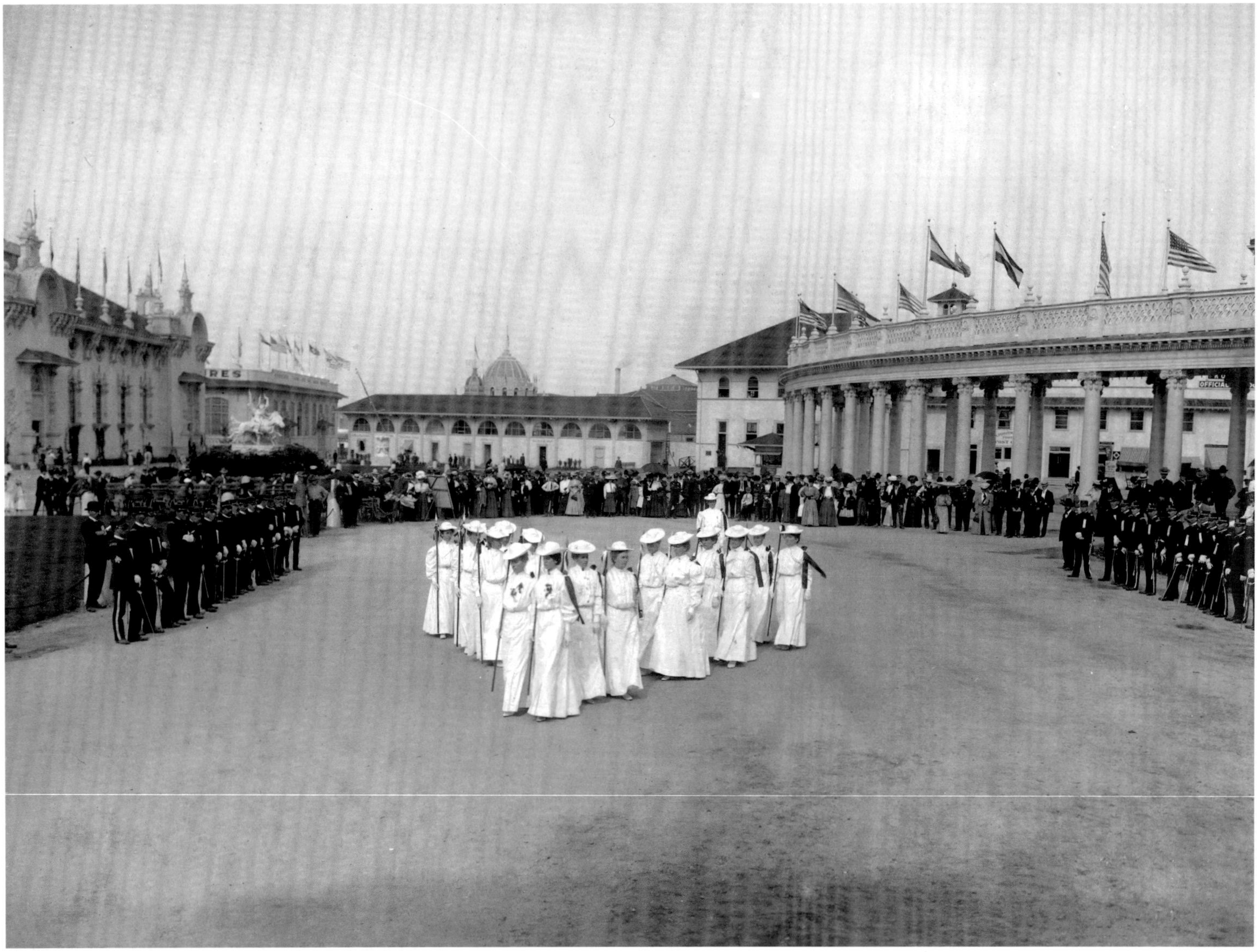

A procession at the Lewis and Clark Exposition of 1905 is the center of attraction of assembled onlookers. The fair not only lured settlers and commerce to the region, but it was a financial success as well, realizing $85,000 (in 1905 dollars) in profit. East Coast journalists called the exposition "Portland's pride."

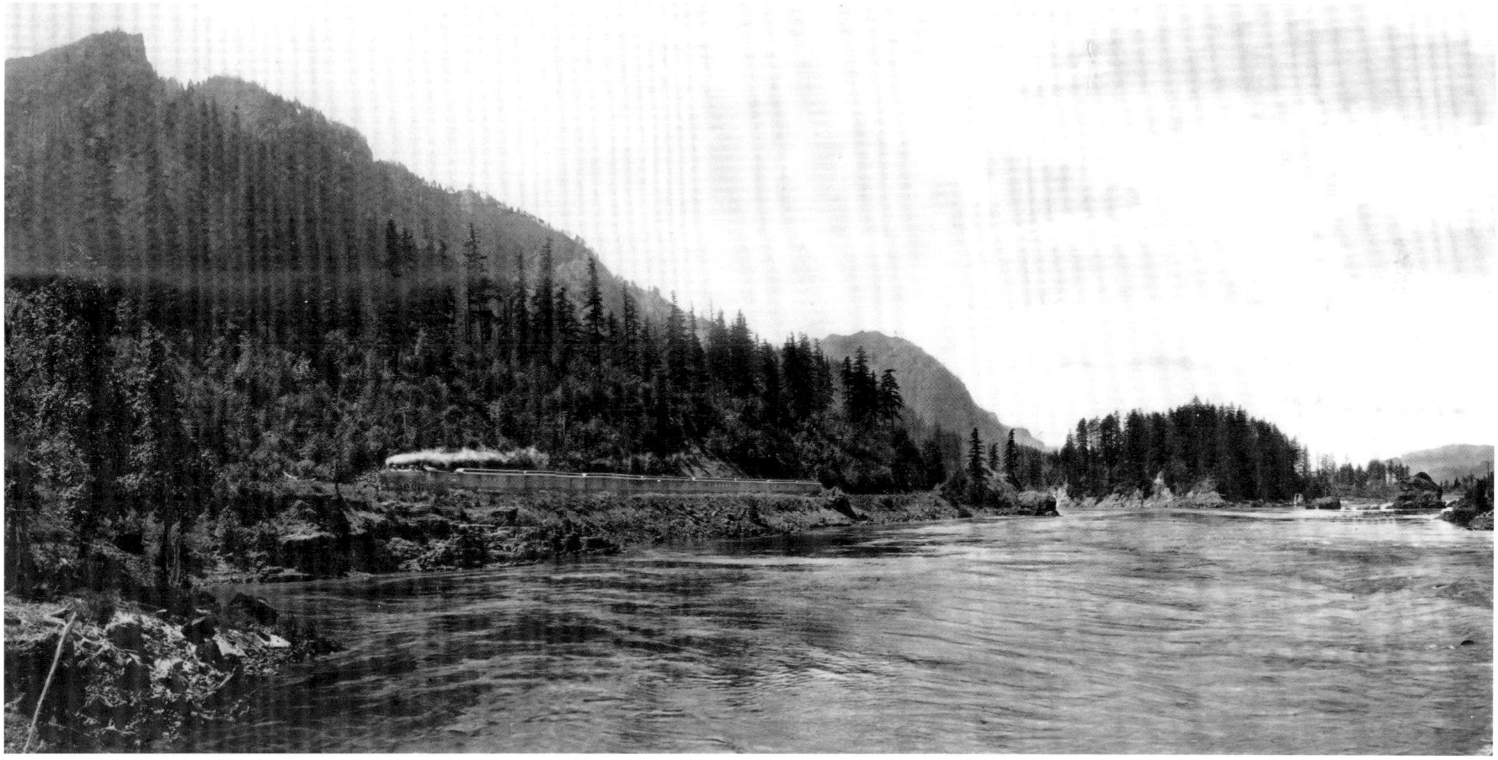

The Middle Cascades Mountains of the Columbia River as they appeared around 1906. The Columbia River is 1,243 miles long, flowing from Columbia Lake in British Columbia through Washington State and along the Oregon-Washington border. The river empties into the Pacific Ocean at Astoria.

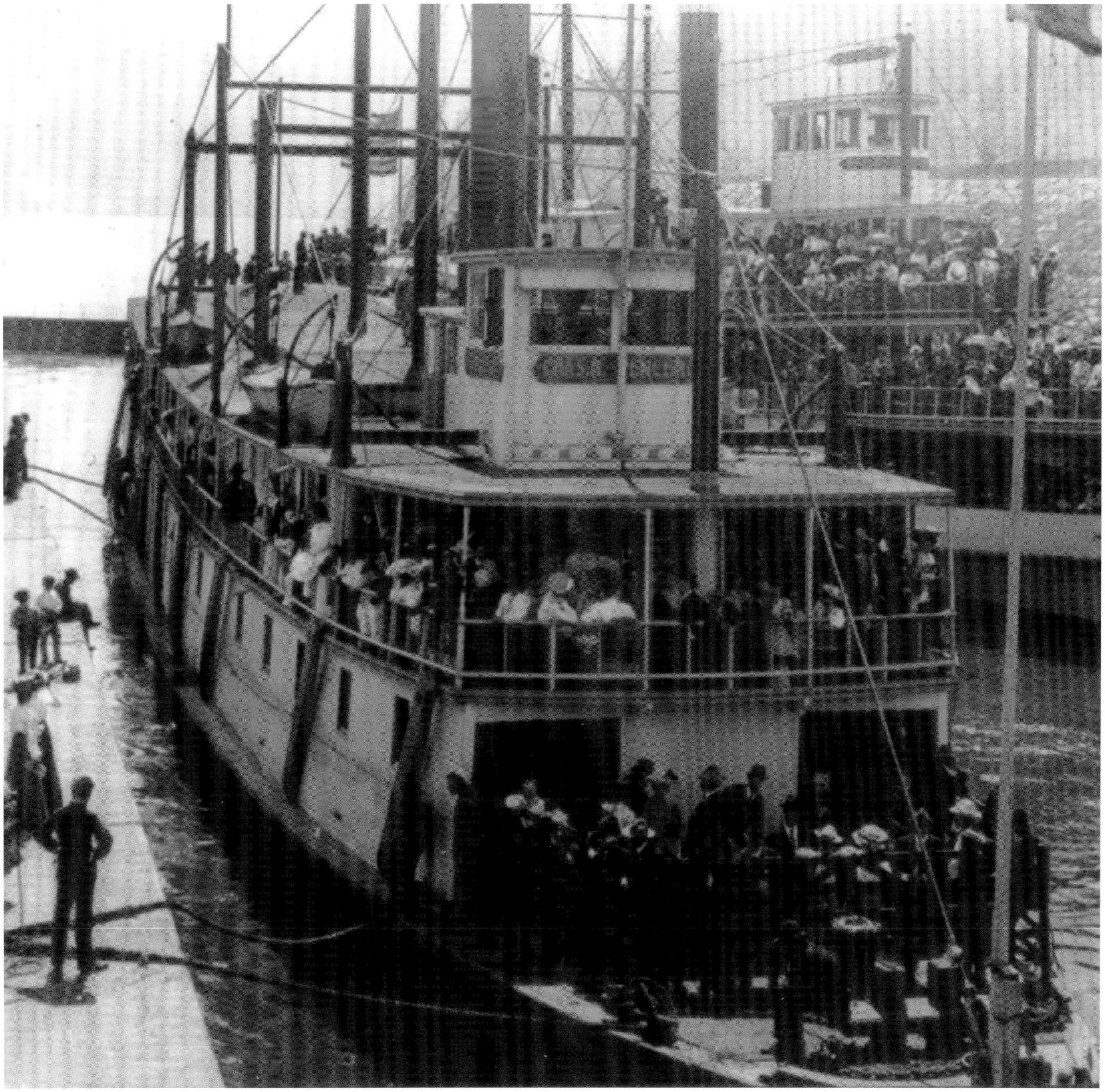

Steamers in the Cascade Locks, Columbia River, are filled to capacity with passengers in 1906. Sternwheel steamboats traveled the Columbia River from 1850 until the 1920s. Passengers on the upper decks of one boat can be seen holding umbrellas, relied on by Americans of the era as a shield against rain as well as the sun. Passenger traffic on steamboats had ceased on the Columbia River by the 1930s.

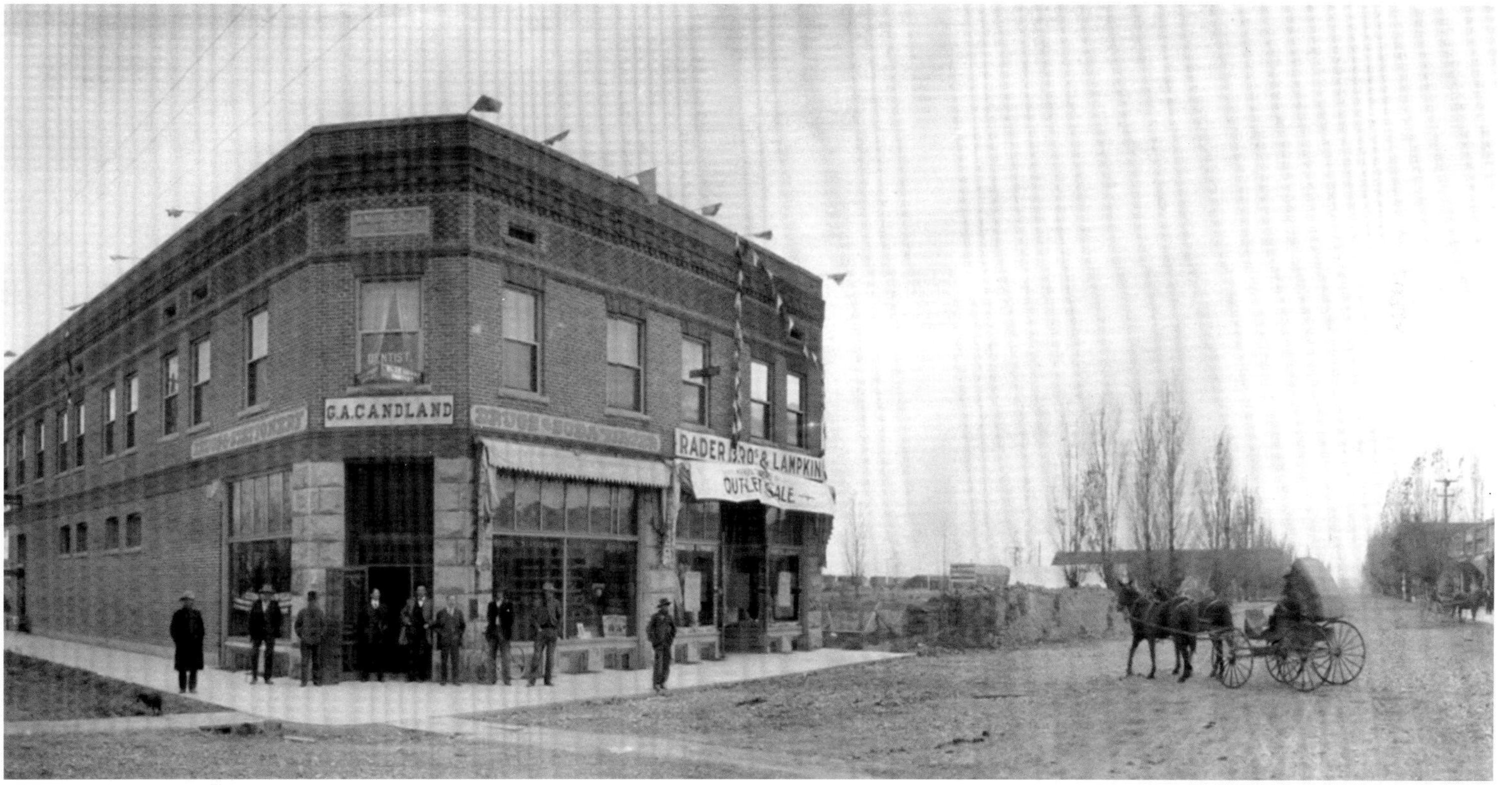

With the coming of the railroad in 1884 and the use of irrigation to boost agriculture, Ontario, Oregon, began to grow. The town would become a center for trade in the region in the twentieth century. This view was recorded in 1907.

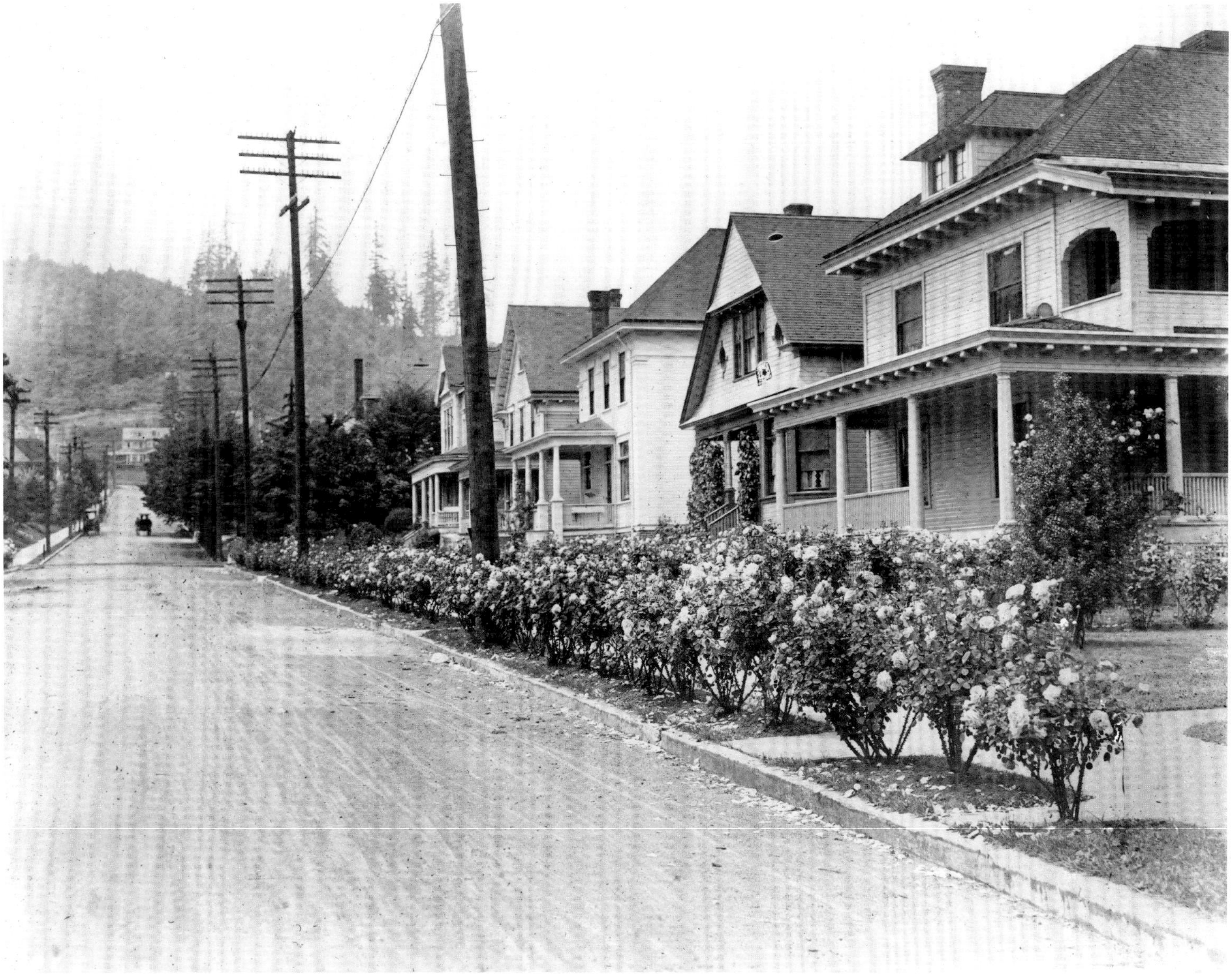

Roses line the curb of a Portland street. The Portland Rose Festival began in June 1907 with three days of events culminating in the grand parade. The festival called attention to Portland's interest in flowers and related activities.

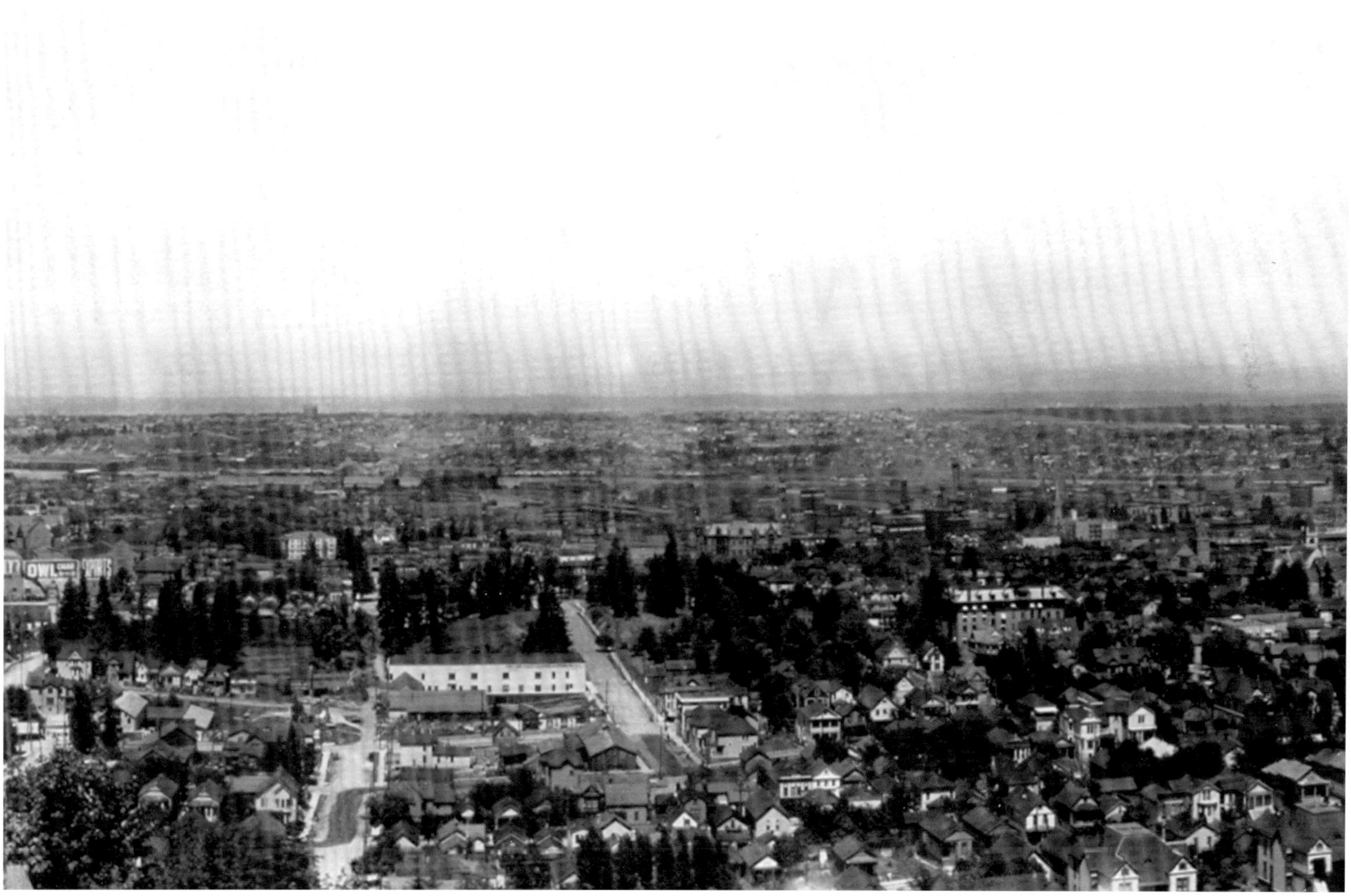

A panorama of Portland, from around 1908. Portland's immigrant communities continued to grow as the twentieth century unfolded. Large numbers of Chinese, Italian, Jewish, German, and Russian immigrants settled into what is now downtown Portland.

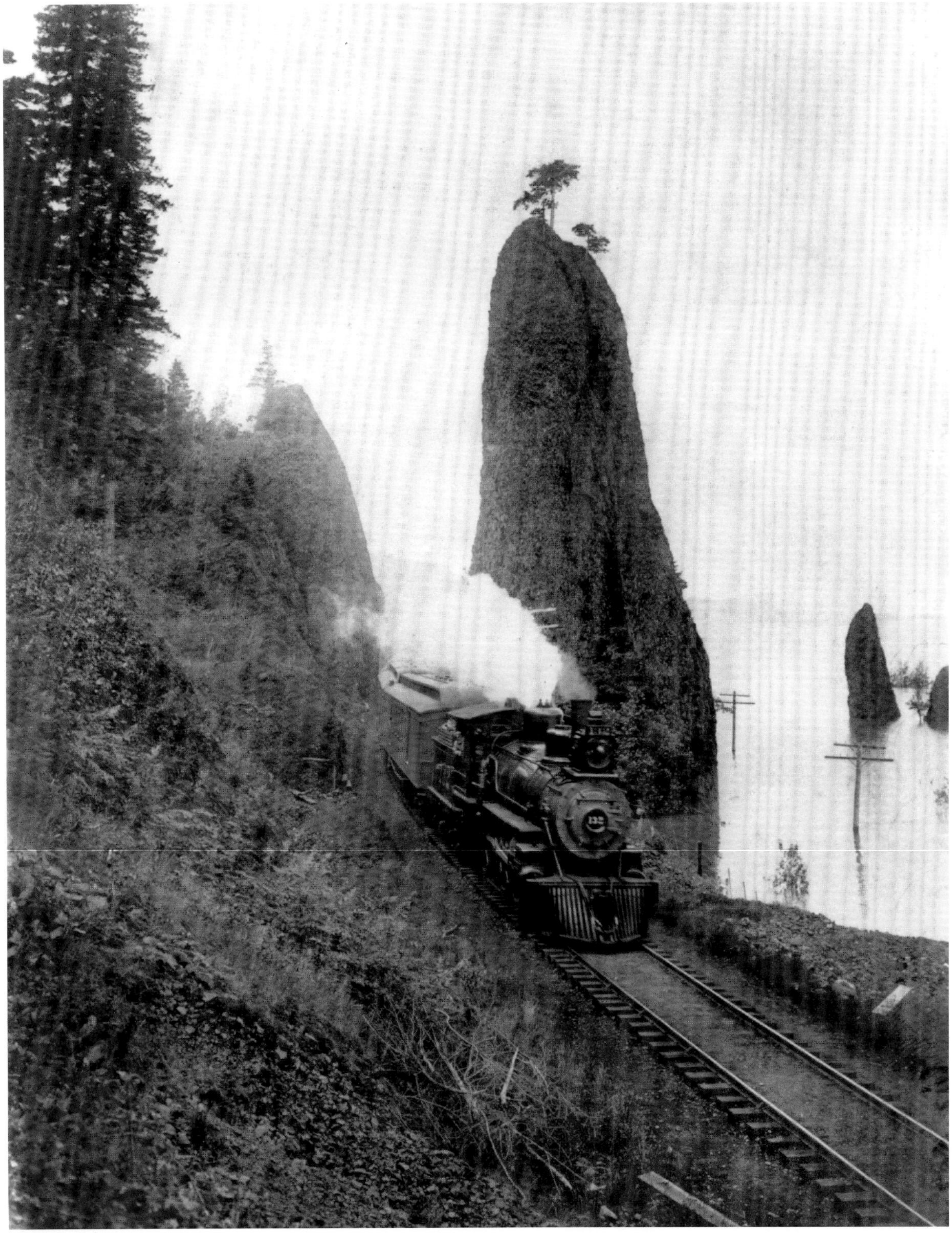

A passenger train makes its way through the Columbia Gorge past the Pillars of Hercules, massive basalt columns of volcanic origin, around 1908. The railroads became vital to the state, making possible the export of products like wheat and lumber and enabling Oregonian farmers and lumberjacks to compete with their California neighbors. The railroad was also important in bringing immigrants and manufacturing to Oregon.

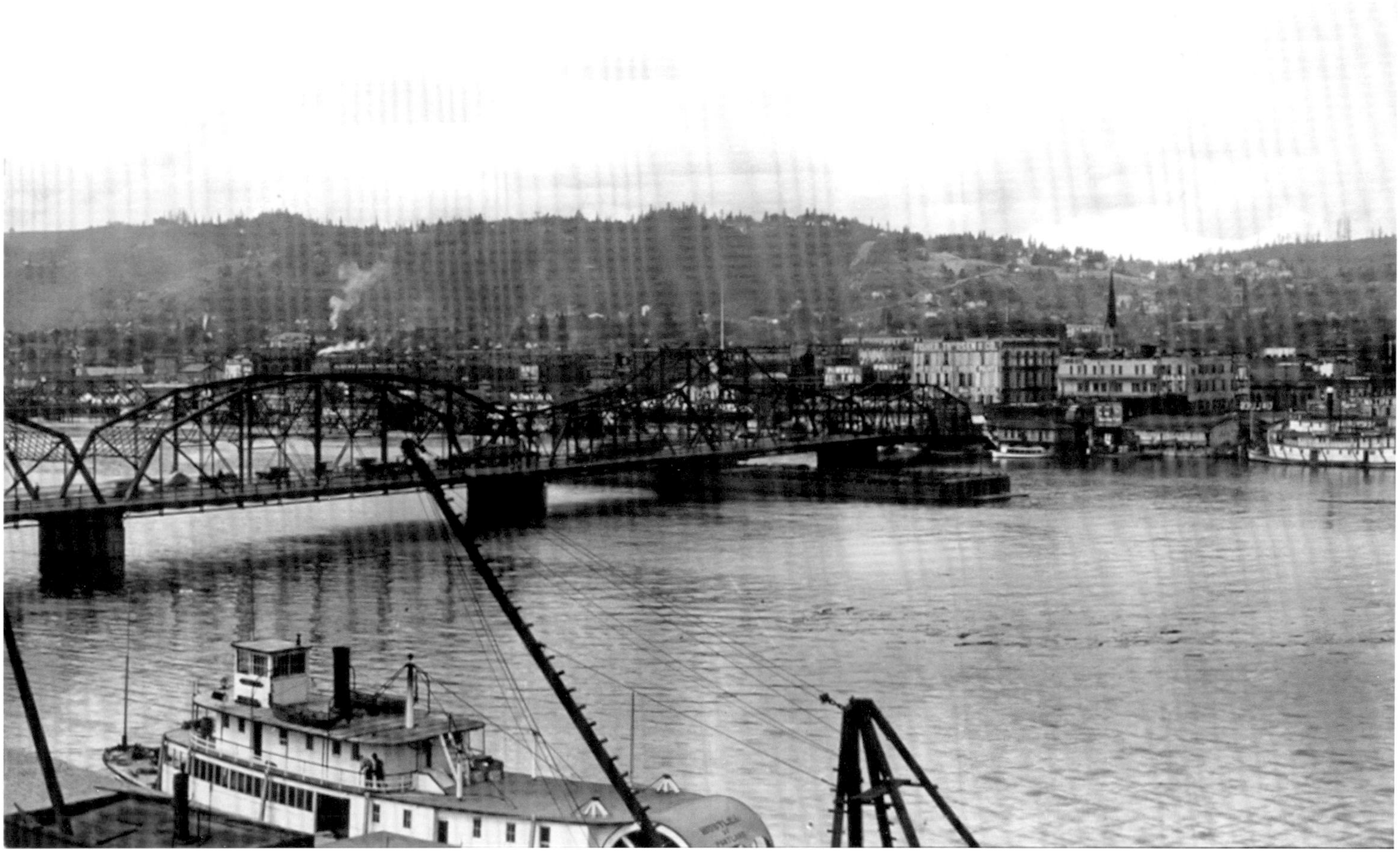

The Willamette River, shown here around 1908, cuts through the middle of Portland. The river is a tributary of the Columbia River and is about 185 miles in length, flowing between the Coast Range and the Cascade Range and its confluence near Portland. Prior to the 1880s, ferries were relied on for transportation across the main channel. By 1908, the waters had been bridged.

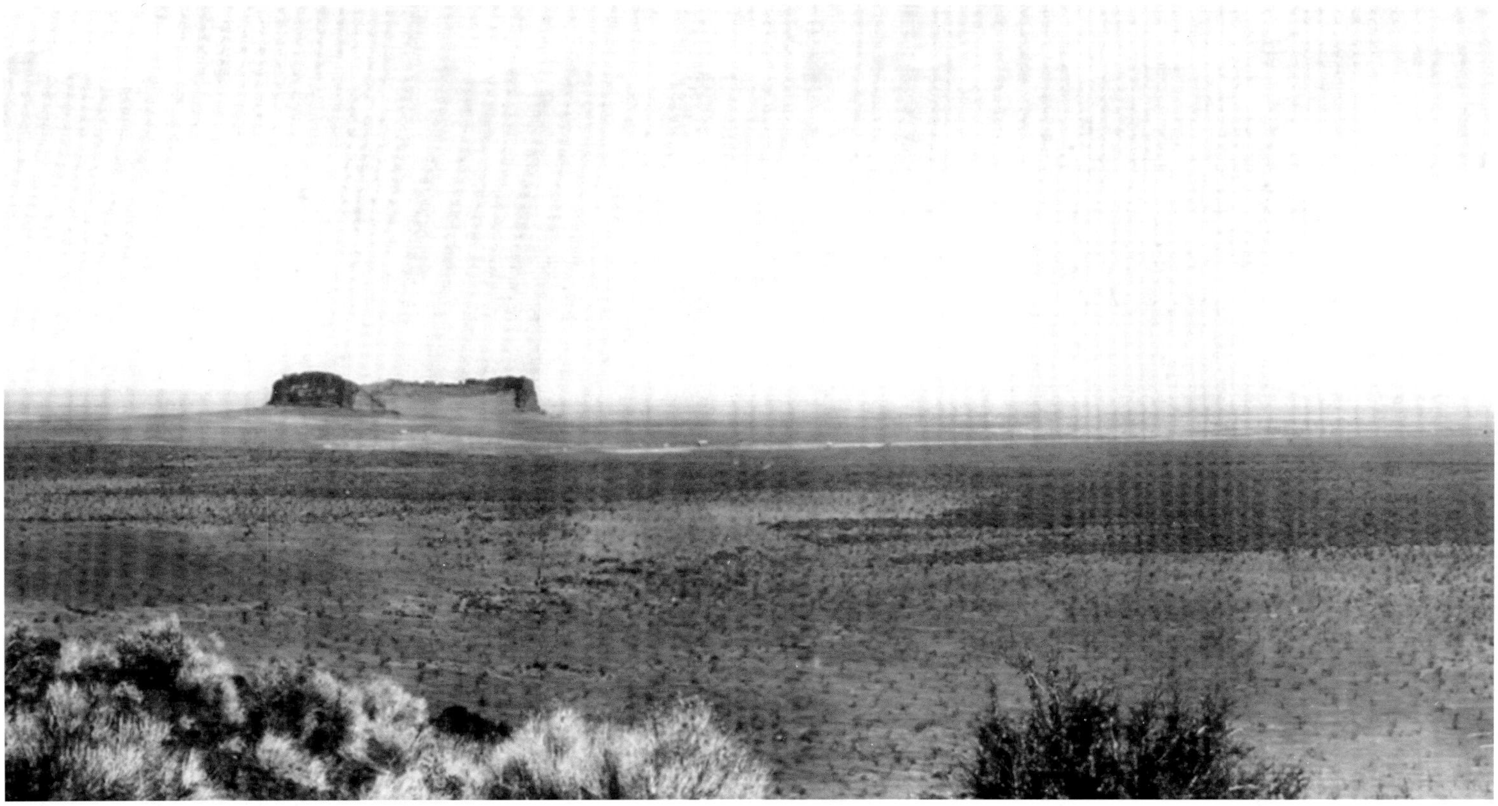

Fort Rock in Lake County, northeast of Christmas Valley, was established in 1908. The town is named for a prominent geological feature, which was the subject of this image. In the 1930s, a pair of sandals found in a cave there were believed to be between 9,000 and 10,000 years old, among the artifacts unearthed that make the Fort Rock formation the site of the earliest-known human remains in the state.

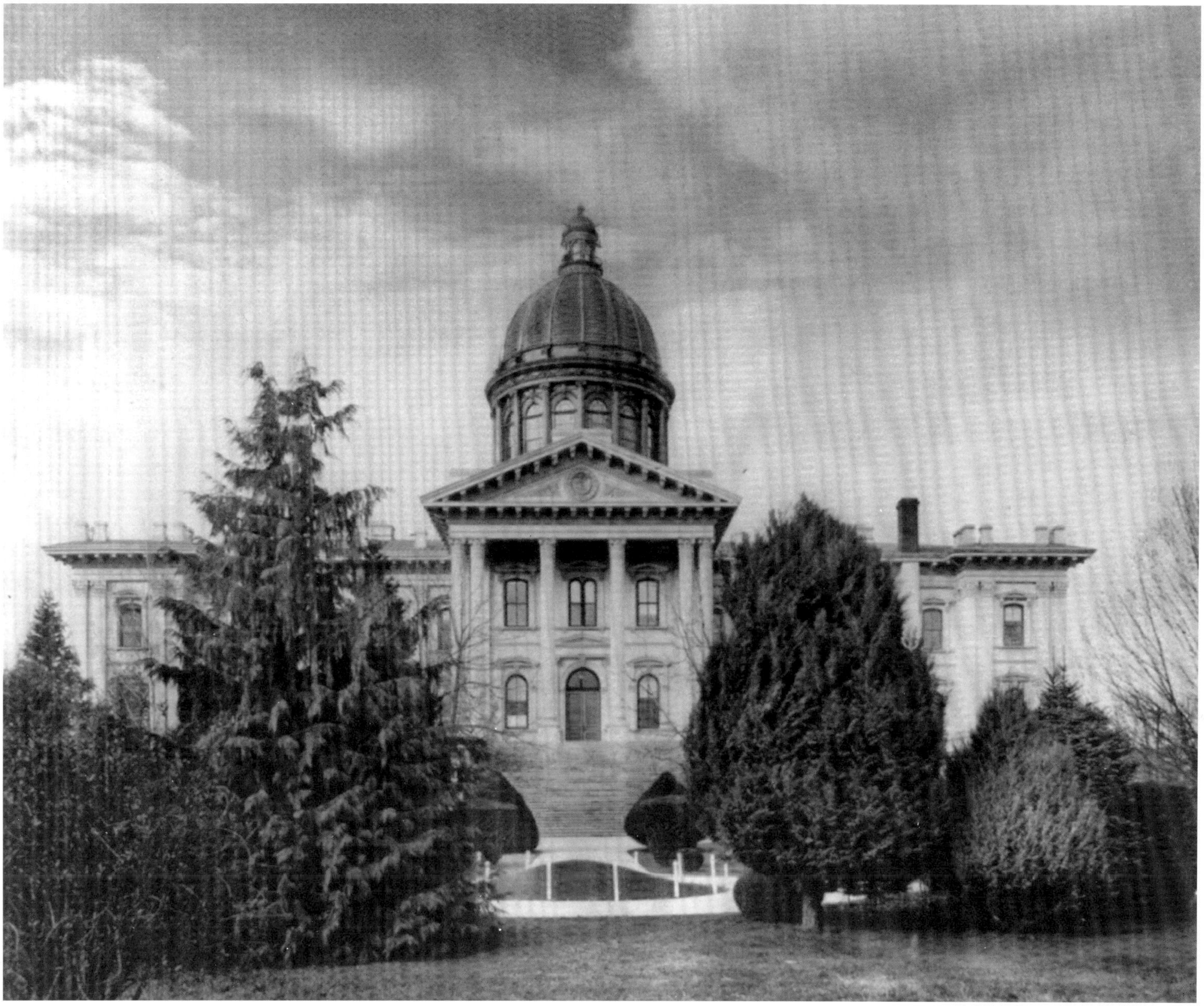

Salem's second State Capitol, shown here in 1909, would burn down in 1935. The first capitol, built in 1855, also succumbed to fire. A third capitol was built in 1938 in the Art Deco style on designs by New York architects Trowbridge and Livingston, and this building continues to house state government today.

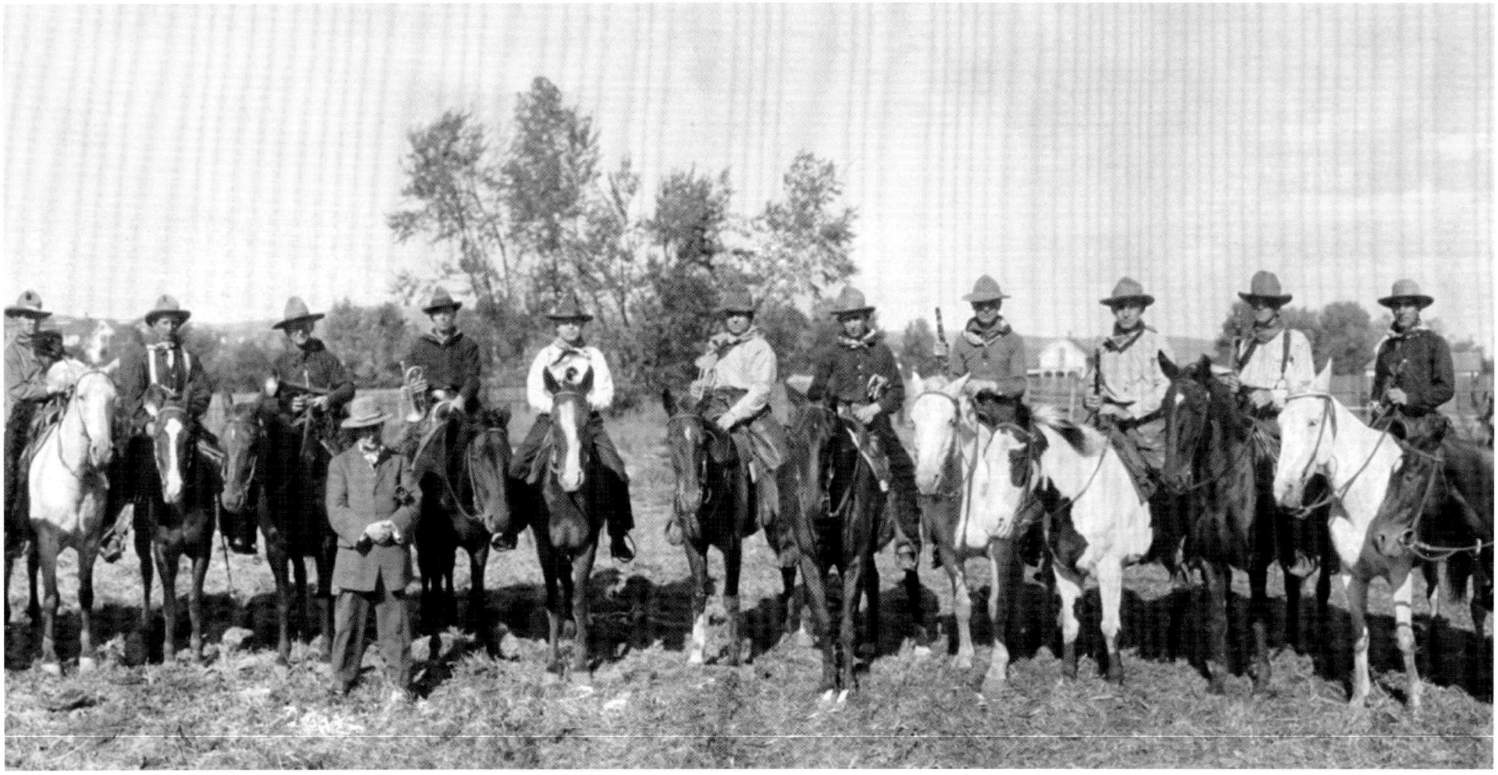

The Pendleton Round-up, which was first held in 1909, is one of the top rodeos in the United States. Events include bronco riding, foot races, Indian dances, feasts, and more. The slogan of the round-up is "Let 'er Buck."

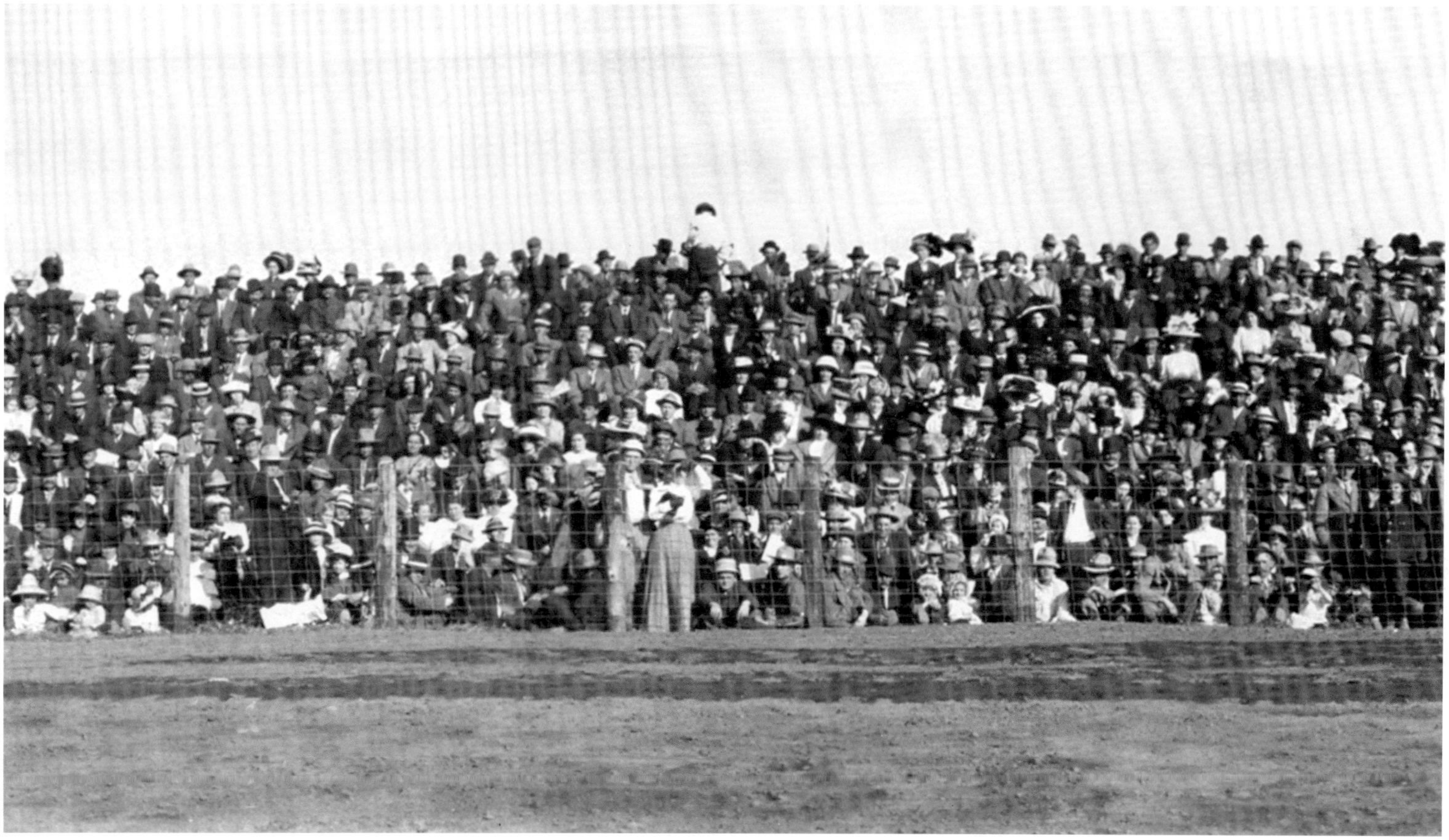

East end bleachers at the Pendleton Round-up in 1911. The Round-up has been held at the same location since 1910 and is attended by rodeo fans each September.

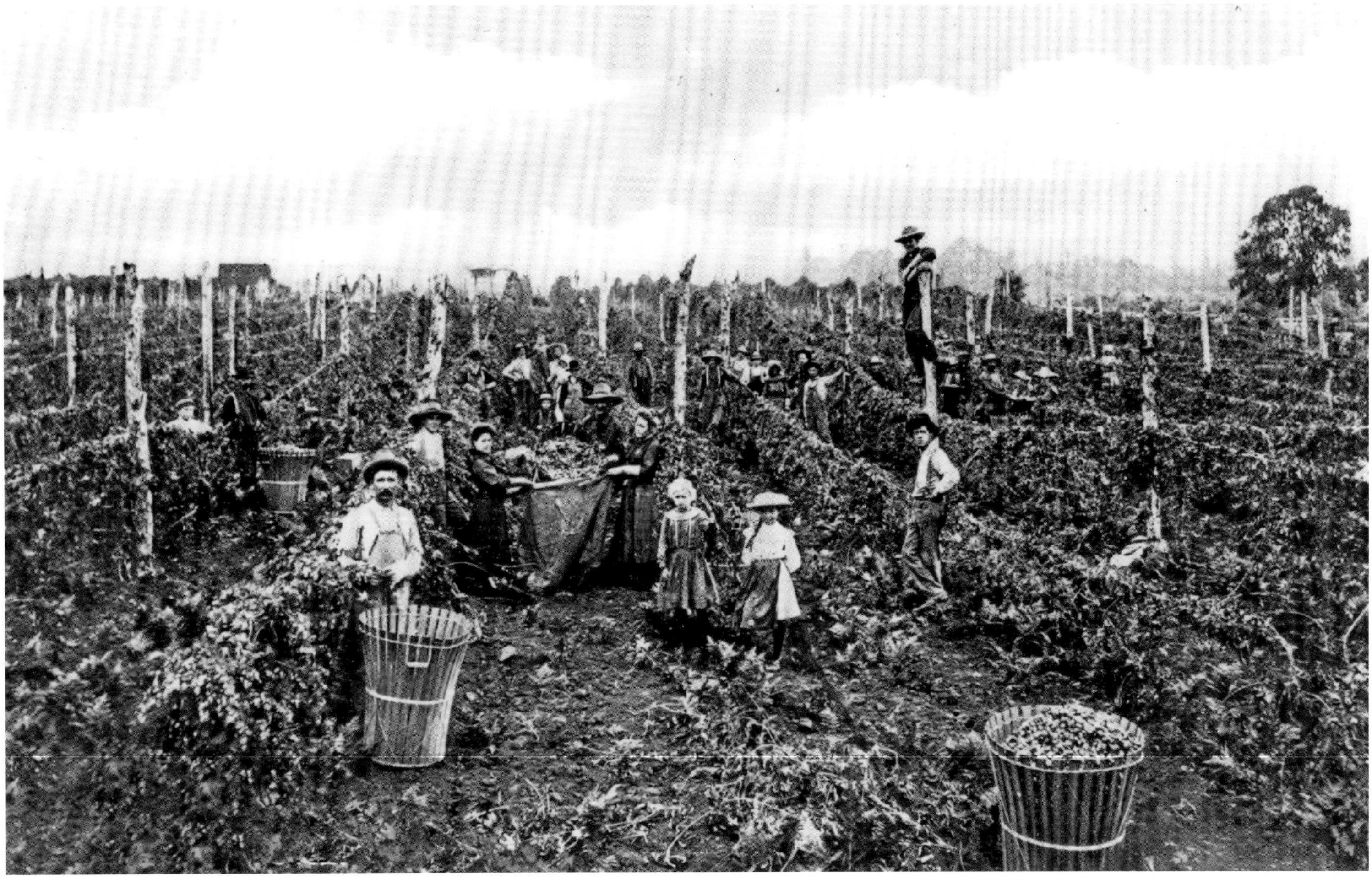

Pausing for a photographer early in the twentieth century are Oregonians at work picking hops in the Willamette Valley. The valley was settled early by pioneers who found the land extremely fertile for growing crops.

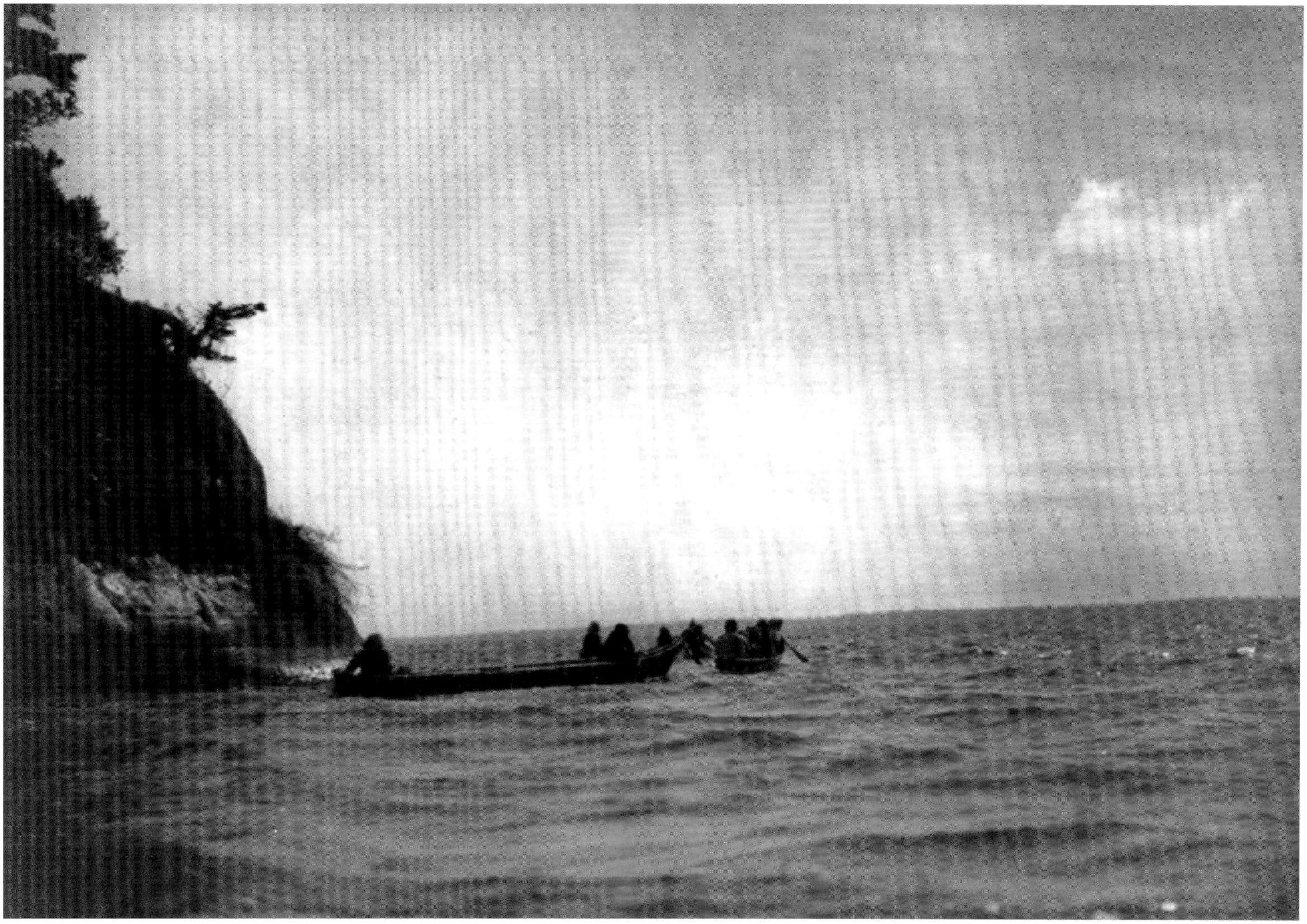

Edward S. Curtis spent his life documenting a vanishing way of life among the indigenous peoples of the American West. Many of the thousands of images Curtis recorded, along with his written accounts, are the only record of these cultures. In the foreword to Curtis's *North American Indian,* Teddy Roosevelt wrote, "Mr. Curtis in publishing this book is rendering a real and great service; a service not only to our own people, but to the world of scholarship everywhere." Curtis took this photograph of Chinook Indians, shown paddling the Columbia River around 1910.

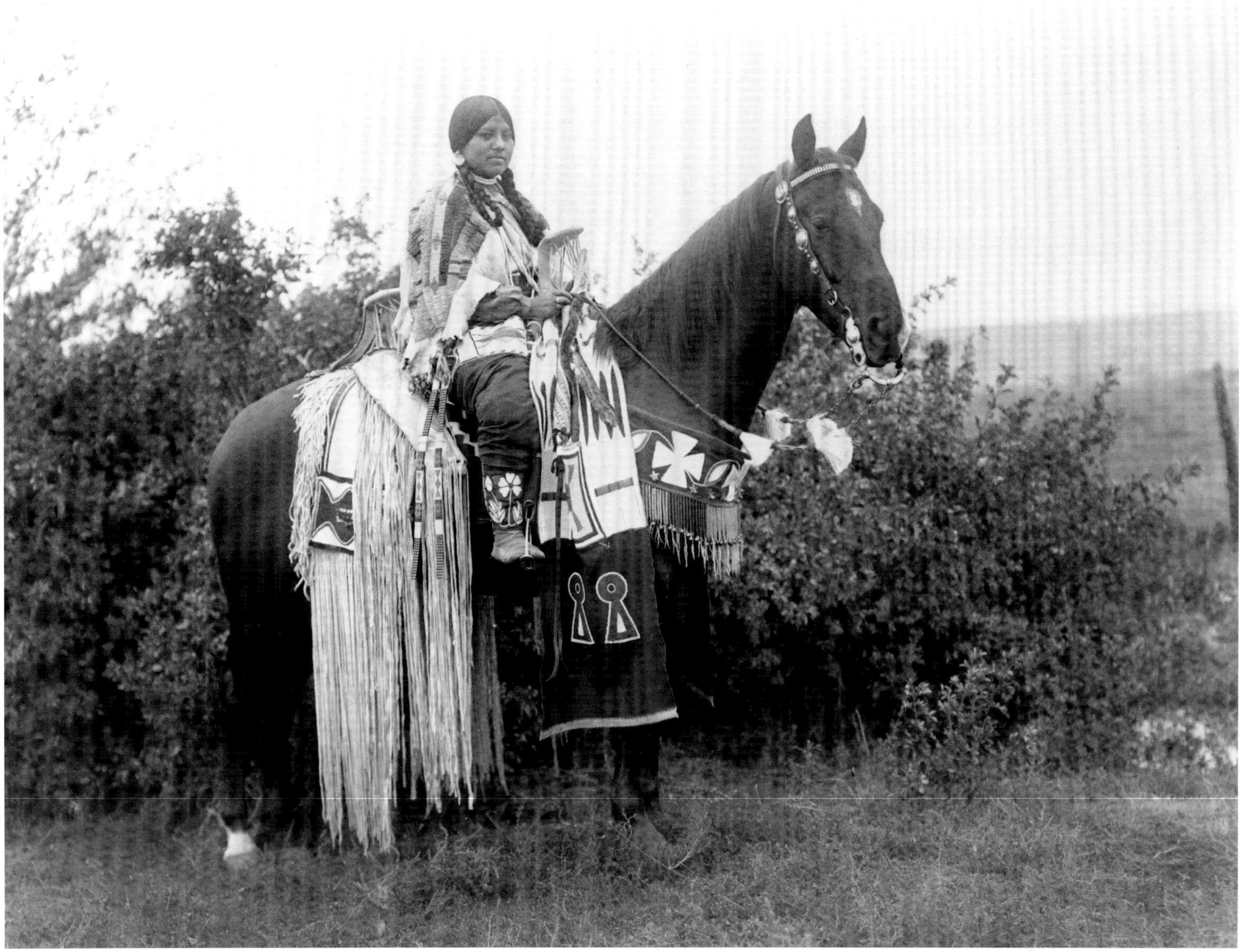

Edward Curtis photographed this Cayuse woman, in full regalia on horseback around 1910.

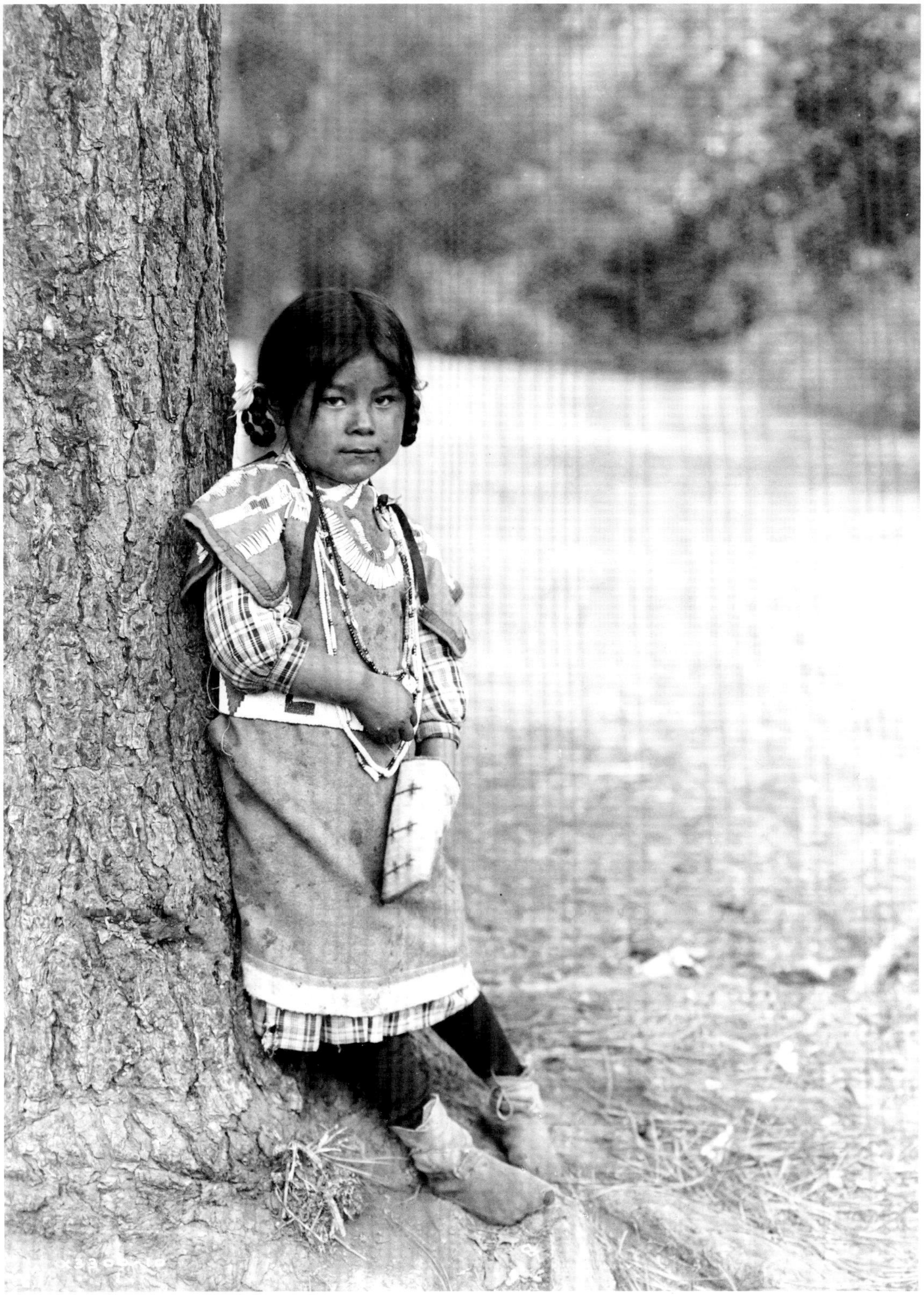

This Curtis photograph, titled "Innocence," shows an Umatilla girl.

A view of The Dalles with a distant Mount Hood in the background. In the vicinity of Celilo Falls, The Dalles was an early settlement for Protestant missionaries seeking to convert Native Americans to the Christian faith. The Dalles was also important for settlers traveling along the Oregon Trail on their way to Portland. During the early part of the twentieth century, the town became a center for the cultivation of fruits and vegetables.

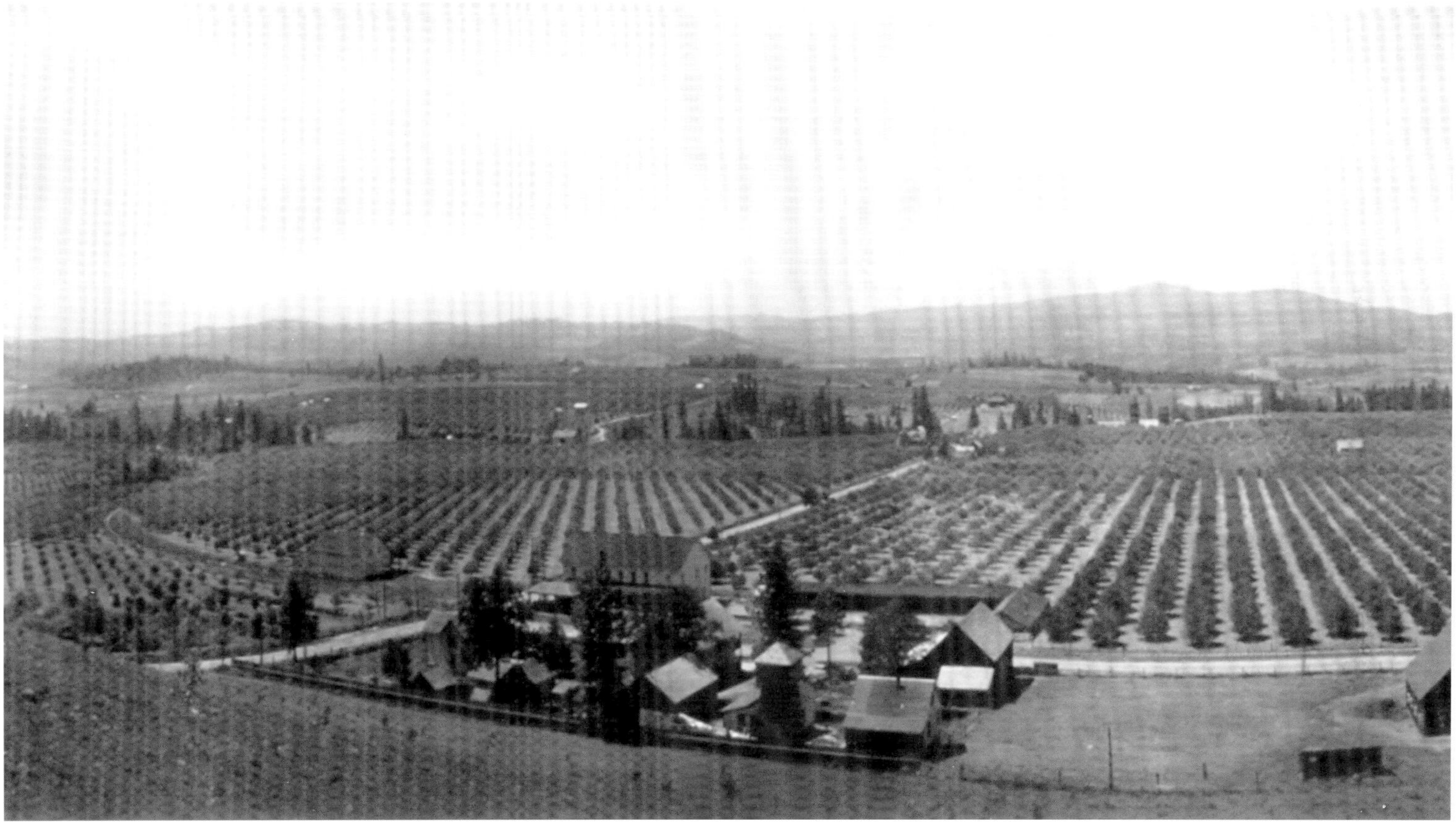

The Hood River Valley as seen from Van Horn Butte. A small but important group of Americans of Japanese descent came to the area to work in the orchards and fields, and several became leading growers.

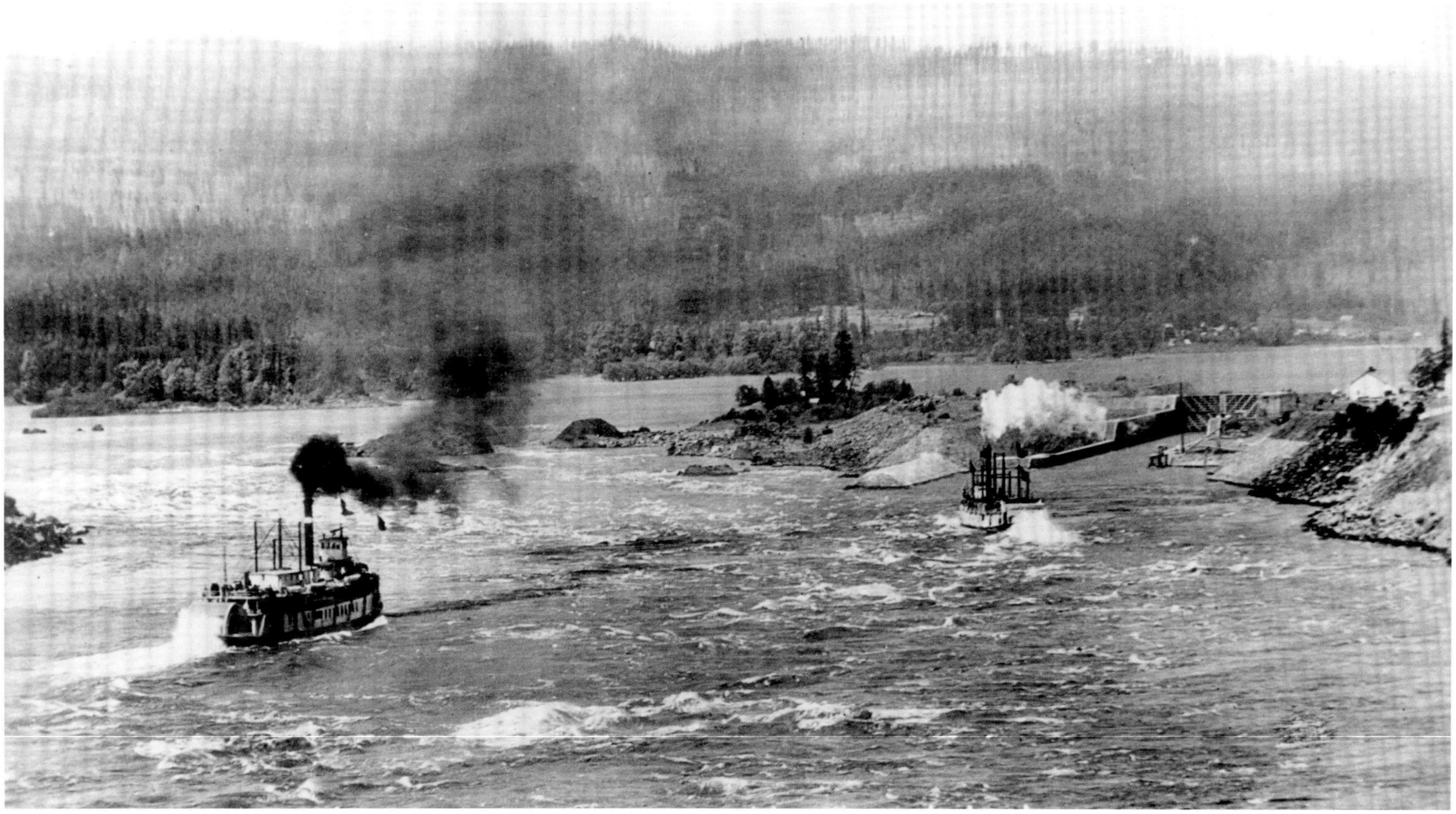

Steamboats plying the rapids approach Cascade Locks, on the Columbia River. The Columbia River Highway would open much later, in 1922, providing transportation by automobile through the region.

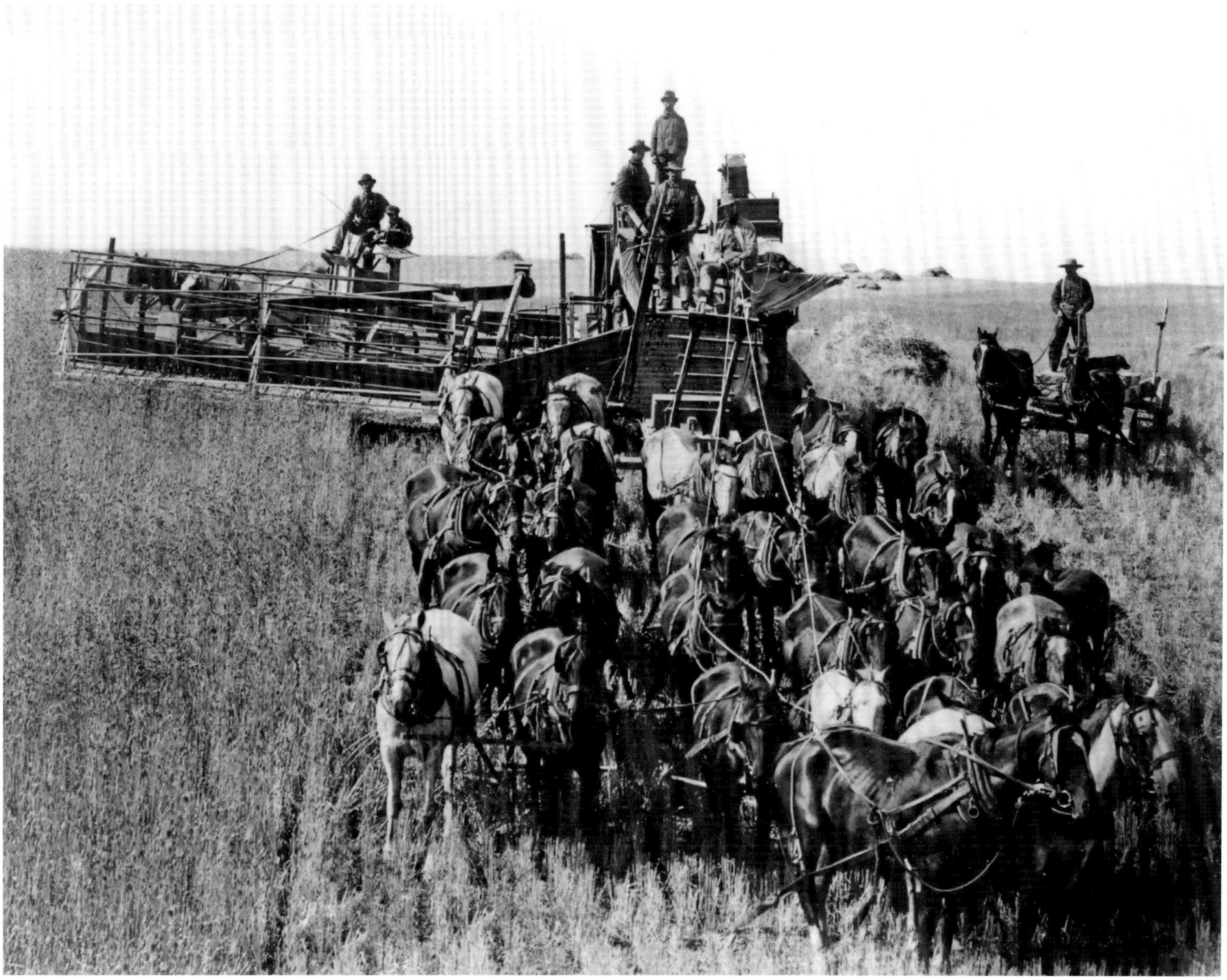

Wheat is being harvested in this view of an early horse-drawn combine and the farmers who made it run. Harvest time was labor-intensive, even after the advent of mechanization, and chores were generally divided. While men toiled in the fields, the women prepared meals to feed them. Much changed from a century ago, today's combines often feature air-conditioned cabs with stereos and other amenities.

Theodore Roosevelt made multiple tours of the West as president, pursuing big game on hunting trips, meeting with conservation-minded leaders like John Muir, and fulfilling speaking engagements to admiring Americans. Here he speaks to a group of Oregonians from the observation deck of a passenger car in Eugene, in 1911. William Taft was now president, but Roosevelt would mount a campaign the following year in a bid to return to the White House for a third term. Roosevelt's Bull Moose party split the Republican vote, giving the White House to Democrat Woodrow Wilson.

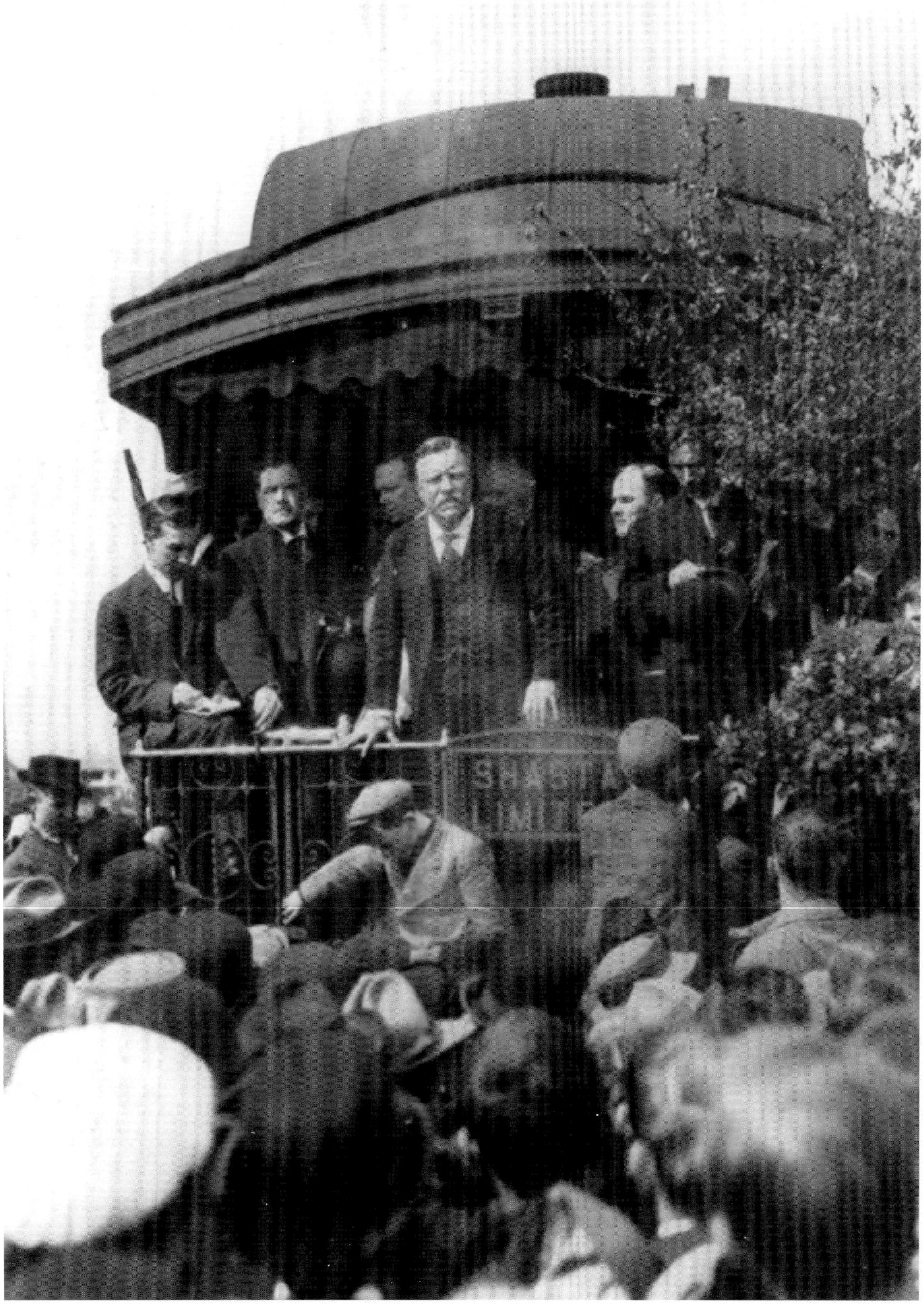

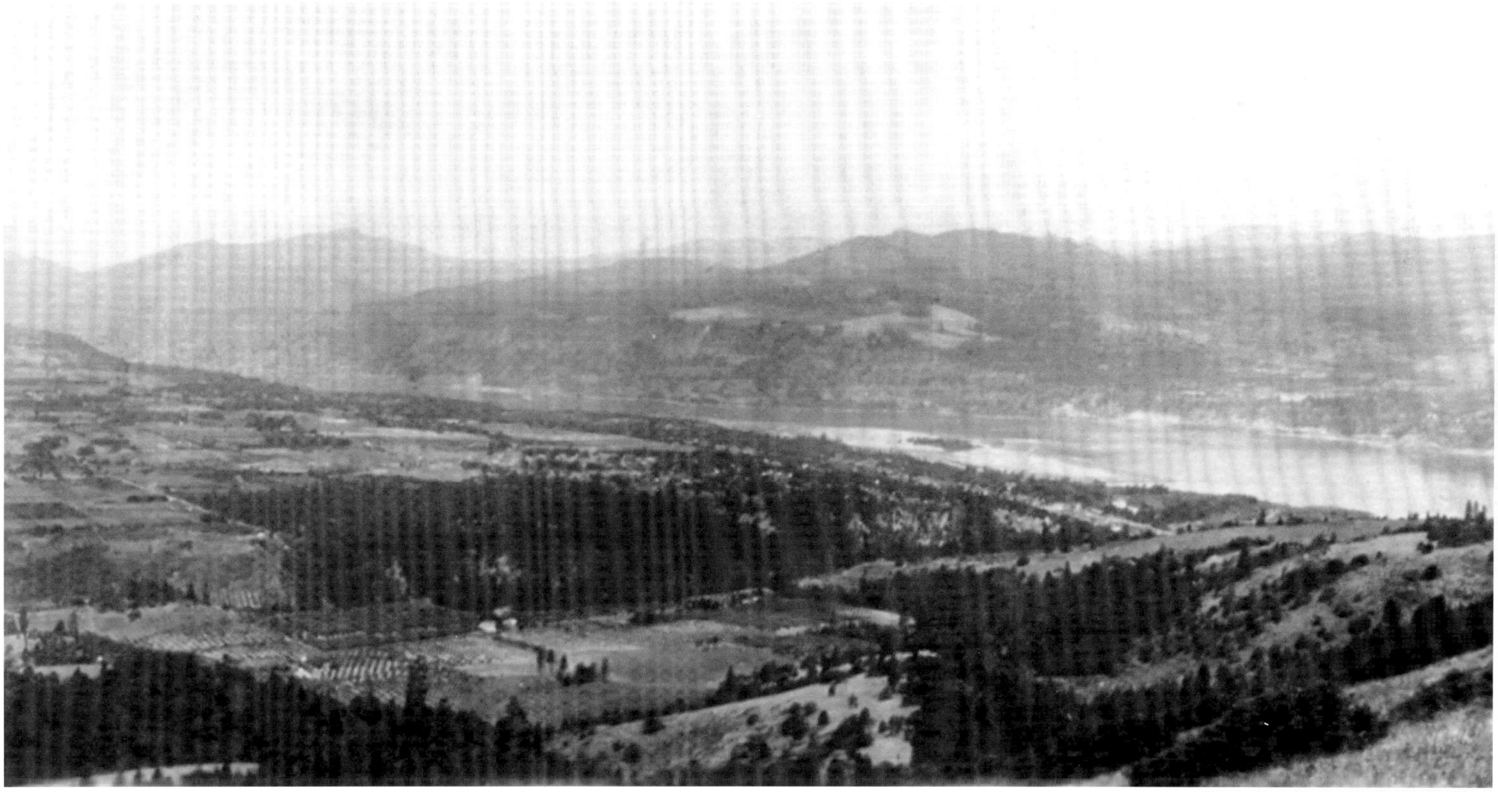

The Hood River Valley, around 1912. The upper valley was planted in orchards after World War I.

St. Mary's Church at Mt. Angel, Oregon, around 1912. The Swiss priest Father Adelhelm Odermatt built a chapel atop Graves Butte, which he renamed Mount Angel. The butte itself became the site of Mt. Angel Abbey and Mt. Angel College. The town of Mt. Angel was originally an agricultural community, home to farmers of German descent. Each October, the community celebrates the harvest with an Oktoberfest.

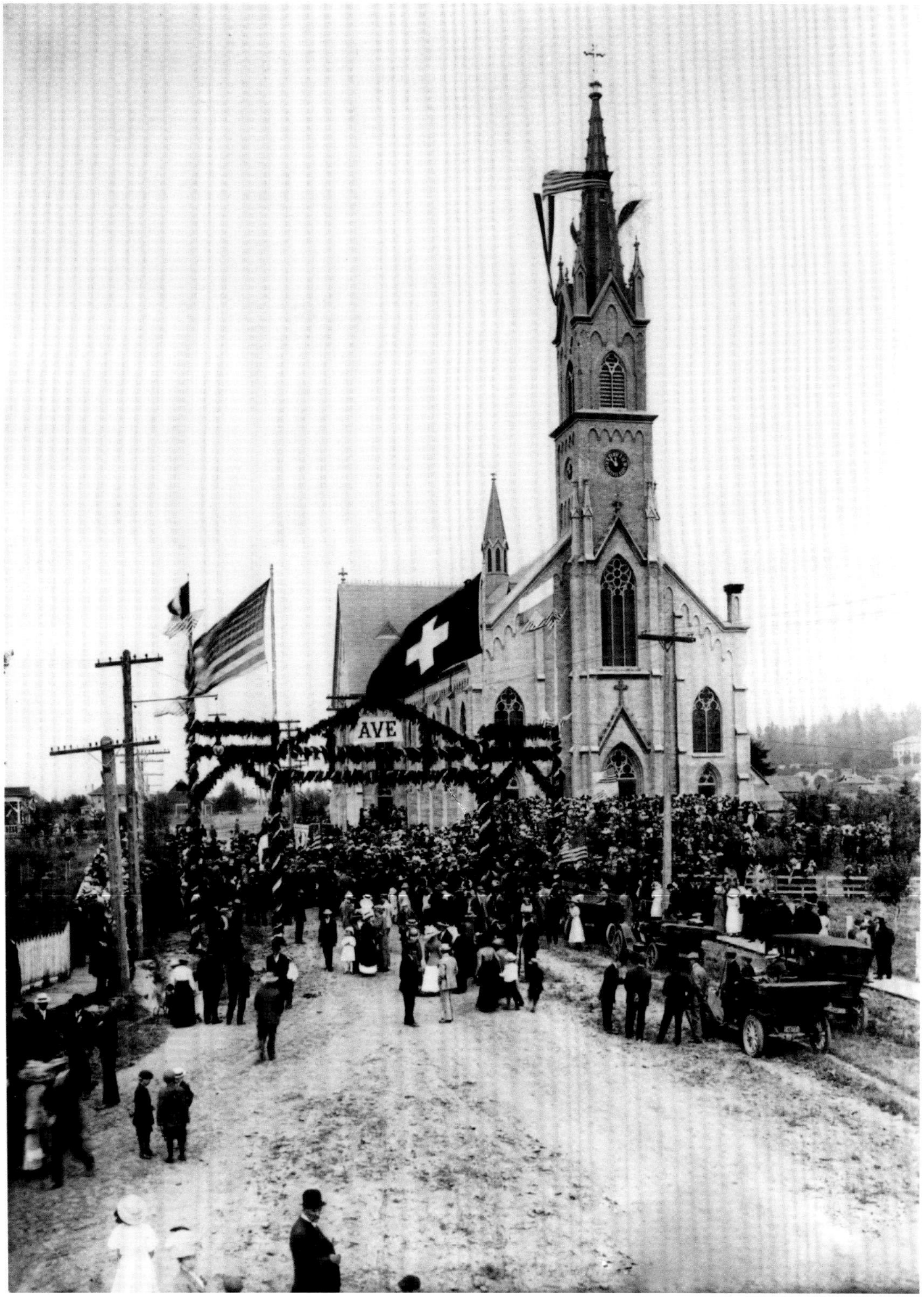

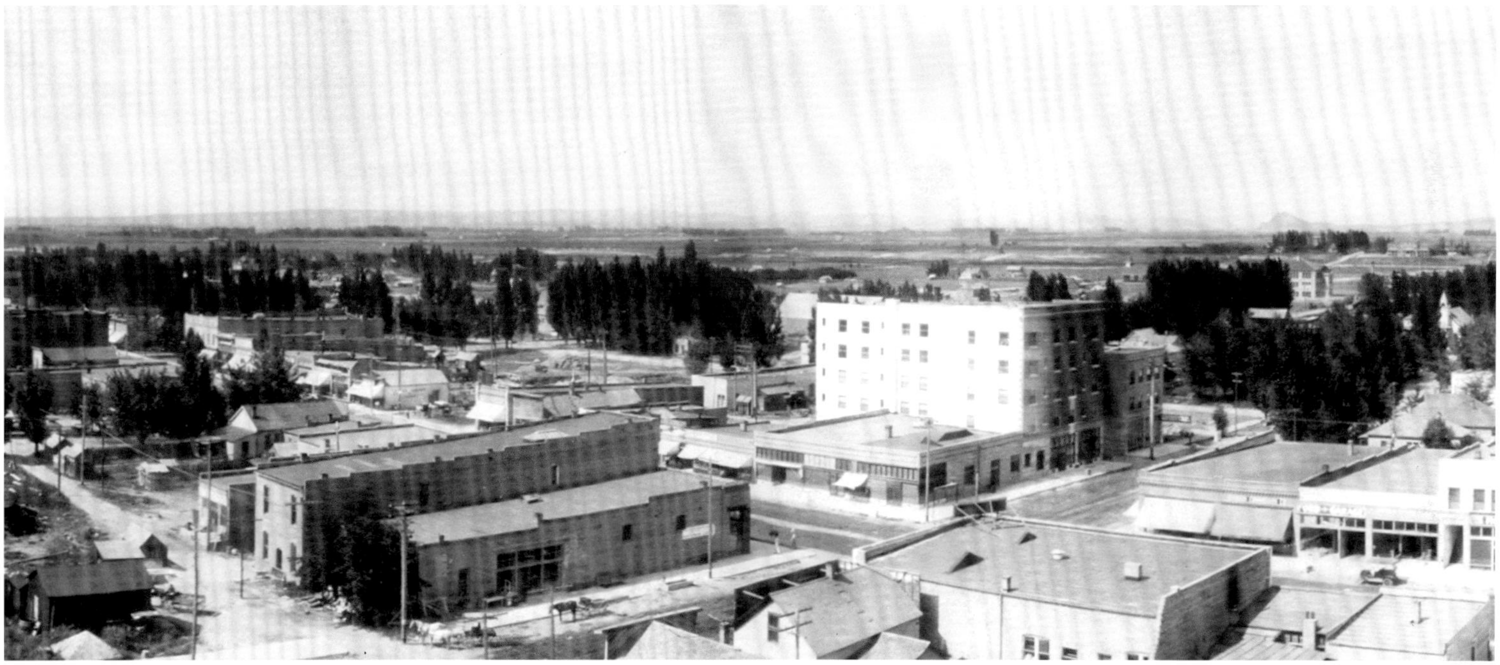

A view of Ontario, Oregon, as it appeared around 1912. Railroad transport, fruit and vegetable farming, and livestock production (especially sheep) made the area prosperous.

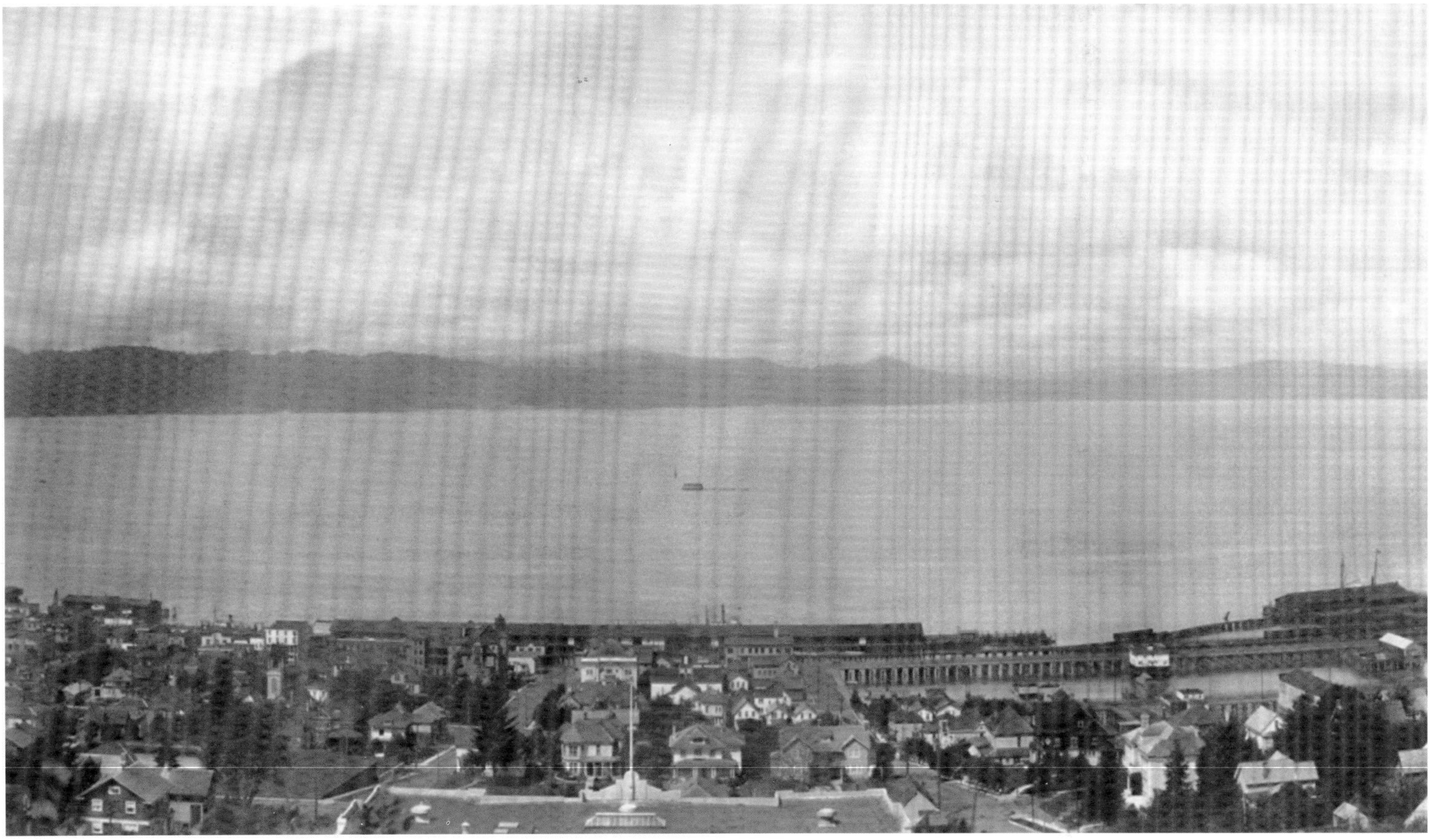

Bird's-eye view of Astoria as it appeared around 1912, at the mouth of the Columbia River, with Washington State in view in the distance. Astoria was established in 1811 by John Jacob Astor's Pacific Fur Company. By the early twentieth century, Astoria was a state leader in the commercial fishing and canning industry.

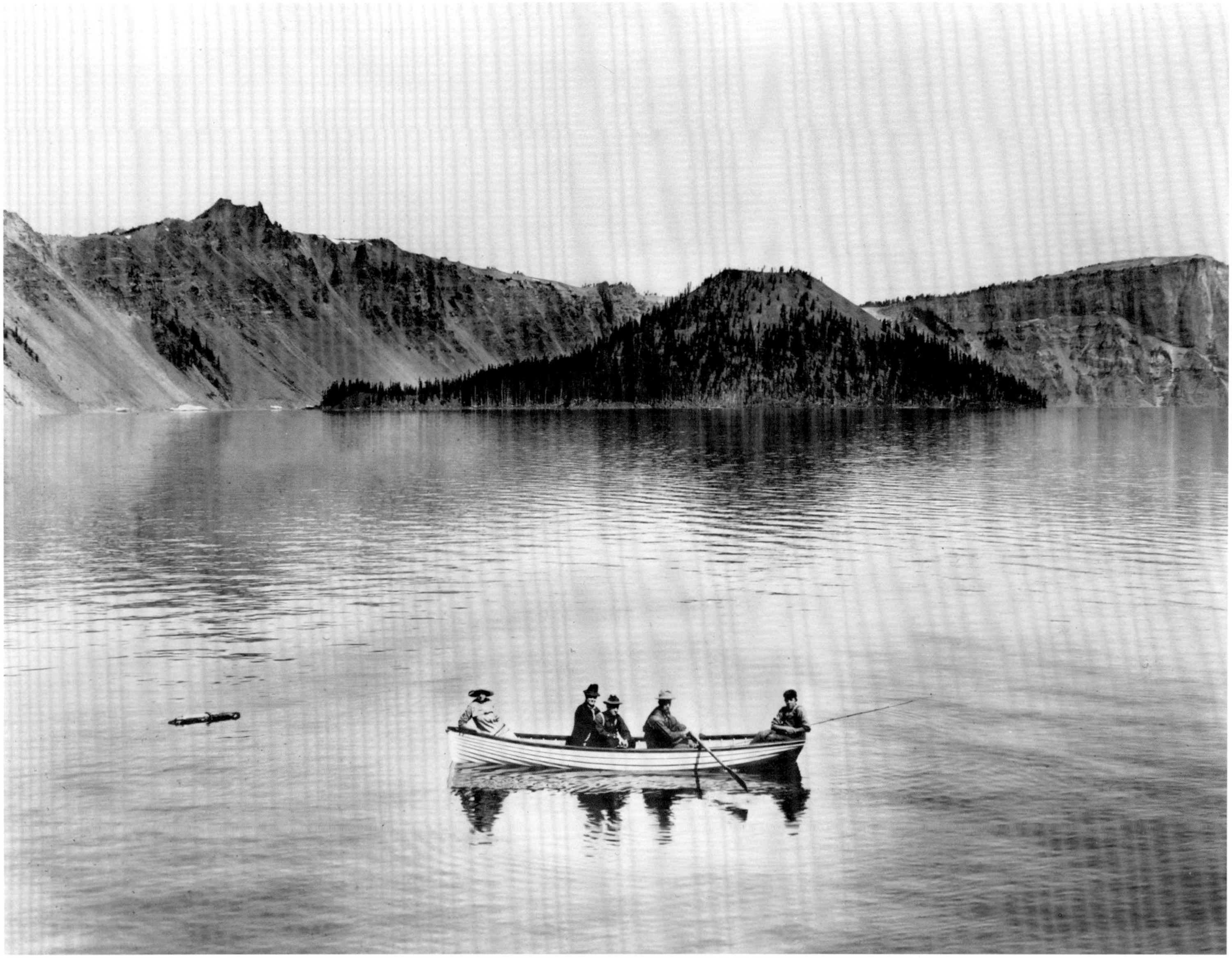

Boaters pose for a photograph in the middle of Crater Lake, with Merriam Cone in the background, around 1912. Crater Lake was not seen by explorers until 1853. In 1974, Peter Britt took the first photograph of Crater Lake, and in 1902, William Steel publicized Crater Lake and was successful in having it declared a national park. The lake fills a collapsed volcanic caldera six miles in diameter and is one of the deepest lakes in the world. It is renowned for its clarity and deep blue color.

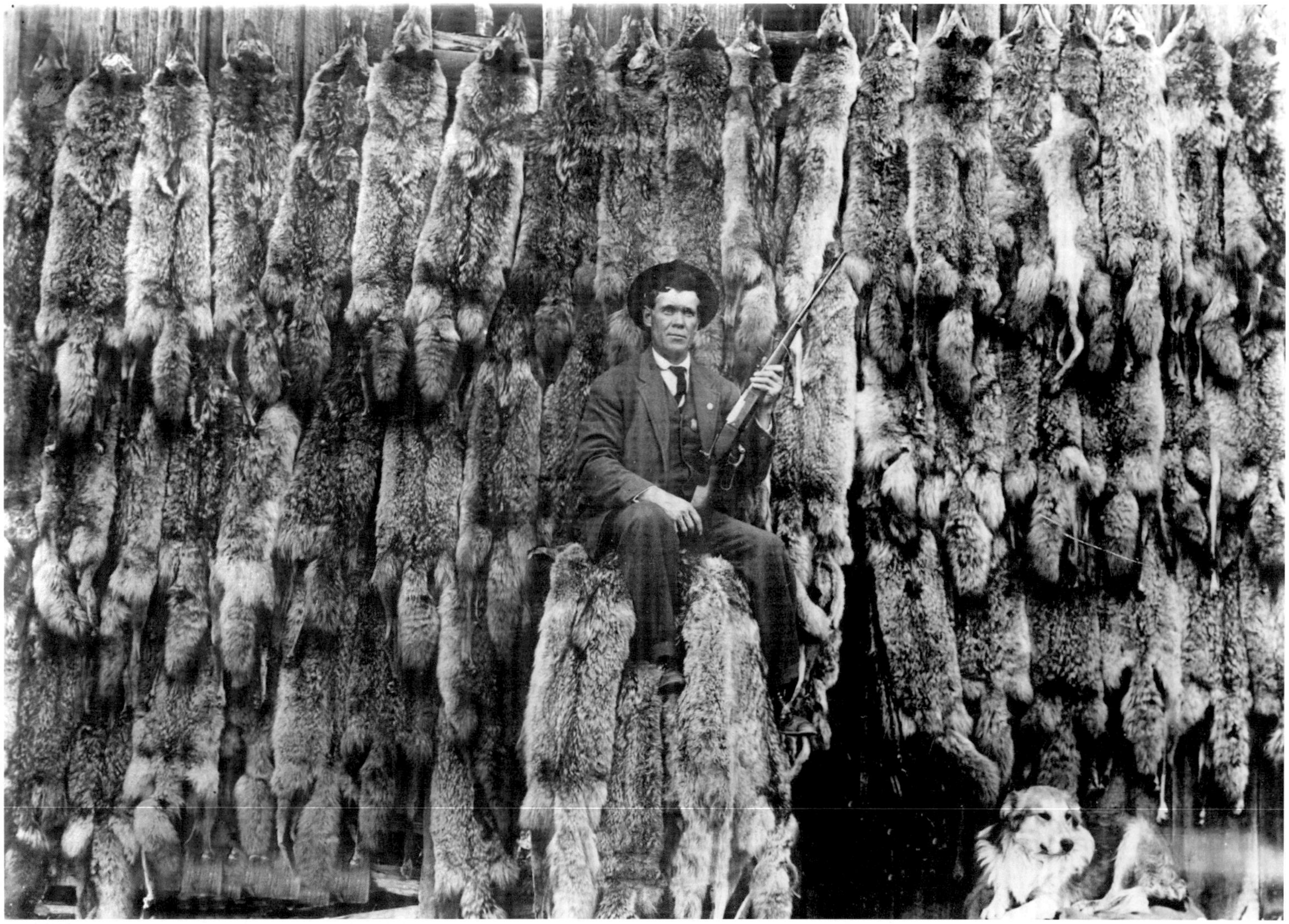

A ranger displays coyote pelts, from kills in the Malheur National Forest in southeastern Oregon, around 1912. As Oregon's second-largest county, Malheur County contains nearly 10 percent of the state's land.

Abigail Scott Duniway is pictured here with Governor Oswald West and Viola M. Coe signing Oregon's Equal Suffrage Proclamation on November 30, 1912. Abigail Scott Duniway enjoyed the distinction of being Oregon's most prominent suffragette.

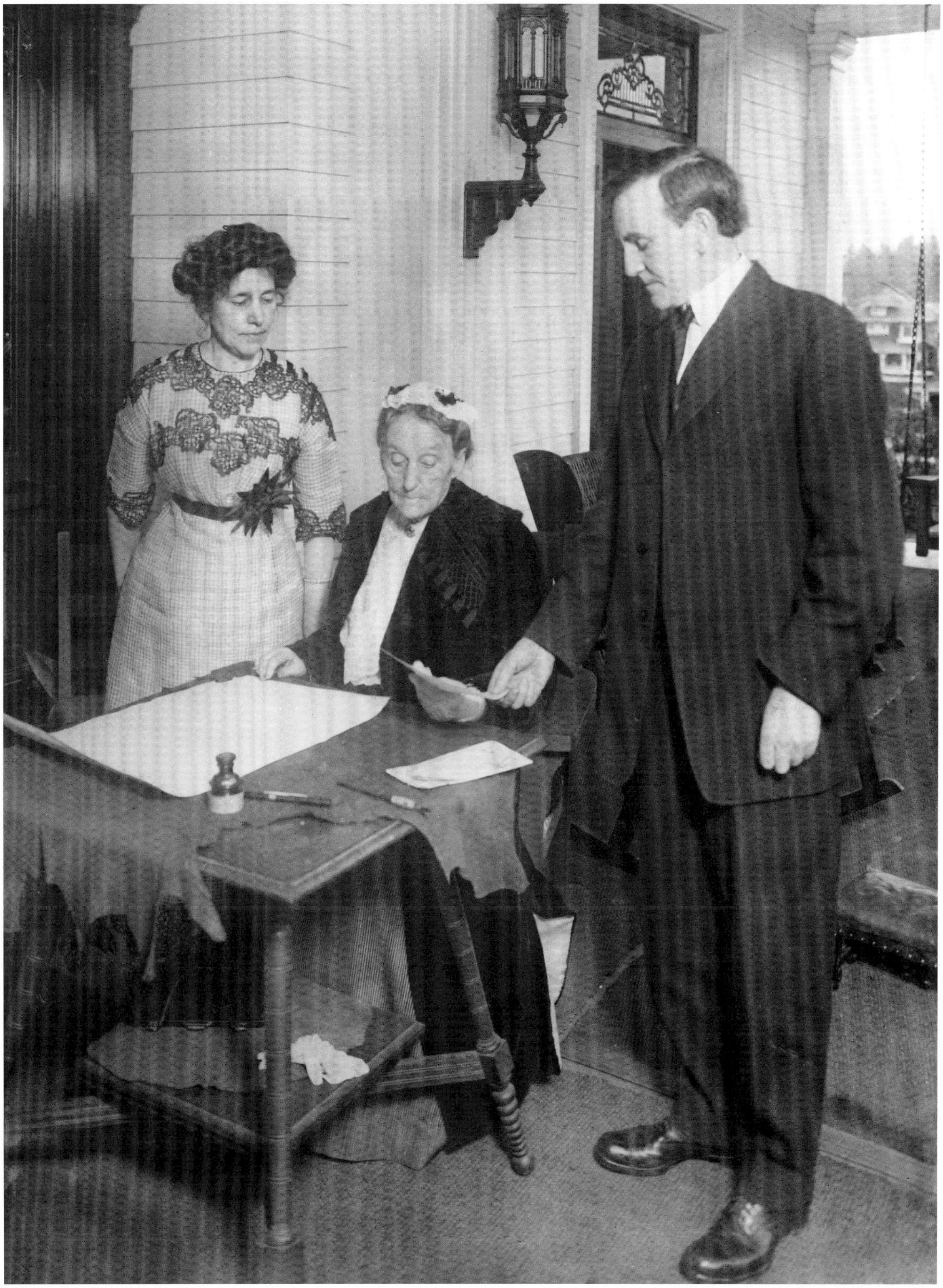

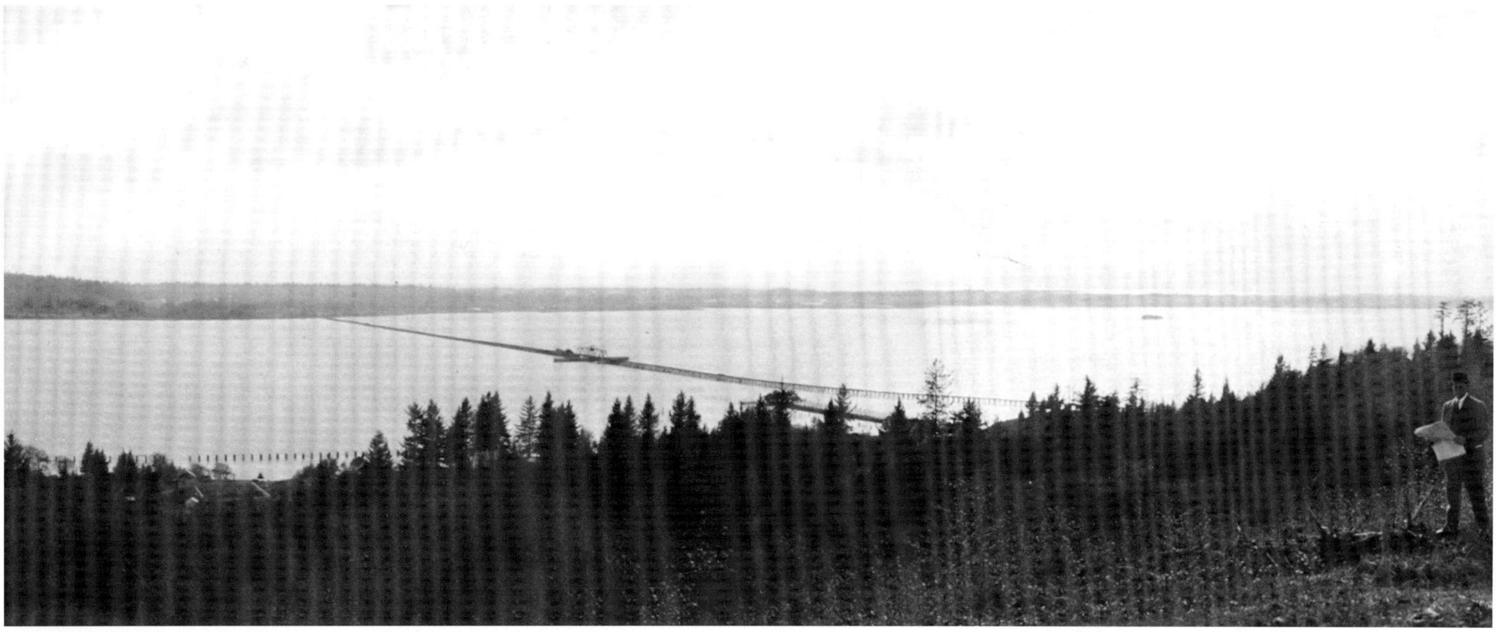

Saddle Mountain and the mouth of the Columbia River at Astoria, around 1913. Saddle Mountain has an elevation of 3,283 feet above sea level and is part of the Coast Range. The mountain was once used as a landmark by sailors seeking the entrance to the Columbia River.

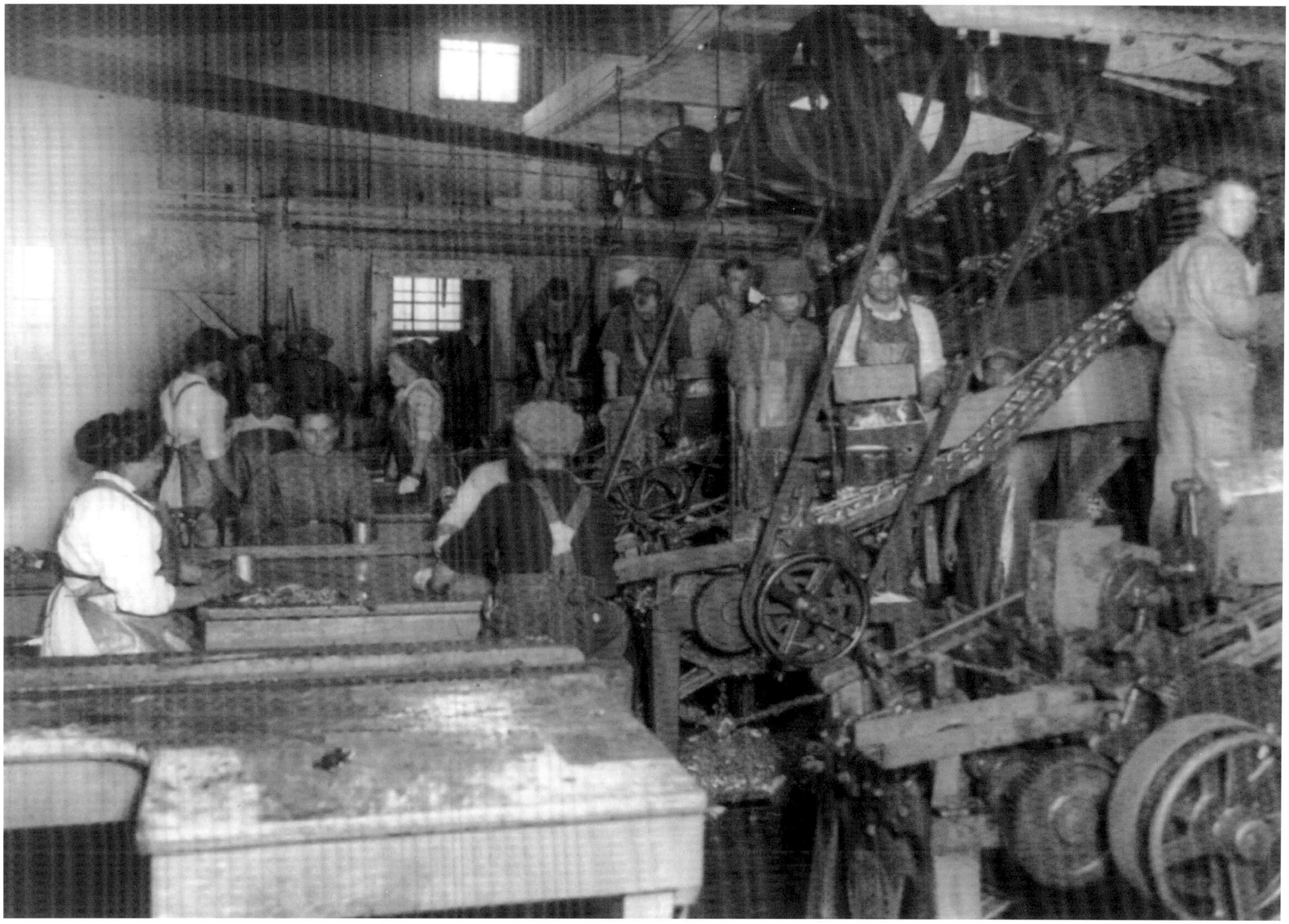

A salmon canning factory, around 1913. The indigenous inhabitants of the Pacific Northwest relied on fishing for their livelihood, and nineteenth-century settlers came to rely on fish as well, industrializing the natural resource in the 1860s. By the early twentieth century, salmon fishing and canning had become the dominant commercial enterprise in Oregon and Washington.

A crowd is assembled to watch the first pile driven for the Hill railroad terminal at Flavel around 1914. The town was named for George Flavel, a legendary seaman. By 1915, Flavel was the northernmost terminus of the Great Northern Pacific Steamship Company, which, in its heyday, transported travelers between San Francisco and Flavel, and from there to Portland. The town intended to rival Astoria as a port, but the plan failed and in 1918 Flavel was annexed by the town of Warrenton.

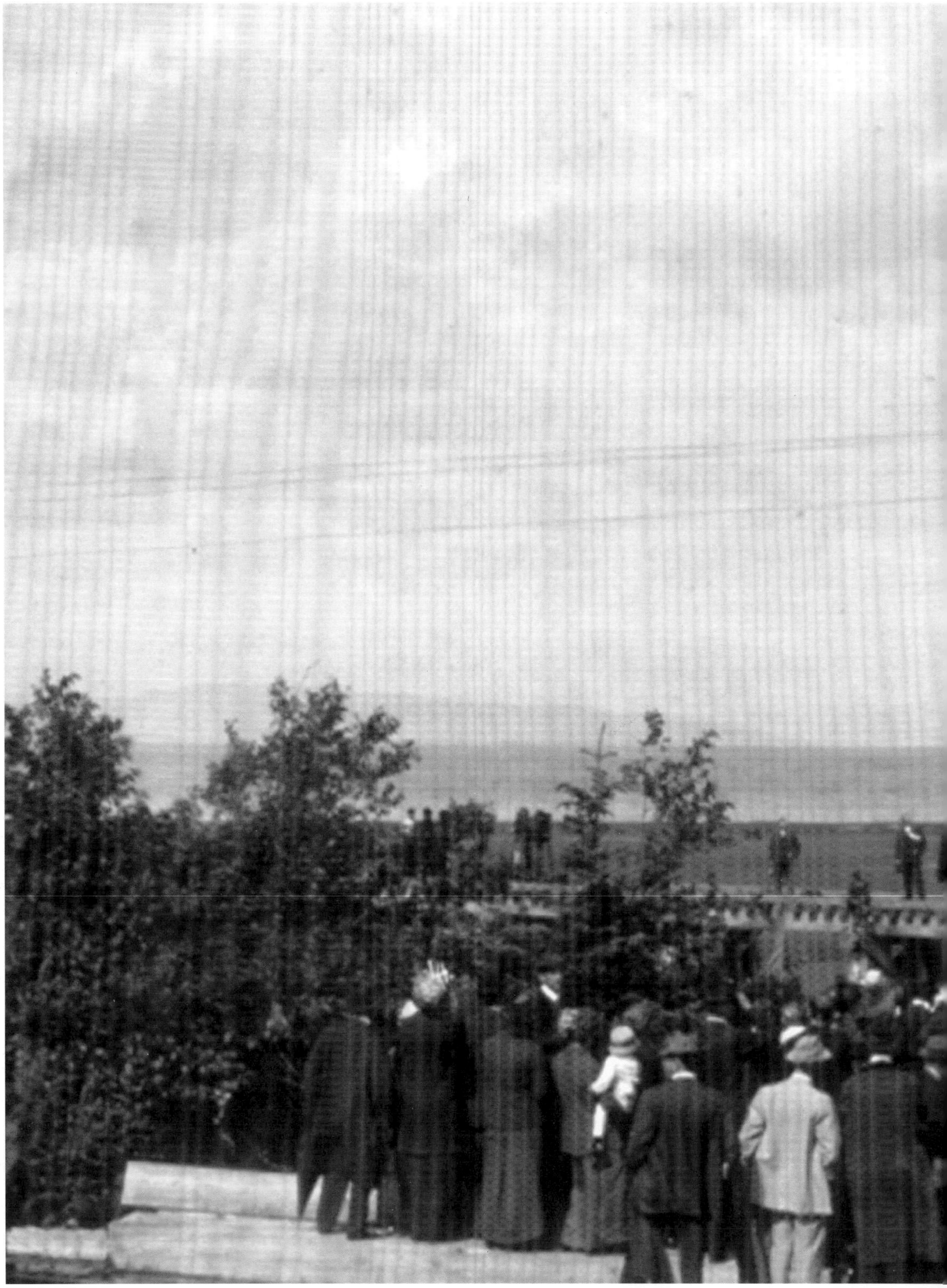

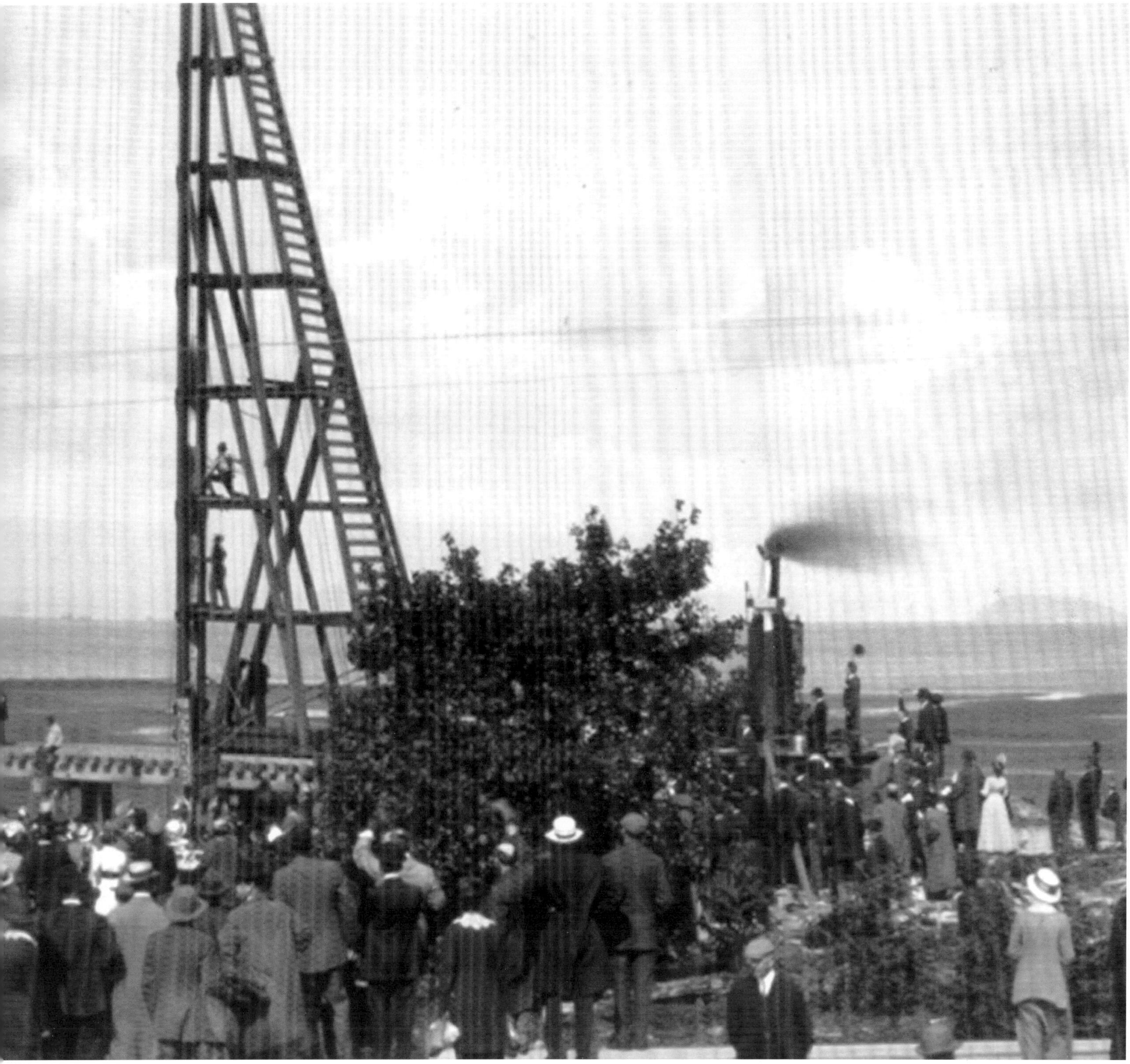

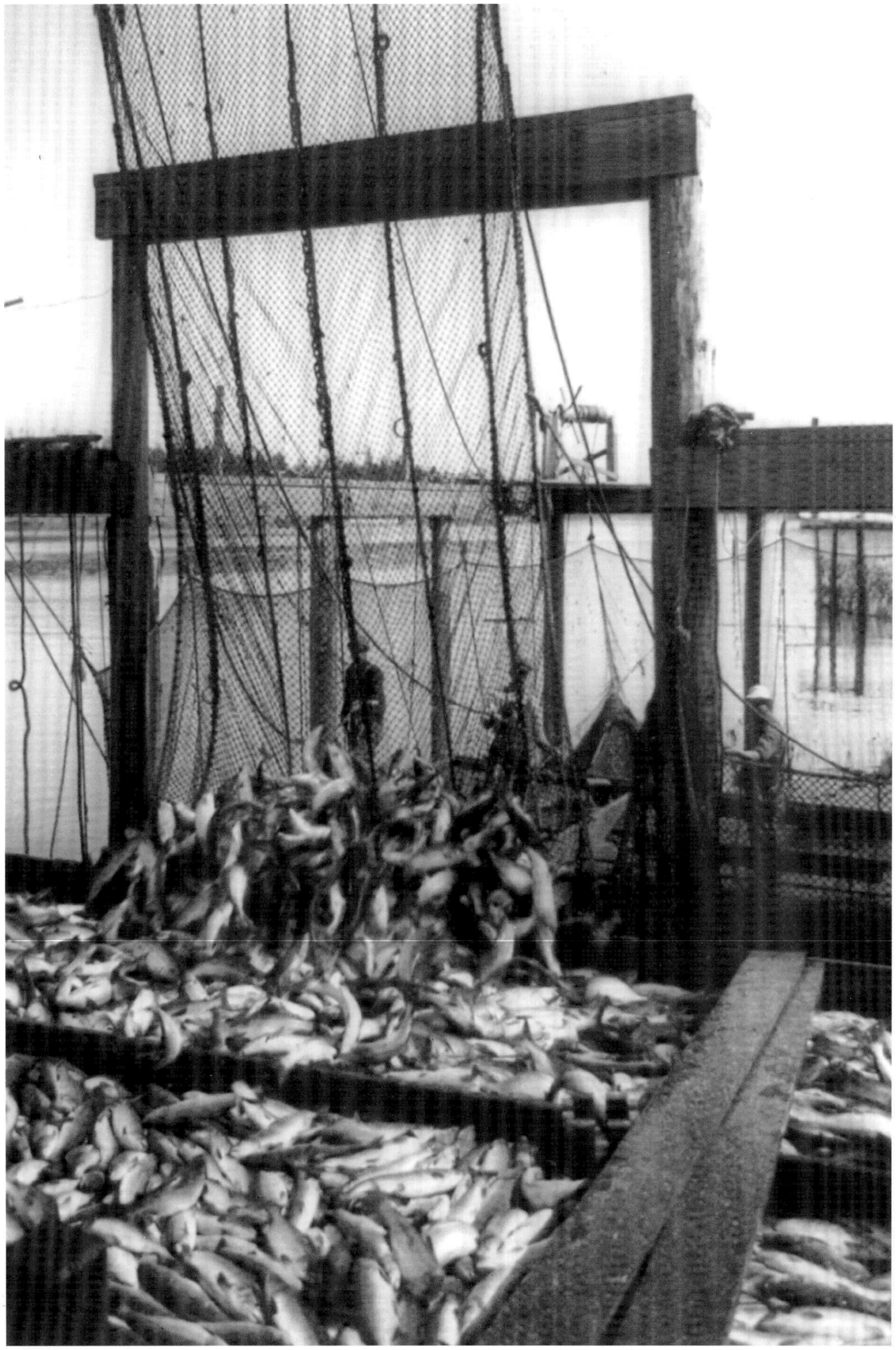

A bounty of salmon, around 1913. Salmon fishing took place not only on the Columbia River, but in coastal locations like Tillamook Bay, at Bay City on the Nestucca and Umpqua rivers, on Coos Bay, and on the Rogue River.

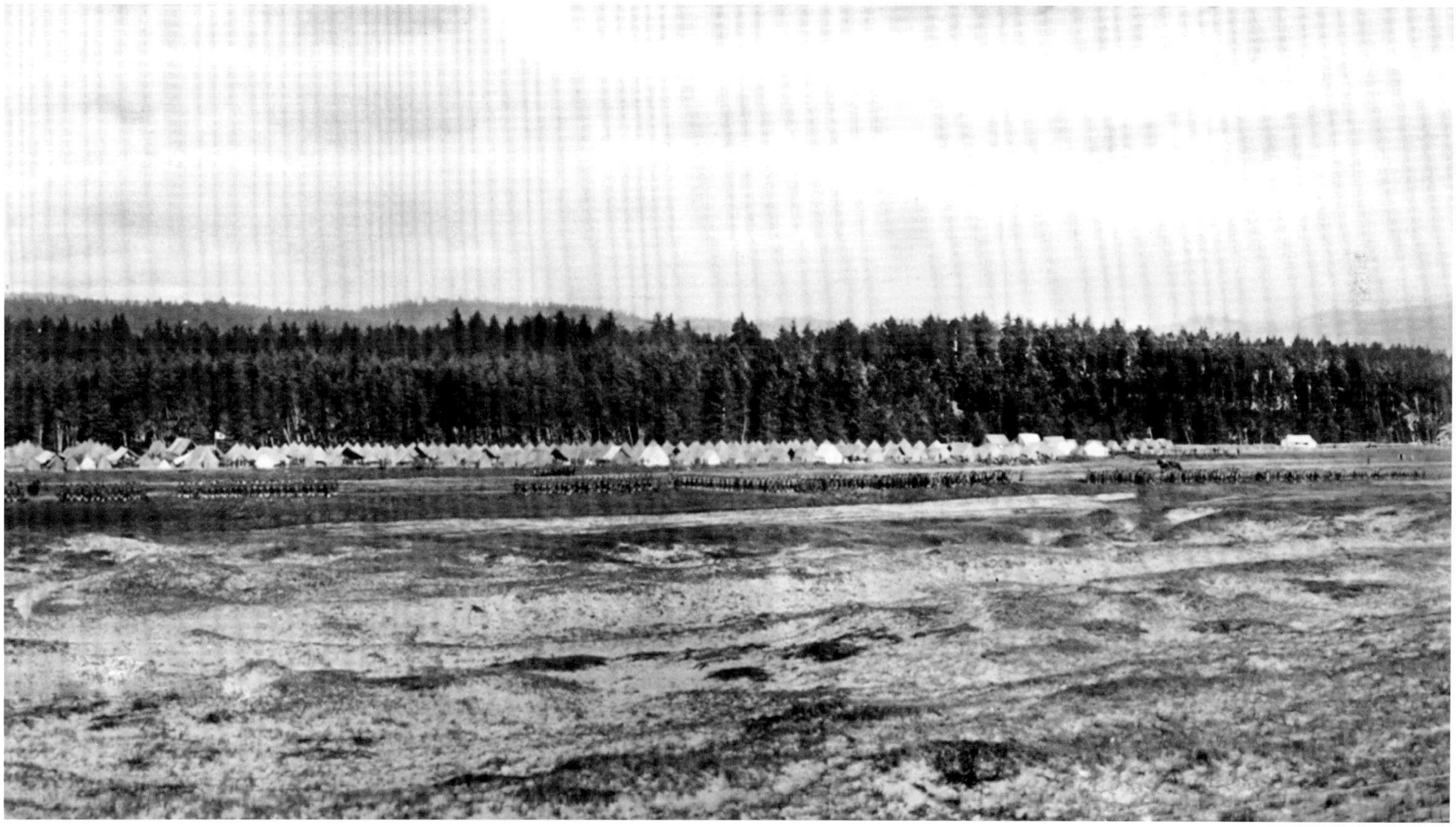

Camp Murray, at Gearhart, home to the Idaho National Guard and 21st Infantry. Gearhart was established in the 1880s as a private beach and golfing community on the Oregon Coast. James Beard, the noted food expert, wrote about the summers he spent there as a young man in the early twentieth century.

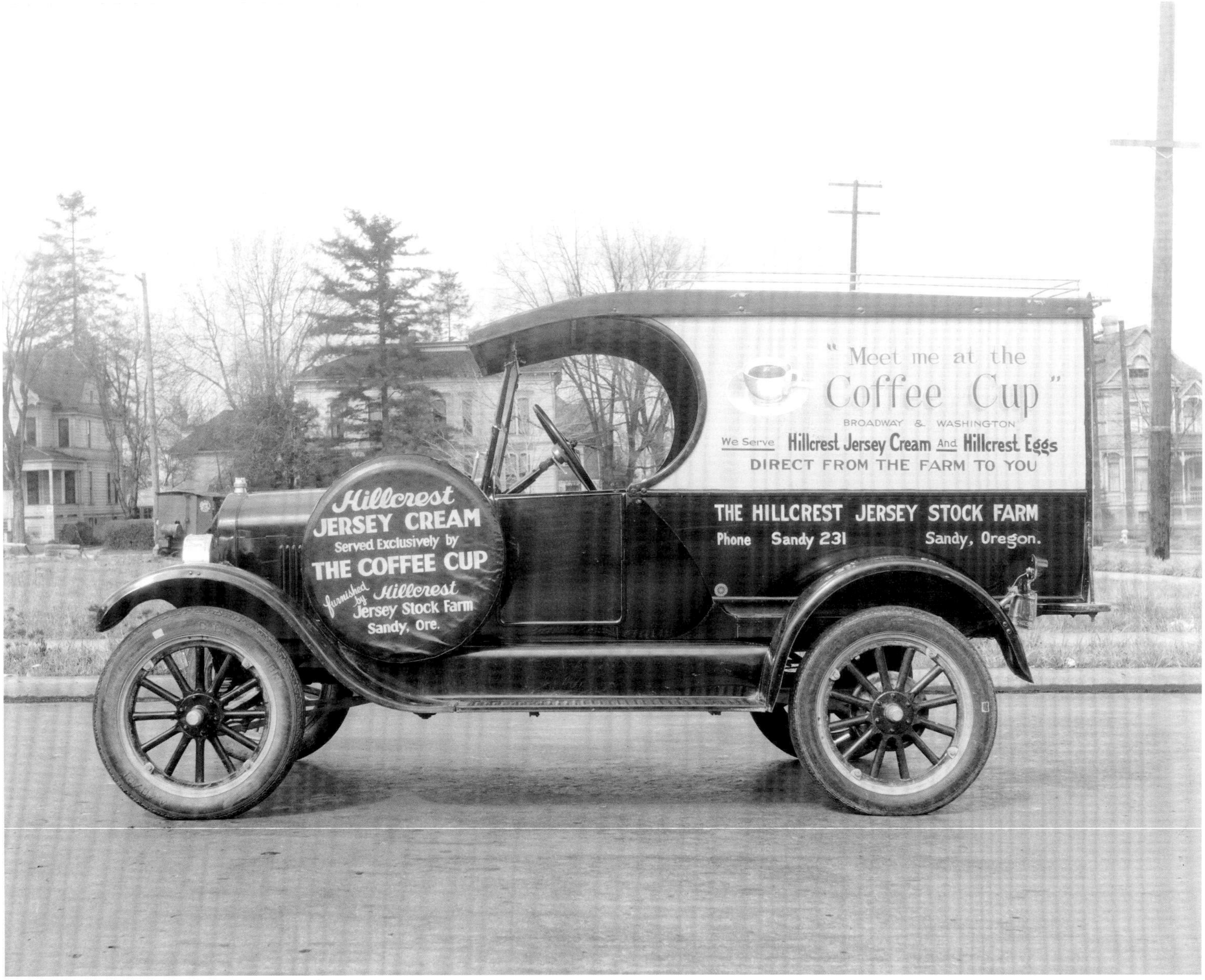

A Hillcrest Jersey Stock Farm delivery truck. During the 1910s, paved roads and the vehicles built for them began to replace dirt roads and horsepower. The farm advertised here was located near the town of Sandy, in northwestern Oregon.

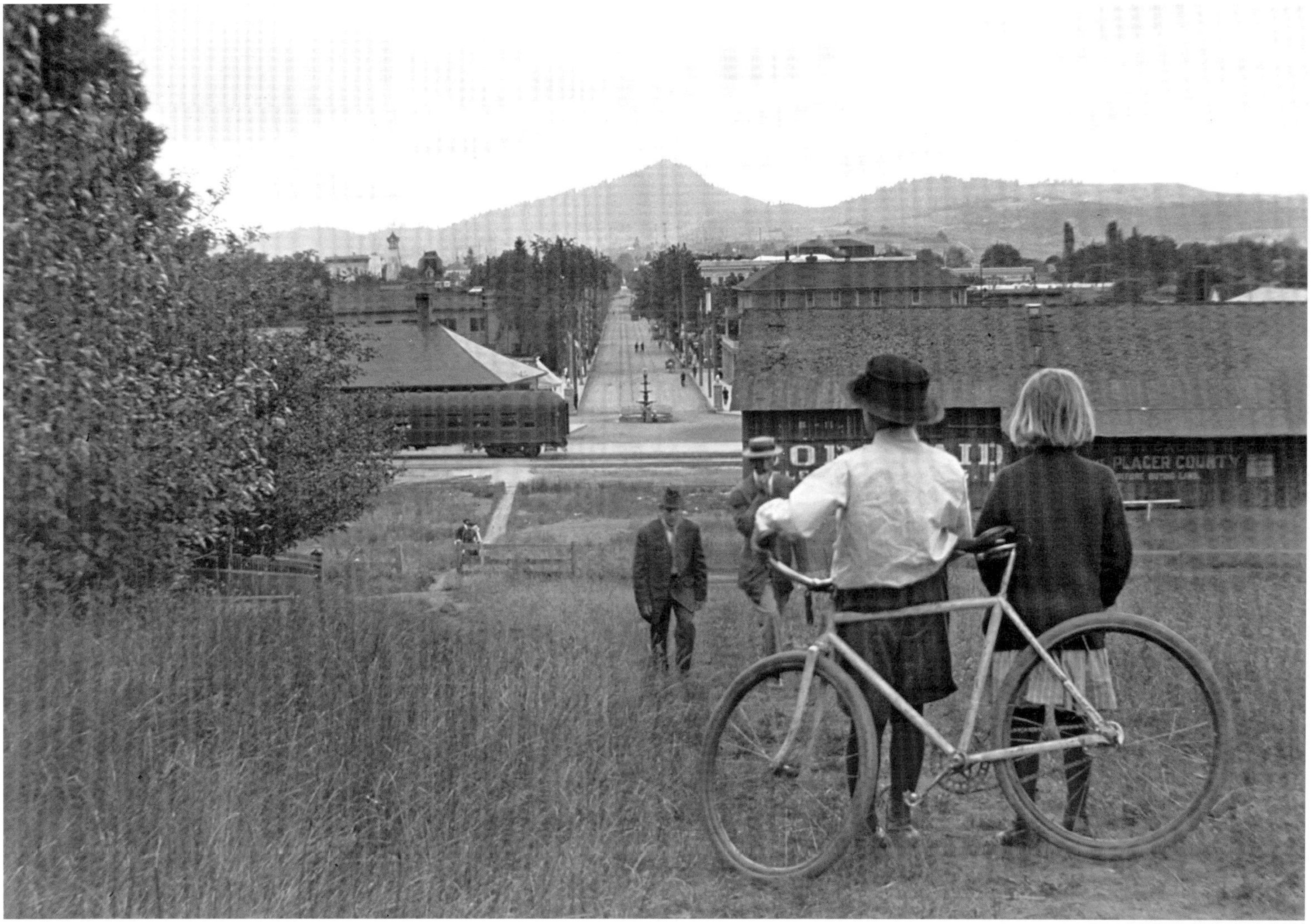

Two youngsters gaze toward Skinner's Butte in Eugene. The butte is named for Eugene Skinner (1809–1864), for whom the city itself was named. Skinner was born in New York, immigrating west and eventually settling in the area. In 1851, he donated land for public buildings and helped plat the town.

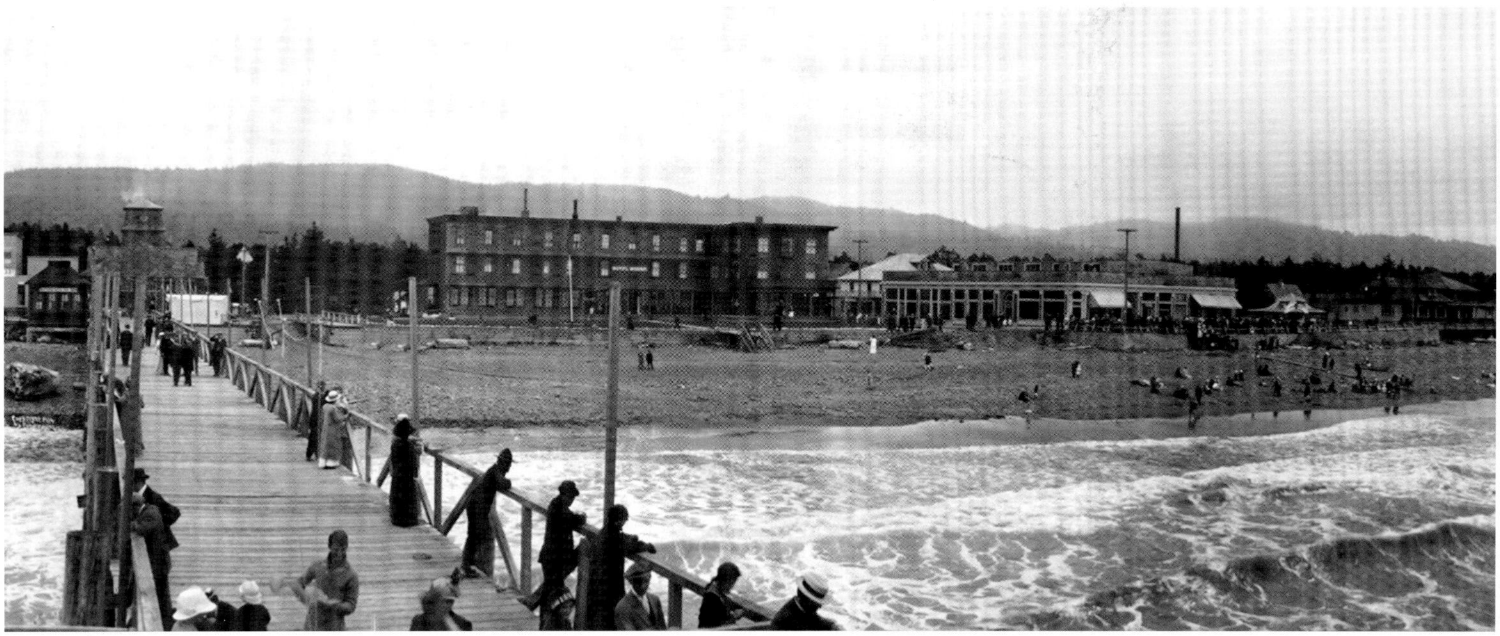

Vacationers enjoy the pier at Hotel Moore, on Tillamook Head at Seaside. Wealthy Portlanders wanting a rustic vacation in the 1910s traveled to Seaside, going by steamboat down the Columbia River and then by wagon to the beach community.

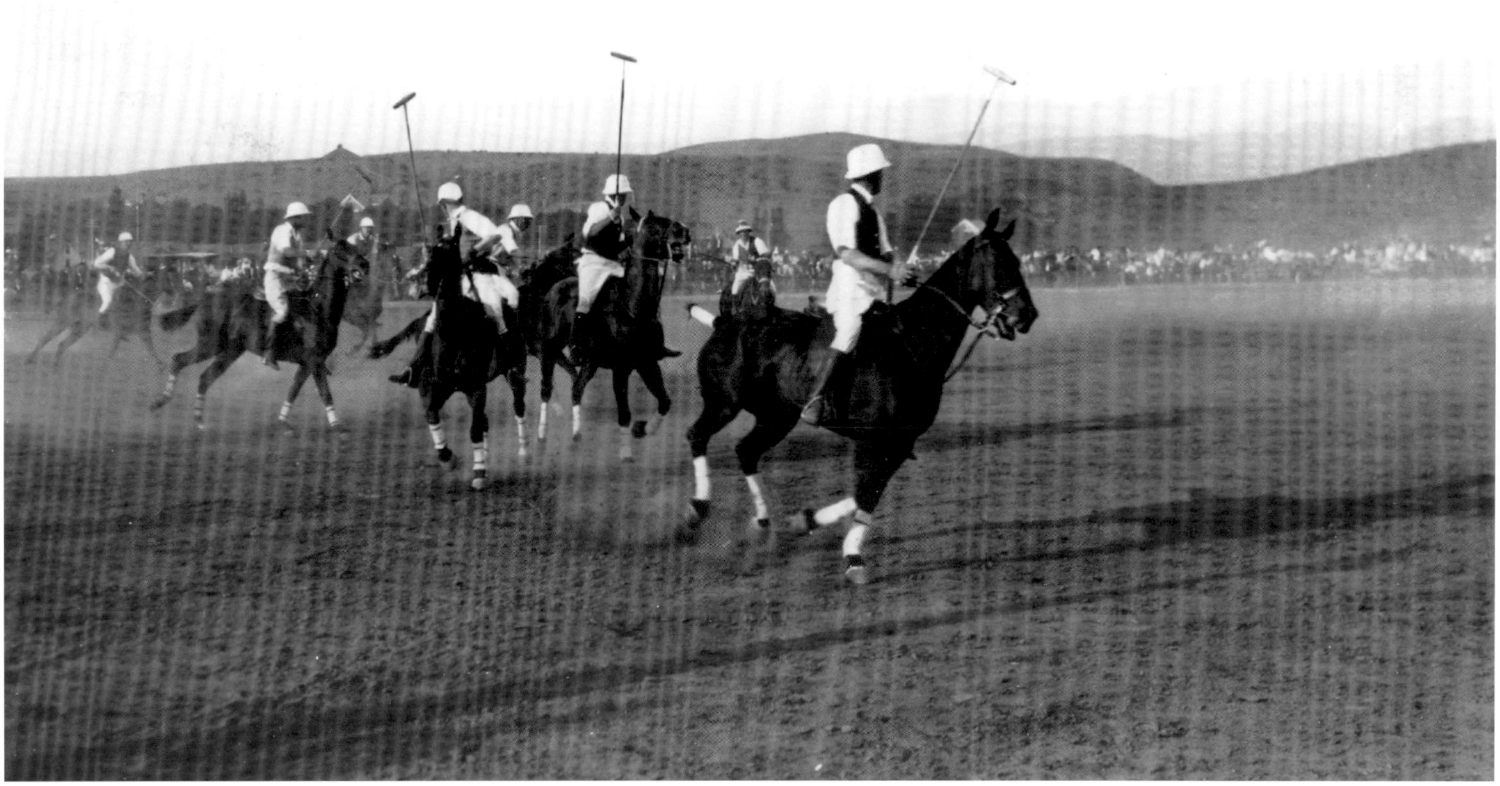

The city of Portland turned out for this polo match around 1915. The game of polo dates from ancient times and was given worldwide popularity by the British in the late nineteenth century.

Following Spread: Terminal for the Great Northern Pacific Steamship Company at Flavel, around 1915. The stacks of one of its two ships rise above the terminal in the distance. The line was opened to complement passenger service by railroad but would prove to be a financial disappointment for its owners. When World War I erupted, the line ended.

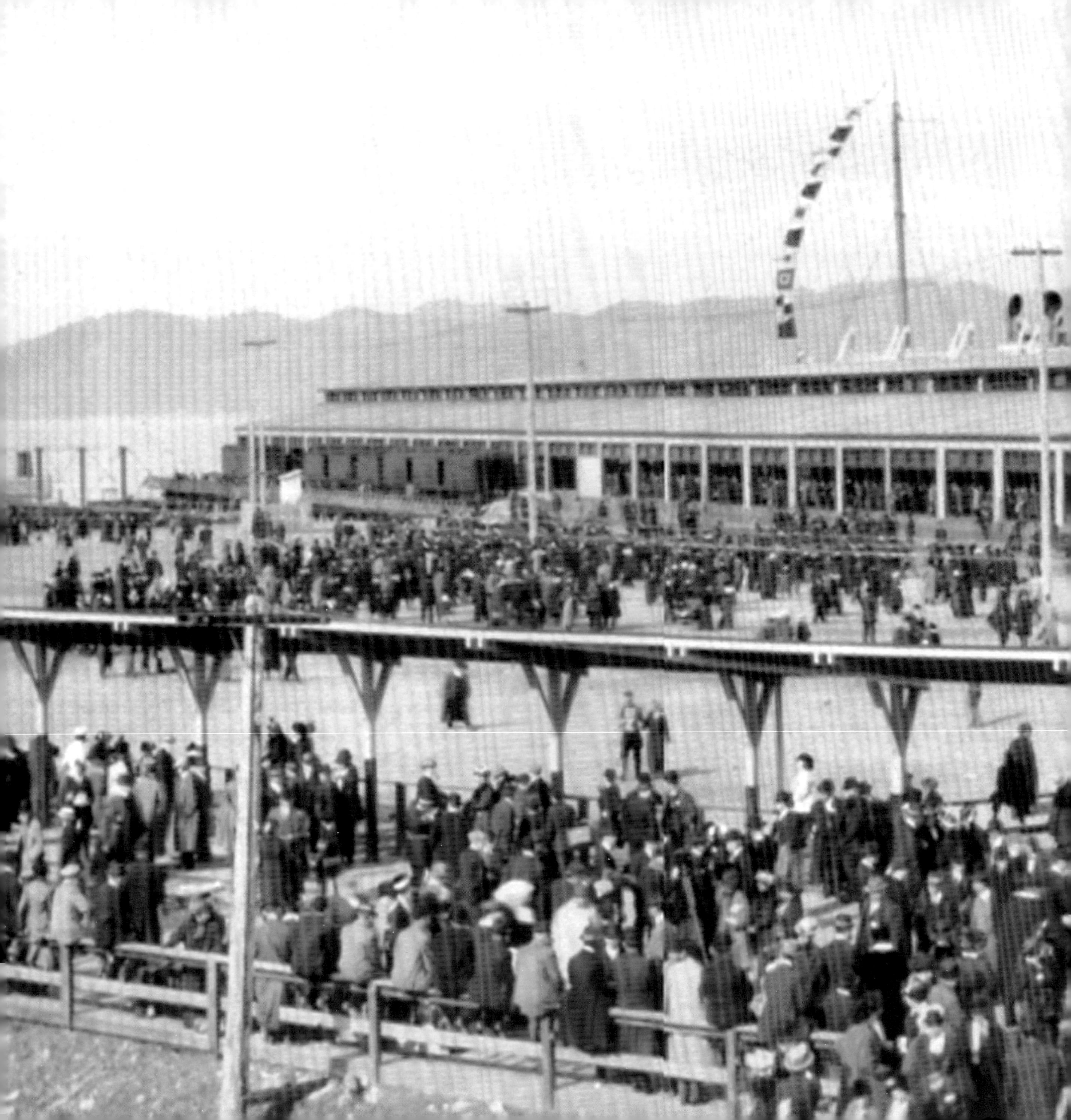

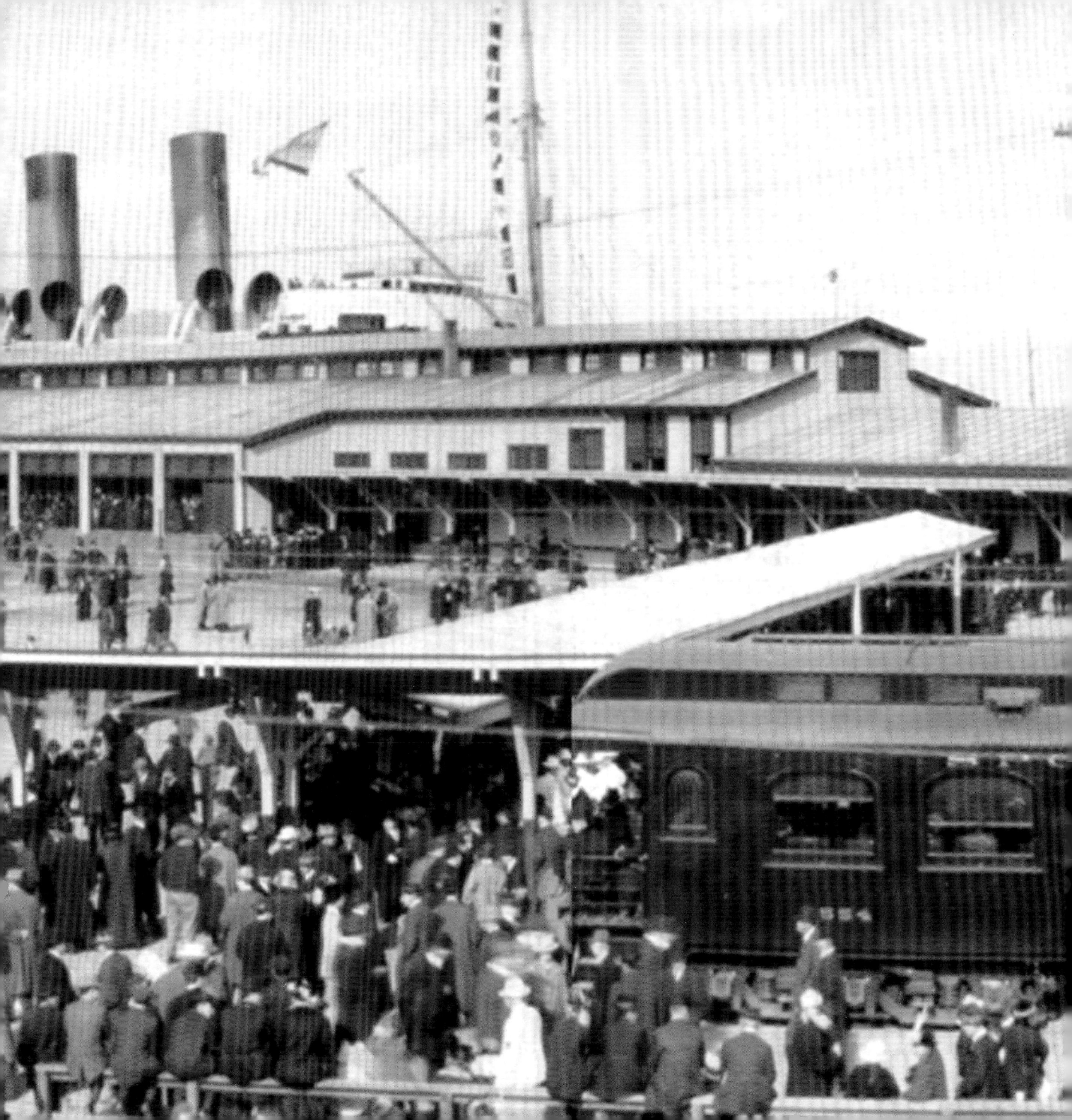

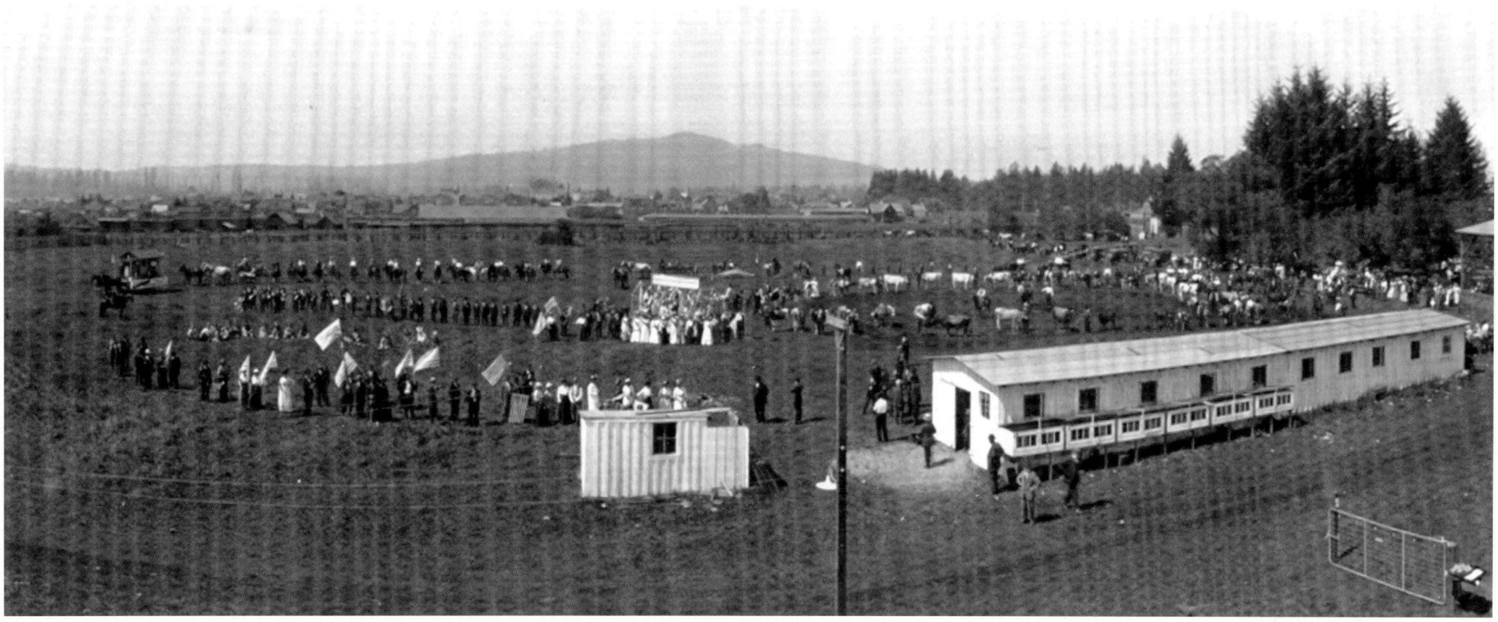

The Tillamook County Fair is under way around 1915. Established in 1866 along the northern Oregon coast, Tillamook is known for its dairy, logging, and lumber milling industries.

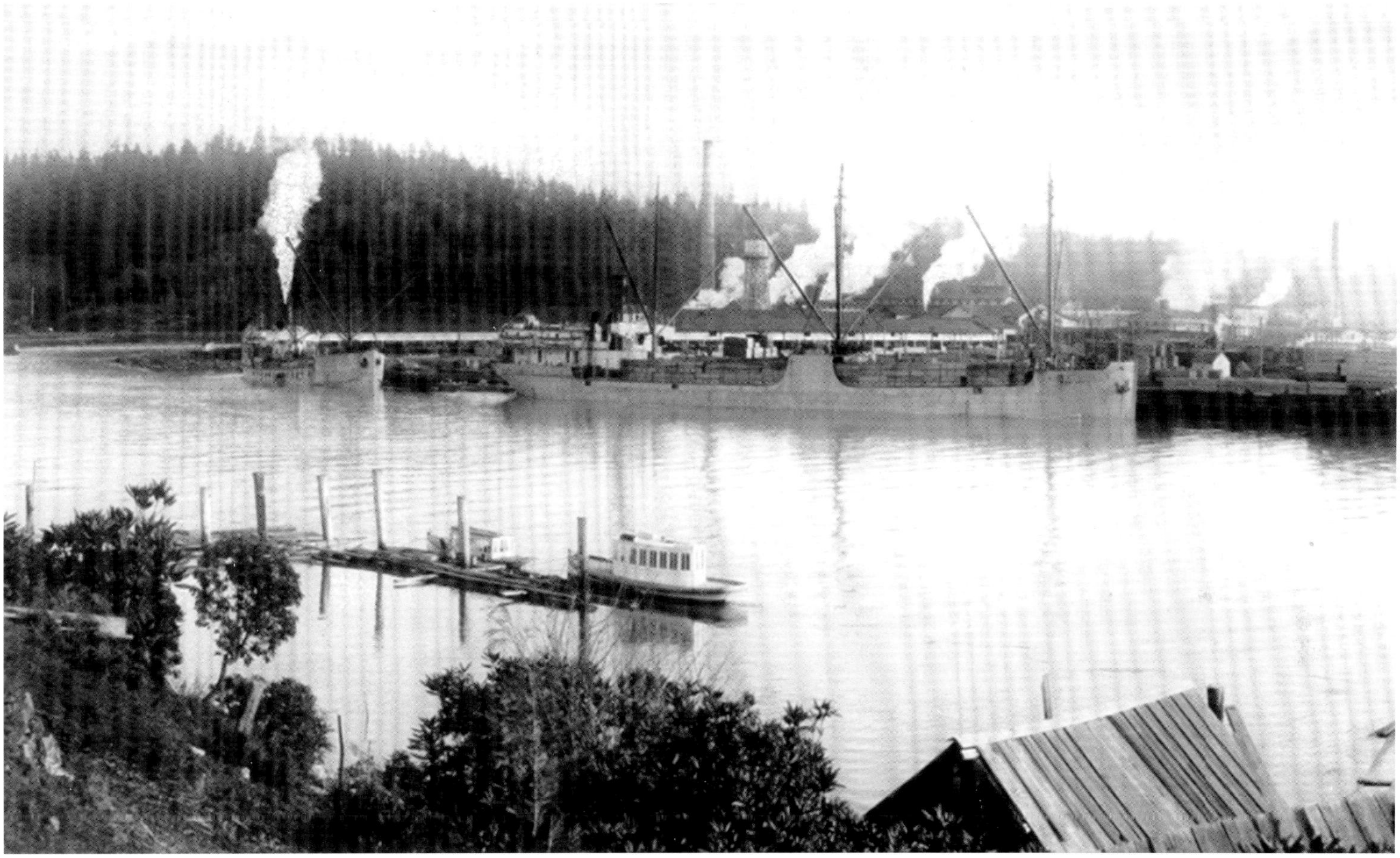

The steamships *Adeline Smith, Nann Smith,* and *Redondo* are being loaded at the C. A. Smith Lumber and Manufacturing Company in Marshfield around 1915. Marshfield would change its name to Coos Bay in 1944.

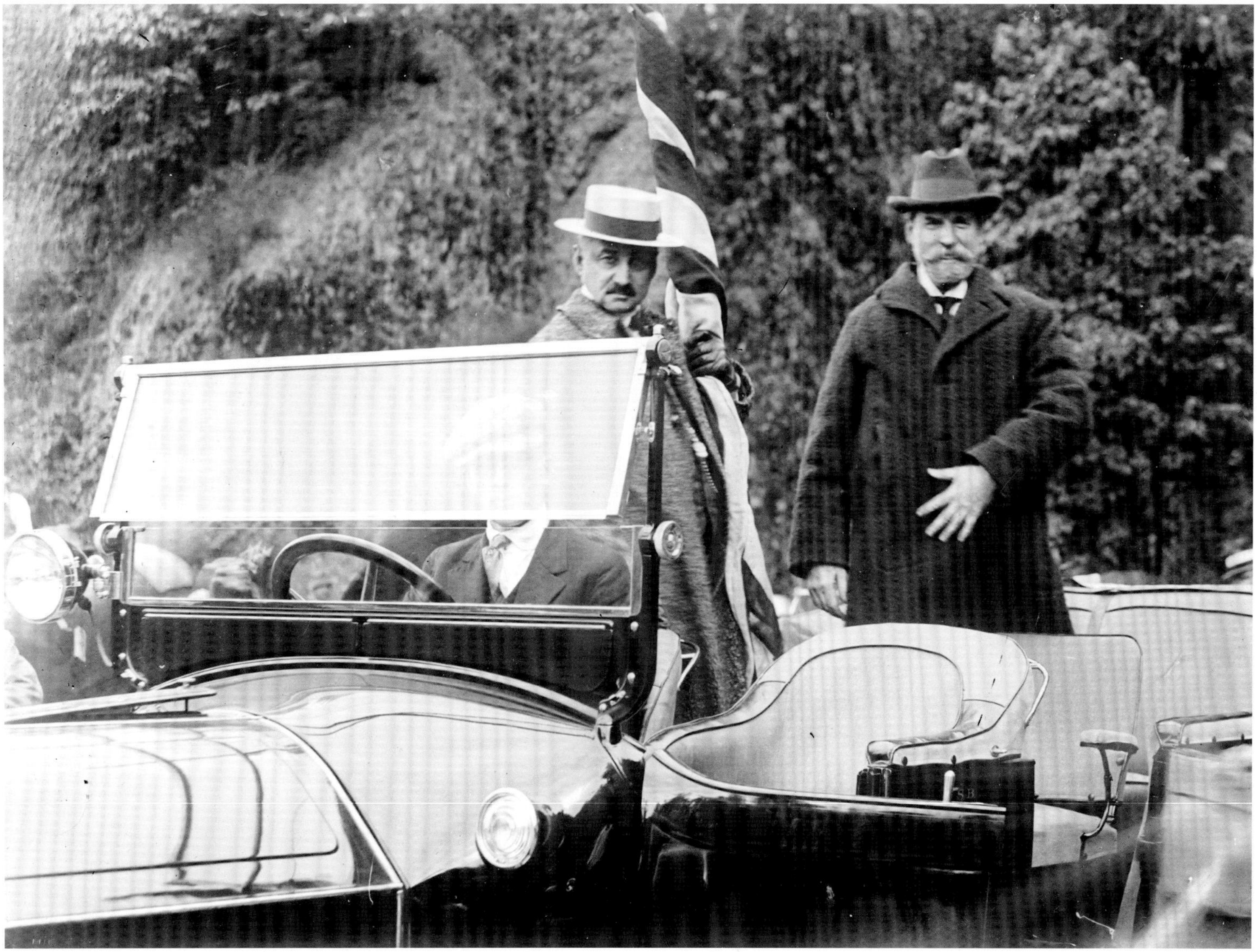

Charles Evans Hughes (at right) during an appearance in Portland, around 1916. Hughes was the Republican candidate for president that year, running against and defeated by Woodrow Wilson in the November elections. Hughes had served as governor of New York and would later become chief justice of the Supreme Court.

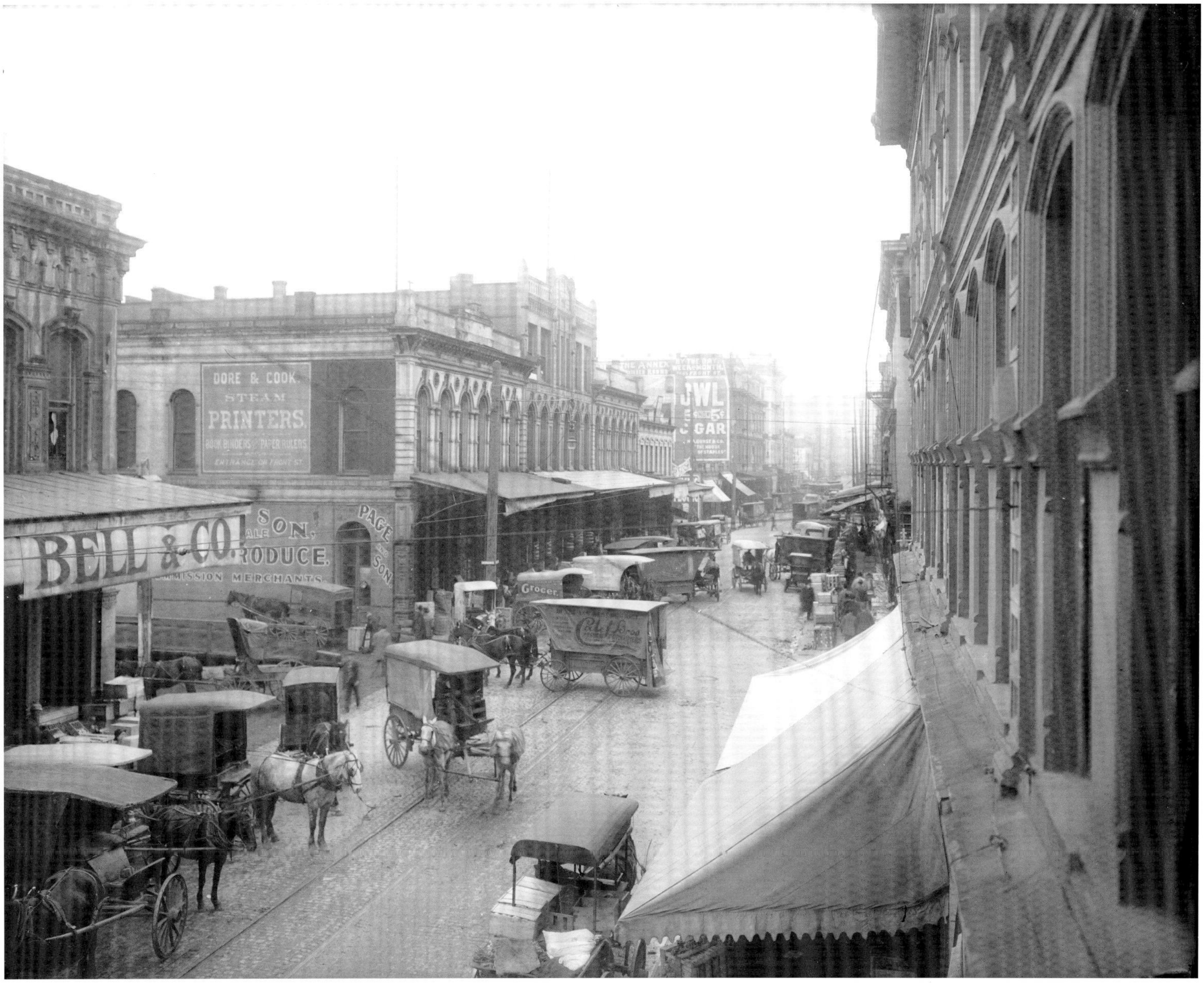

Business is brisk around 1916 on Front Street in Portland.

Southwest Morrison Street at Fourth Avenue in Portland. The retail giant F. W. Woolworth building is visible in the foreground in this view from the 1910s.

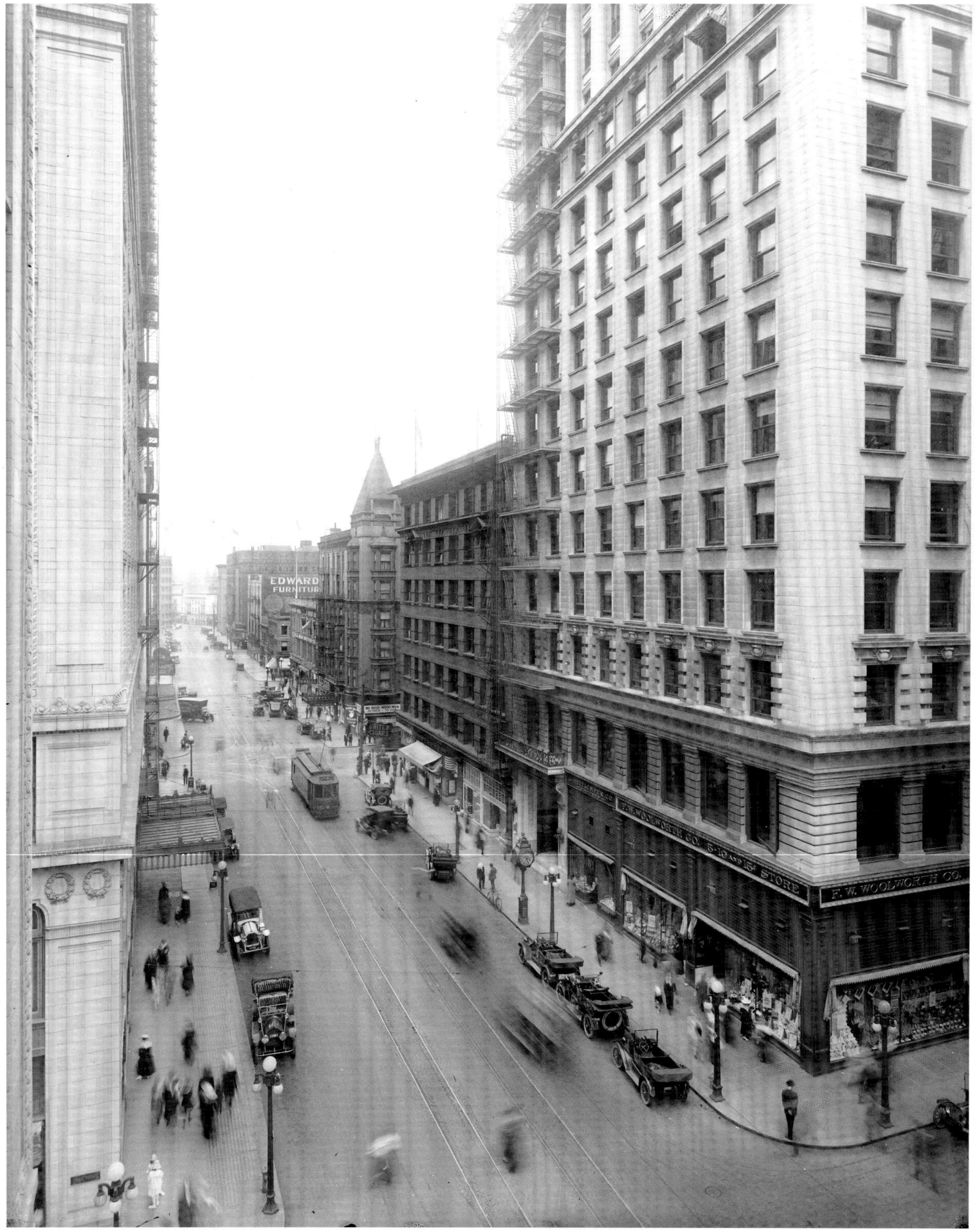

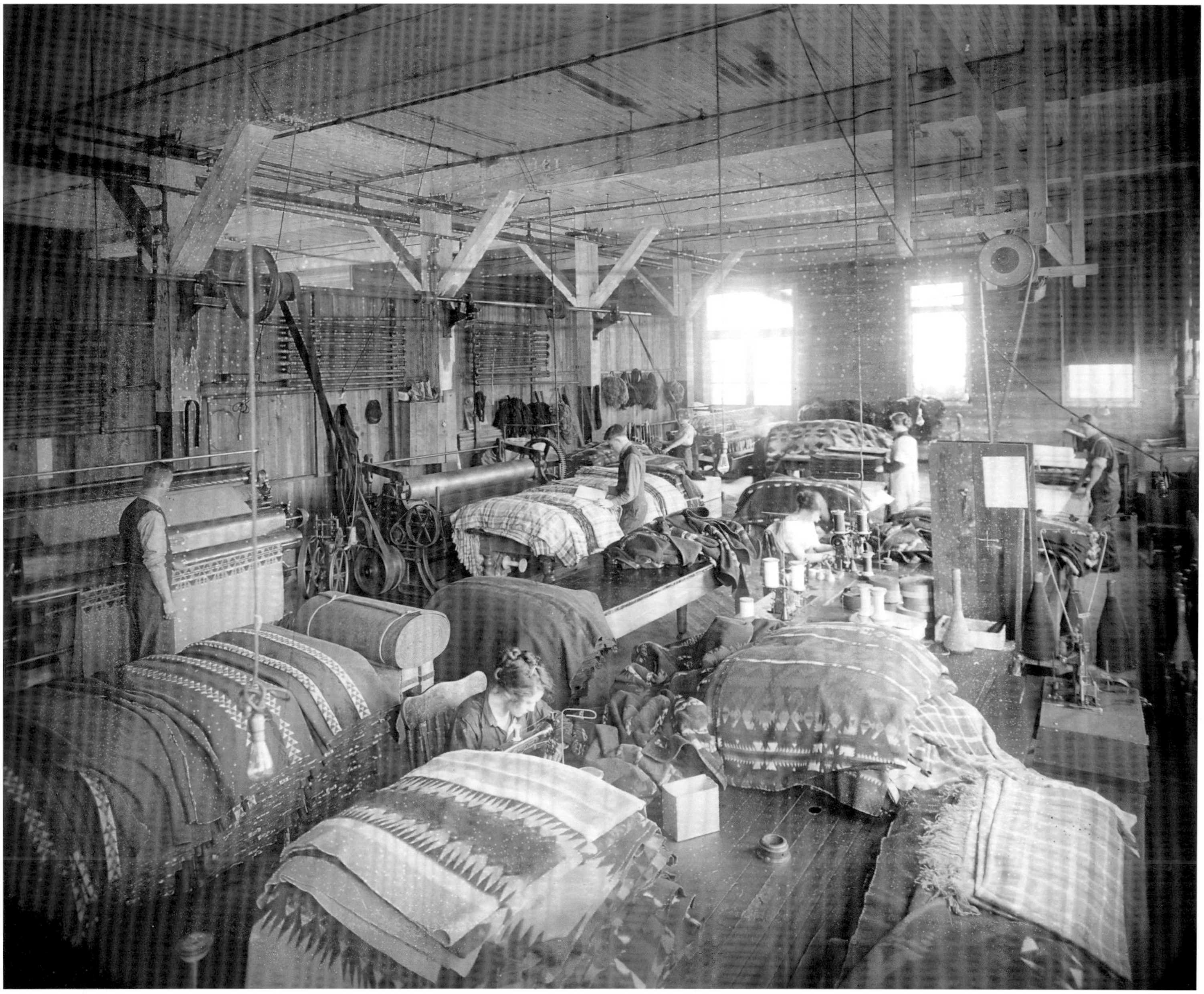

Interior view of the Pendleton Woolen Mill Factory founded in 1909 by the Bishop family. The company's main business was trade with Southwest and Pacific Northwest Indian tribes.

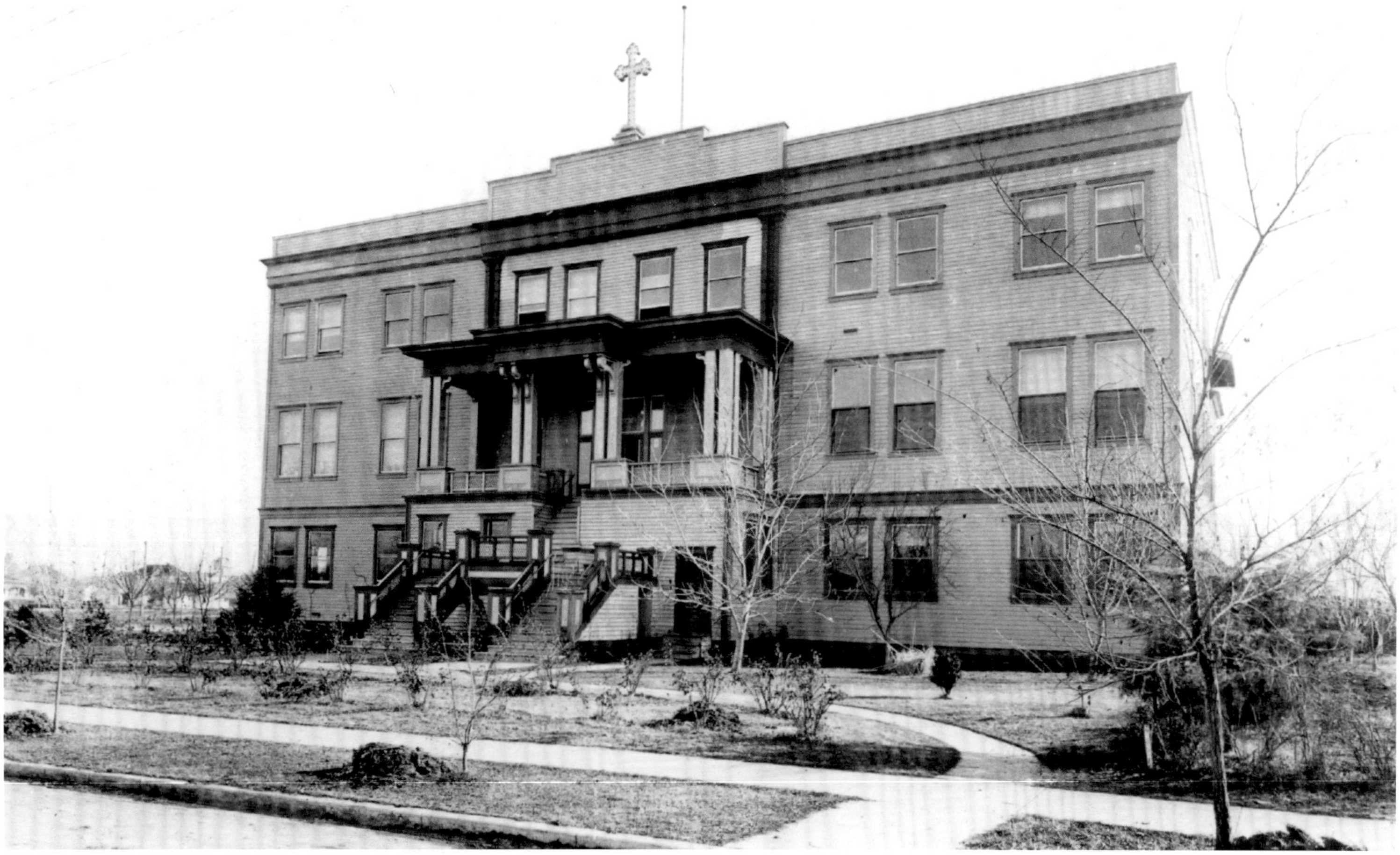

St. Mary's Academy relocated to Medford in 1908. Medford's economy flourished owing to the Oregon & California Railroad and the fruit growing and packing industry. Today, more than 75,000 Oregonians make their home in Medford, the largest city in southern Oregon, and St. Mary's continues to operate as a school for the city's youth.

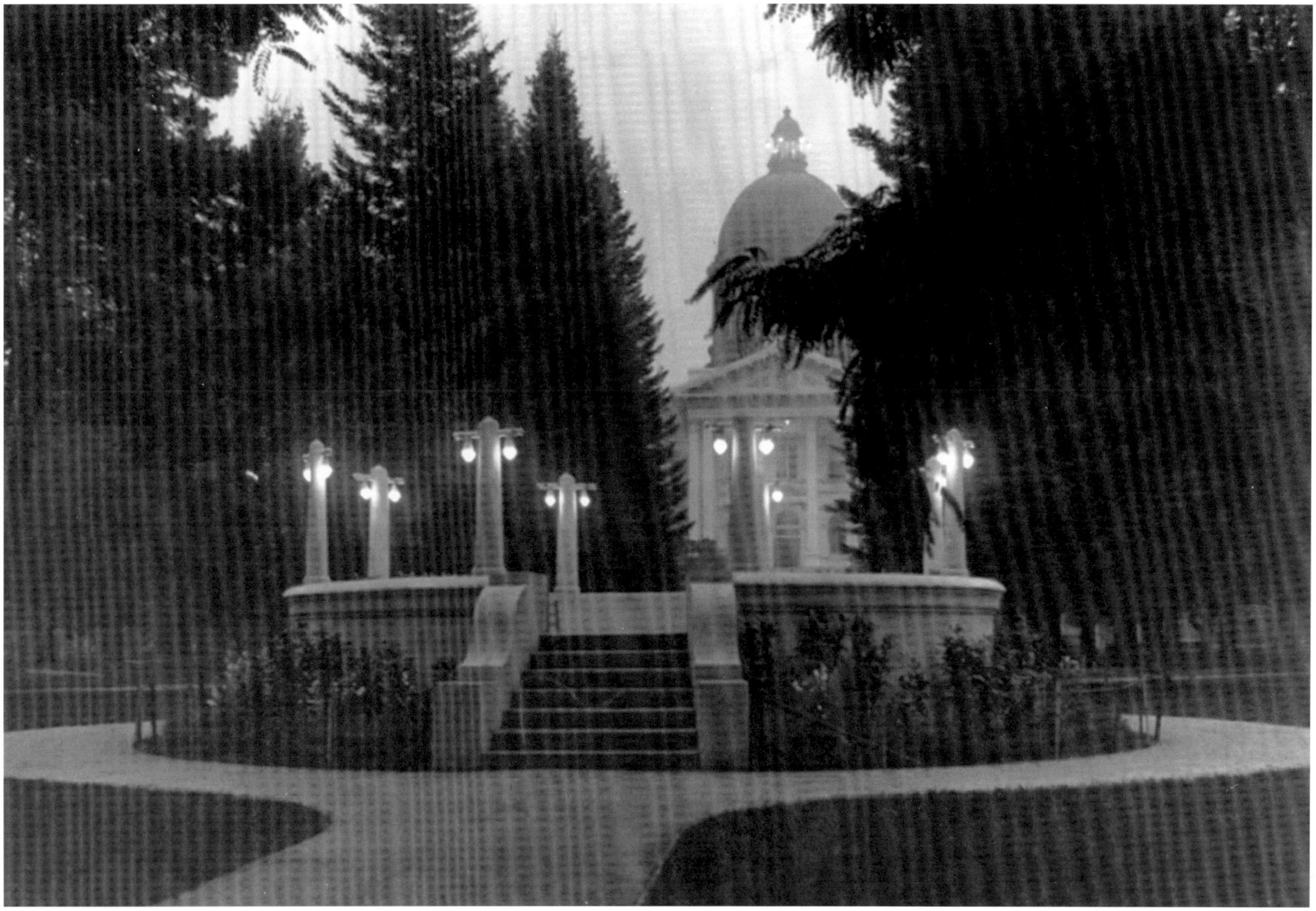

A park in Salem at night with the capitol in the background, around 1917. Salem has been Oregon's state capital since 1851 (Corvallis served briefly as the capital in 1855) and was incorporated as a city in 1857. This is a view of the second state capitol, which would be replaced in the 1930s after it caught fire and burned.

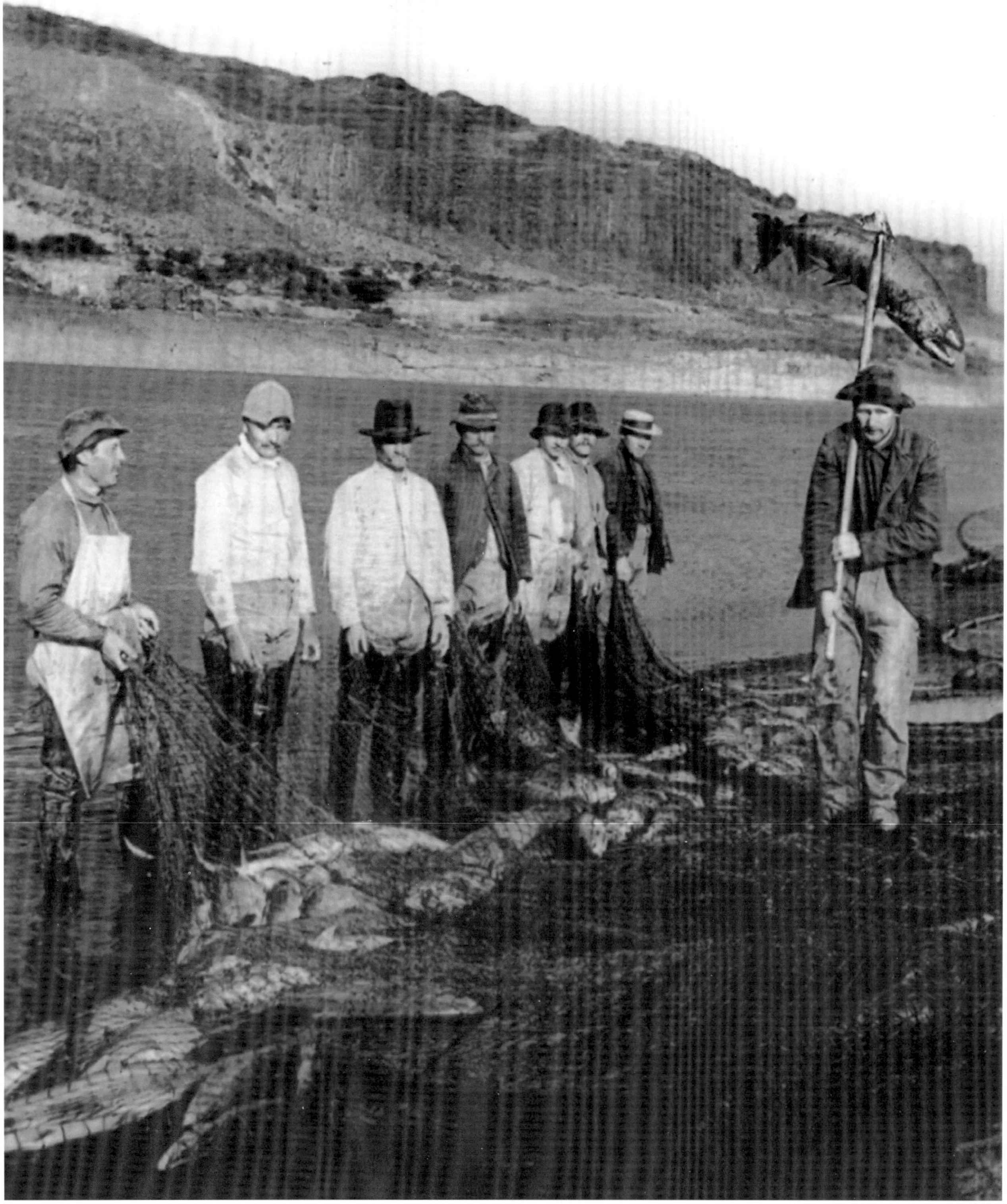

Salmon caught with nets on the Columbia River. The Columbia River supported an abundance of fish until overfishing and the building of dams beginning in the 1930s cut into populations. Fish ladders were built alongside the dams, enabling many fish to continue their annual migrations.

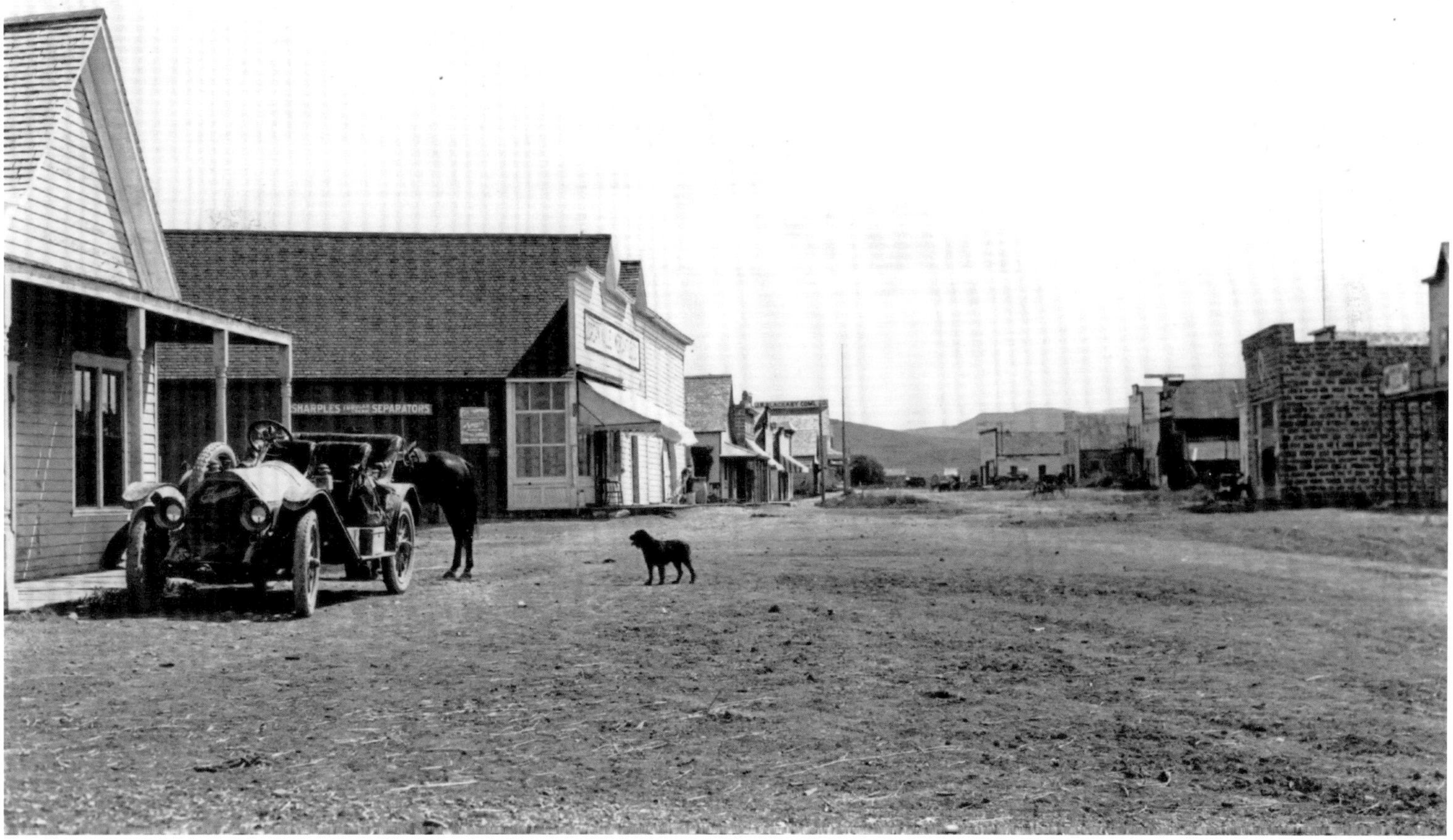

The community of Jordan Valley, located in Malheur County, was incorporated in 1917. The area became famous for the Basque people, who came from Spain to raise sheep in the early twentieth century.

Following Spread: Crown Point and Vista House on the Columbia River. Designed by Portland architect Edgar W. Lazarus, Vista House opened in 1918 as a memorial to Oregon pioneers and as a rest station for those traveling the Columbia River Highway. Towering 733 feet above the Columbia River, the octagonal structure was reopened to the public in 2005 following extensive renovations.

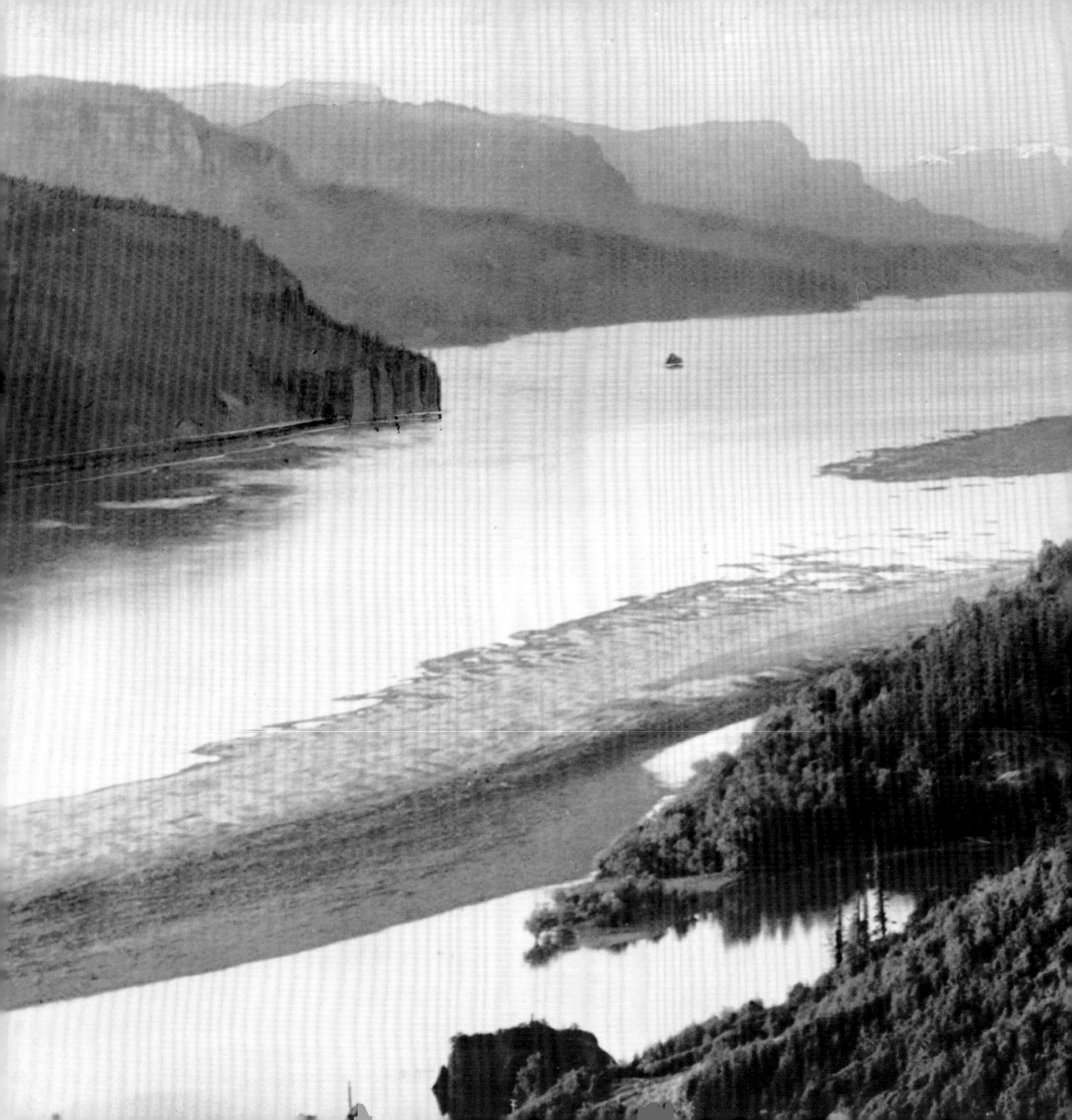

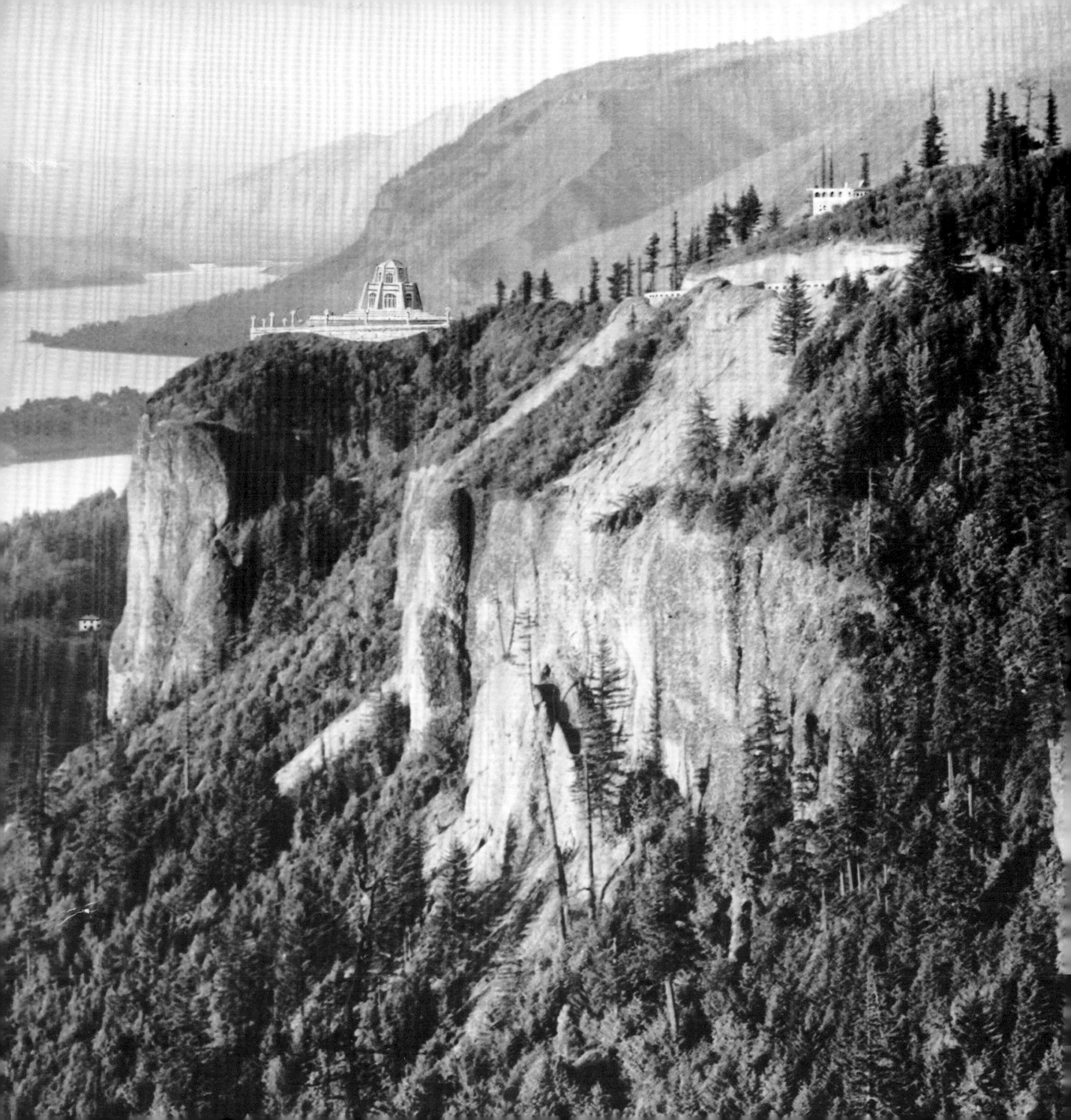

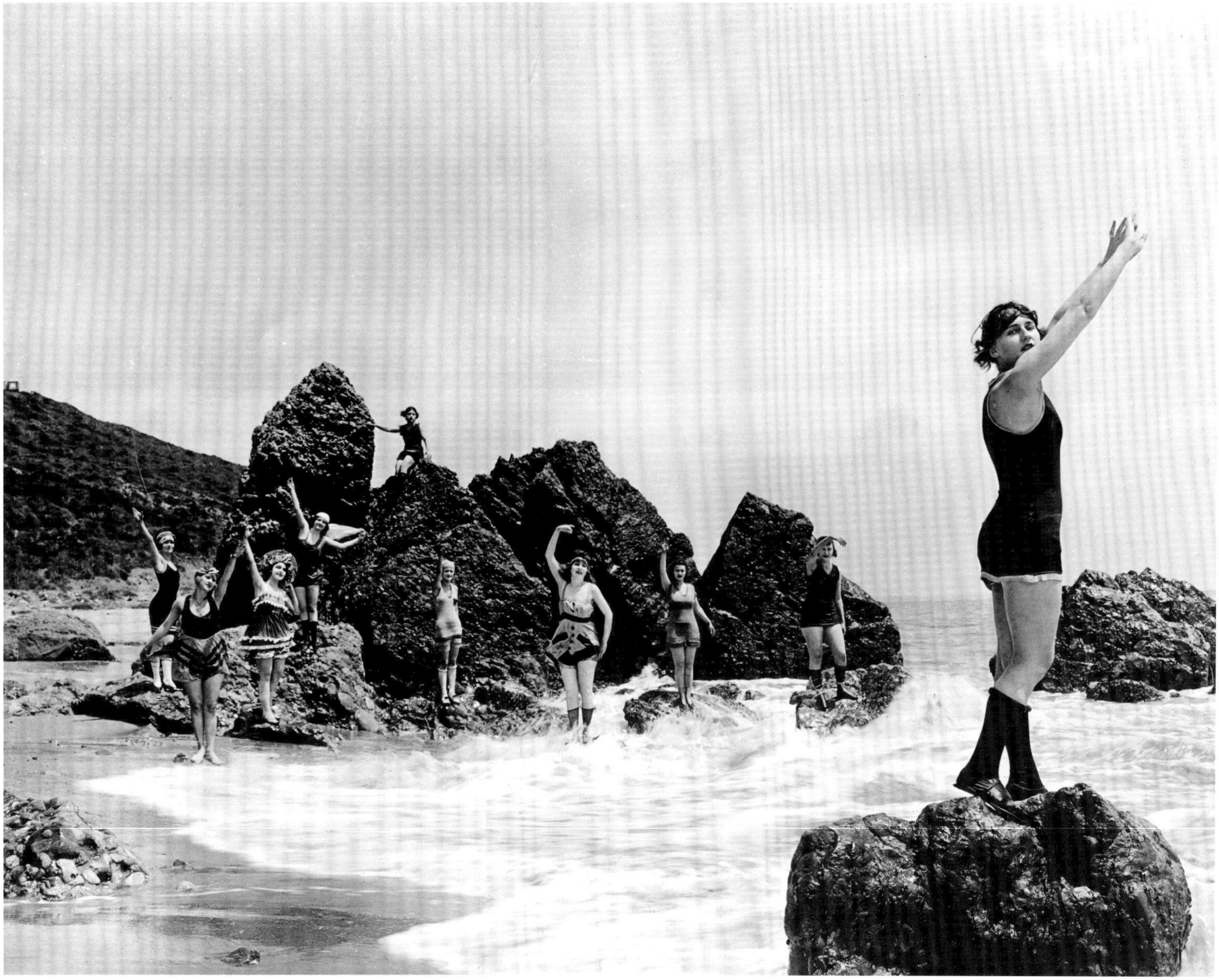

Young women pose in the swimsuits of yesteryear on a rocky Oregon beach. Many beaches on the Oregon coast were not accessible by automobile until completion of the Oregon Coast Highway (in 1932) and Sunset Highway (in 1949).

Between the Wars

(1920–1940)

During the 1920s, agriculture and timbering remained economically crucial to the state economy. Efforts both public and private brought more people to the state's rural areas to pursue these activities. Arid areas in the eastern part of the state were irrigated. West of the Cascades, large land companies bought areas of good land with excellent rail connections and planted fruit-bearing trees, and then sold them in five-to-ten-acre plots to buyers. Shipbuilding, in part owing to European demand, also flourished during the decade.

The building of roads and increased automobile ownership contributed much to growth in the state. By 1929, one out of every four Multnomah County residents owned an automobile. More roads in Oregon resulted in people being able to visit attractions such as Crater Lake National Park in southern Oregon, the state's only national park, and Jantzen Beach Amusement Park in Portland.

The second incarnation of the Ku Klux Klan, which had been organized in 1915, sprang up in the state in 1921, but its wide influence was shortlived. After several years of mistreatment of minorities and controversial legal decisions, the public turned against the Klan, and the group as a single, widely influential organization largely disappeared from Oregon and other states by the end of the decade.

In 1929, the stock market crash on Wall Street would mark the beginning of the Great Depression, which brought hardship to Americans nationwide. Based more on agriculture and to a less extent on manufacturing, Oregon's economy weathered the hard times better than some. Franklin D. Roosevelt's New Deal programs in the 1930s, among them the Civilian Conservation Corps, the Works Progress Administration, and the Rural Electrification Administration, would bring relief by providing jobs through tax dollars to unemployed Americans. Oregonians given work by the federal government completed numerous building projects, including Timberline Lodge and Bonneville Dam, and helped to reforest the state, particularly after the Tillamook Burn. The New Deal was not a cure-all for the economic woes that had befallen the state, but the relief it provided Oregonians during a difficult time in the nation's history would have far-reaching effects on the thinking of citizens, who began looking to government for answers to economic crises.

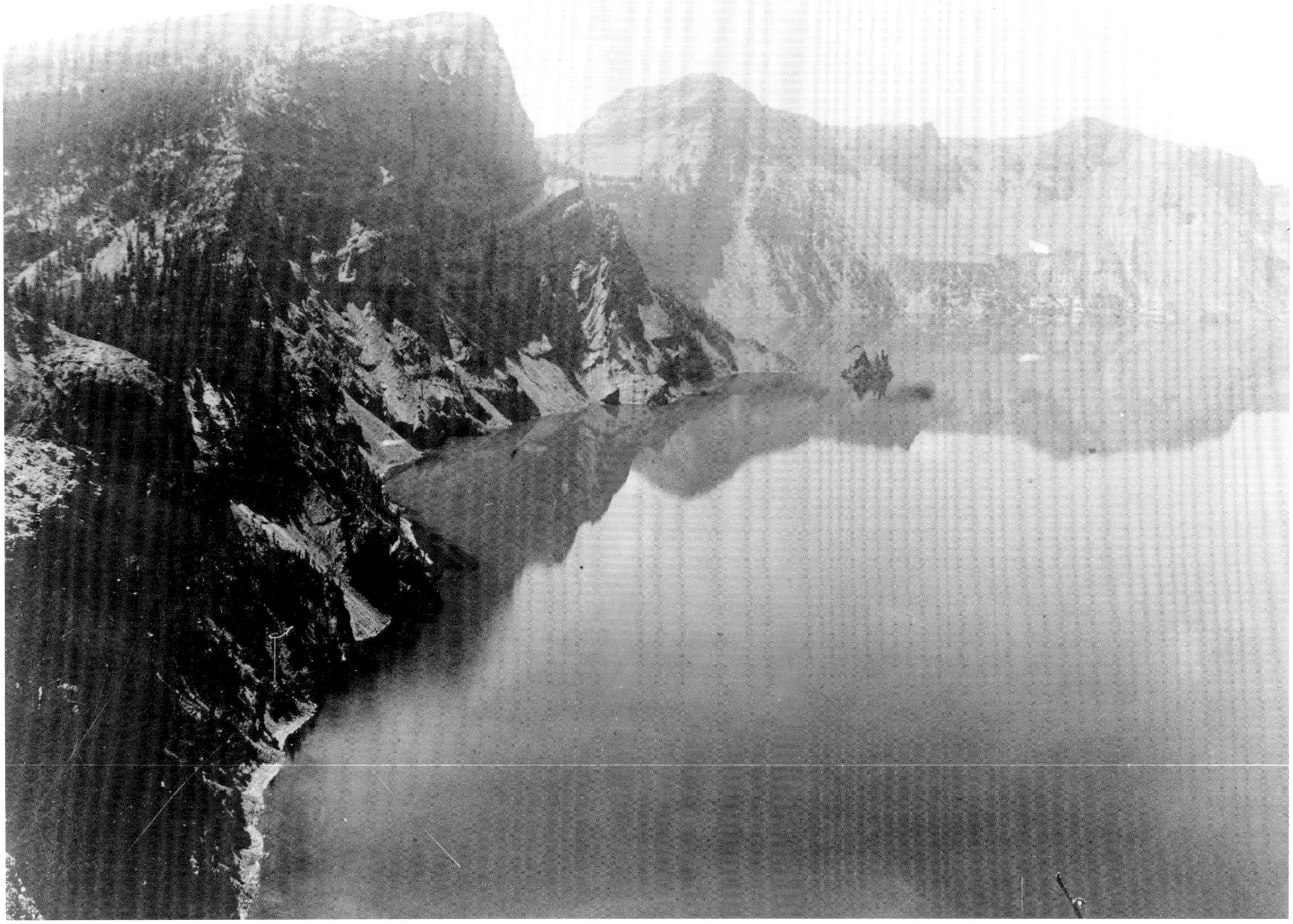

This image gives a vivid look at Dutton Cliff, Eagle Point, and Garfield Peake at Crater Lake National Park.

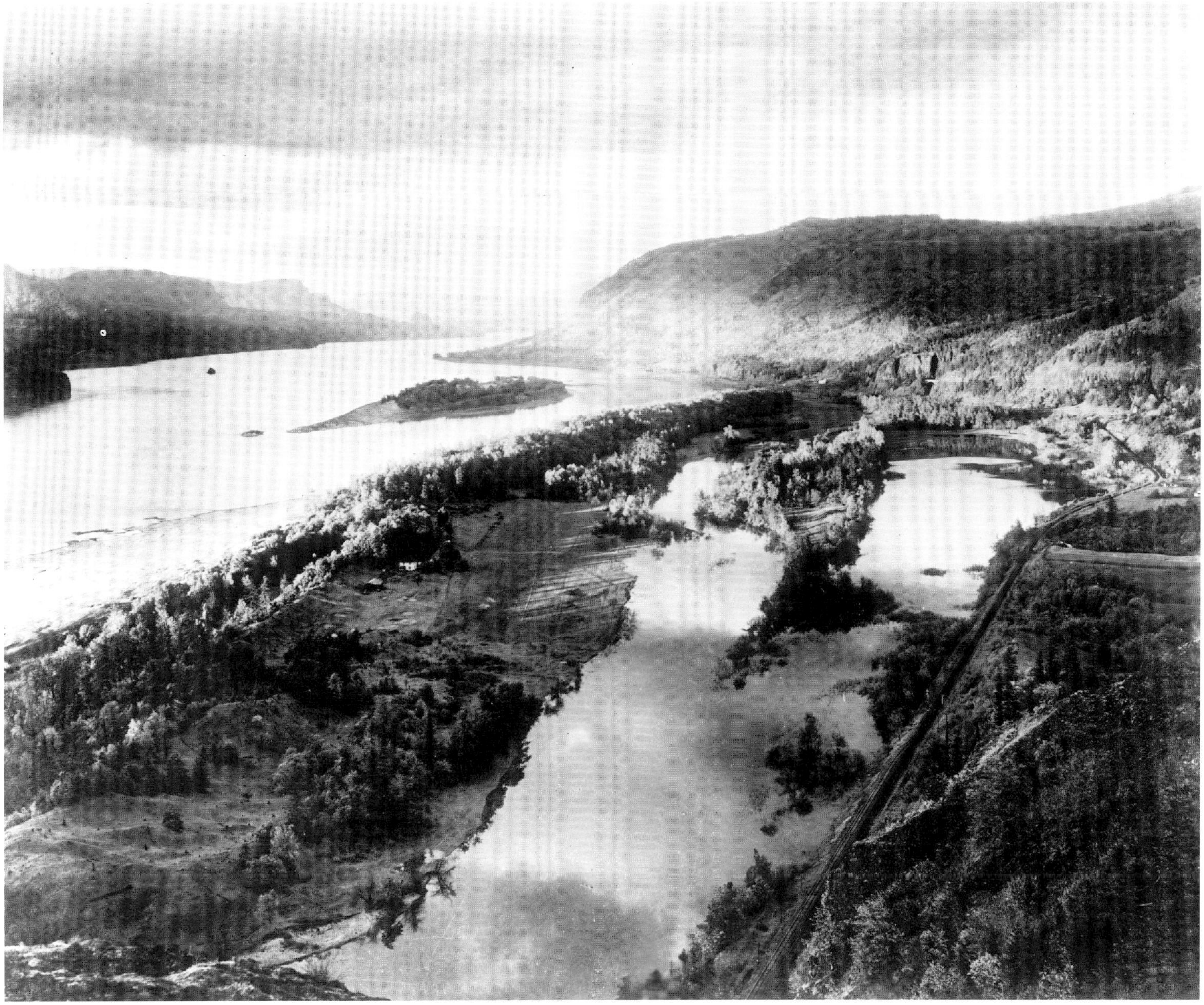

Highways joined rivers and railroads as a third, and increasingly vital, transportation system in Oregon early in the twentieth century. The (Historic) Columbia River Highway was built along the Columbia River between 1913 and 1922 to become the first planned scenic highway in the nation. A grand opening was held in 1916. The 75-mile-long highway linking The Dalles with points west would later become U.S. Highway 30 and was placed on the National Register of Historic Places in 1983.

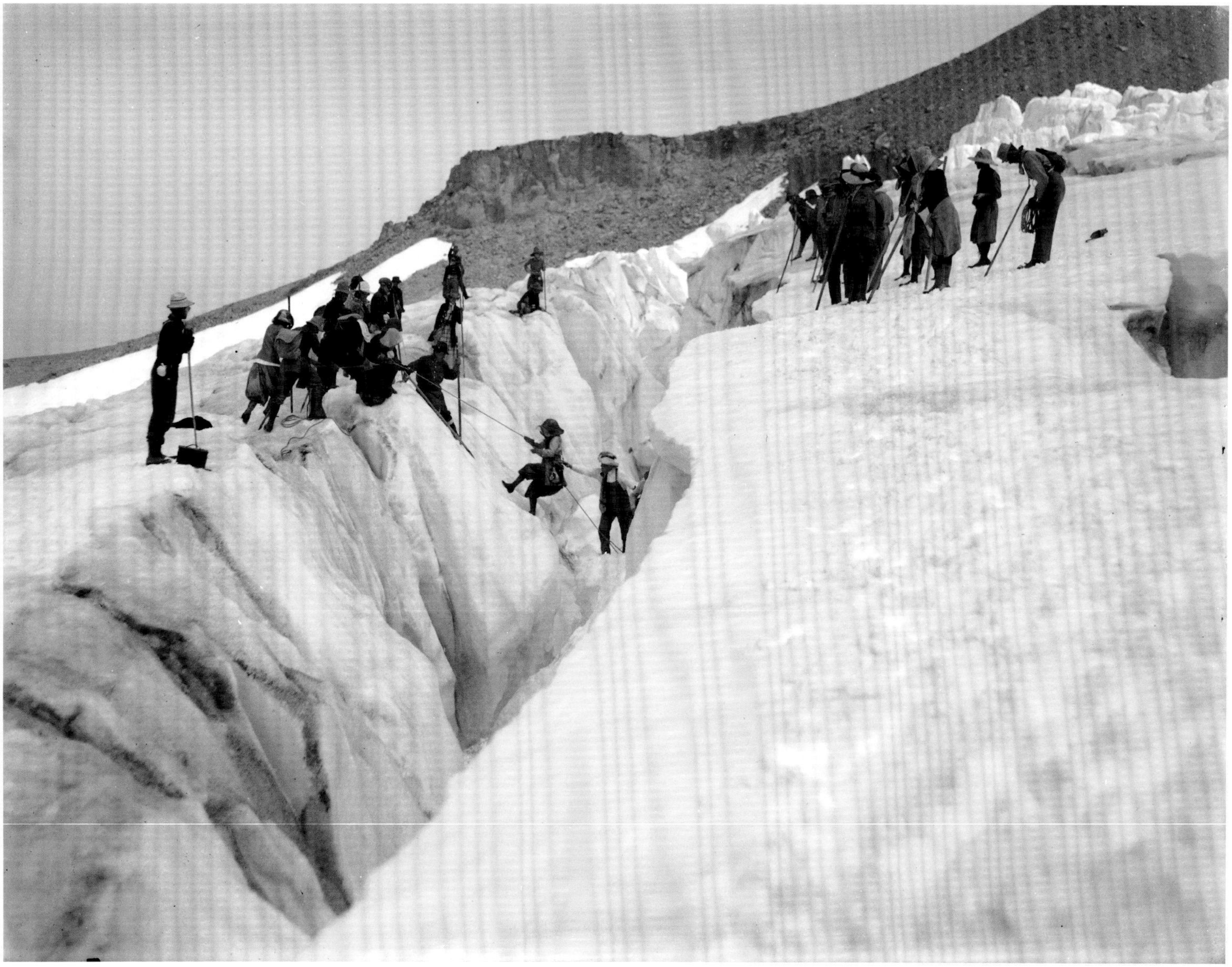

A group of climbers rappel into a large crevasse on a glacier on Mount Hood. The mountain holds 12 glaciers and occasionally shows signs of volcanic activity.

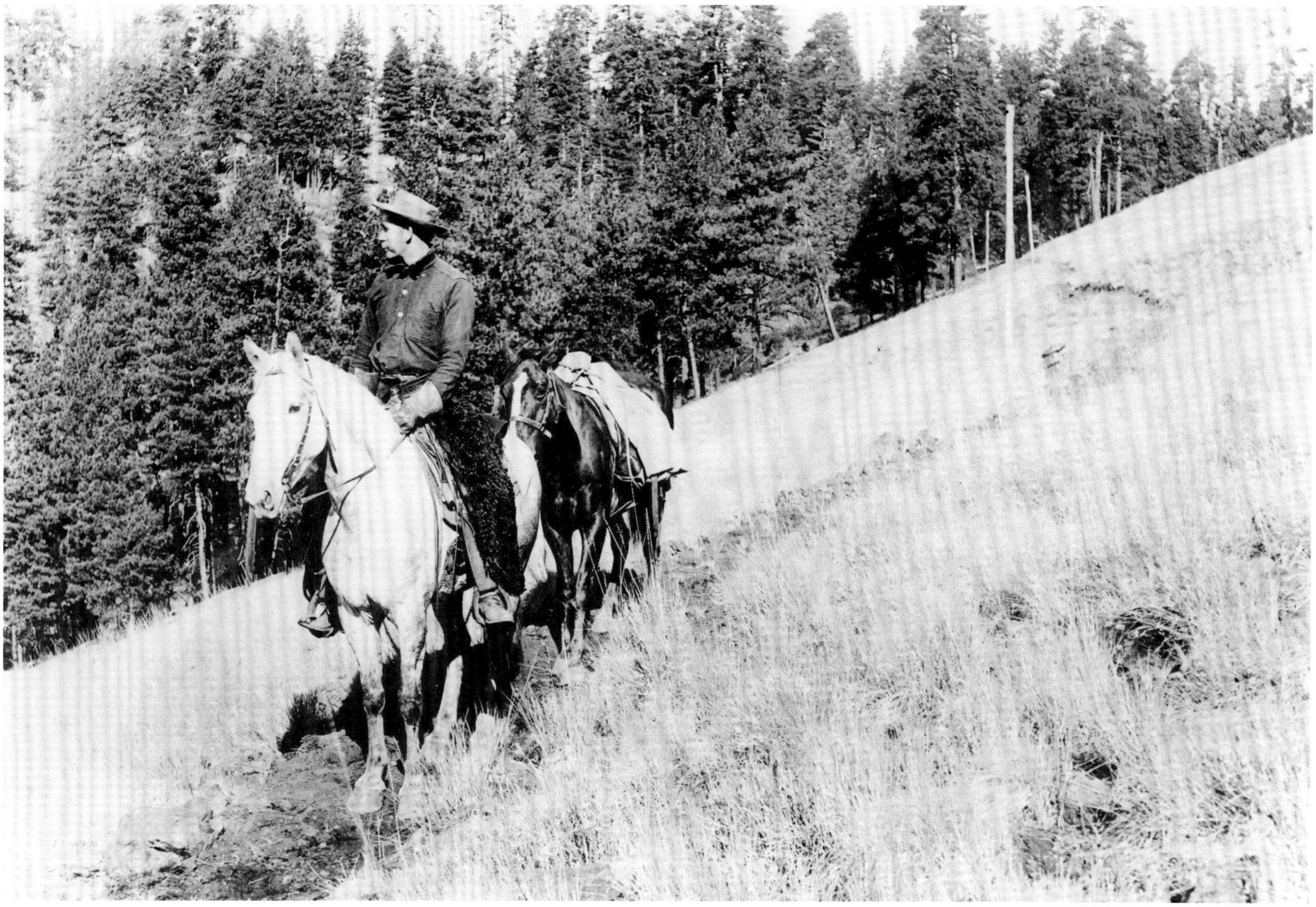

A man on horseback explores Davis Creek Canyon, in Wallowa National Forest. The highest point in the Wallowa Mountains is Sacagawea Peak (at 9,838 feet above sea level), the sixth-tallest peak in the state.

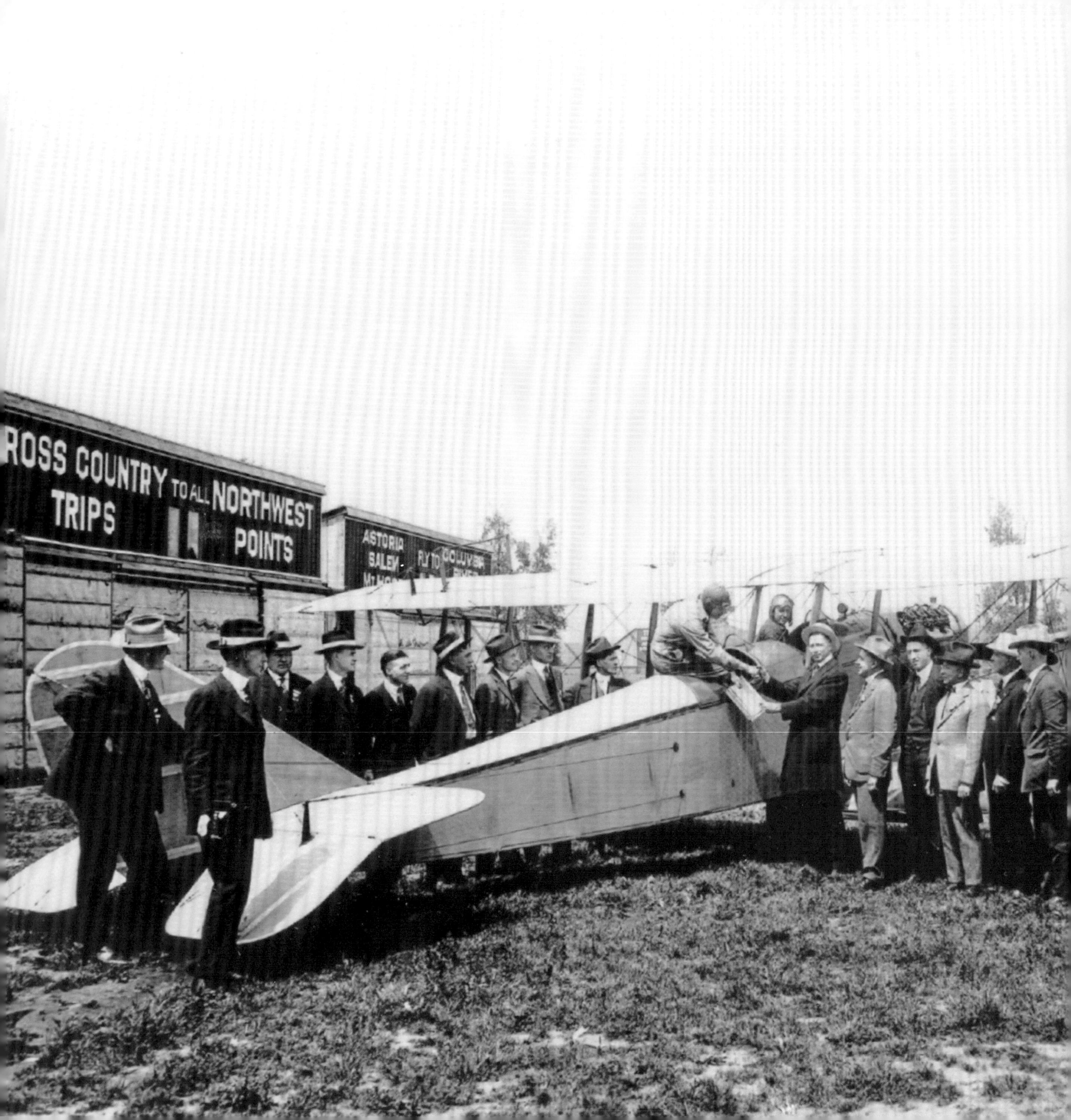
ROSS COUNTRY
TRIPS
TO ALL
NORTHWEST
POINTS
ASTORIA
SALEM

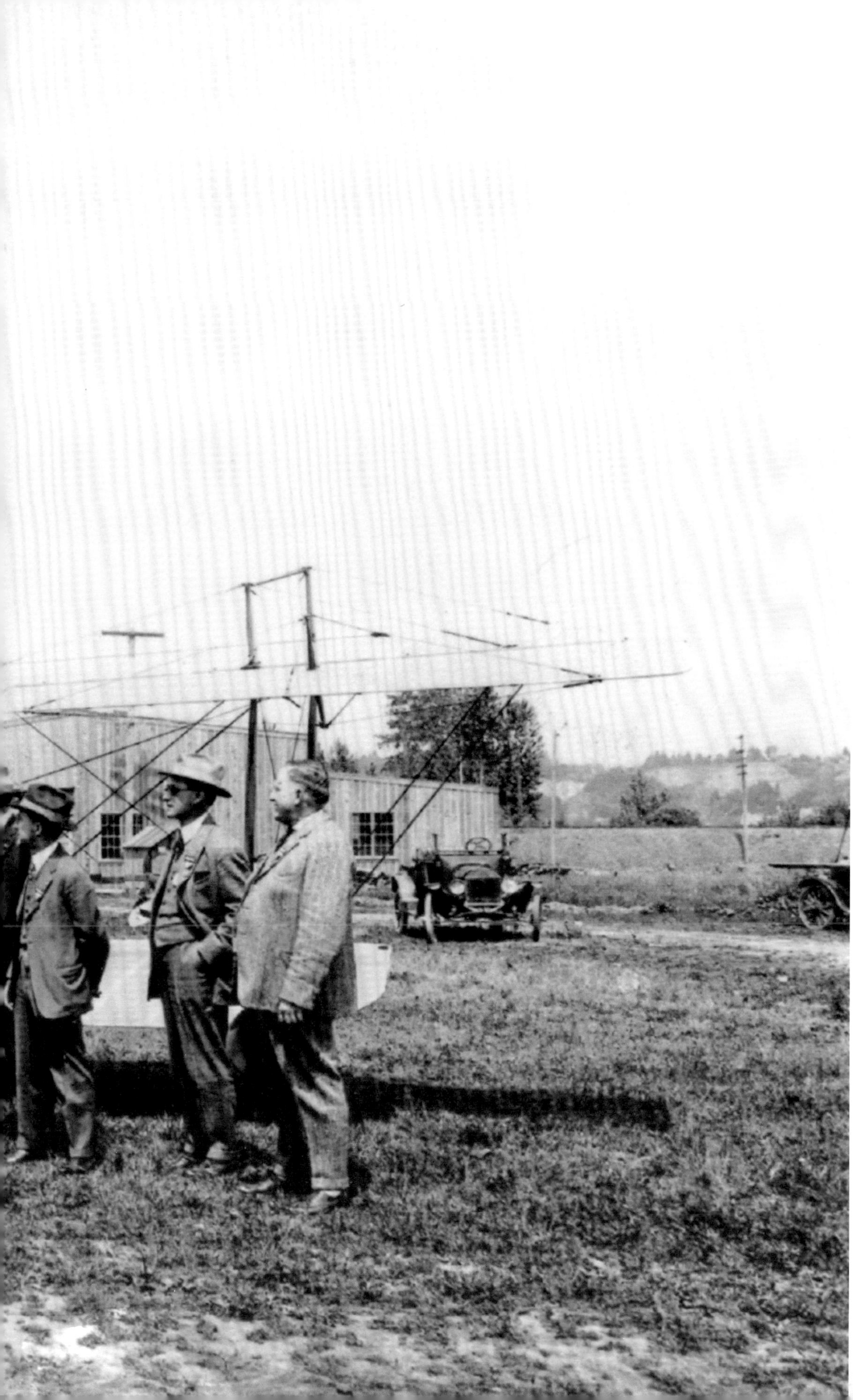

An early aircraft in Portland, around 1920. Commercial passenger air service began in Portland in 1926 with Pacific Air Transport. Portland's first large airport opened in 1927 on Swan Island and was dedicated by Charles Lindbergh.

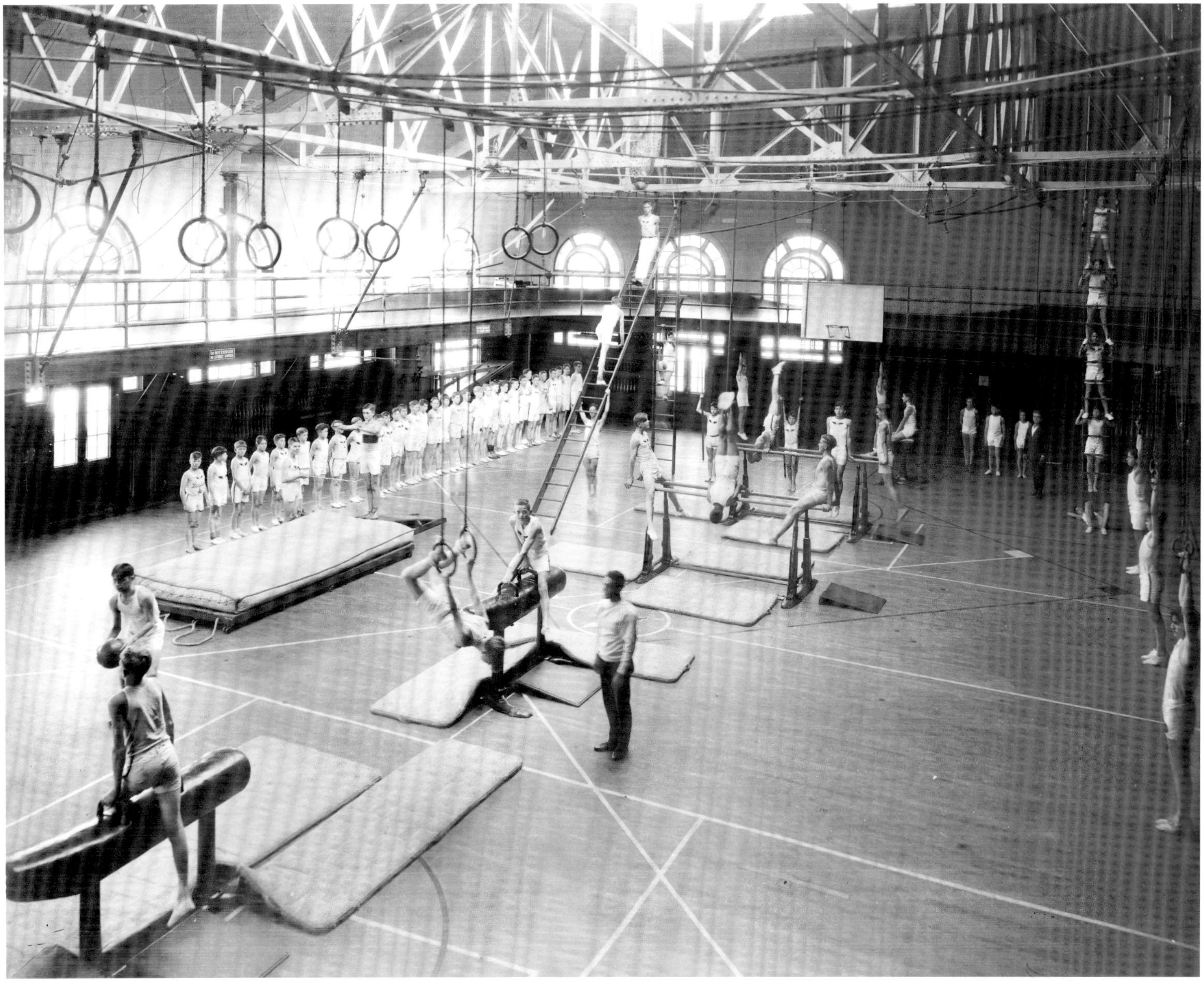

The Multnomah Athletic Club was founded in 1891 as the Multnomah Amateur Athletic Club. In 1893 the club purchased Multnomah Stadium and continued to grow. Today it is one of the largest indoor athletic clubs in the nation, with 20,000 members.

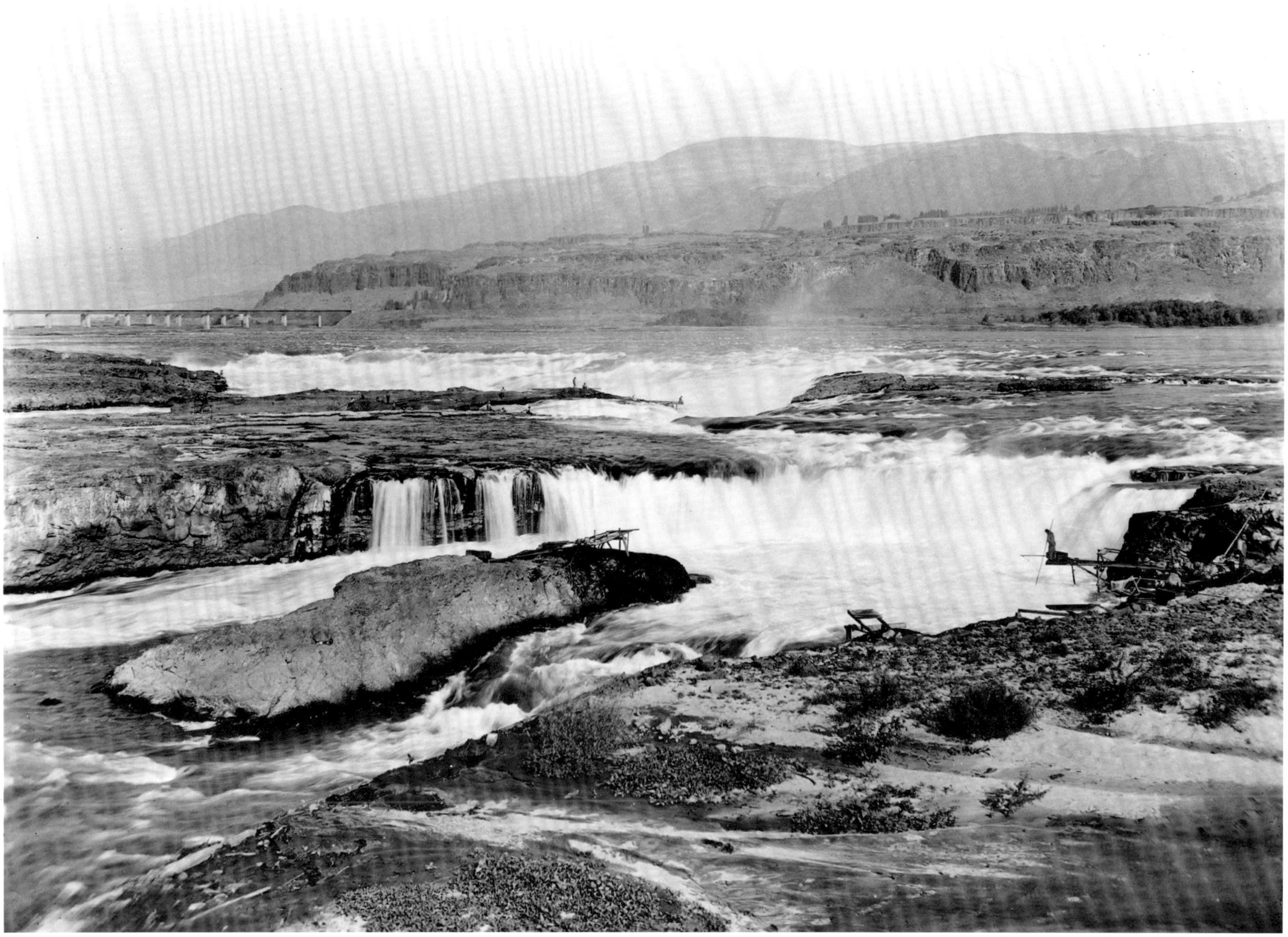

Celilo Falls on the Columbia River was a fishing and trading site for Native Americans for thousands of years. Demand for inexpensive hydroelectric power, a clear navigation route, and the need to prevent floods would prompt the construction of The Dalles Dam in 1957 by the U.S. Army Corps of Engineers. The dam erased Celilo Falls and with it the prime fishing that so many had prized for so long.

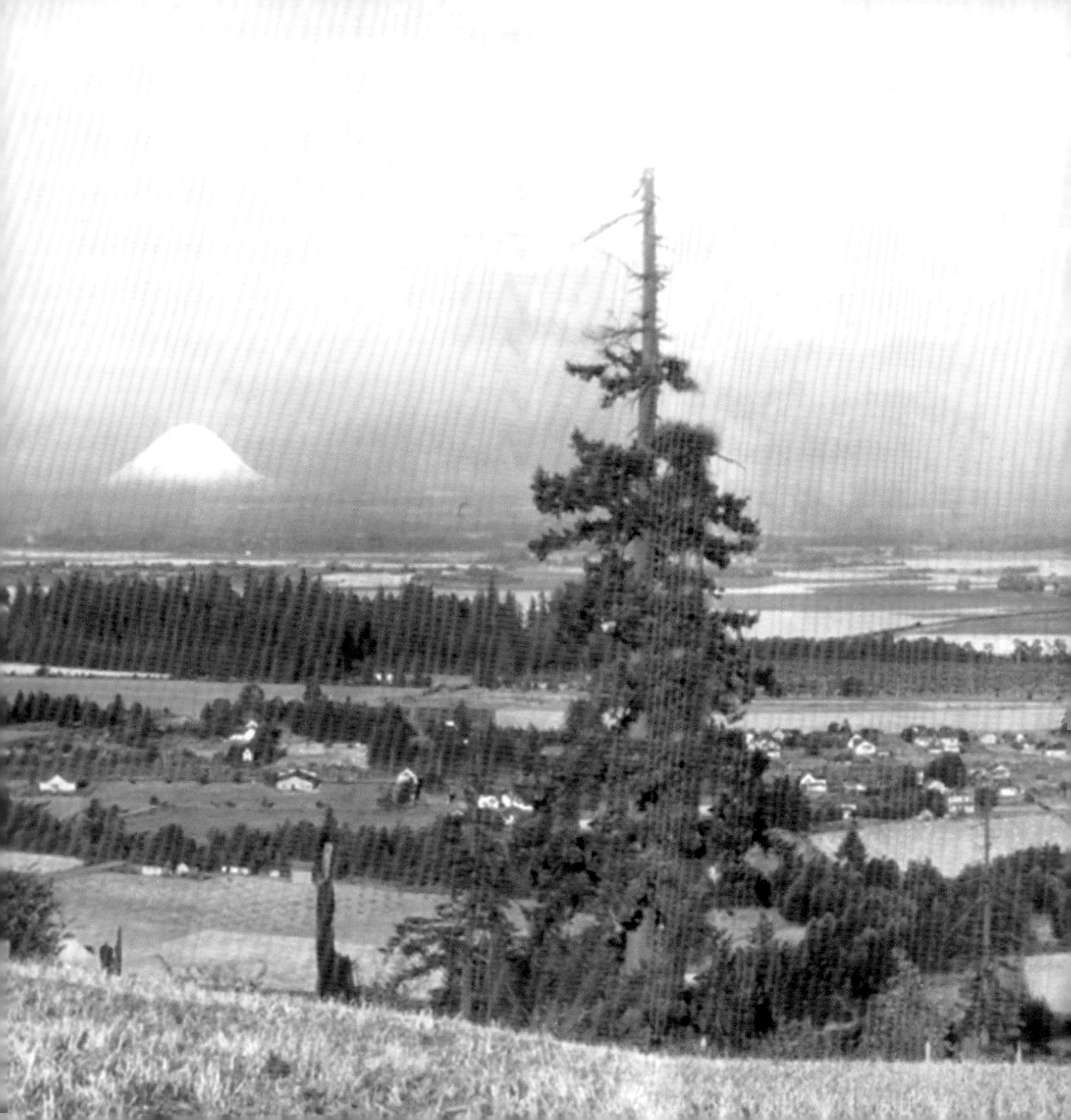

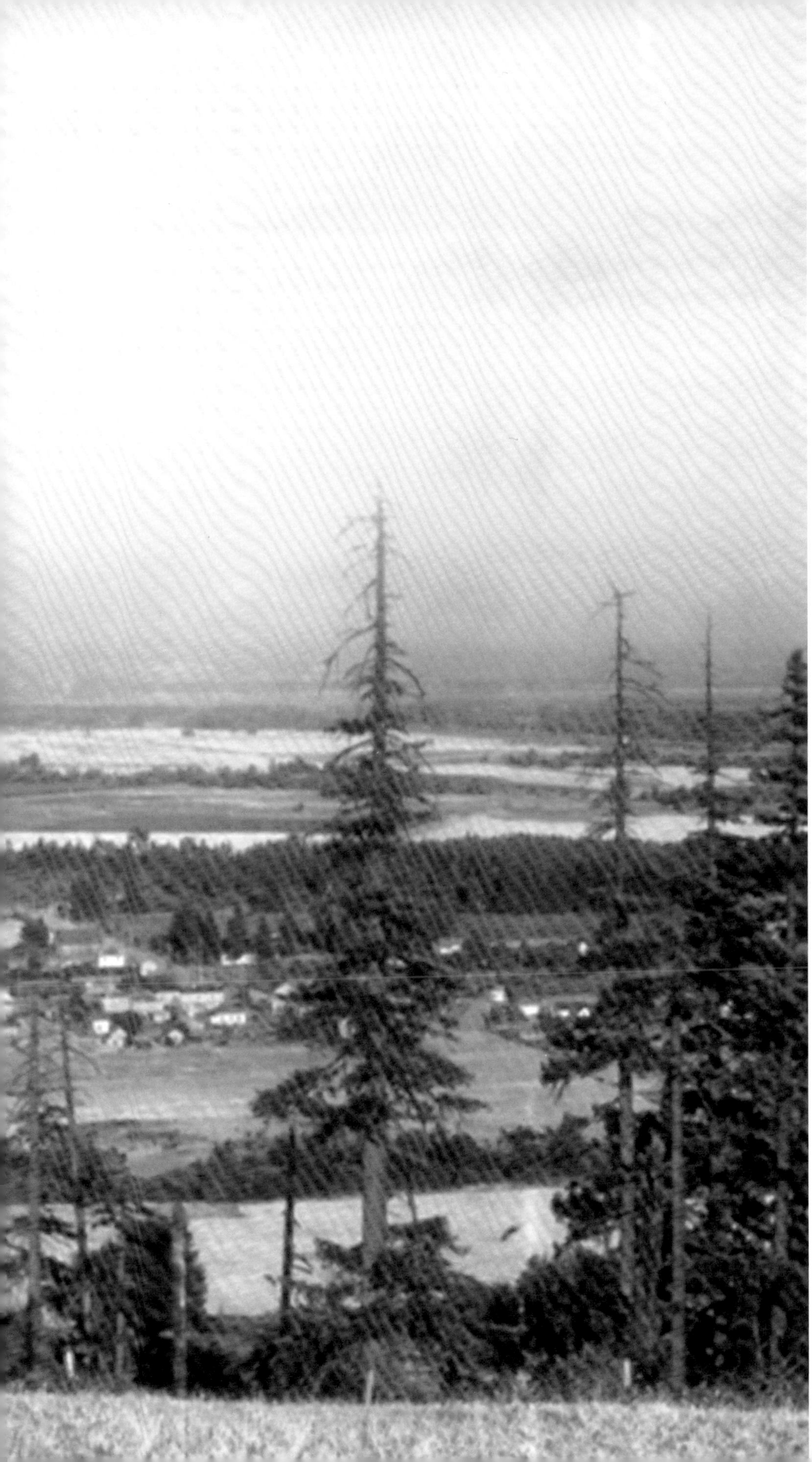

A panorama of Scappoose and its environs. Thomas McKay and his Chinook wife Tomee first came to the area in 1828, on assignment by the commander of nearby Fort Vancouver to find pasture for the fort's horses. In 1842 the first wagon train reached the area, and by 1853 the town had organized its first school. Railroad service from Portland began in 1883, and the townspeople were enjoying electricity by 1927. The Scappoose economy would get a boost when the Columbia River Highway opened in the 1920s.

Edward S. Curtis photographed this Klamath man in the Klamath Basin around 1923. Curtis spent his life documenting the American West and its indigenous peoples. He would live into the modern era, dying in 1952 at the age of 84.

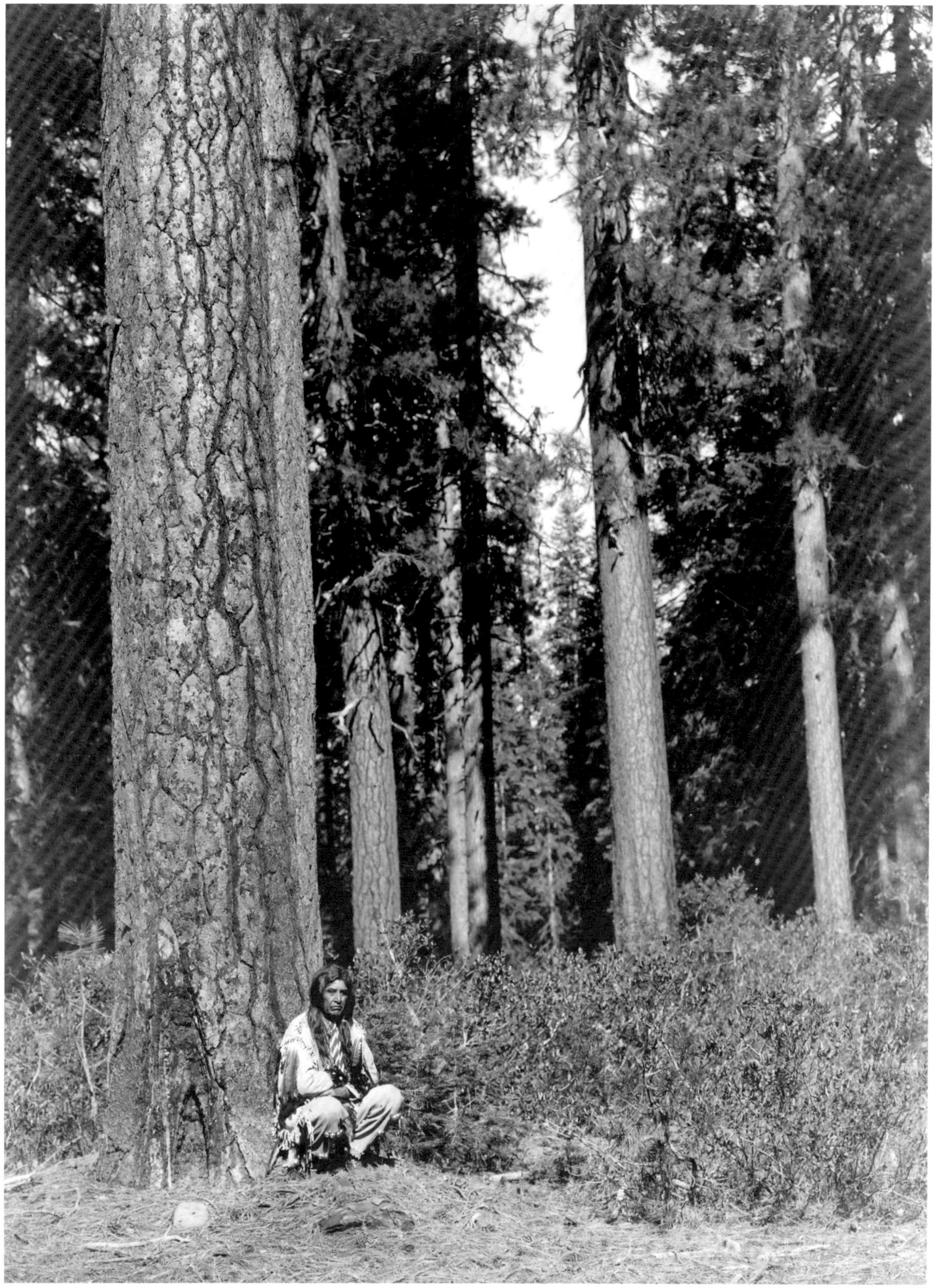

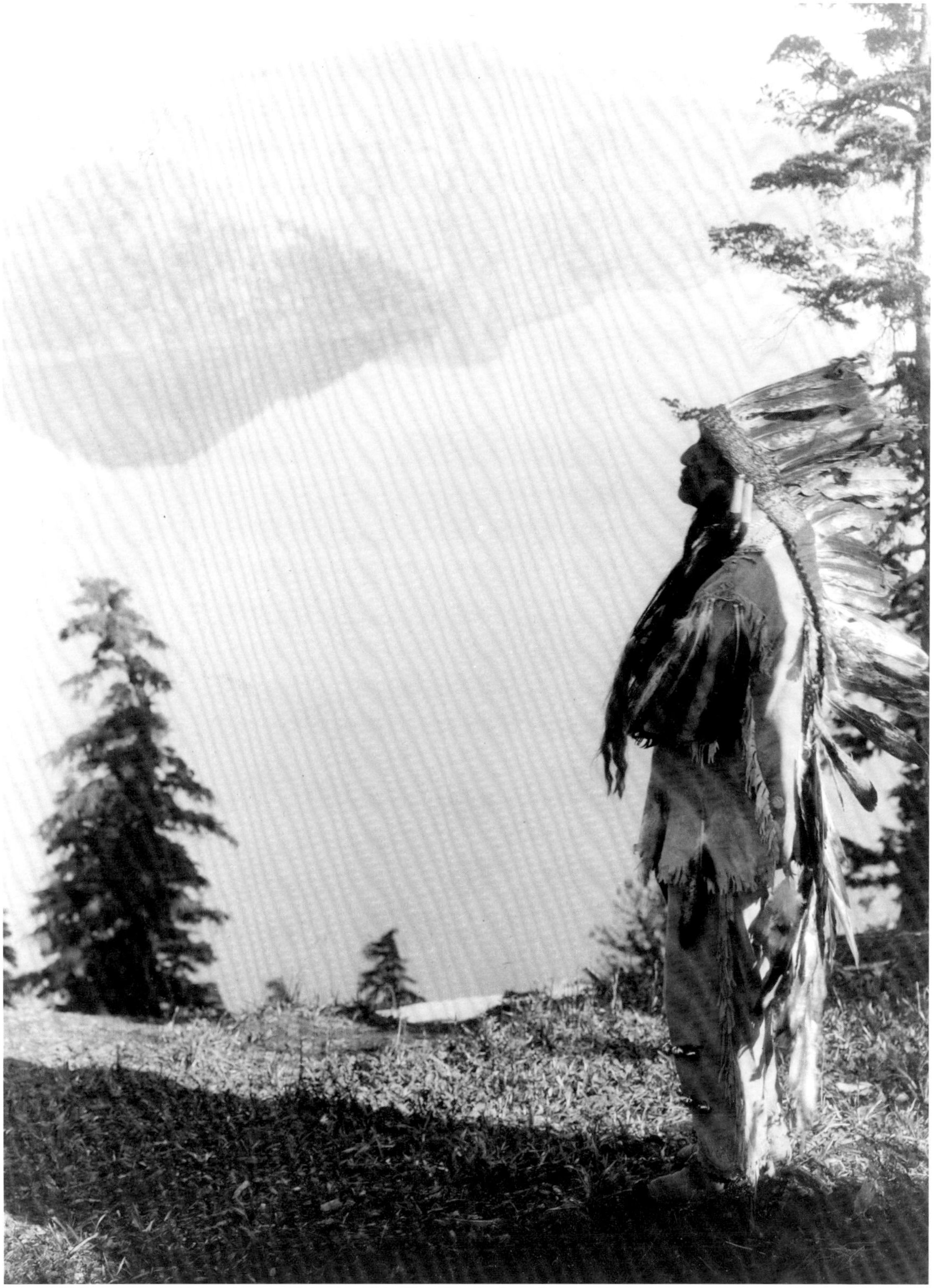

Curtis photographed this Klamath Indian at Crater Lake around 1923.

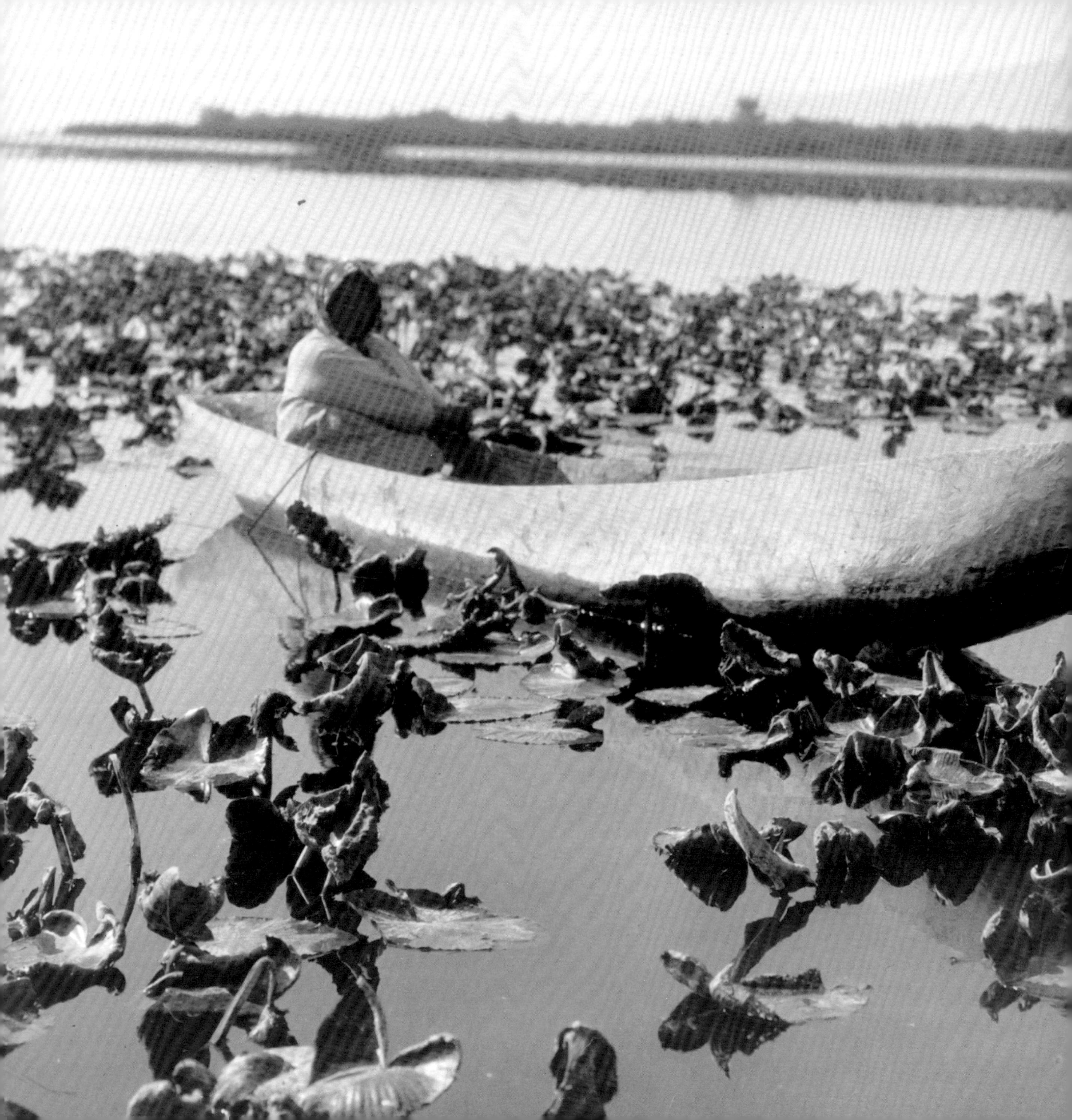

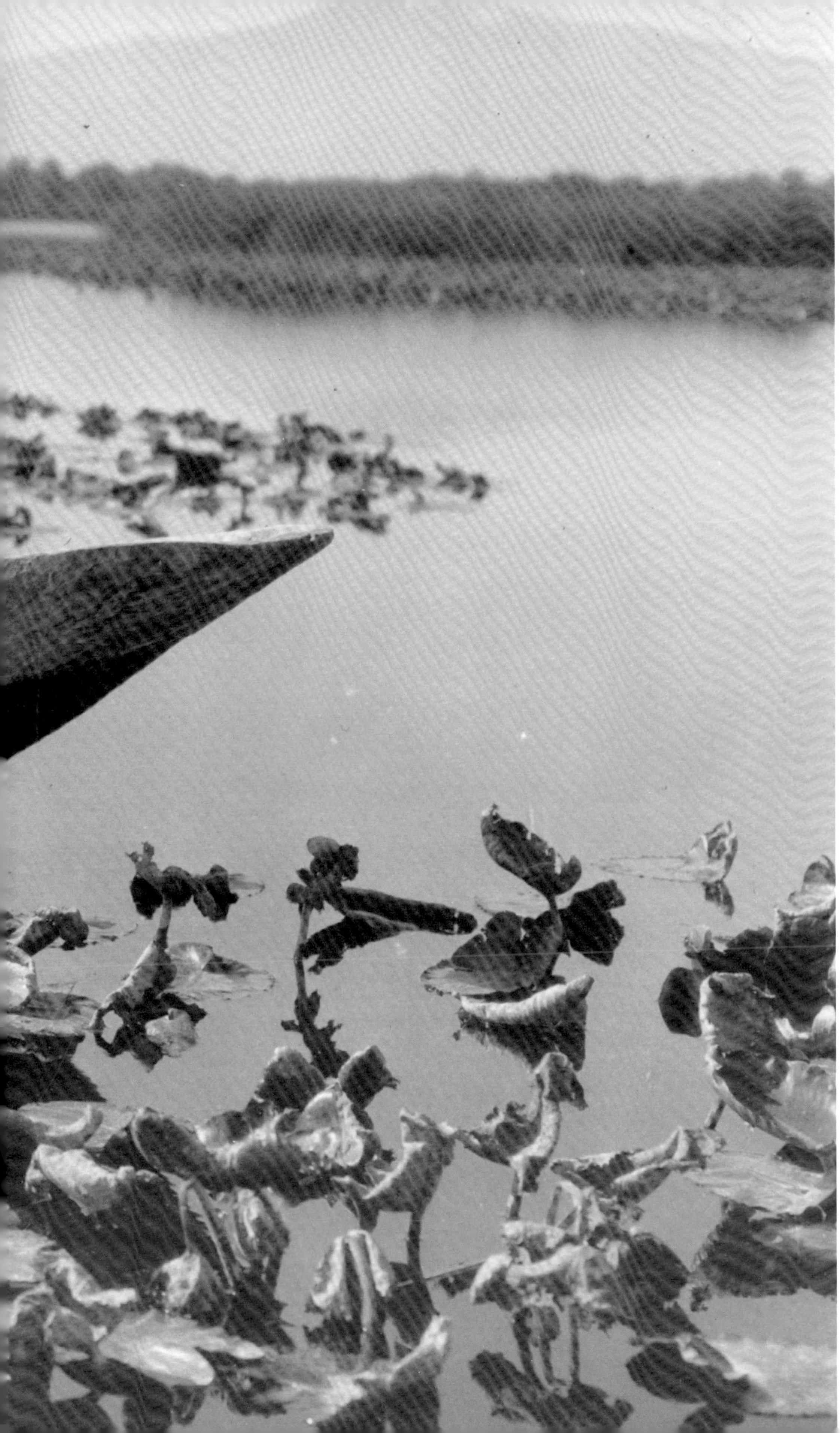

Edward Curtis recorded this image of a Klamath woman in a dugout canoe in the Klamath Basin around 1923. The canoe is at rest in a field of wokas, known also as yellow water lilies, which yielded seeds the Klamath people gathered, roasted, and ate.

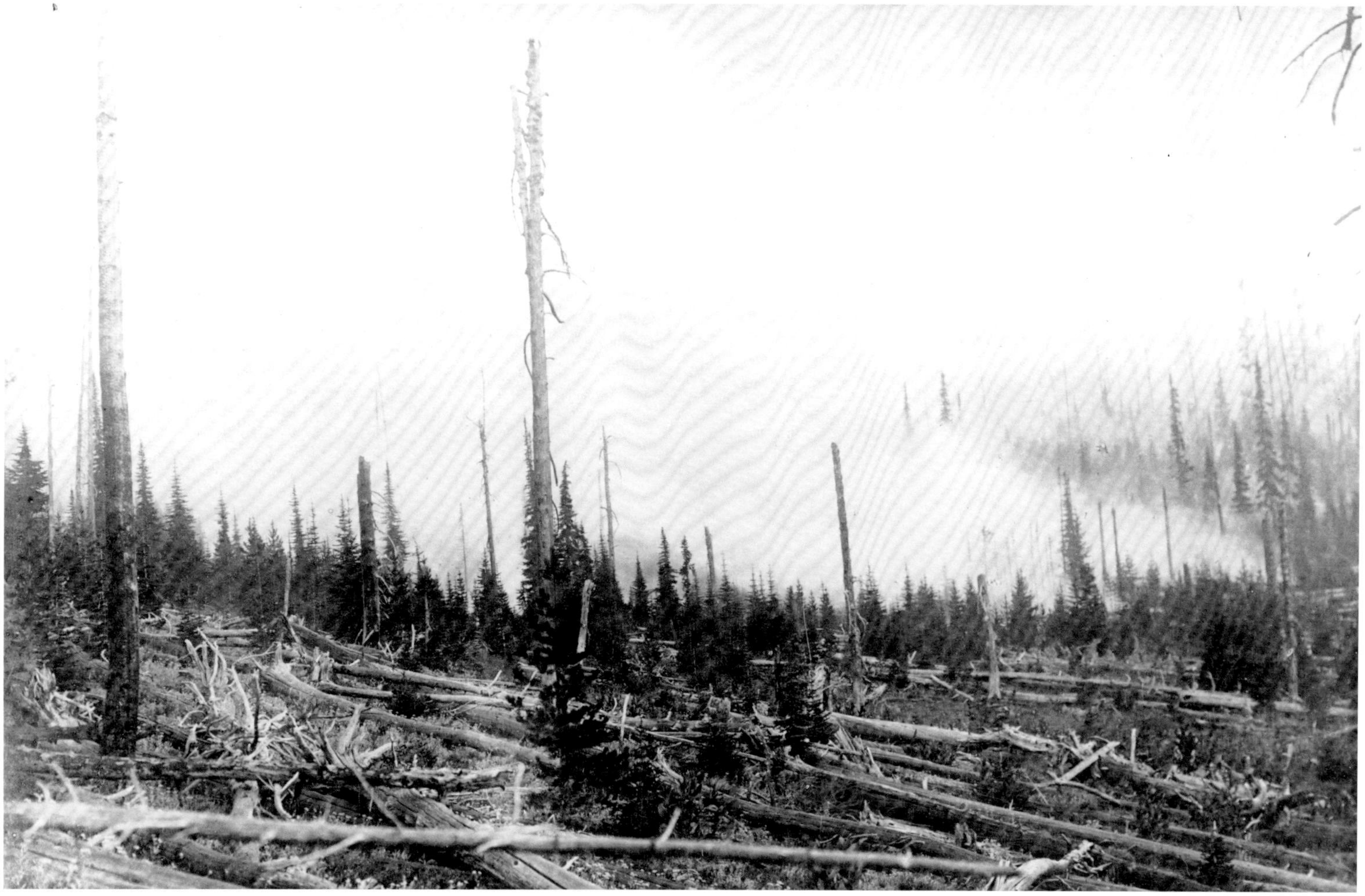

Wallowa County was created in 1887 and includes the land at the northeastern tip of the state. The region's economy was based on a combination of lumber, gold mining, and agriculture. The county is known as the homeland of the Wallowa band of the Nez Perce and Chief Joseph is buried at the foot of Wallowa Lake. By 1920, the population of the county had risen to 9,778. This image depicts a fire in progress in the Wallowa National Forest.

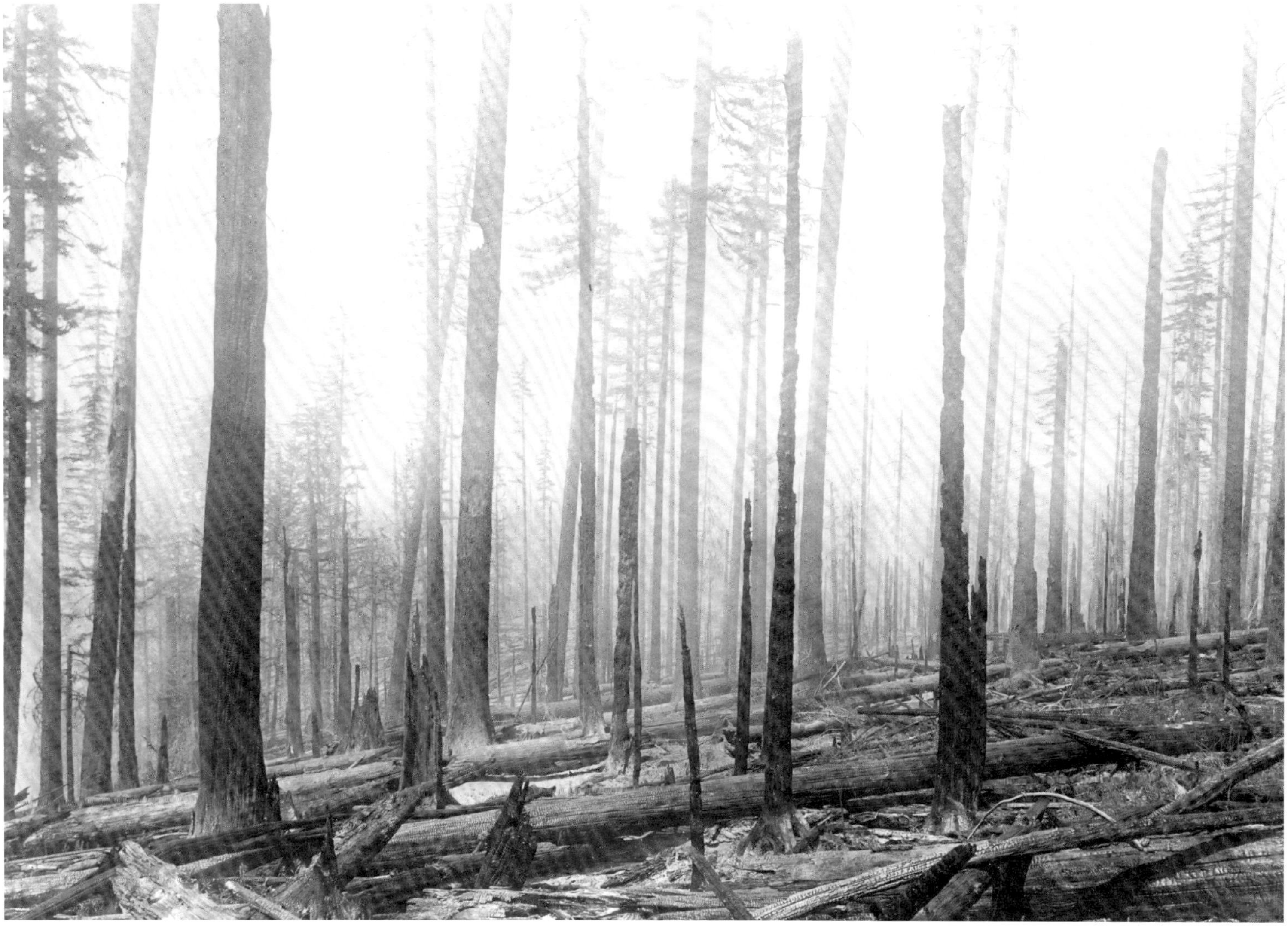

Forest fires in Oregon were once very common. Native Americans used fire to encourage the growth of plants for foraging animals, among many other purposes. Settlers saw the forests as wealth and were bothered by the massive fires they witnessed. After a series of large forest fires culminating in the Tillamook Burn in 1933, a painstaking effort was made to prevent forest fires in the state.

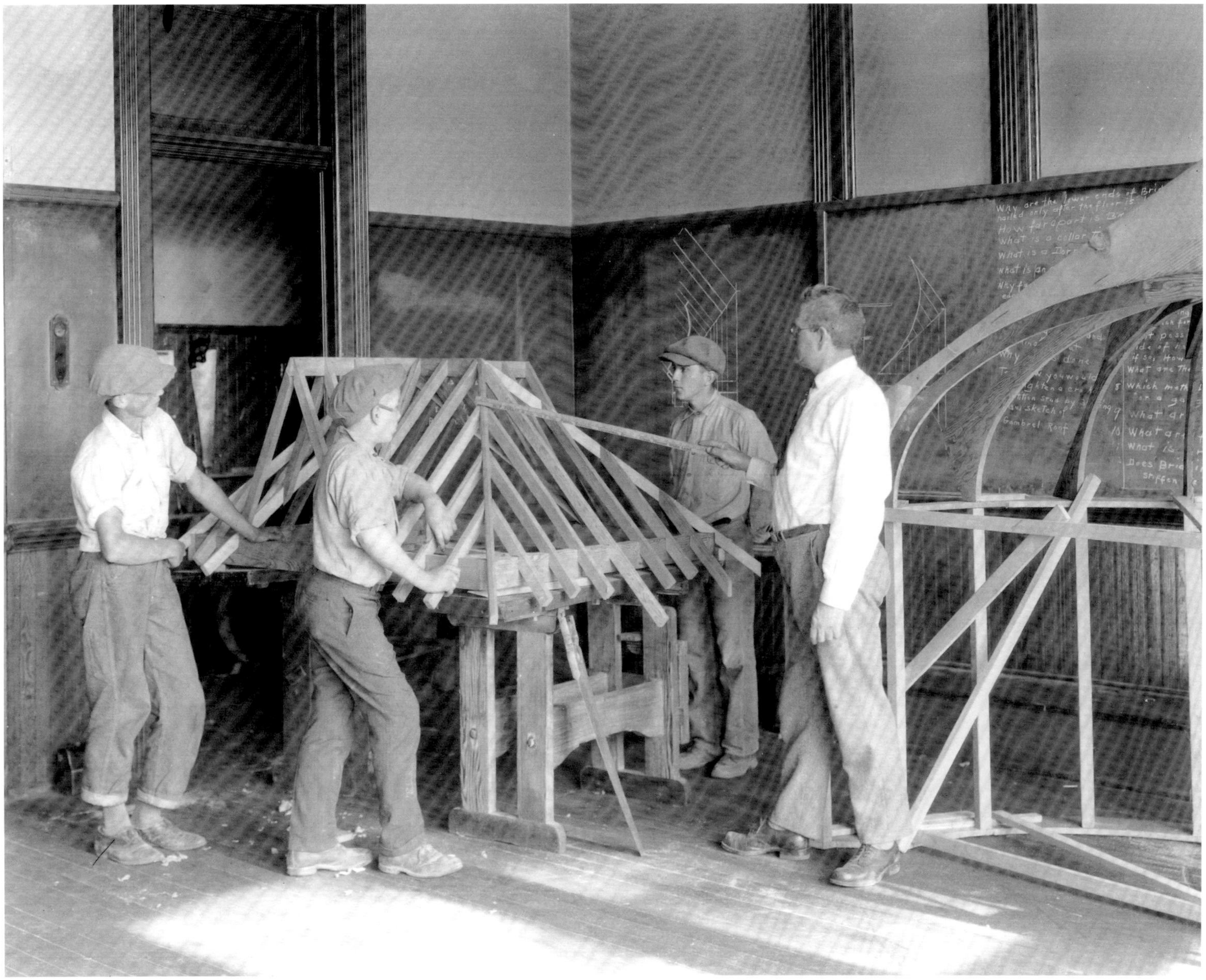

Scene at a State Board of Vocation Education classroom. Students study construction methods in this Salem classroom in 1925.

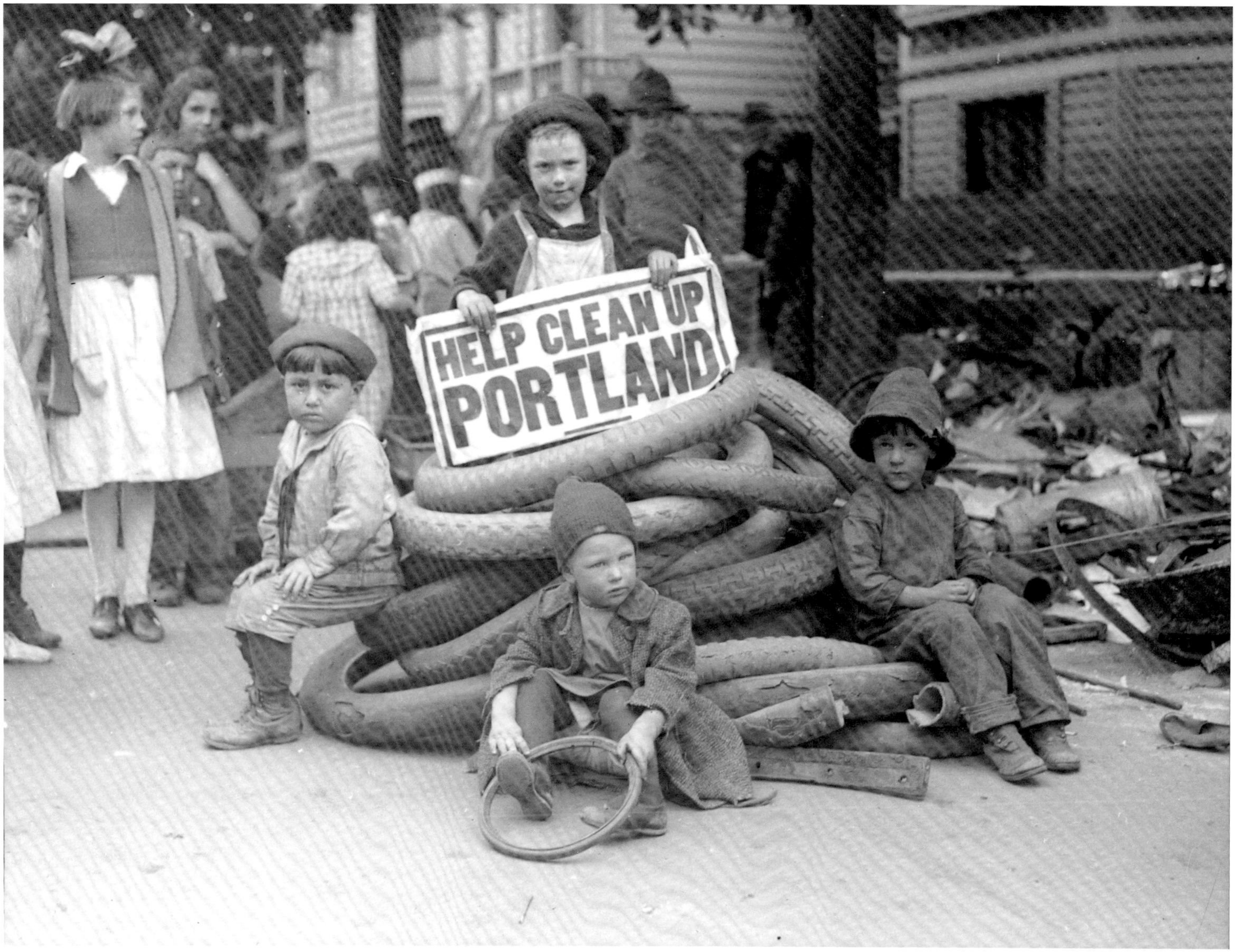

Portland children participate in a cleanup drive on March 11, 1929.

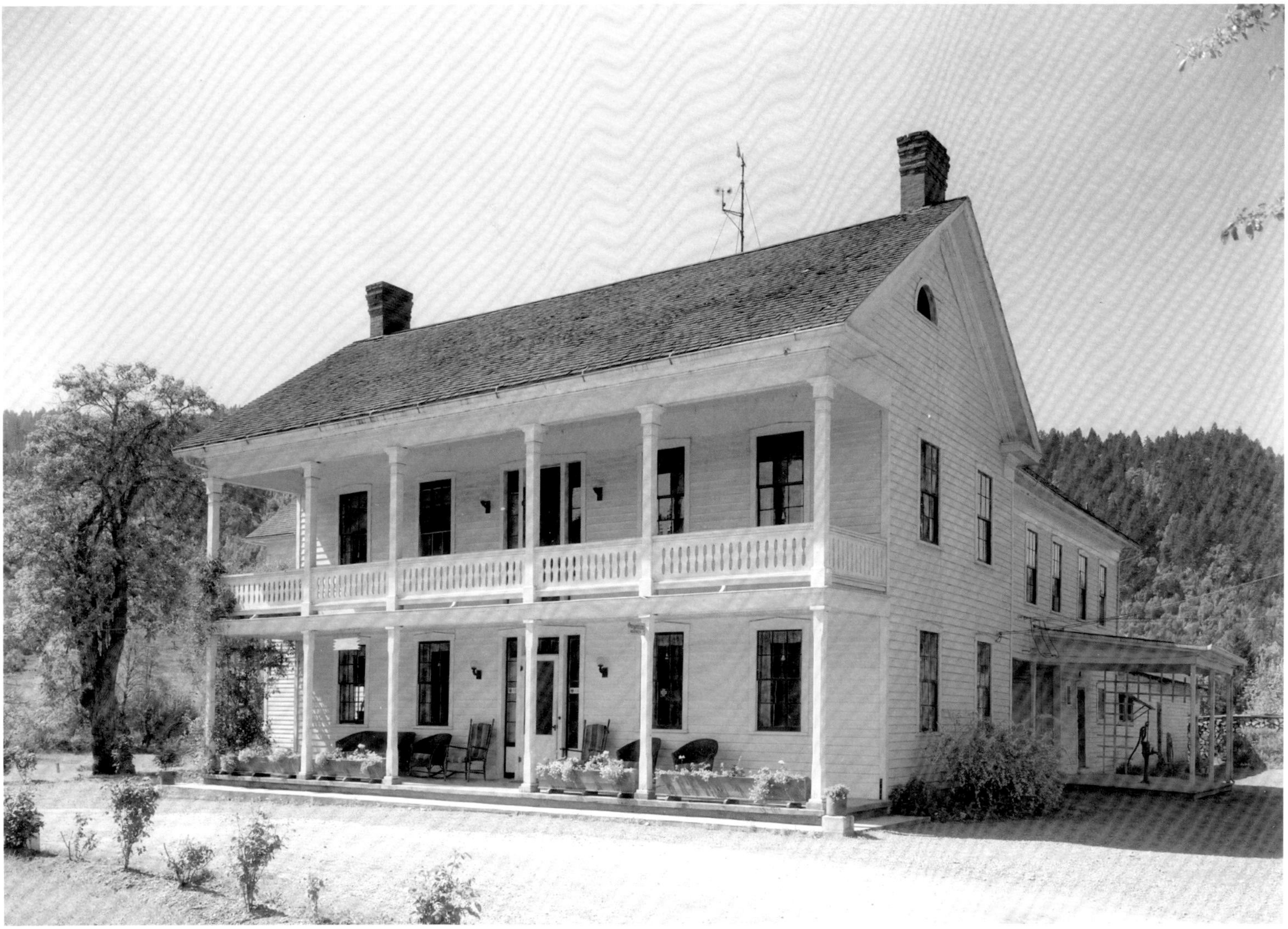

The Wolf Creek Tavern was built near Medford on the California-Oregon Trail, opening around 1883. It became a popular rest stop on the Pacific Highway for many years, visited by celebrities from far and wide, including writer Jack London and Hollywood actor Clark Gable.

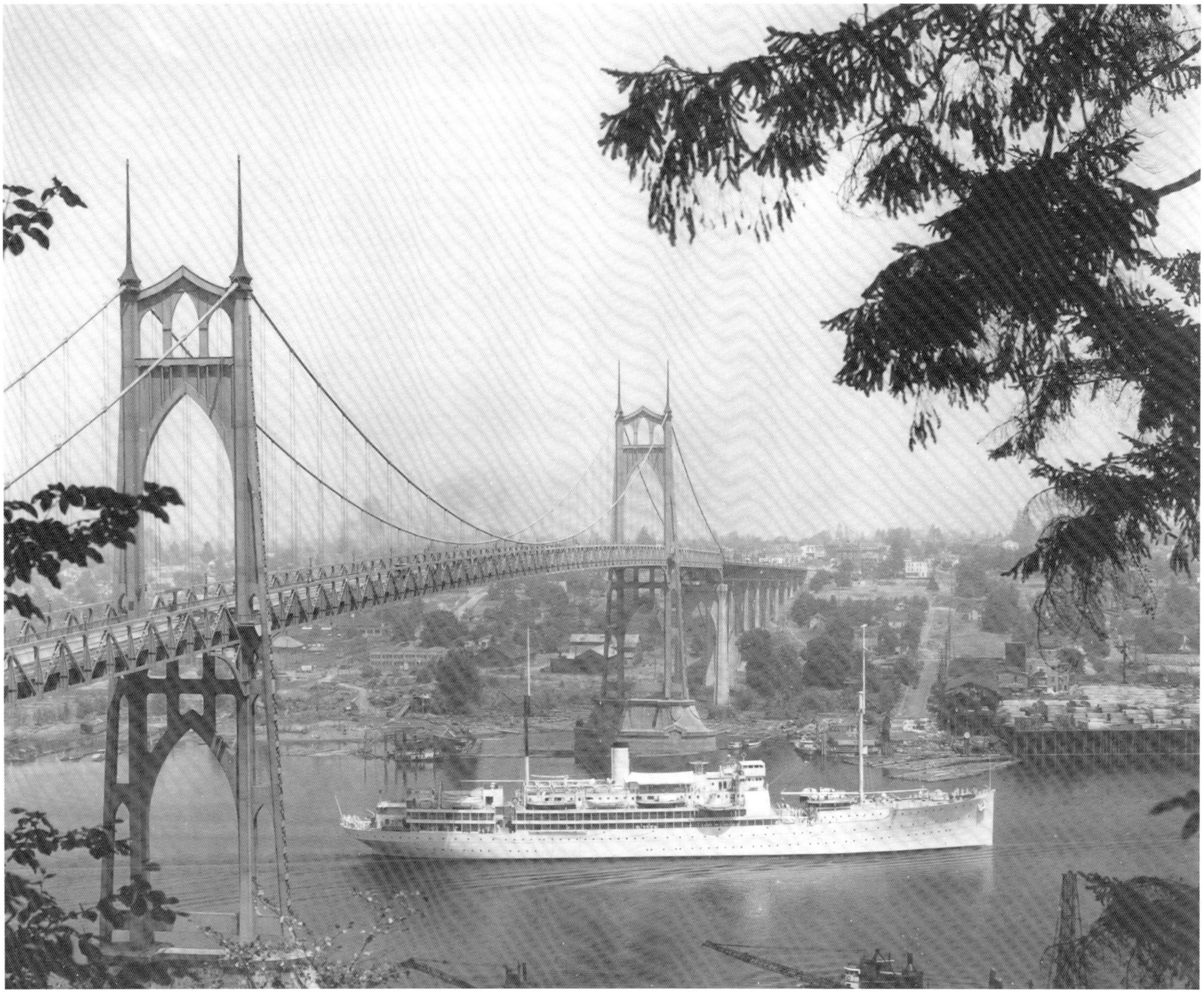

The USS *Relief* sails under the St. John's Bridge on the Willamette River in Portland. The graceful structure with its 400-foot-tall Gothic towers was completed in the Great Depression year 1931 a million dollars under budget.

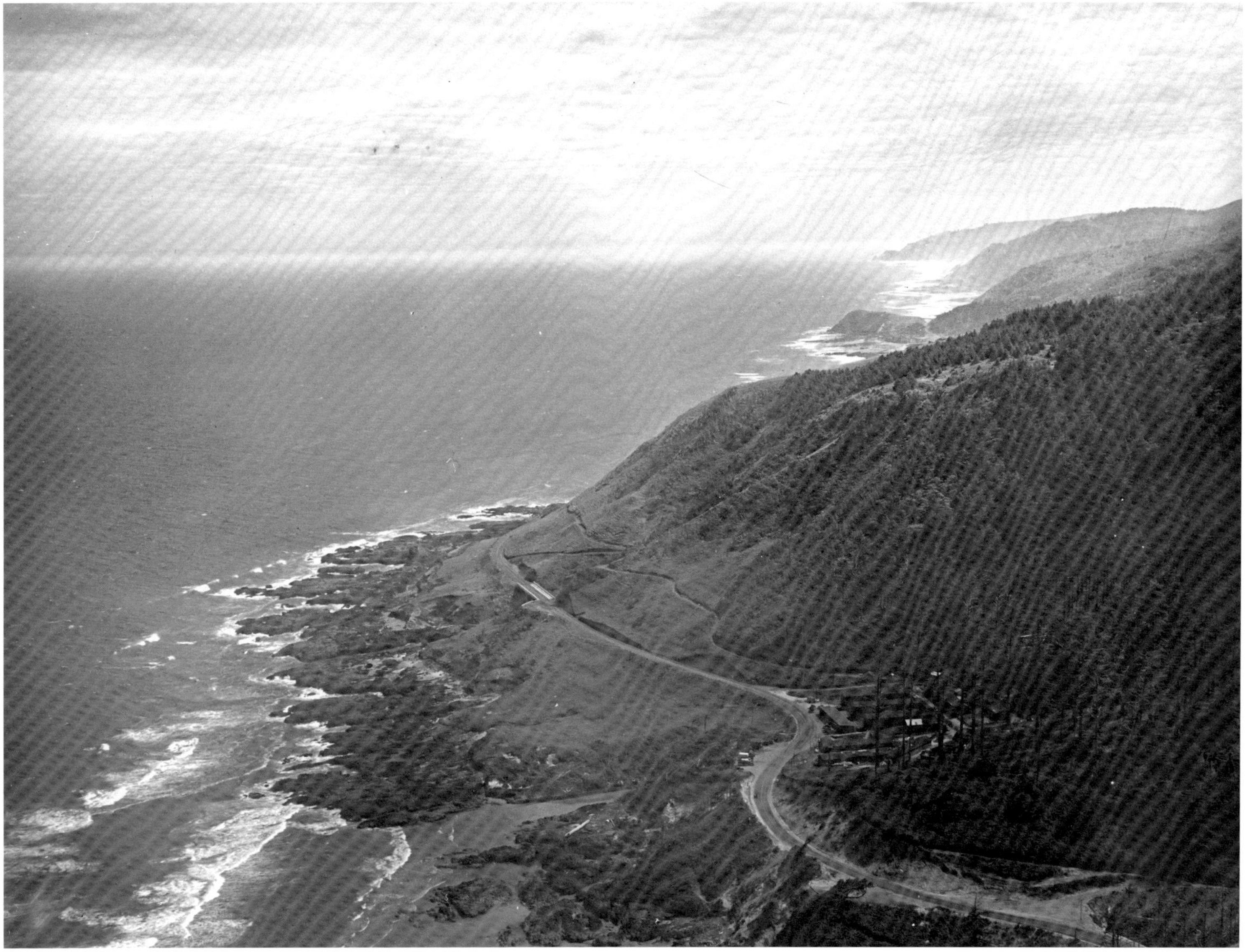

The building of the Oregon Coast Highway began in the 1920s and was completed in 1932. For the first time, visitors to the Oregon coast had a direct route by automobile. It remains a scenic route enjoyed by motorists and the most direct link between some communities in the region.

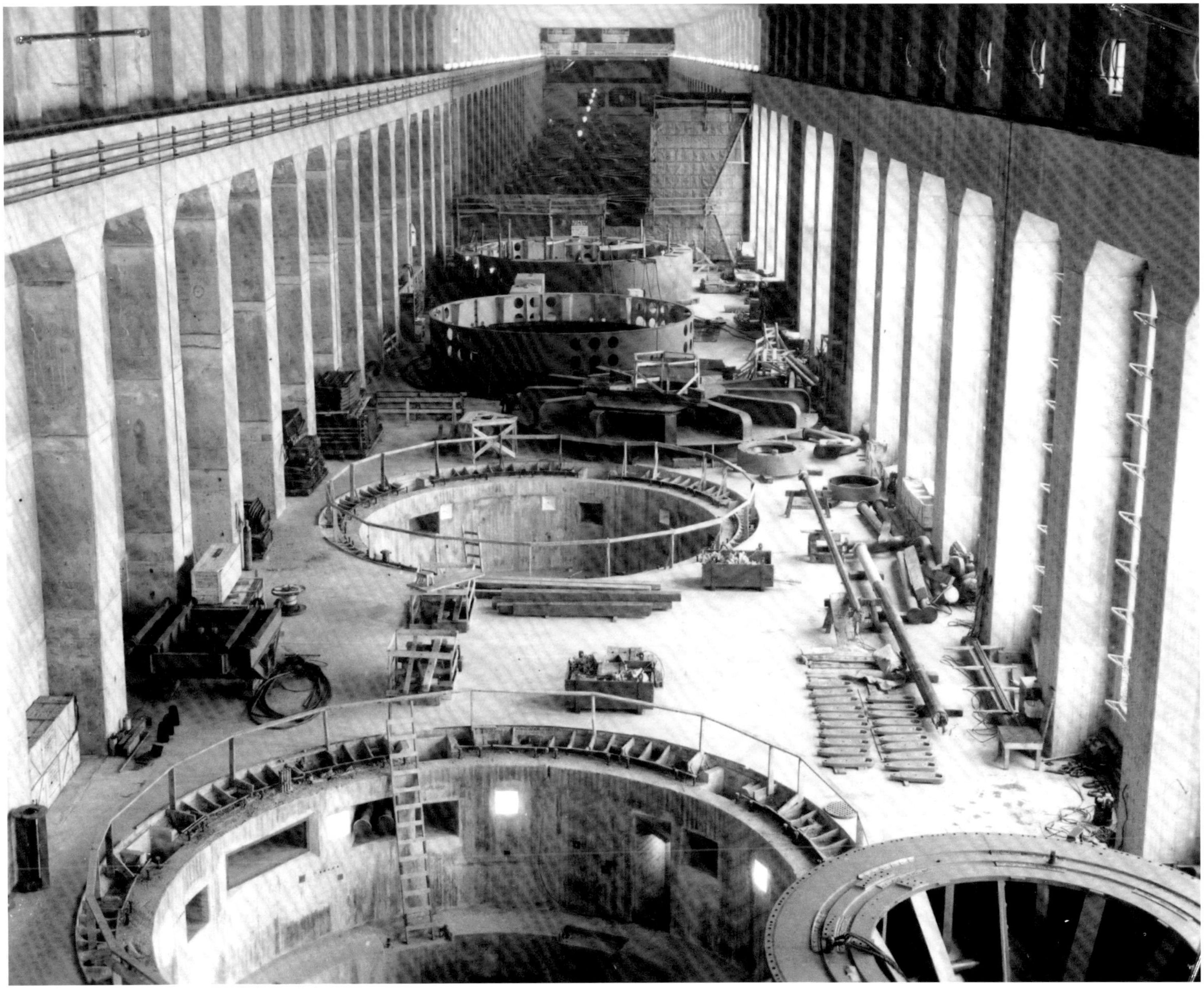

Interior of the powerhouse at Bonneville Dam on the Columbia River. A second powerhouse would open decades later in 1981, increasing the dam's electrical output and lowering electric bills.

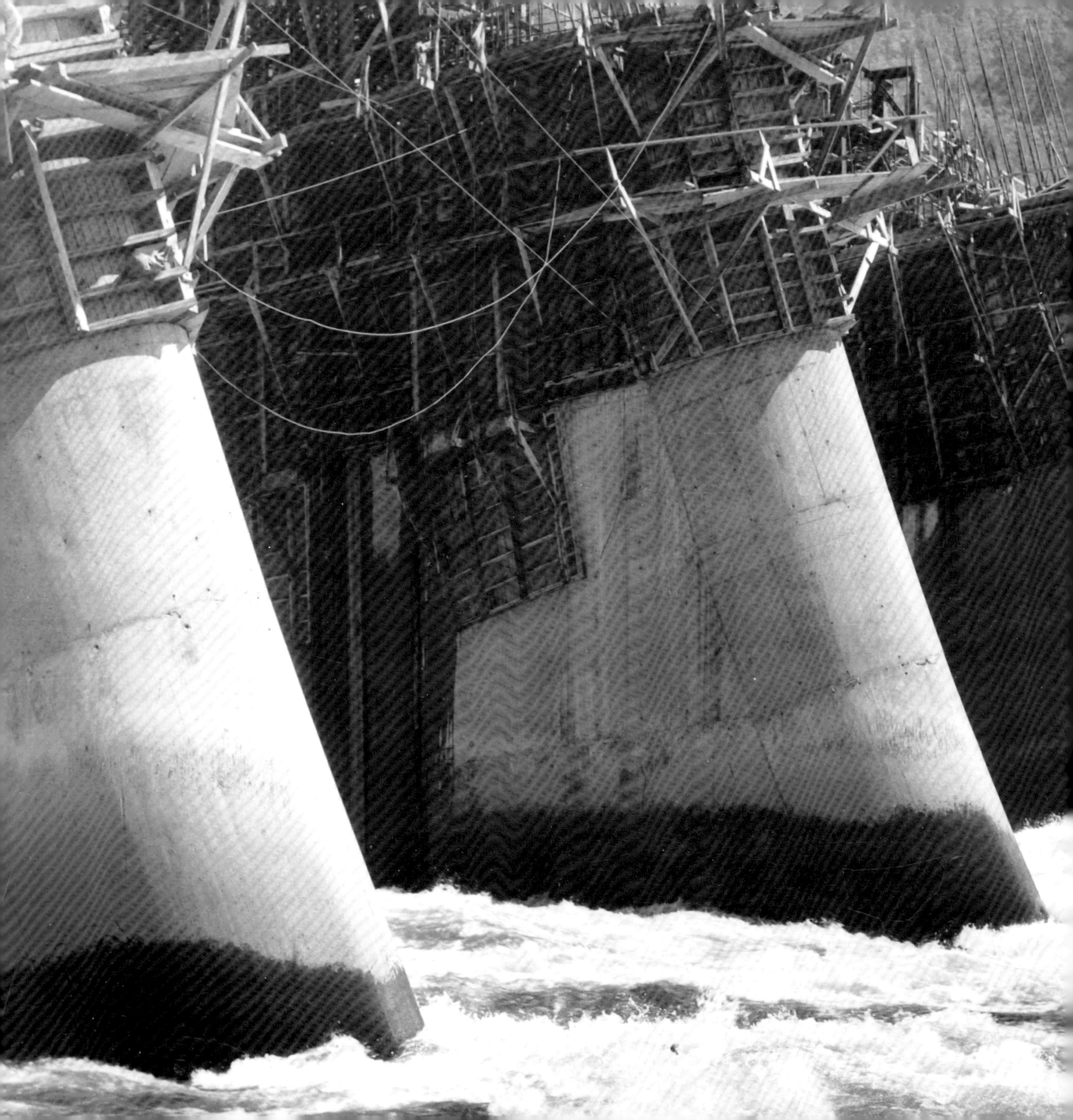

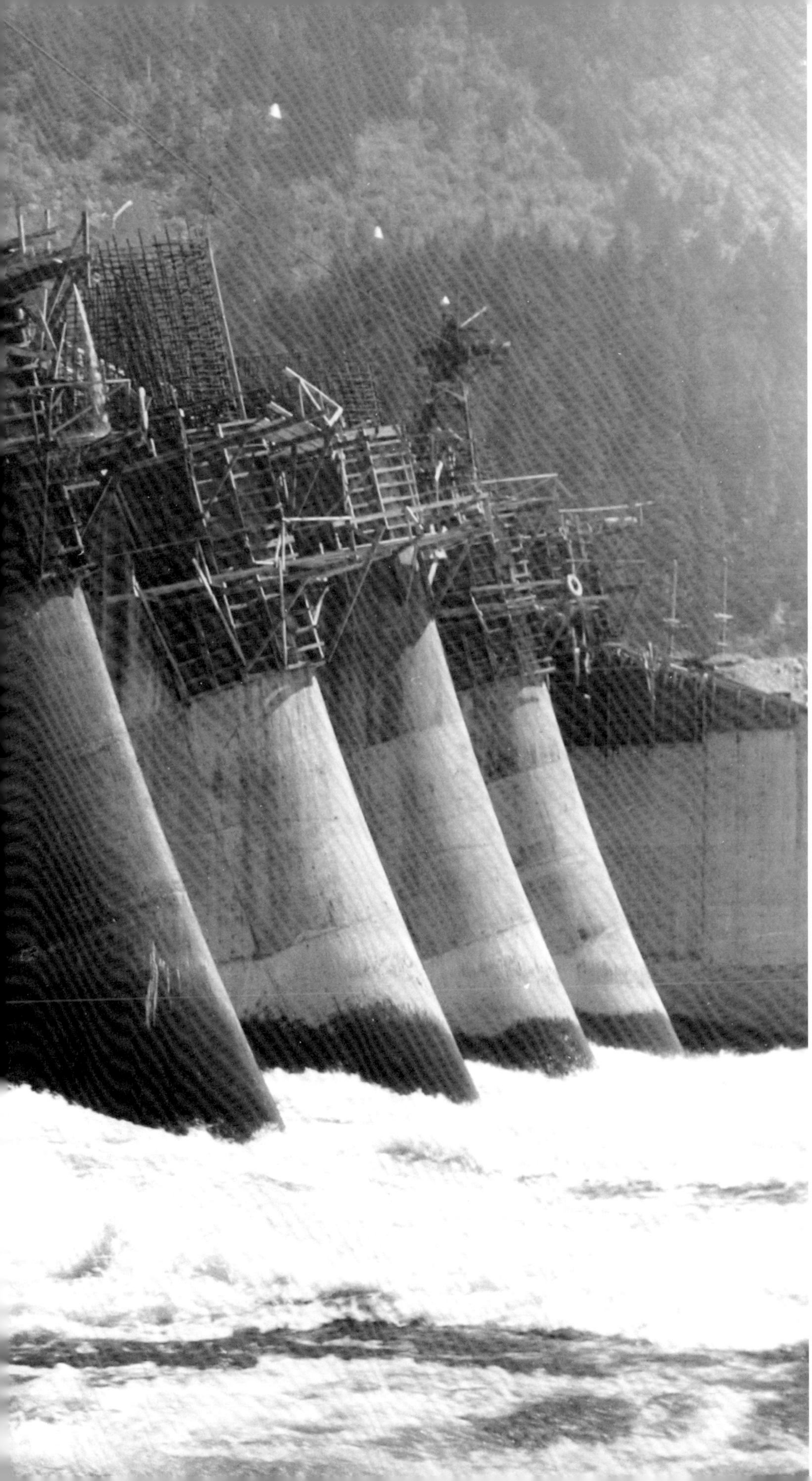

Exterior view of construction of the Bonneville Dam on the Columbia River. The dam was a response to the need to generate inexpensive hydroelectric power and improve river navigation. The dam is operated today by government agency as the Bonneville Power Administration or BPA. It was built with fish ladders, which permitted migrating salmon and steelhead trout to pass through.

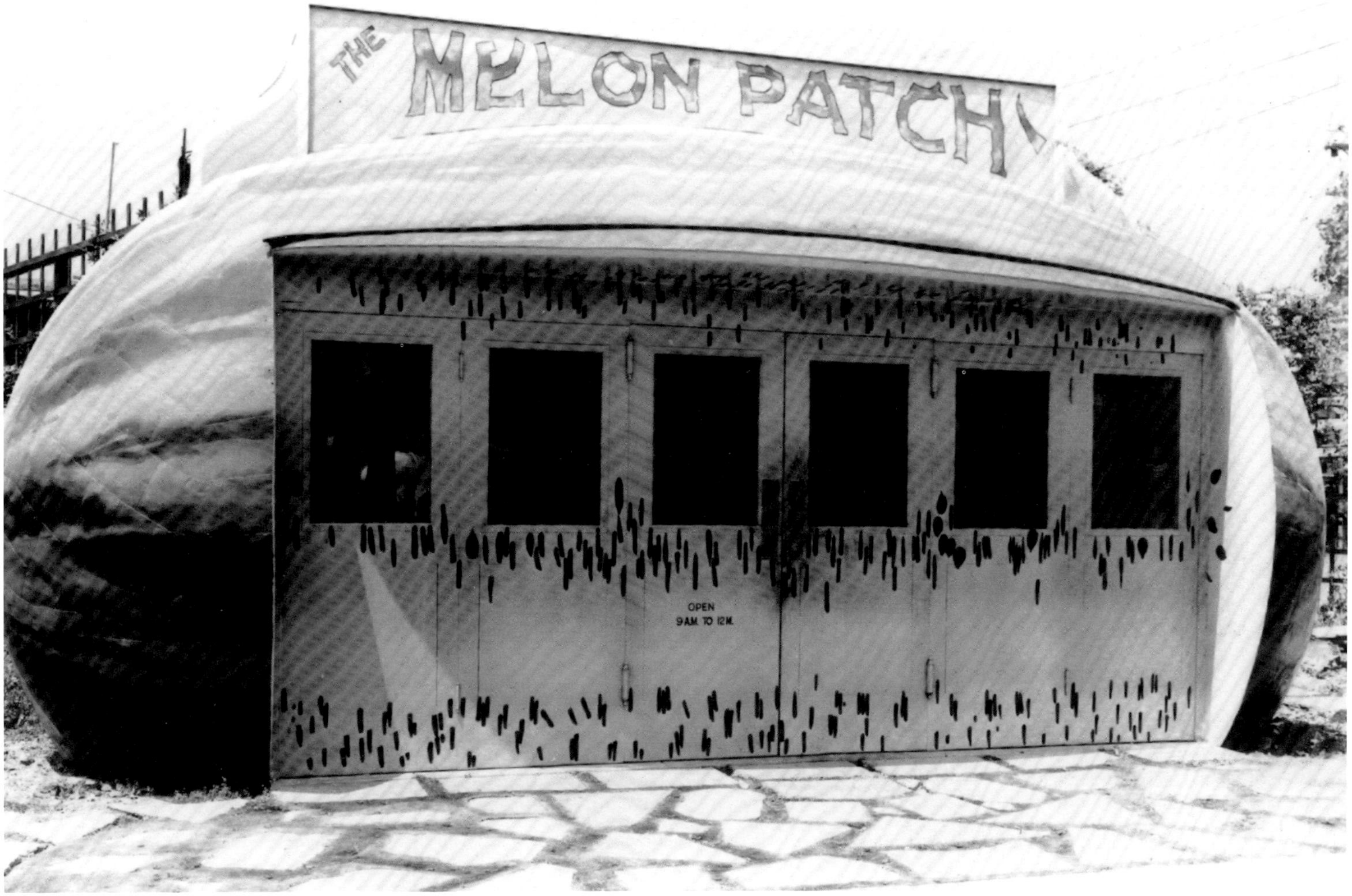

Open-air markets permitted farmers to sell their produce directly to customers, and most communities had one. Photographed in 1934, this creative facade ushered customers into a market rented to farmers by a local community group.

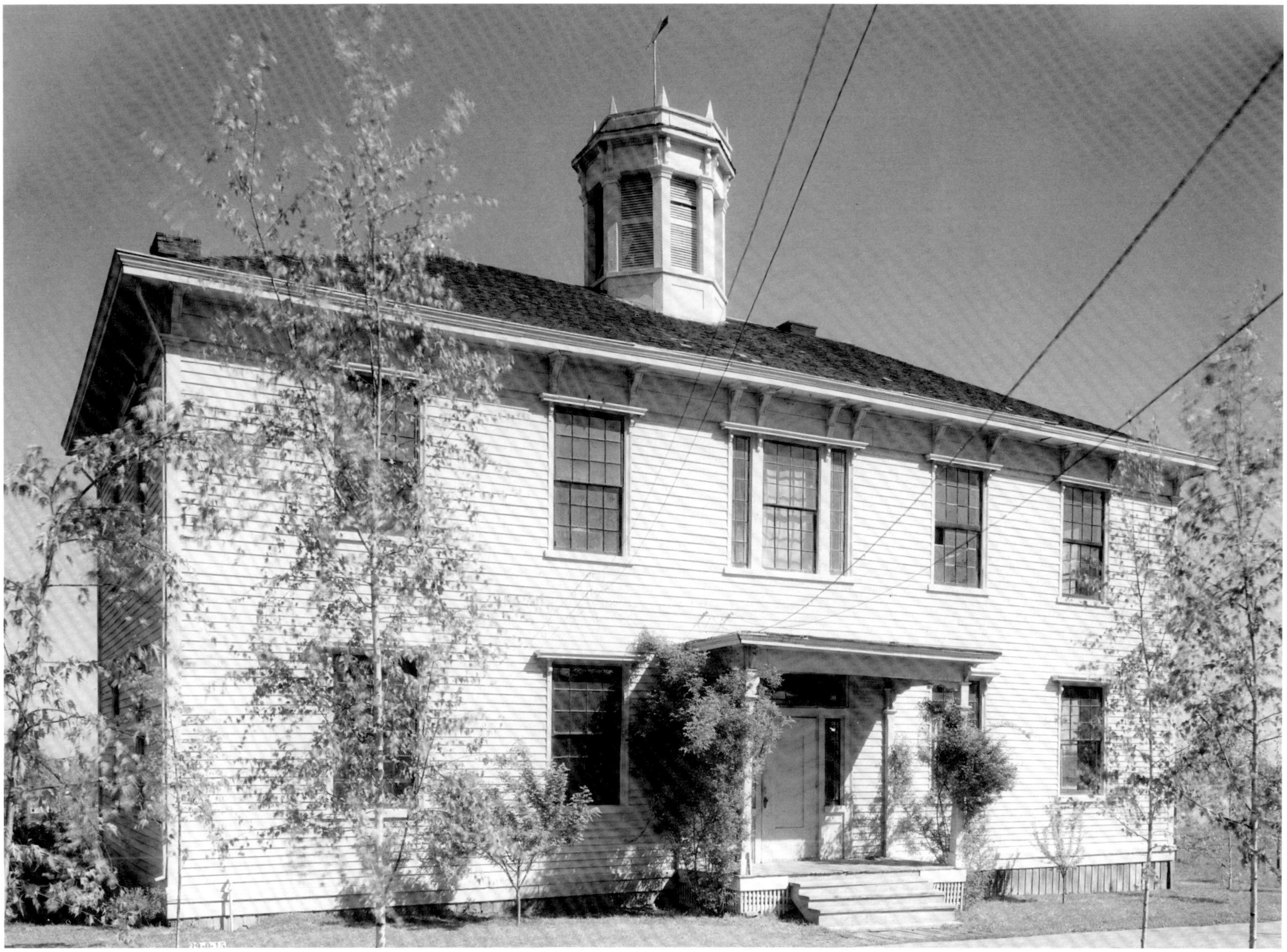

Old College Hall on the campus of Pacific University appears rather youthful in 1933. Located in Forest Grove, Pacific University was founded in 1849 by leaders of the Congregational Church. The college is currently known for its academic programs in the fields of health care and the liberal arts.

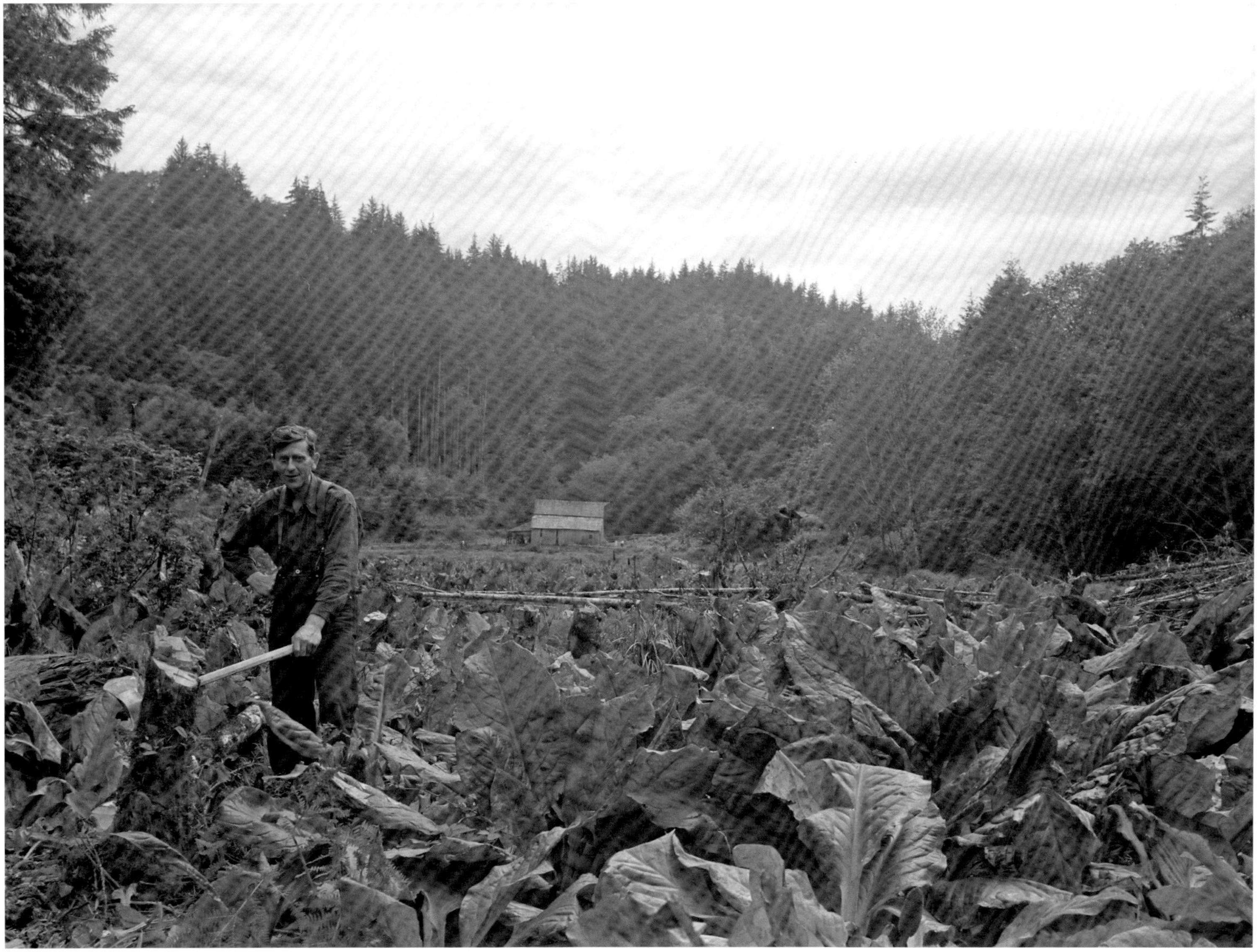

Clearing an abandoned homestead is hard work for this farmer around 1936. He may have been wondering whether saplings or the large-leaved skunk cabbage, a noxious plant with flowers that release enough heat to melt snow, posed the greater challenge for his ax.

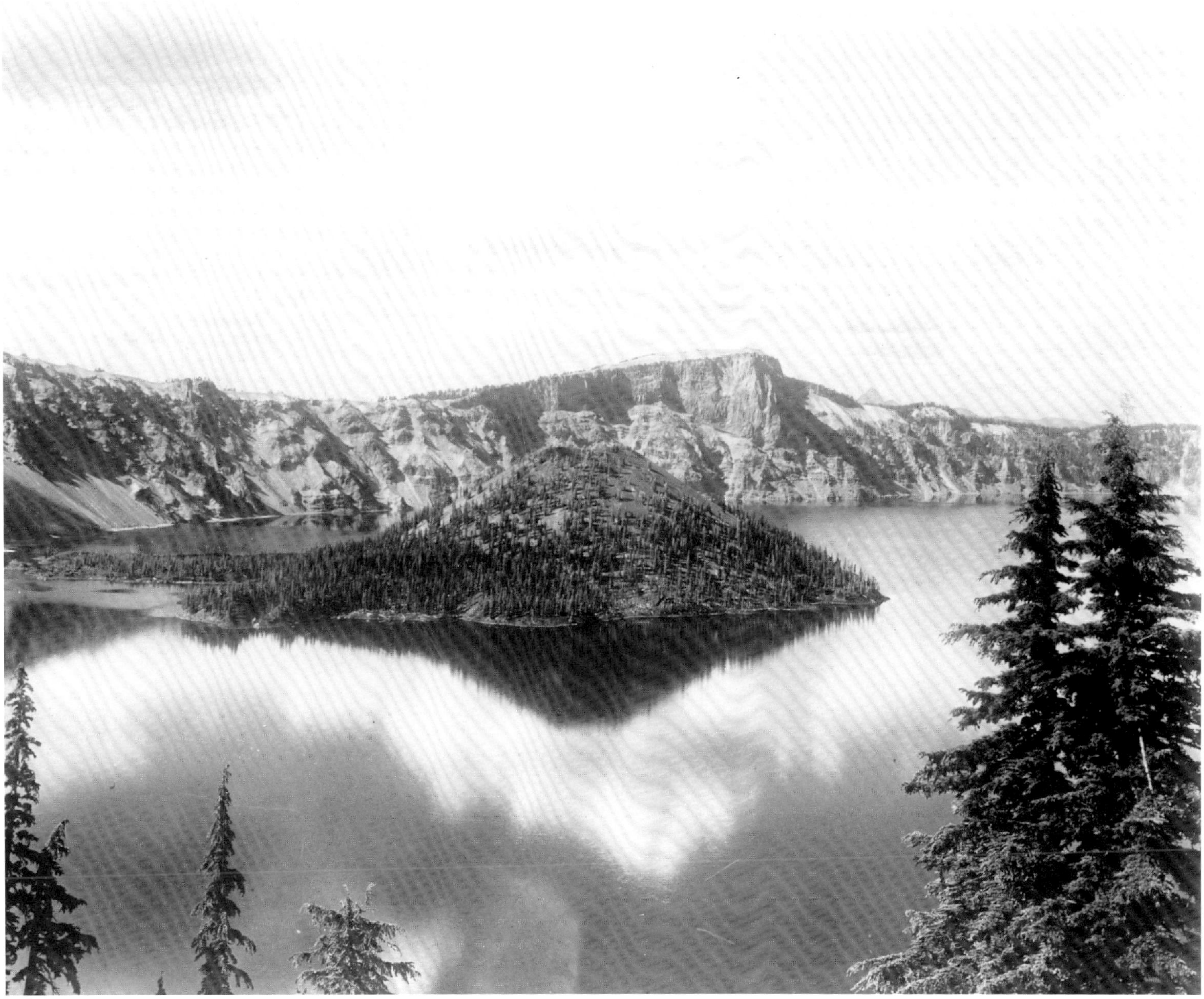

A view of Crater Lake National Park in southern Oregon as it looked in 1936.

The Columbia River takes its name from the ship *Columbia Rediviva.* Captained by American Robert Gray, the ship made the voyage of discovery, sailing 25 miles up the river in 1792. Sunbeams break through cloud cover in this spectacular view of a 1936 sunset by well-known photographer Arthur Rothstein.

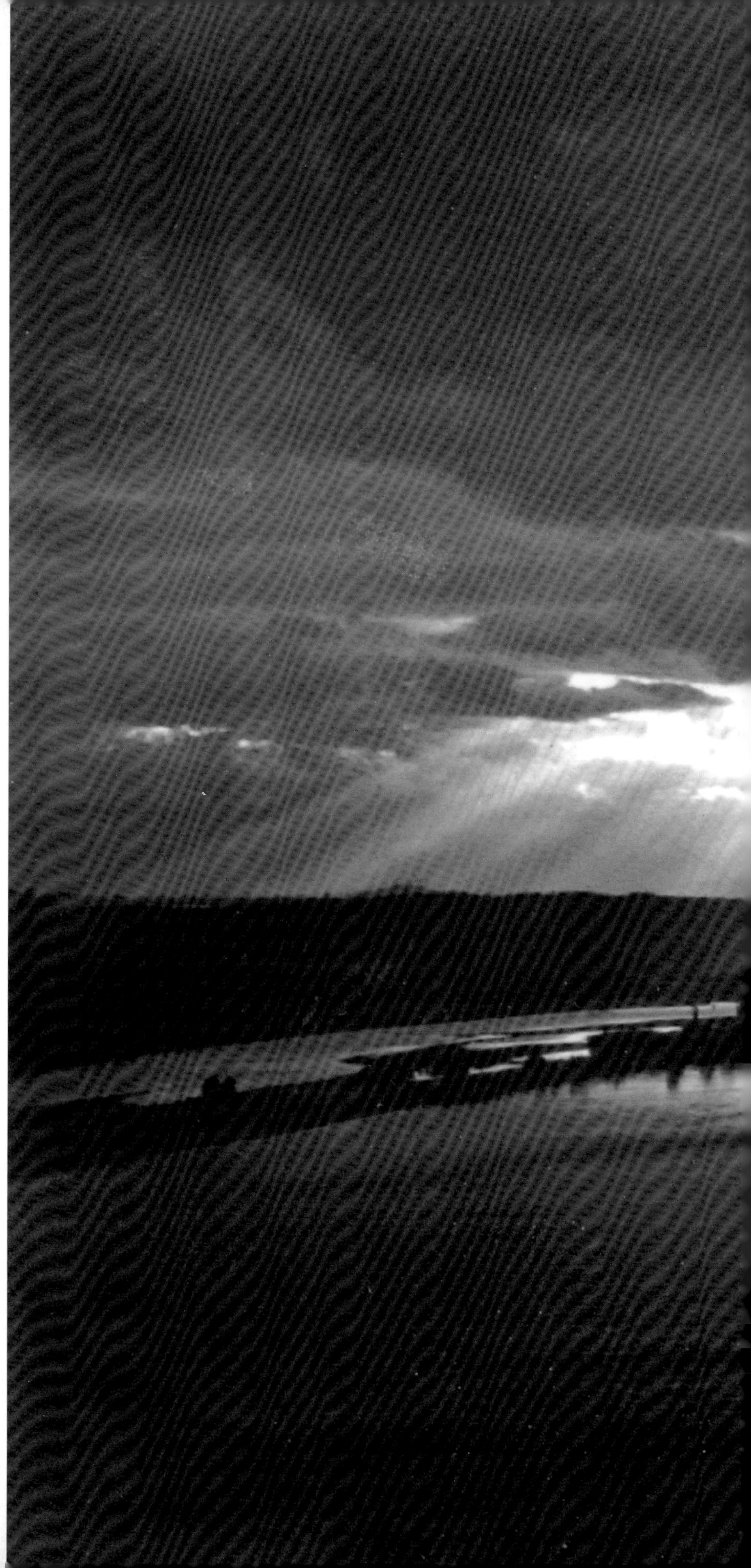

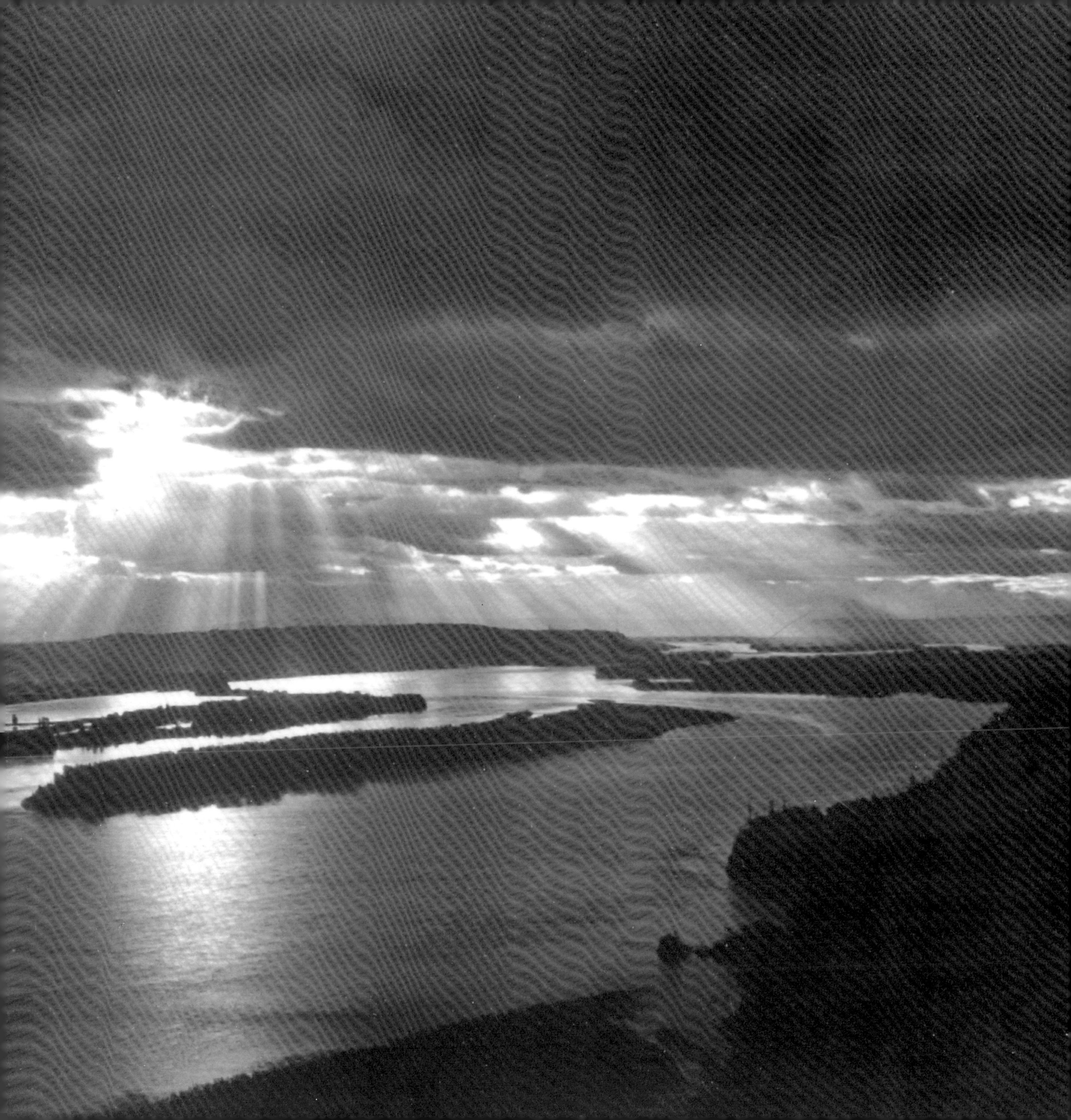

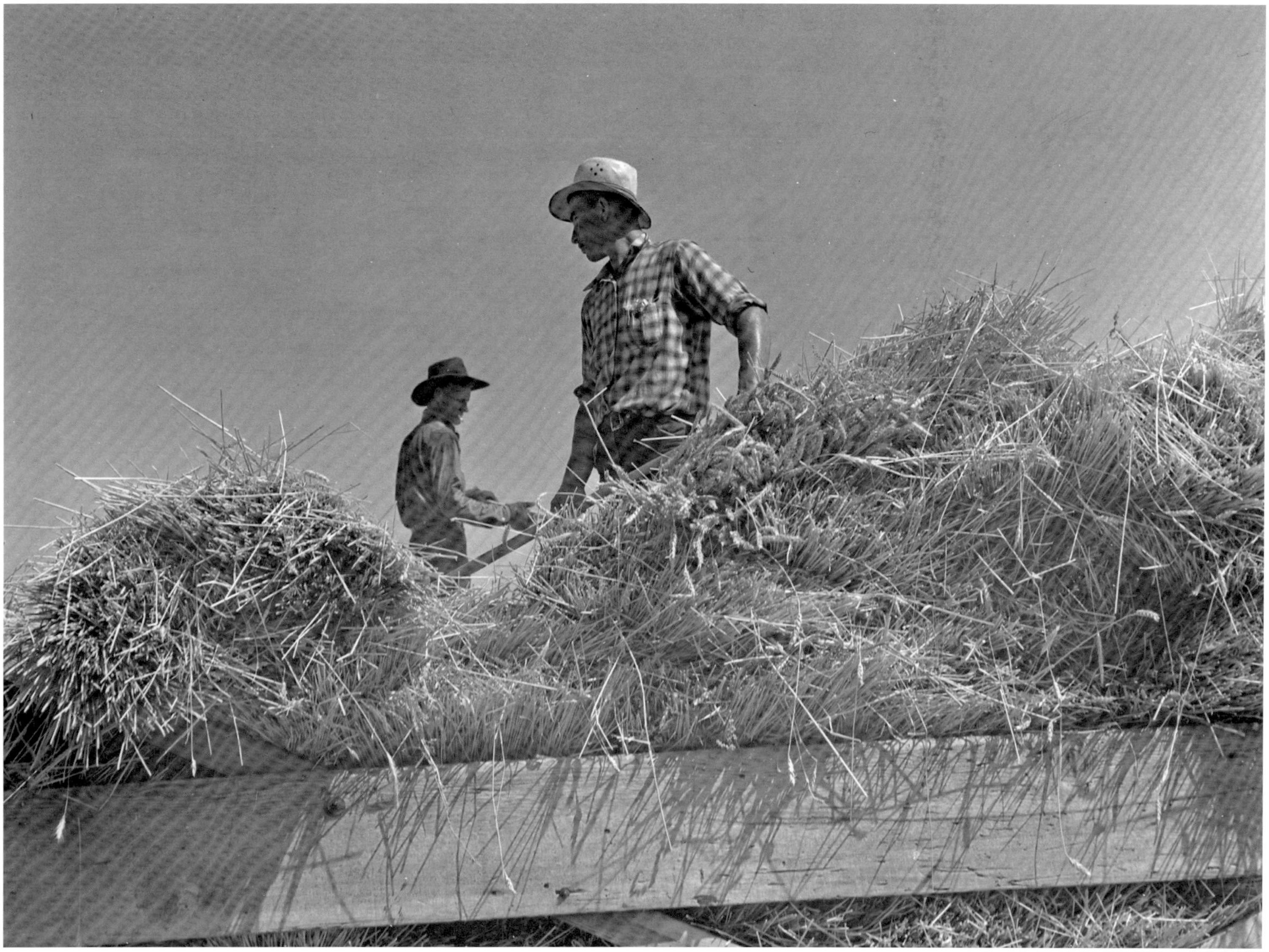

During the Great Depression, the Farm Security Administration became one of the many federal agencies set up under President Roosevelt's New Deal to respond to the crisis. To document unemployment across the nation, the FSA hired a small army of photographers, many of whom would become well known for their well-publicized and widely acclaimed images. Dorothea Lange is perhaps the best known member of the group. A series of images recorded by Lange during her visit to Oregon in 1939, including this view of two farmers at work, follows.

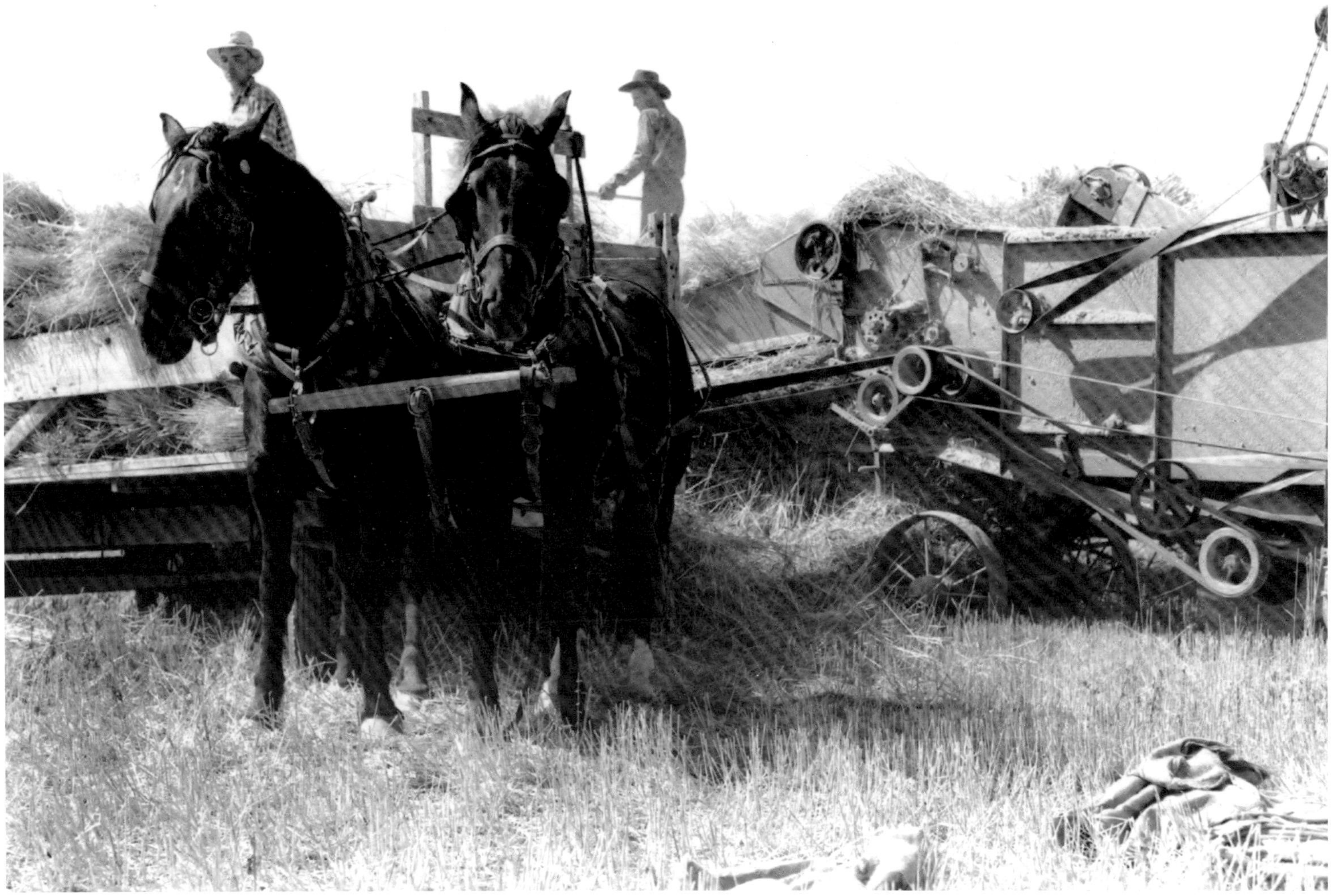

Beginning in 1905, the federal government began making plans to irrigate southern Oregon. The Klamath project irrigated 250,000 acres and contributed to an economic and population boom in the area. These Klamath County farmers are threshing wheat five miles west of Malin in this Dorothea Lange image.

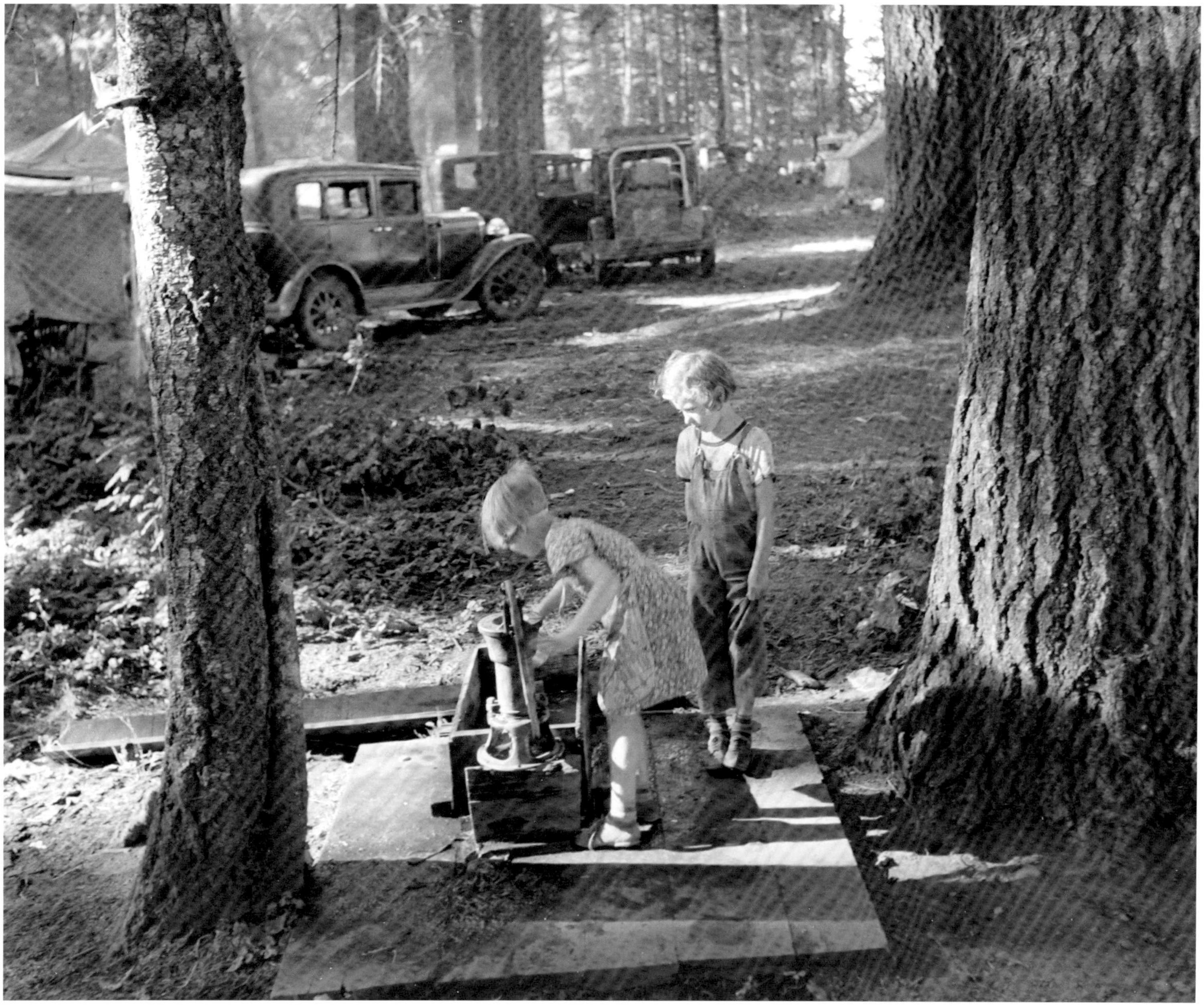

Employment across Oregon dropped by 60 percent from 1929 to 1933. This Lange image records a group of children at a migrant workers camp in Marion County in the mid-Willamette Valley. They are standing beside a water well pump.

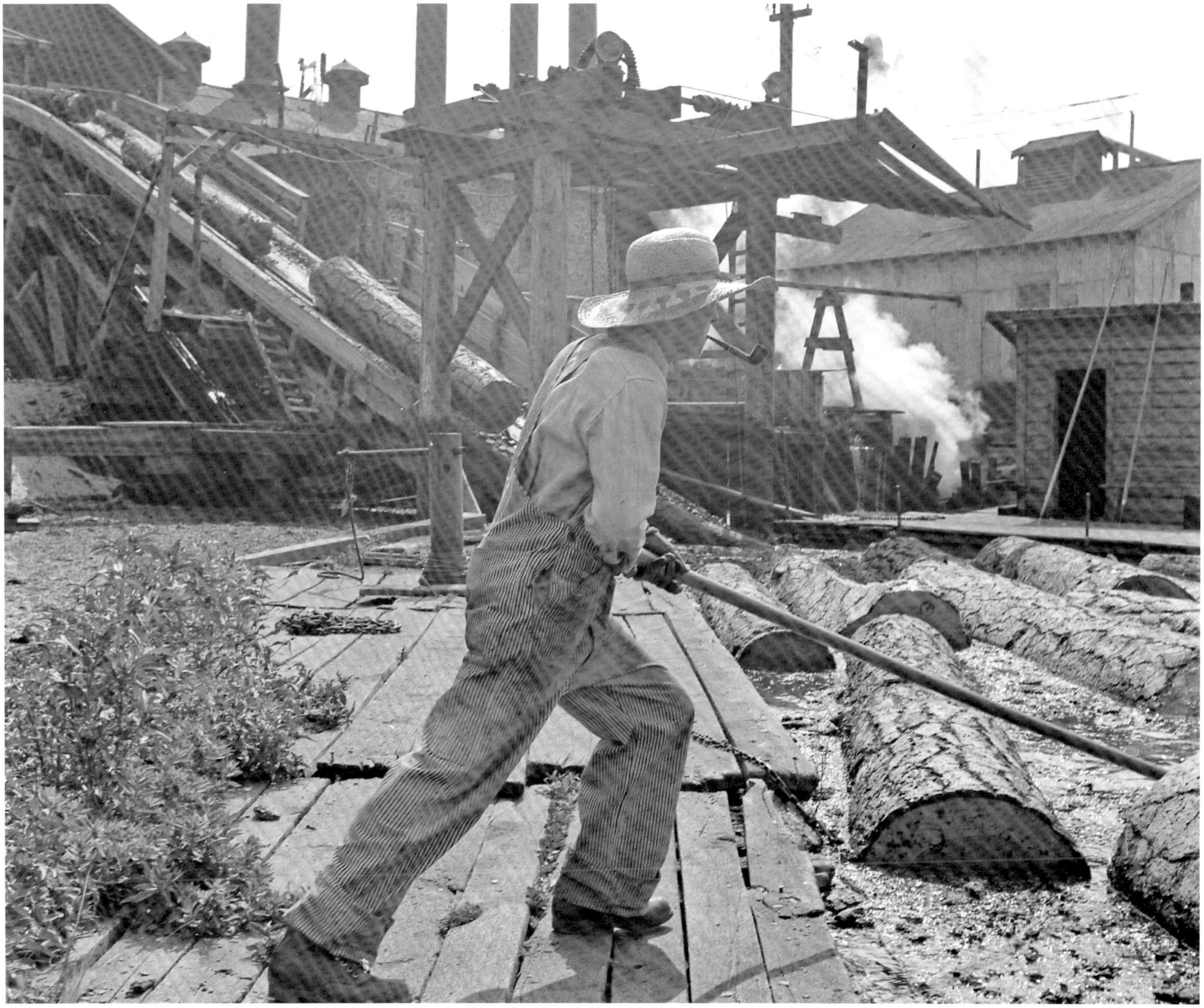

Known as a "pond monkey," this worker guides logs from the mill pond to the chute at the Pelican Bay Lumber Company in Klamath Falls.

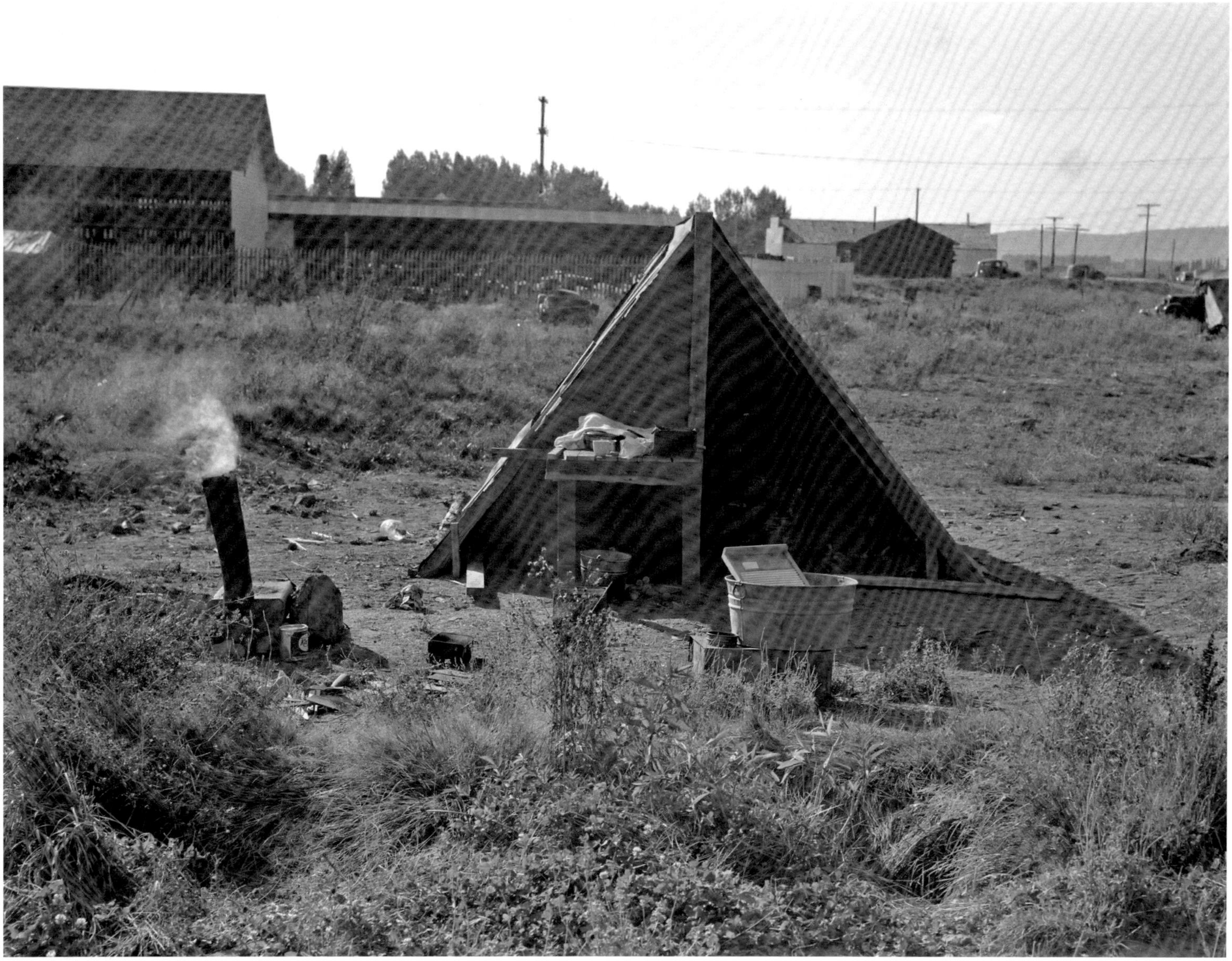

Campsite of a migrant worker in the Klamath County potato fields near the town of Malin. The large tub in front of the shelter includes a washboard, used by many Americans for washing clothes before the days of automatic washing machines.

Lange's camera found this Independence man all smiles in 1939. Perhaps he was looking forward to the Hop Fiesta on August 24, which was to include log rolling, vaudeville, amateur hour, parades, acrobats, a street dance, fireworks, and more. A sign at far-left directs hop picker applicants to the employment service office. Unemployment nationwide still averaged 17 percent in 1939.

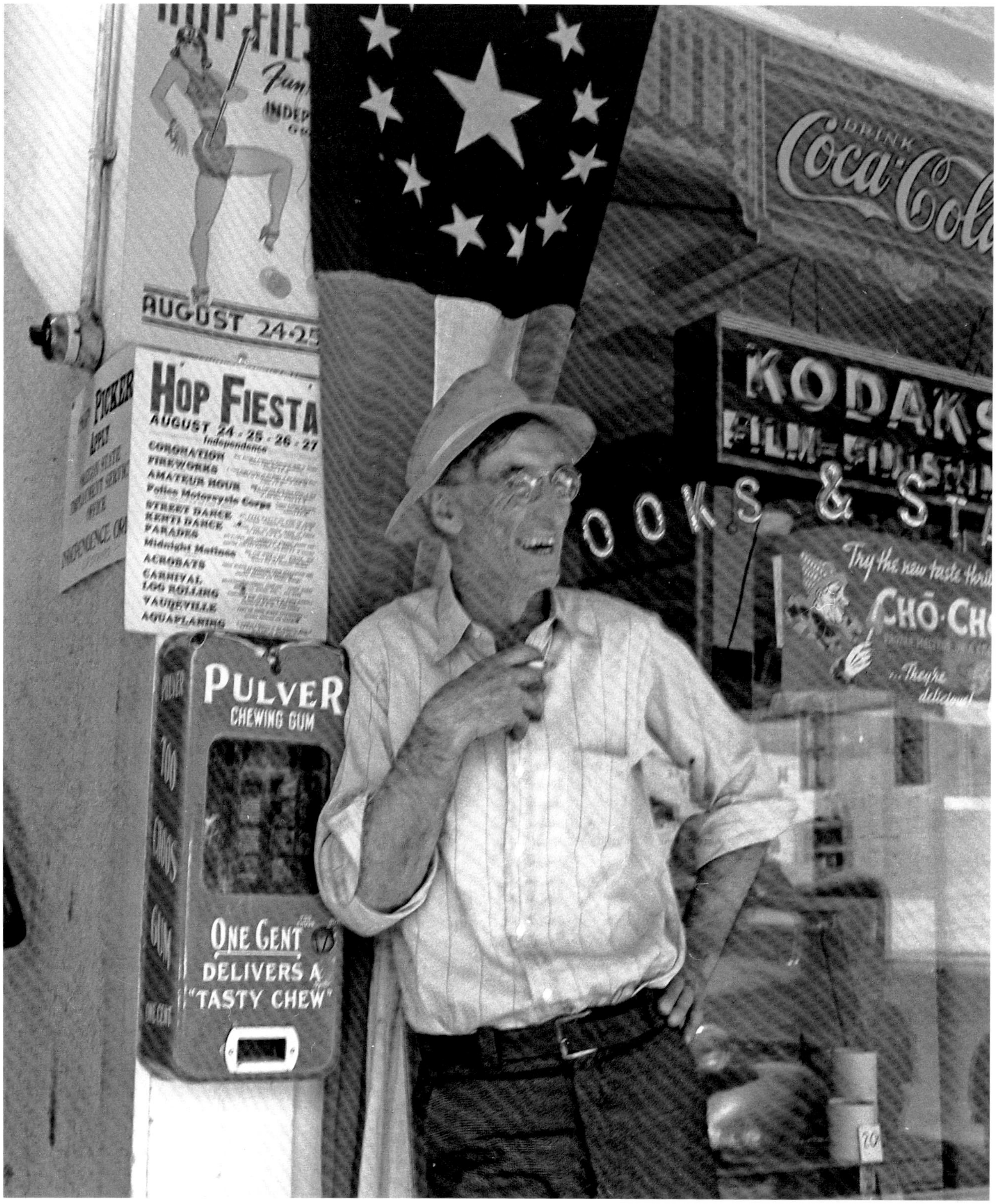

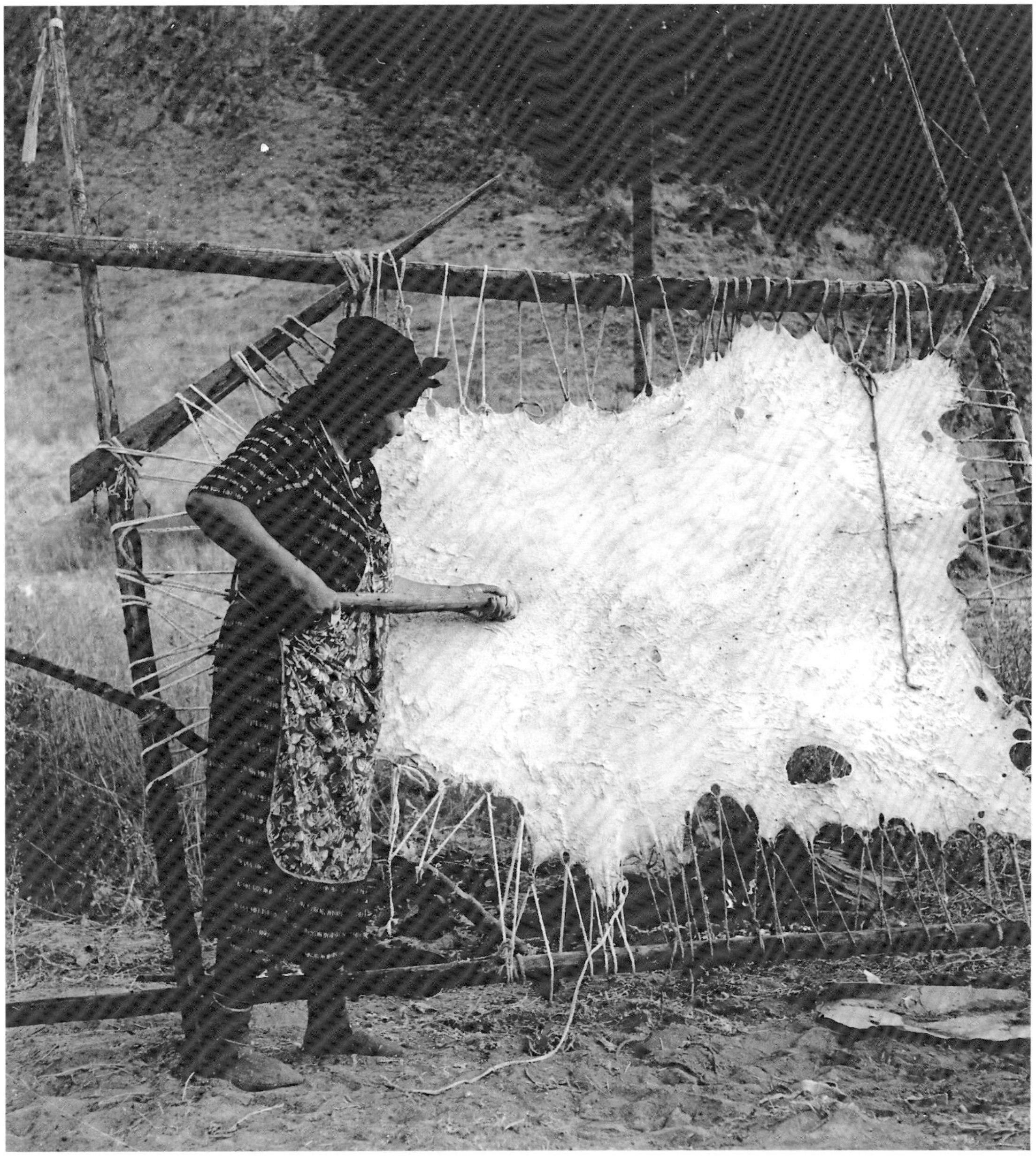

This Lange photograph shows a Klamath Indian woman at a fishing village scraping animal hide.

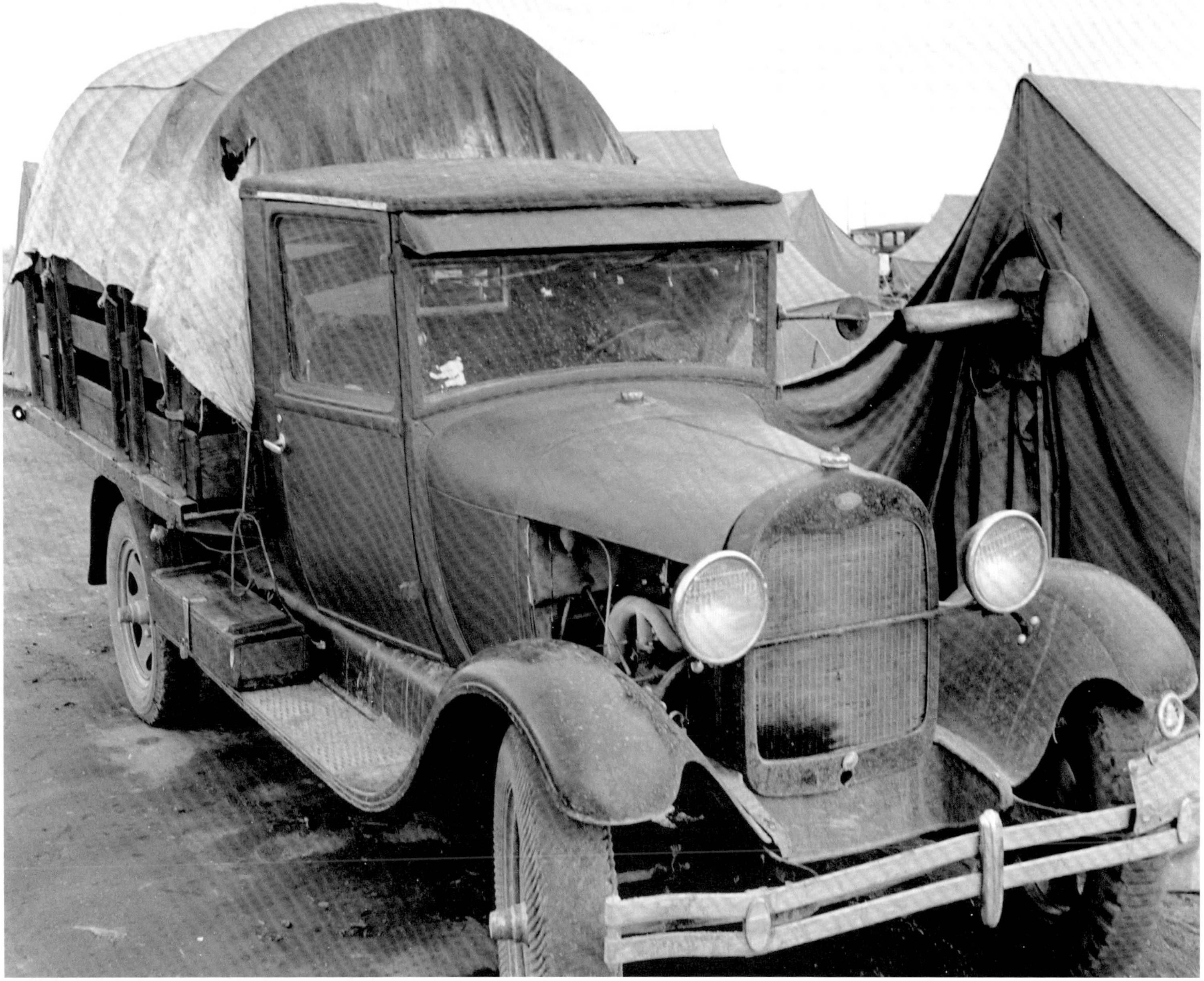

Lange visited a migrant camp operated by the Farm Security Administration in the town of Merrill, focusing her lens on this truck with bald tire and canvas-shelter back end.

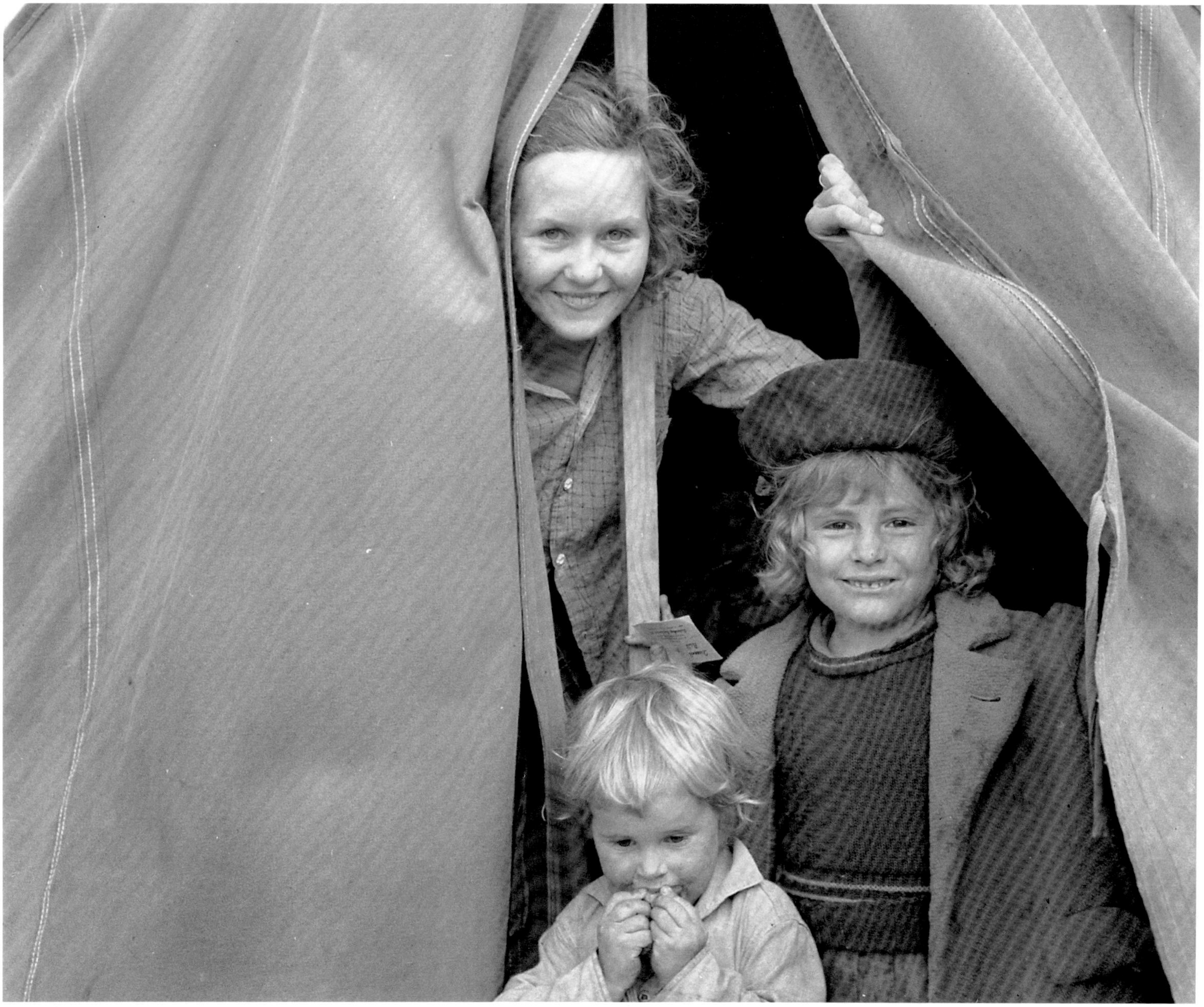

This October view of the FSA migrant camp at Merrill focuses on the younger folks, seen here smiling for Lange's camera from their canvas tent shelter.

In the Willow Creek area of Malheur County, Mrs. Soper draws a cup of water from the well while her youngest tot invests attention in a metal cog. Haystacks are visible in the distance.

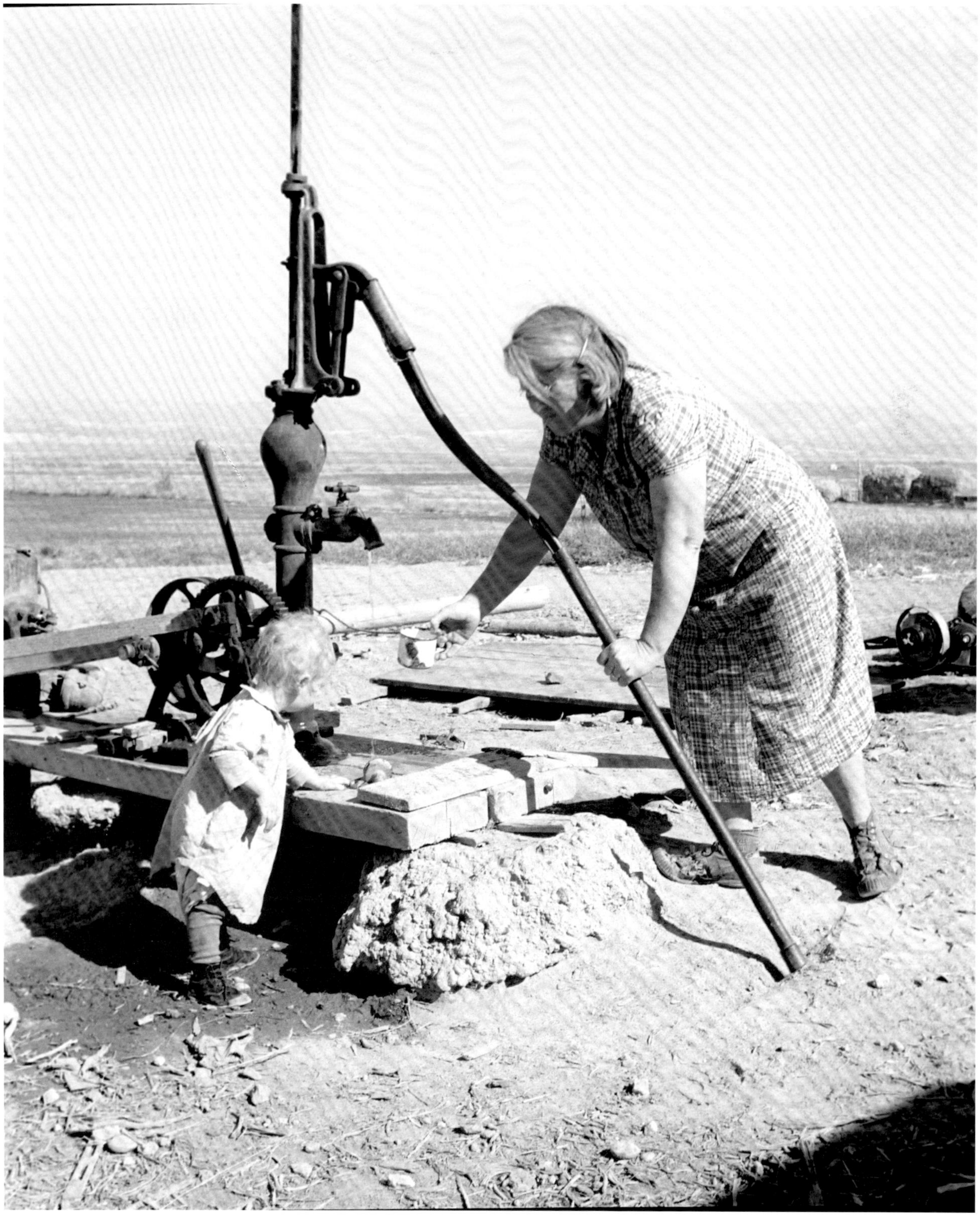

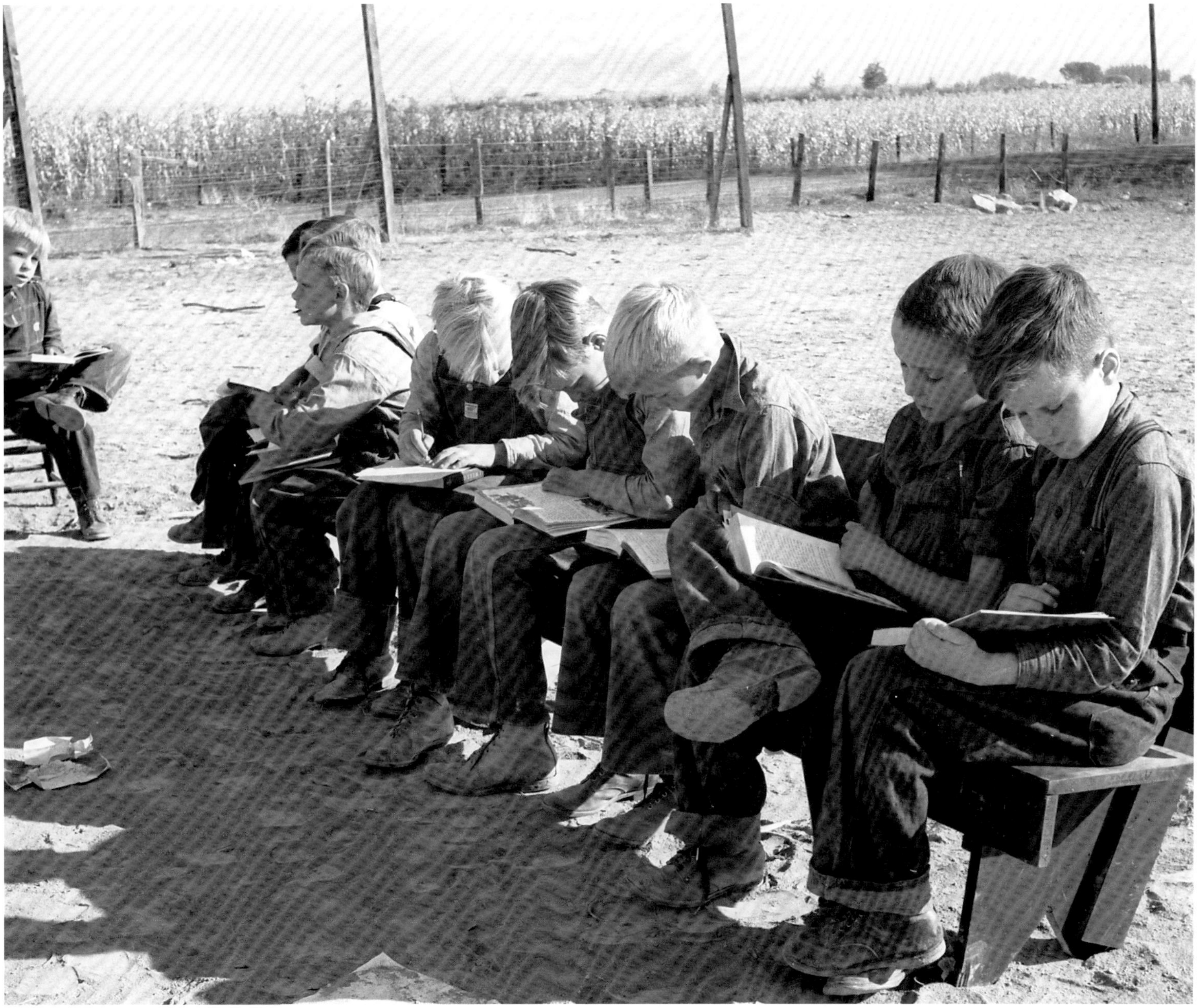

Nine boys, born in six states, study their lessons at Lincoln Bench School. The school was set up at a migrant camp near Ontario, in Malheur County. A field of corn matures in the distance.

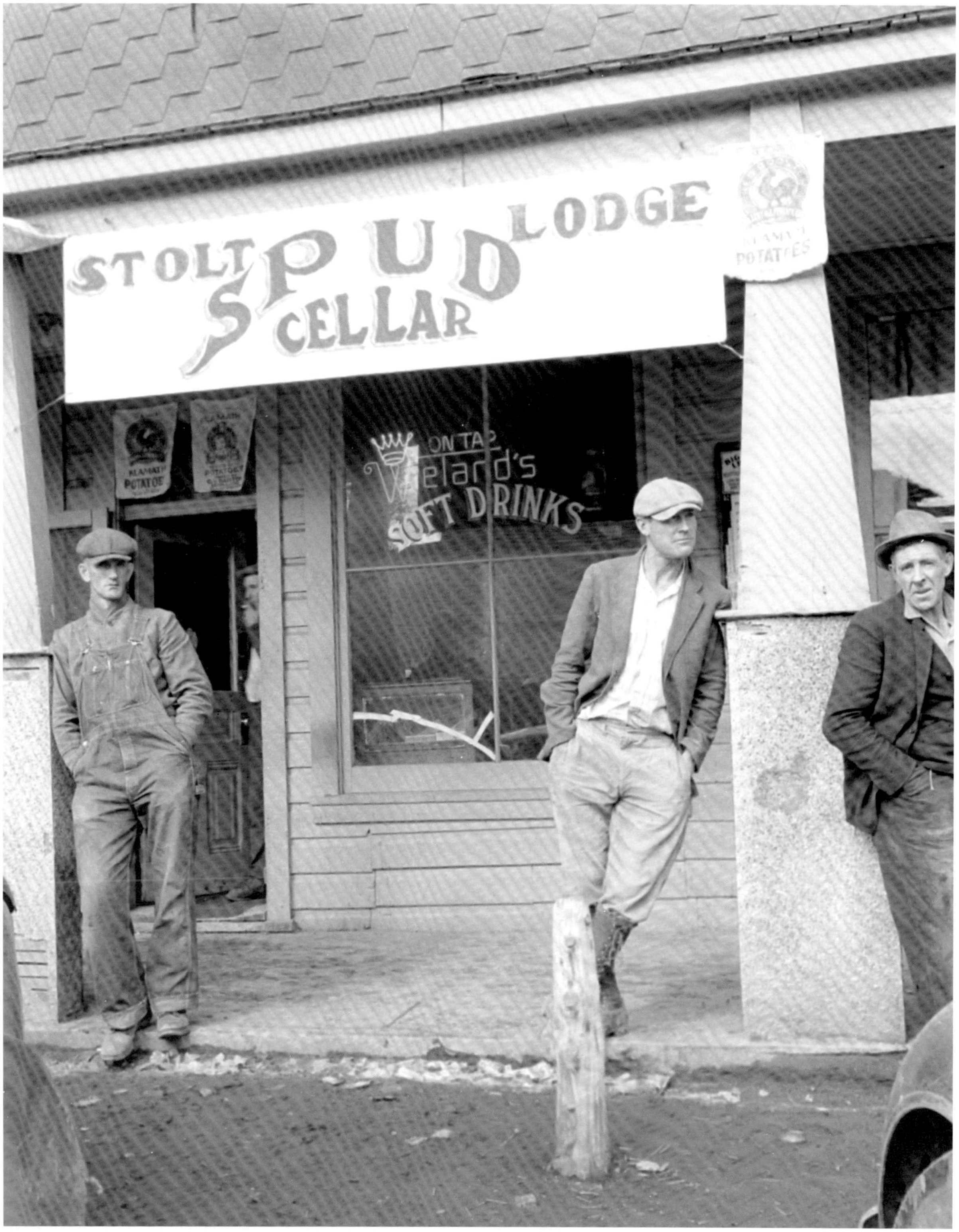

Signs of the times on Merrill's main street during potato harvest season, where Klamath potatoes get top billing. Seldom noted today, the signage on every building front in America was once hand-lettered by skilled craftsmen without recourse to computers, electronic printing devices, or much of anything but paint, brushes, chalk, and a yardstick, and the satisfaction derived from well-executed brushstrokes. "Welard's On Tap" was executed in neon, very popular in the 1930s and 1940s as an alternative to hand-lettering.

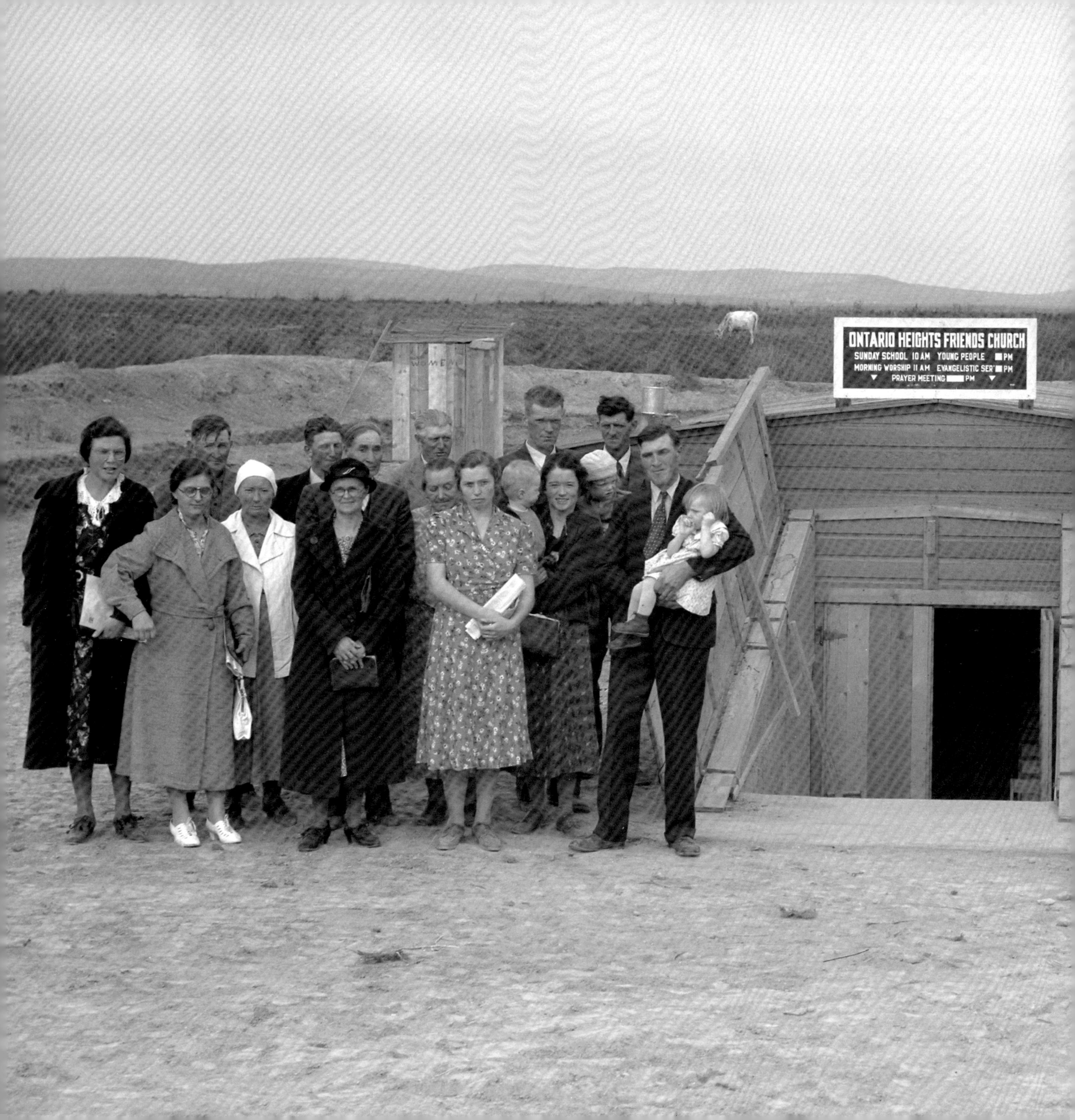
ONTARIO HEIGHTS FRIENDS CHURCH
SUNDAY SCHOOL 10 AM YOUNG PEOPLE PM
MORNING WORSHIP 11 AM EVANGELISTIC SER' PM
PRAYER MEETING PM

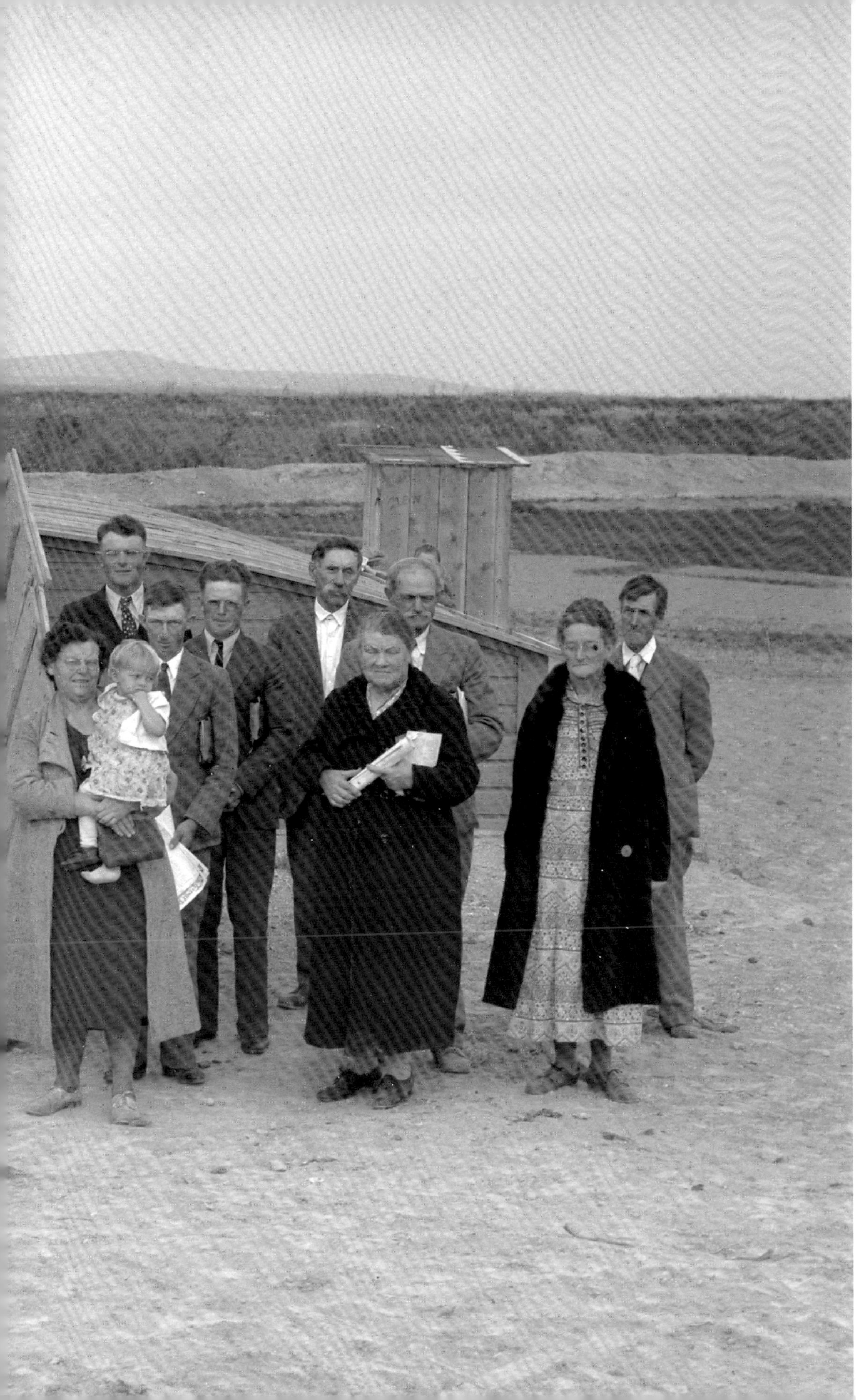

Members of a Quaker congregation in Dead Ox Flat, in Malheur County. Sunday school was held at 10:00 A.M. and morning worship at 11:00. The building was built partly underground, to save on construction costs, for which there was little money, and to leave it less prone to damage from extreme weather.

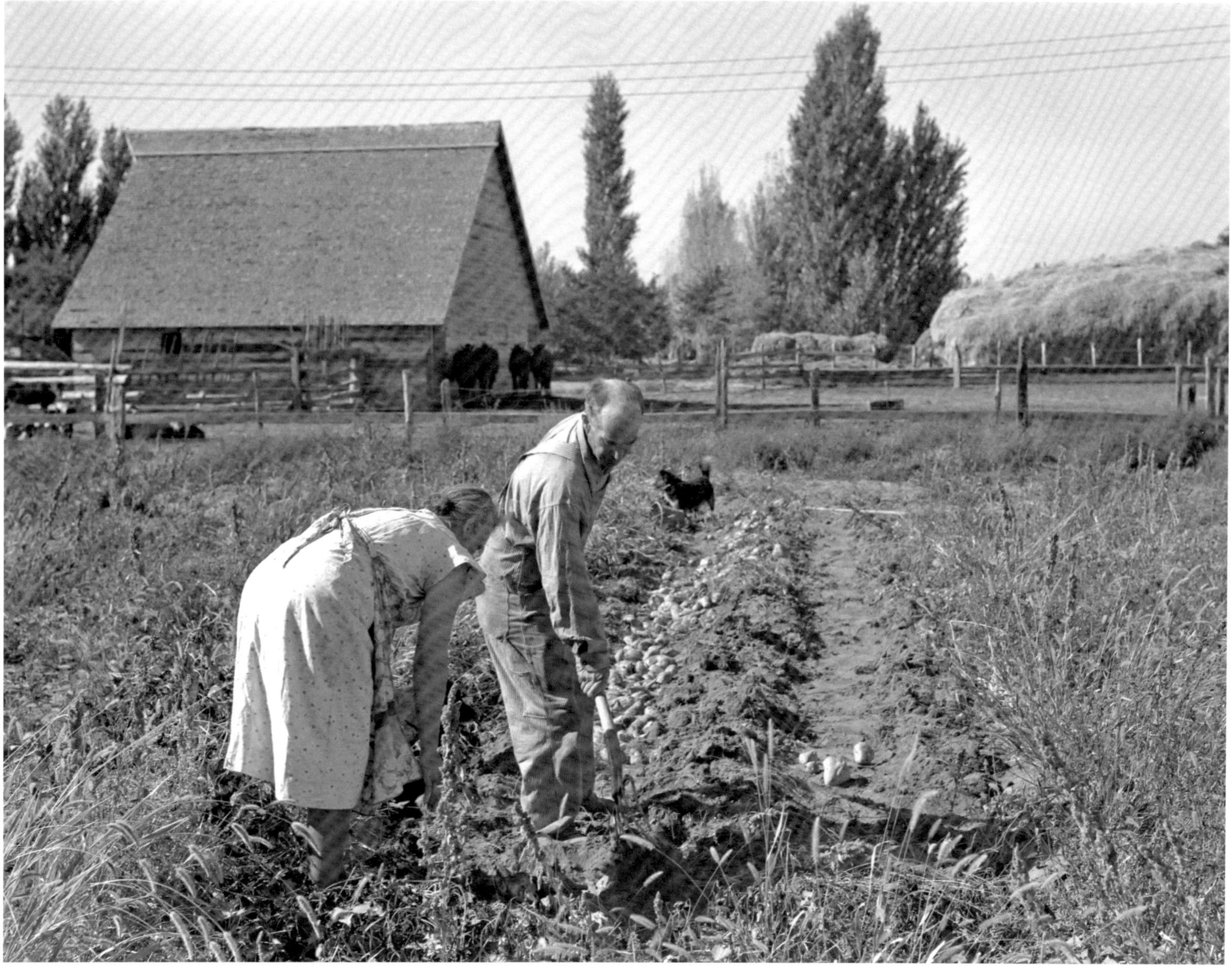

Lange captured this Irrigon couple using a potato fork to harvest sweet potatoes in autumn 1939.

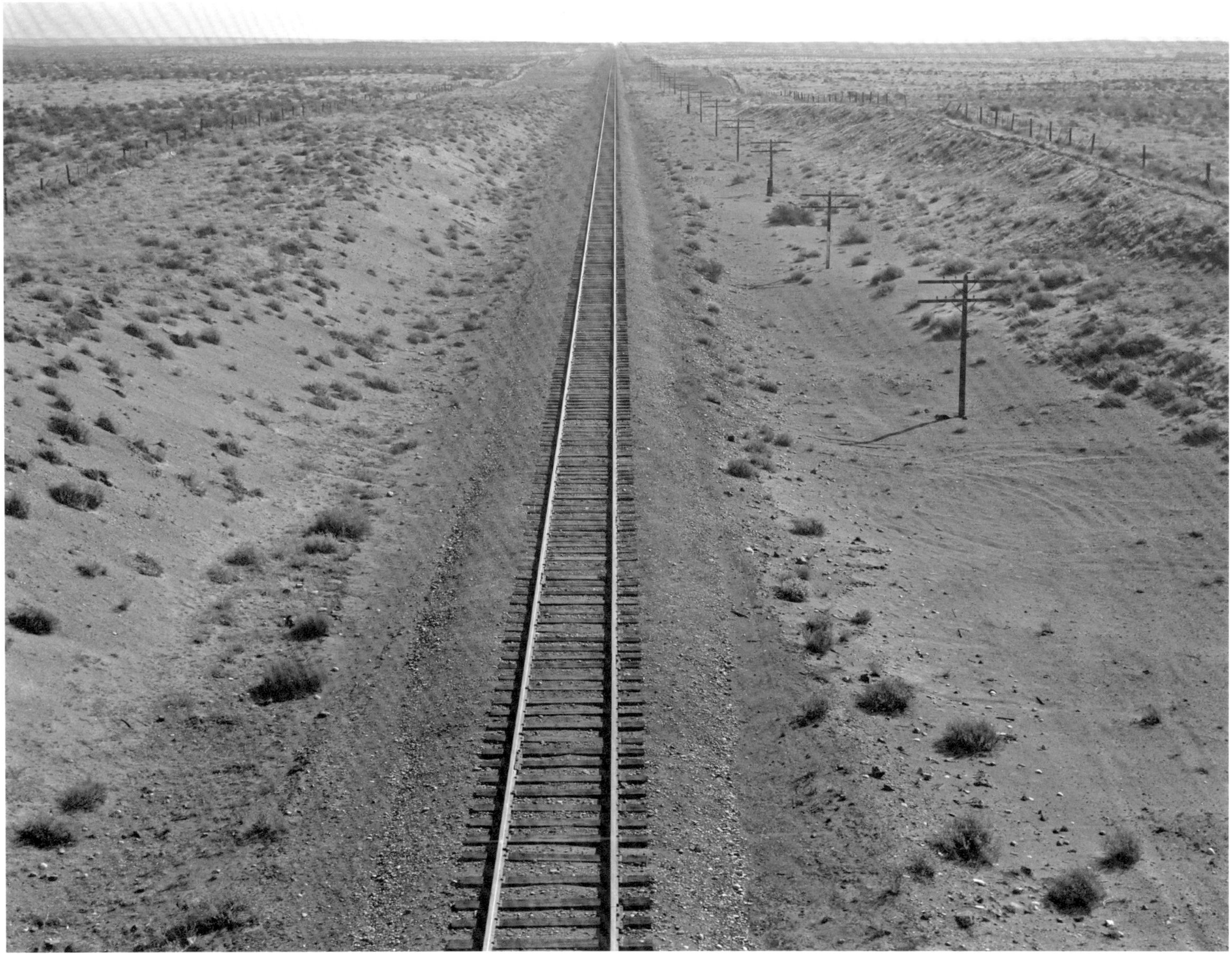

A Western Pacific rail line runs through desert near Irrigon, in Morrow County, just south of the Columbia River. Dorothea Lange must have gone to great heights to capture this image, which concludes the Lange series.

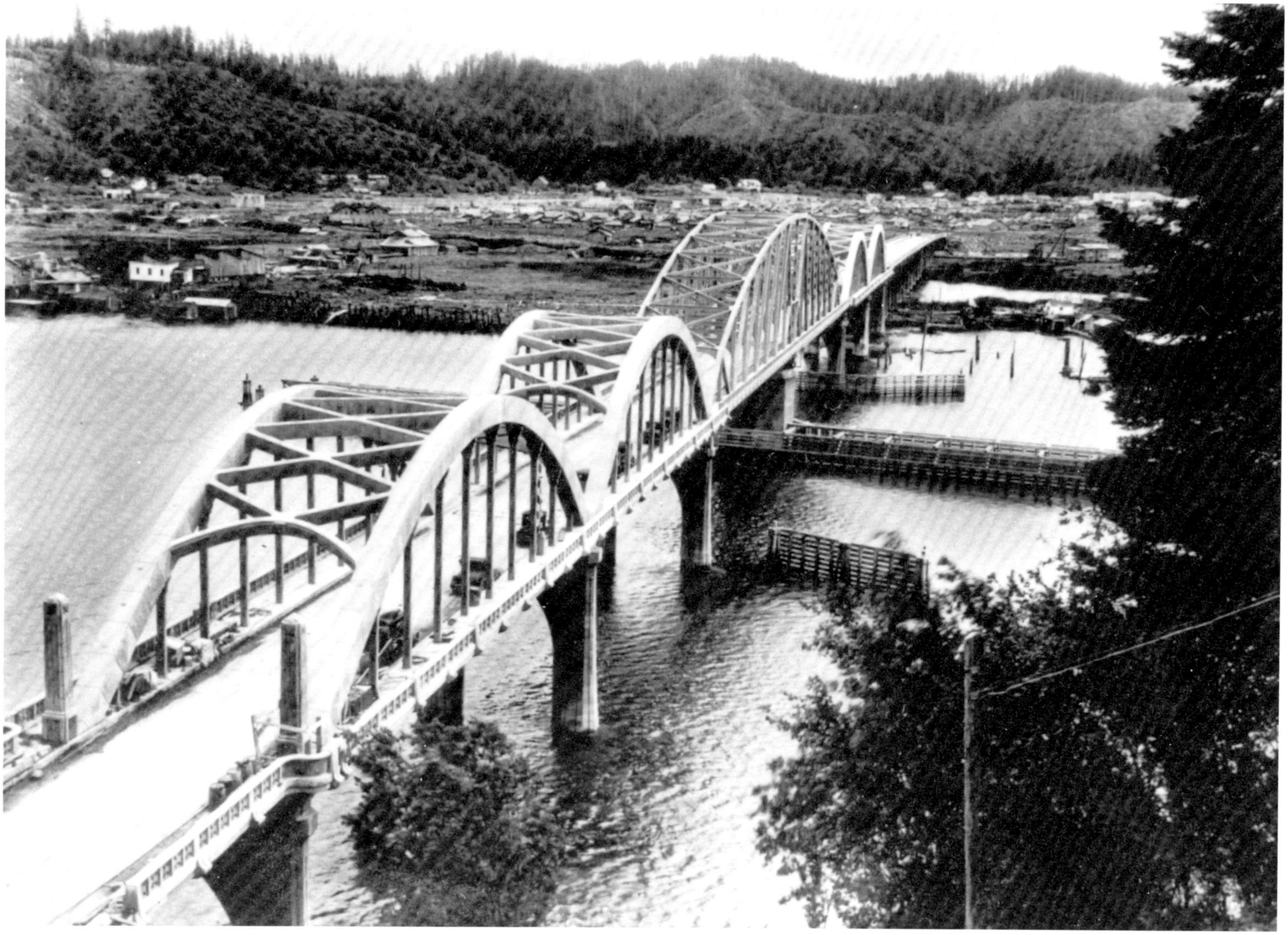

The Umpqua River Bridge spans the Umpqua River in 1939, three years after it was built. It remains the longest swing bridge in Oregon, built to permit tall ships passage upriver.

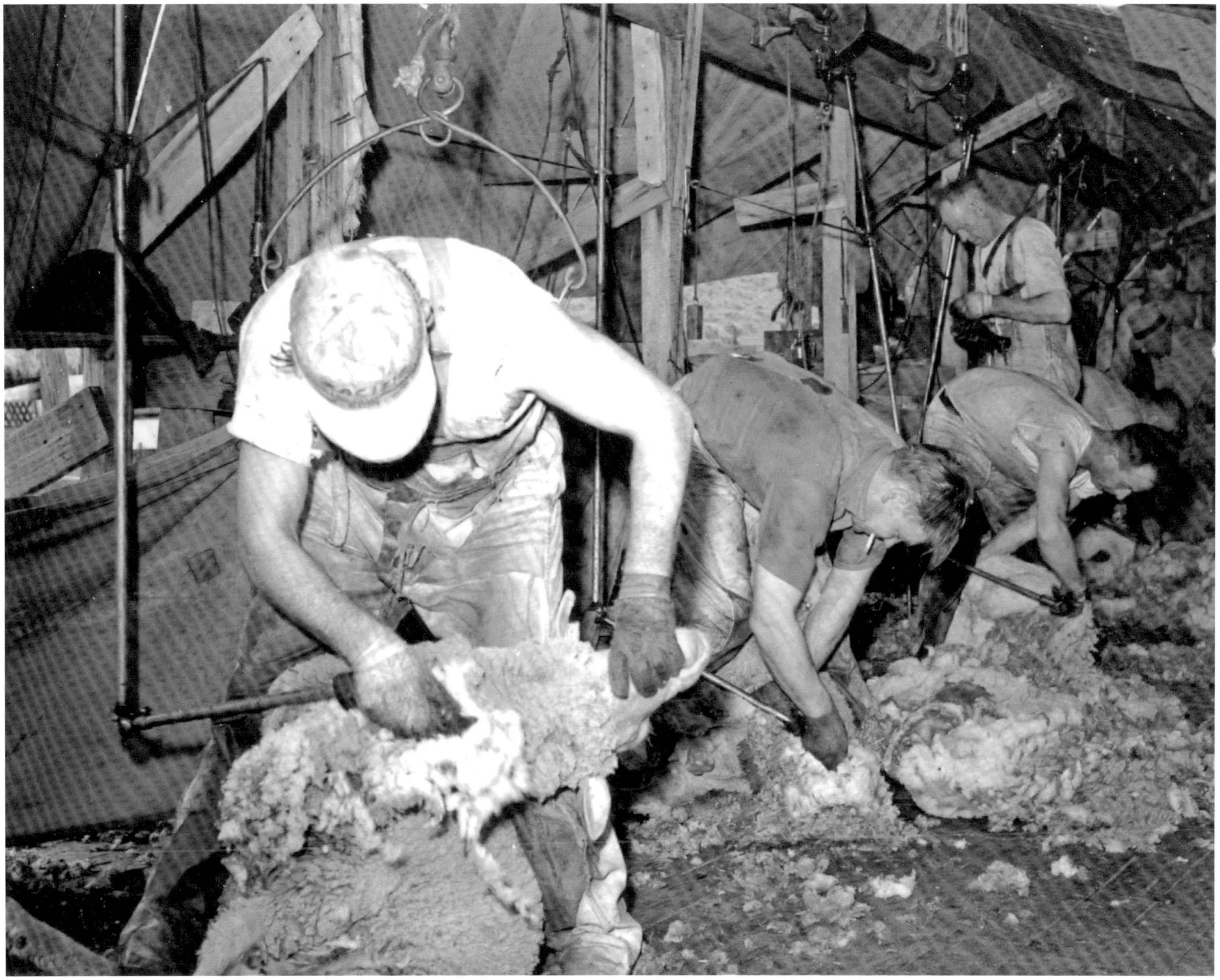

The Basques were often sheepherders in Malheur County after 1900, and sheep are being shorn at this ranch. The wool industry declined after 1902 and lamb meat became a specialty product.

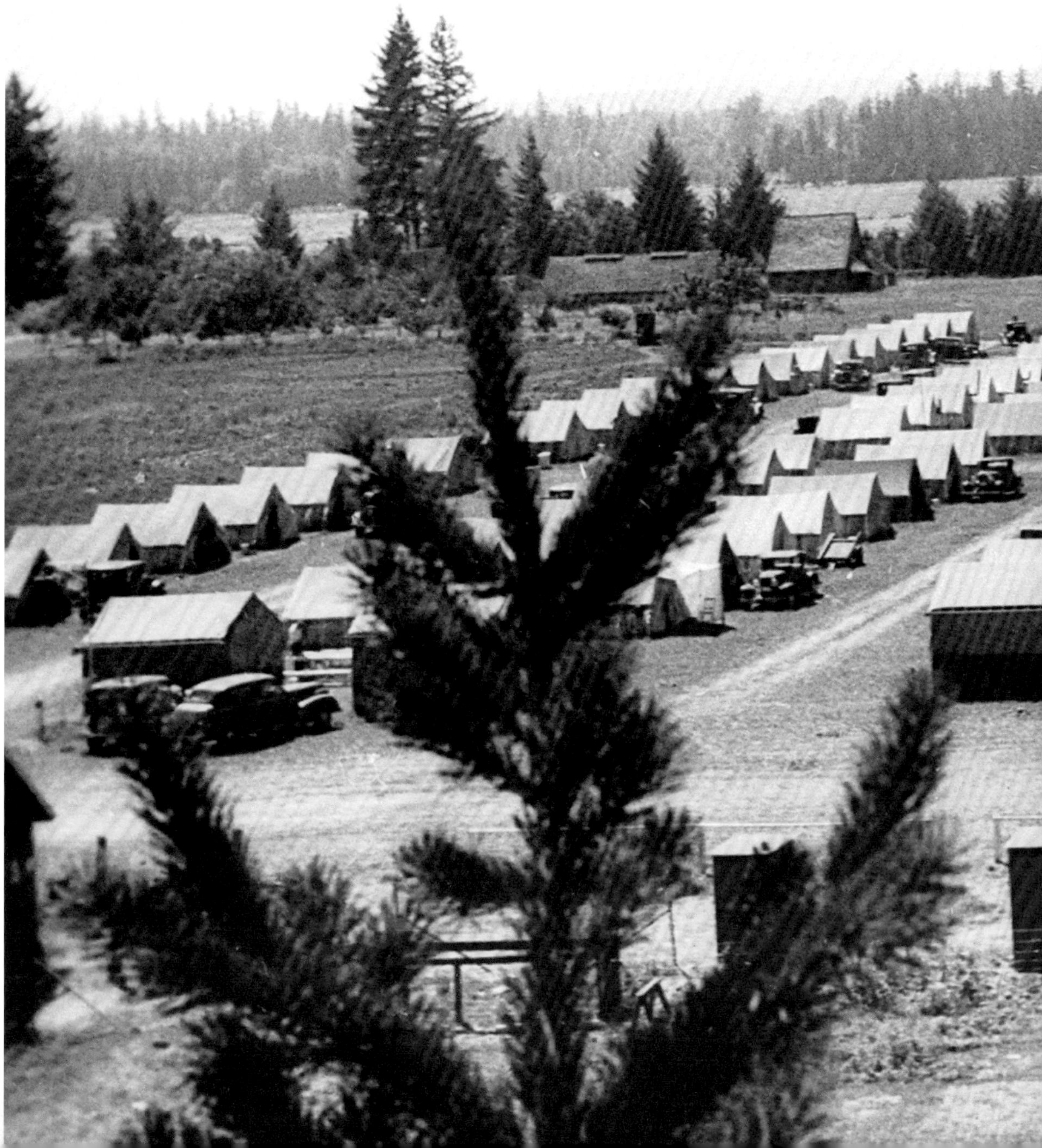

A mobile migrant labor camp, shown here at Stayton, in the mid Willamette Valley, in 1940.

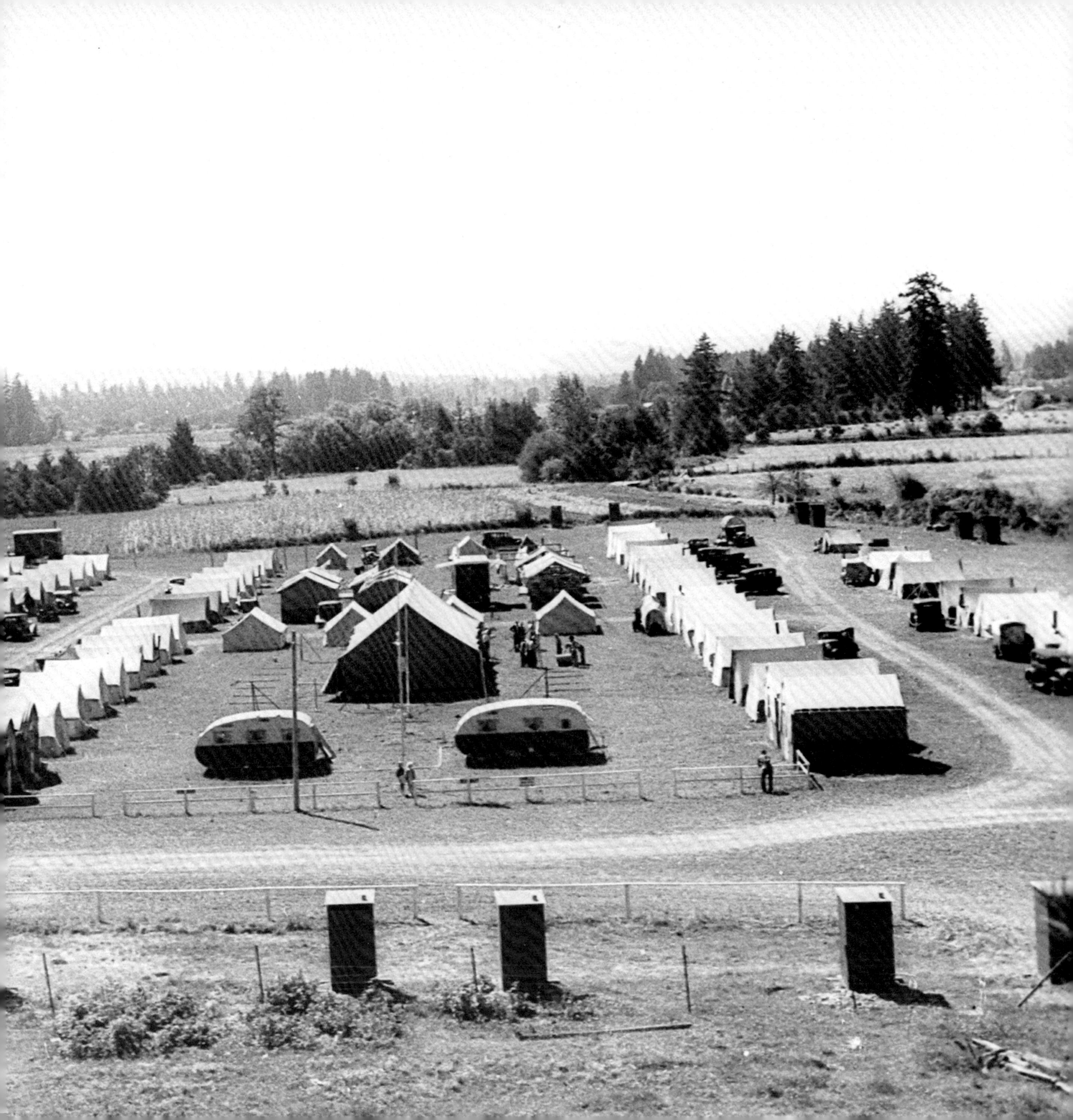

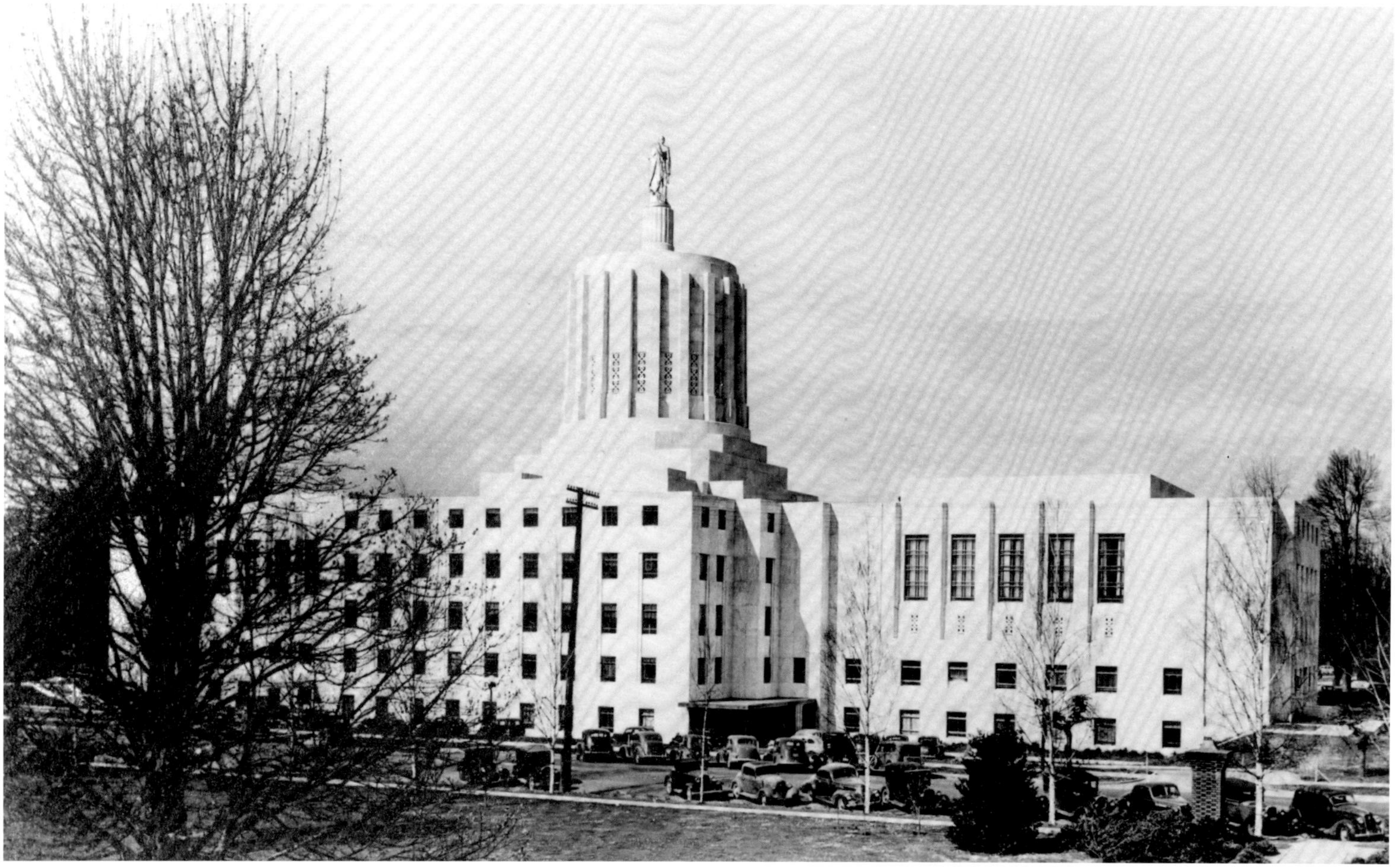

The new Oregon State Capitol, shown here sometime after it was completed, replaced the second capitol when it burned down in 1935.

The War Years

(1941–1945)

The Japanese attack on Pearl Harbor, Hawaii, on December 7, 1941, startled not only Oregonians but Americans up and down the West Coast. It was widely feared that the Japanese would soon attack the coast by sea and by air. Six months later, a Japanese submarine fired a few artillery shells at Fort Stevens near the mouth of the Columbia River. World War II had erupted and would become the pivotal event of the twentieth century, shaping the destiny of Oregon, the United States, and the world in a way that continues into the present.

In response to the crisis, the federal government under President Roosevelt began to establish training bases for the armed forces. The largest in Oregon was Camp Adair near Corvallis. Soldiers came to the state to prepare for overseas duty, boosting the economy by spending money in restaurants, theaters, and other businesses.

Another thrust for the war effort also benefited the state economically, and Portland in particular. The Kaiser Shipyards, led by Henry Kaiser, needed housing for its workers. In response, Edgar Kaiser, Henry's son, began working with the Housing Authority of Portland to build housing for 160,000 shipyard workers. The community of Vanport (which would be destroyed by a flood in 1948) would come to rank as the largest housing development erected under this effort. At peak production in 1943 and 1944, the shipyards launched 1,000 oceangoing ships. The inflow of workers also gave Portland a boost in population, from 501,000 to 661,000 citizens between 1940 and 1944.

The shipyards provided employment for minorities and women, who were needed to fill vacancies left by servicemen fighting and dying overseas. All Americans were asked to make sacrifices, and those who remained on the home front volunteered any way they could, from planting Victory gardens to organizing scrap drives. On the heels of Pearl Harbor, and often criticized in recent times, was the compulsory evacuation of Japanese-Americans and Japanese resident aliens to internment camps in 1942, through FDR's Executive Order 9066. By March 1942, 1,707 residents of Portland had moved to the North Portland Assembly Center (now the Exposition Center), where they departed for internment camps to await the outcome of the war. In 1988, Congress awarded reparations of $20,000 to each of the 60,000 people of Japanese descent still living who had spent the war at an internment camp.

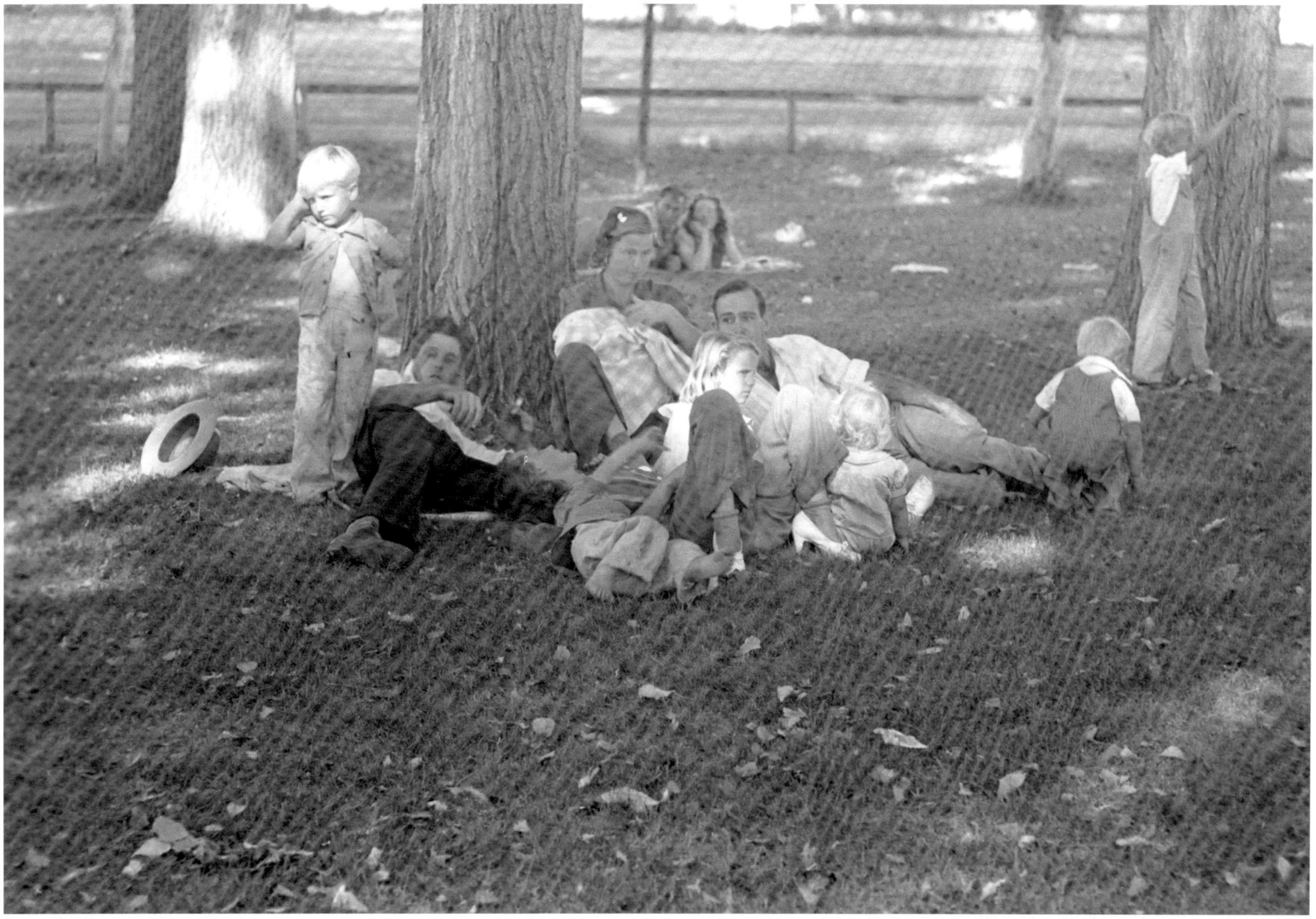

A family picnic on the Fourth of July in Vale, Oregon, in 1941. The population of Vale just before the war was around 1,100.

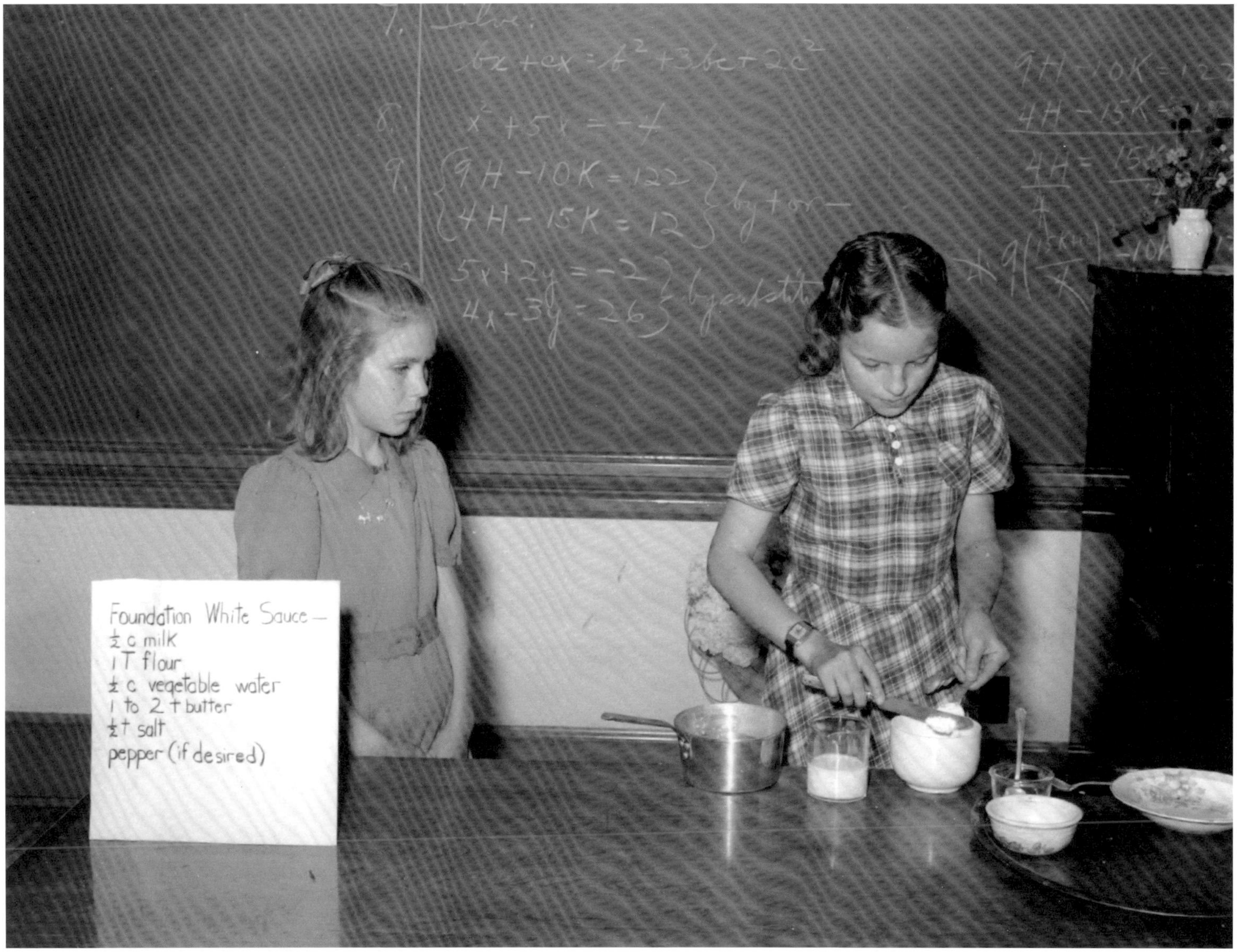

Girls demonstrate cooking methods at the 4-H Club spring fair in Adrian, Oregon, in 1941. This small farming community located in Malheur County originated in 1913 as a station on the Oregon Short Line Railroad.

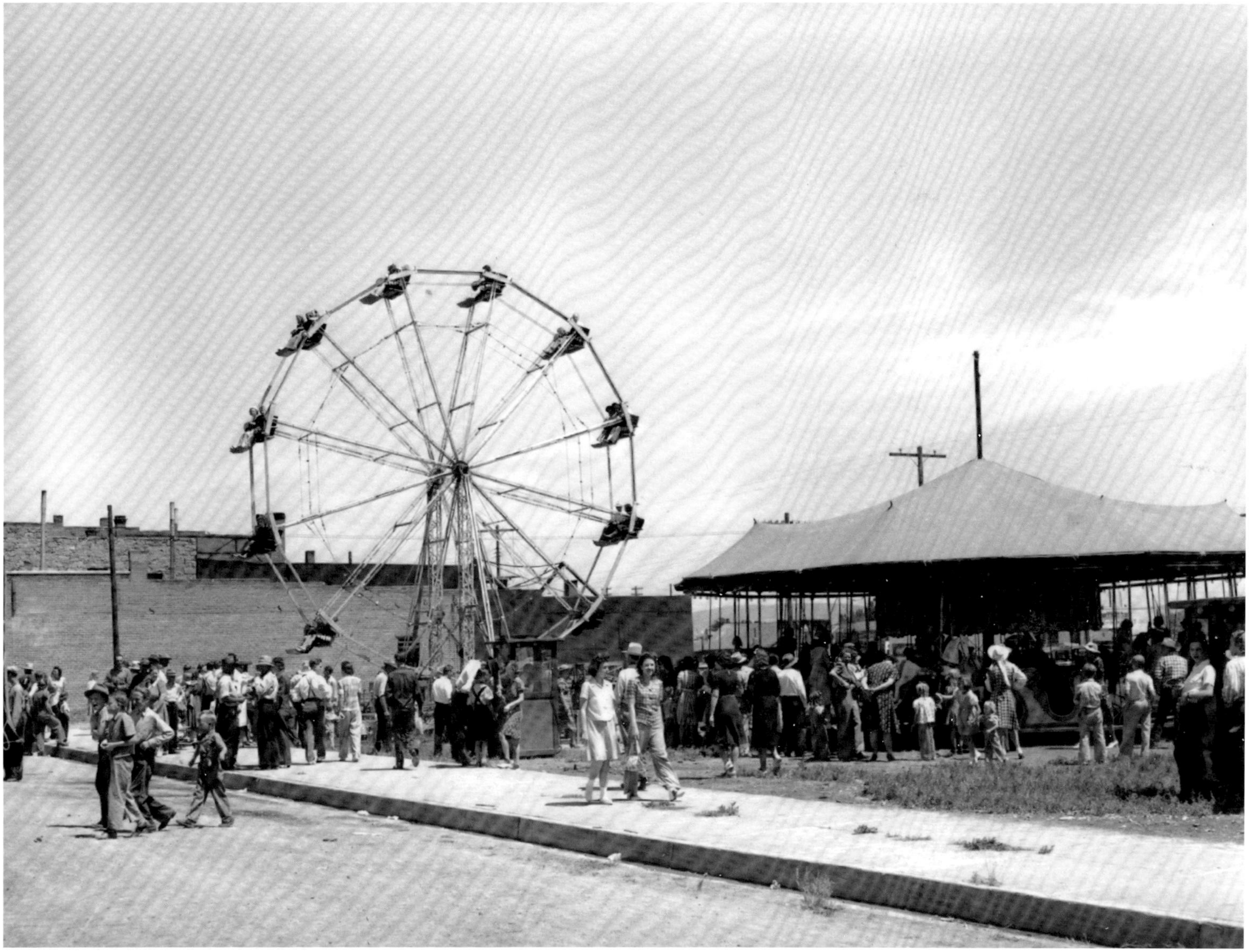

Oregonians enjoy a carnival on the Fourth of July at Vale in 1941.

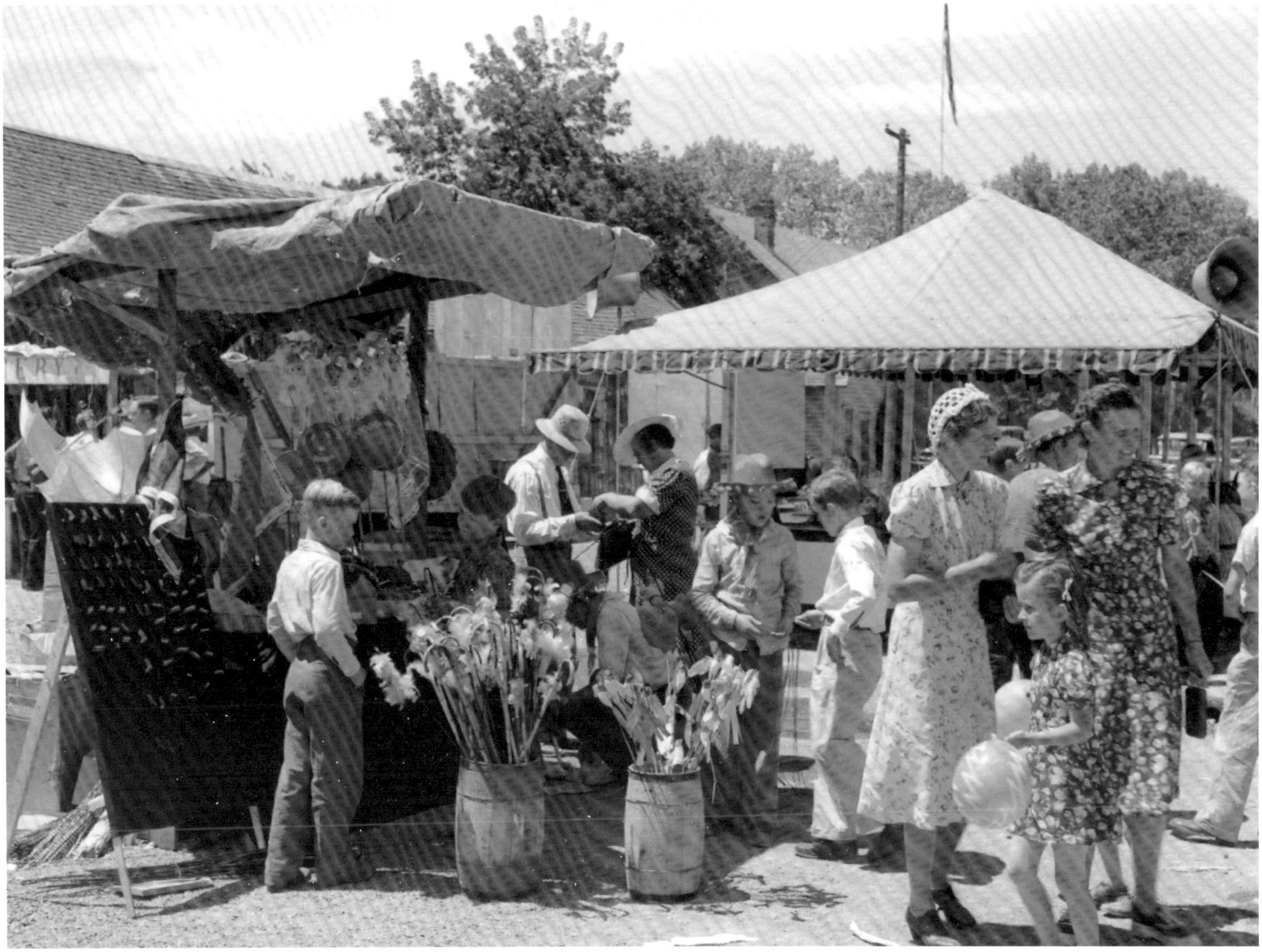

Carnival attractions on the Fourth of July at Vale. Americans of the era always strove to look their best at any public gathering and on the street, usually donning hats, with men in shirts and trousers and often in ties and ladies in dresses, neatly pressed.

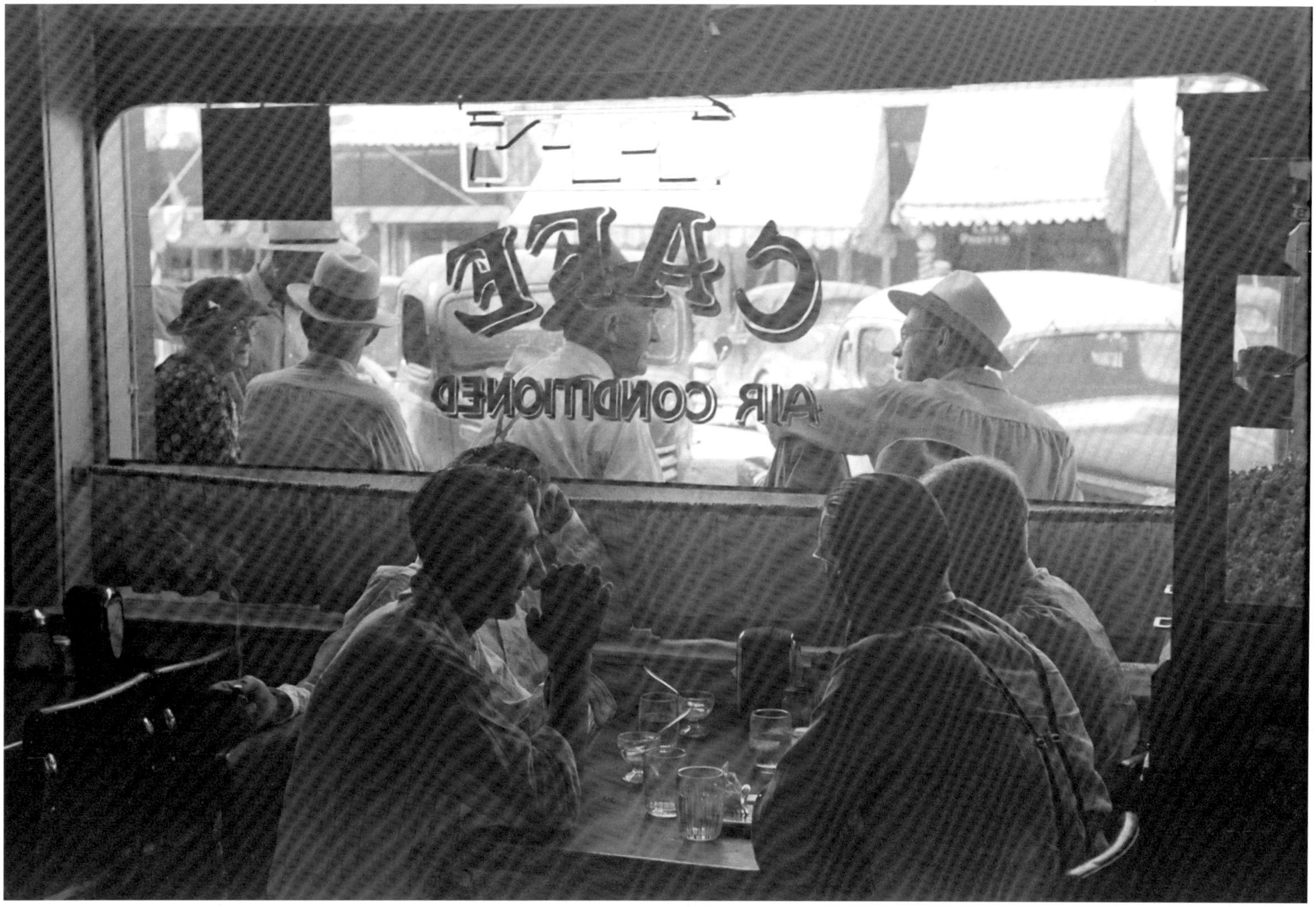

For citizens of Vale uninterested in the Ferris wheel at the Fourth of July carnival, cold drinks were available at this air-conditioned cafe.

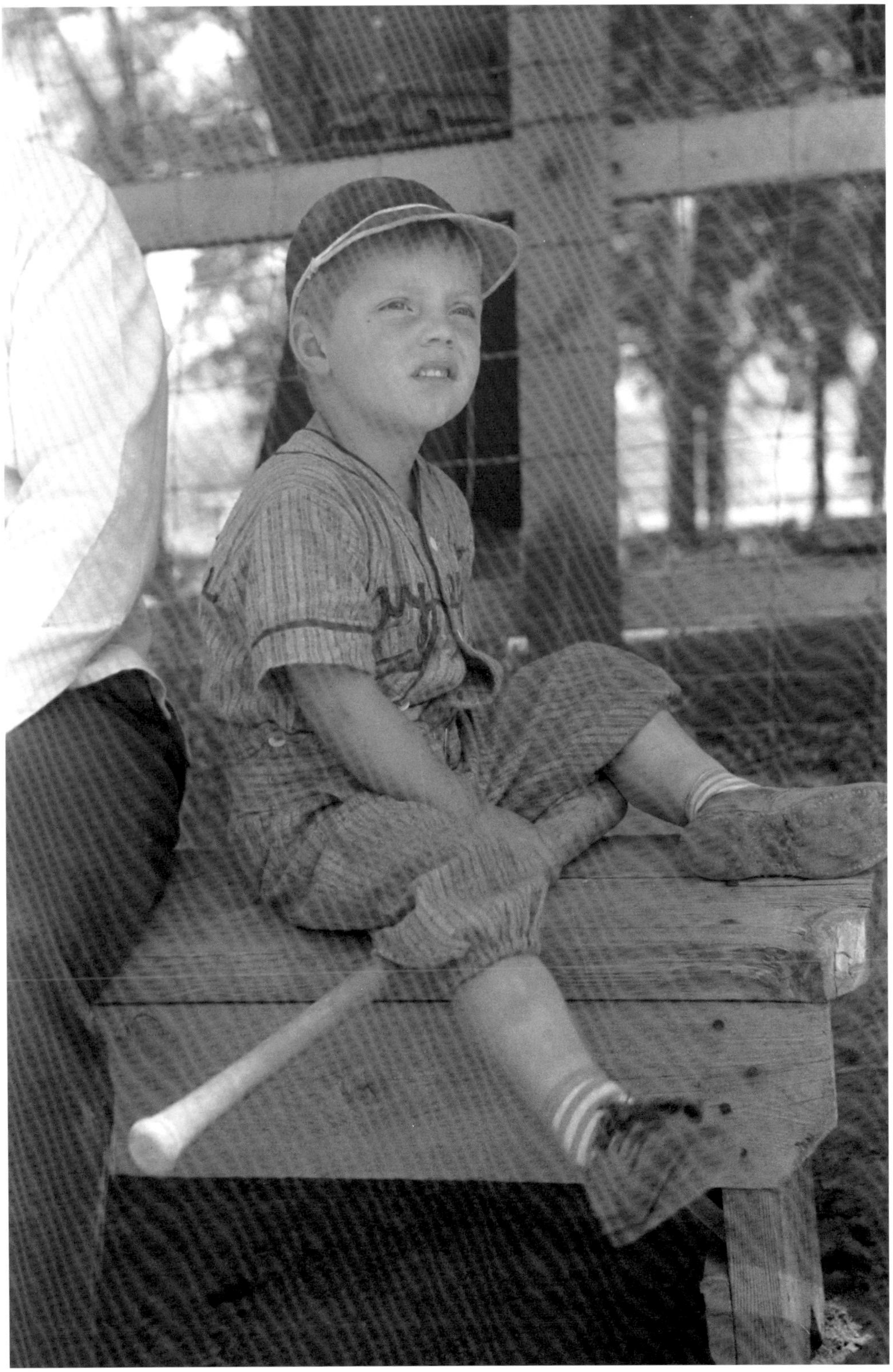

Vale's 1941 Fourth of July celebration wouldn't be complete without a baseball game. This youngster is glued to the action taking place on the ball field.

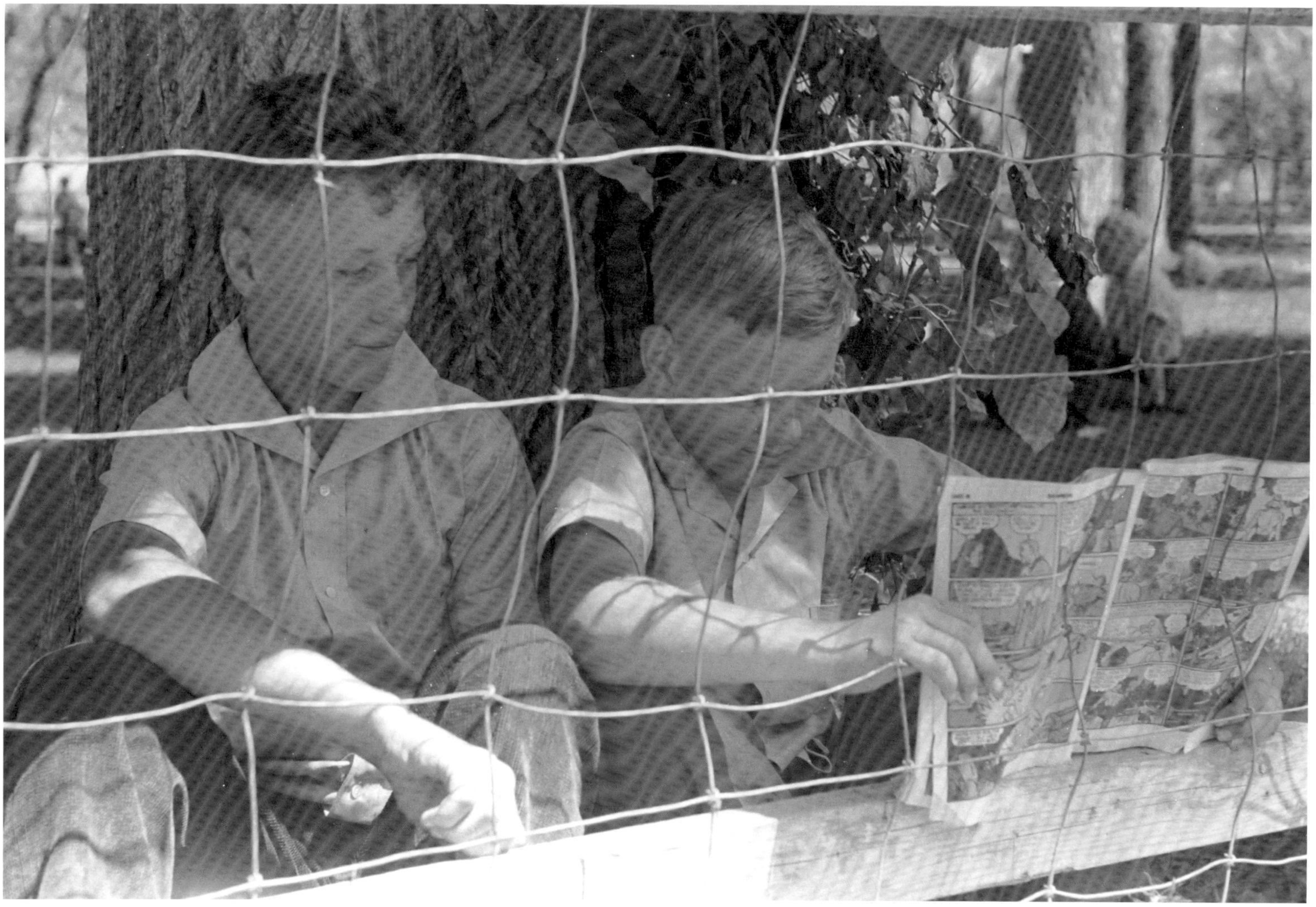

These Vale youngsters are absorbed in a comic book in 1941. Vale was settled in 1883 by ranchers. By the 1910s, the town had been linked by rail to Ontario and was an important agricultural community.

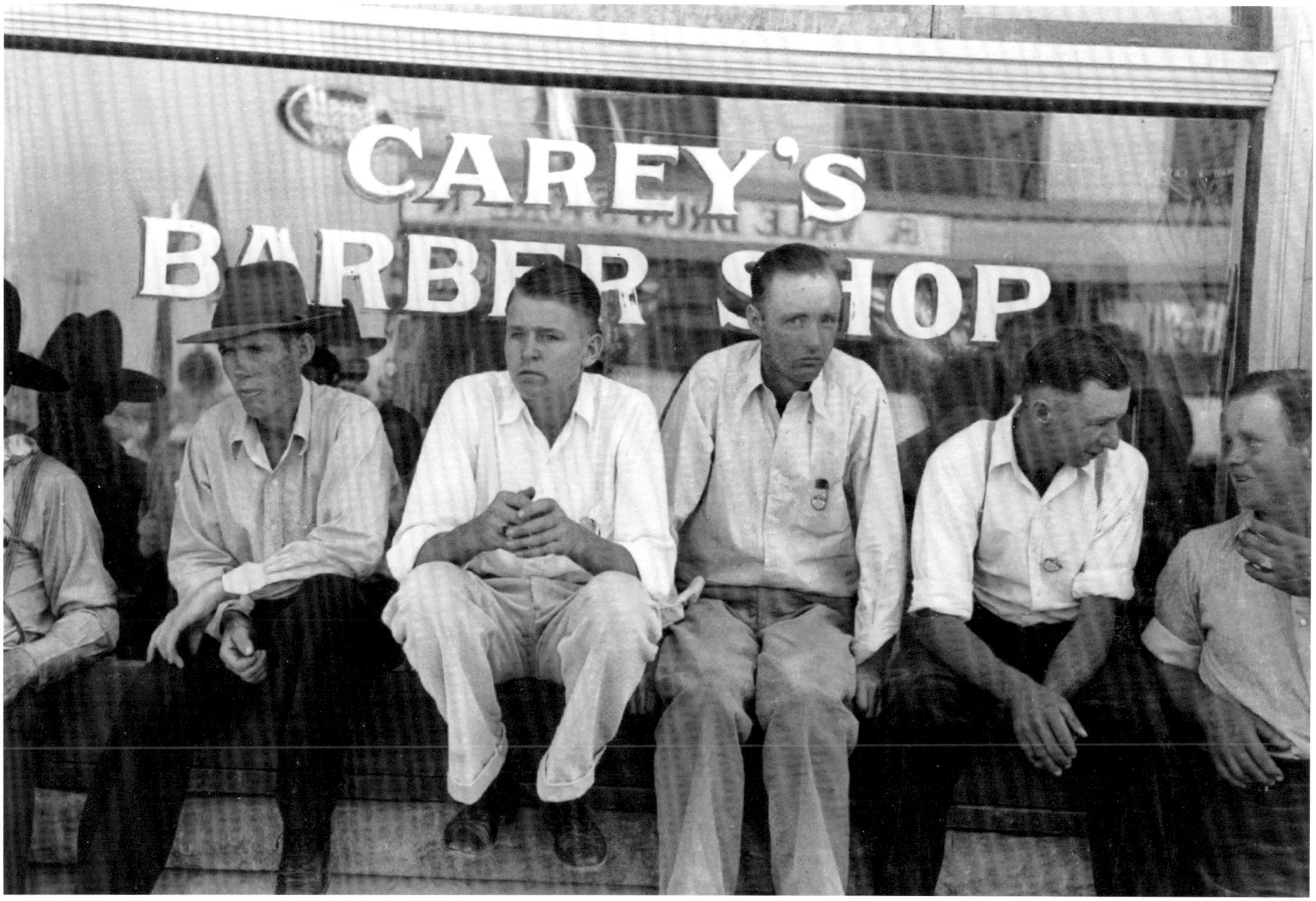

The Fourth of July in Vale, outside Carey's Barber Shop, in 1941.

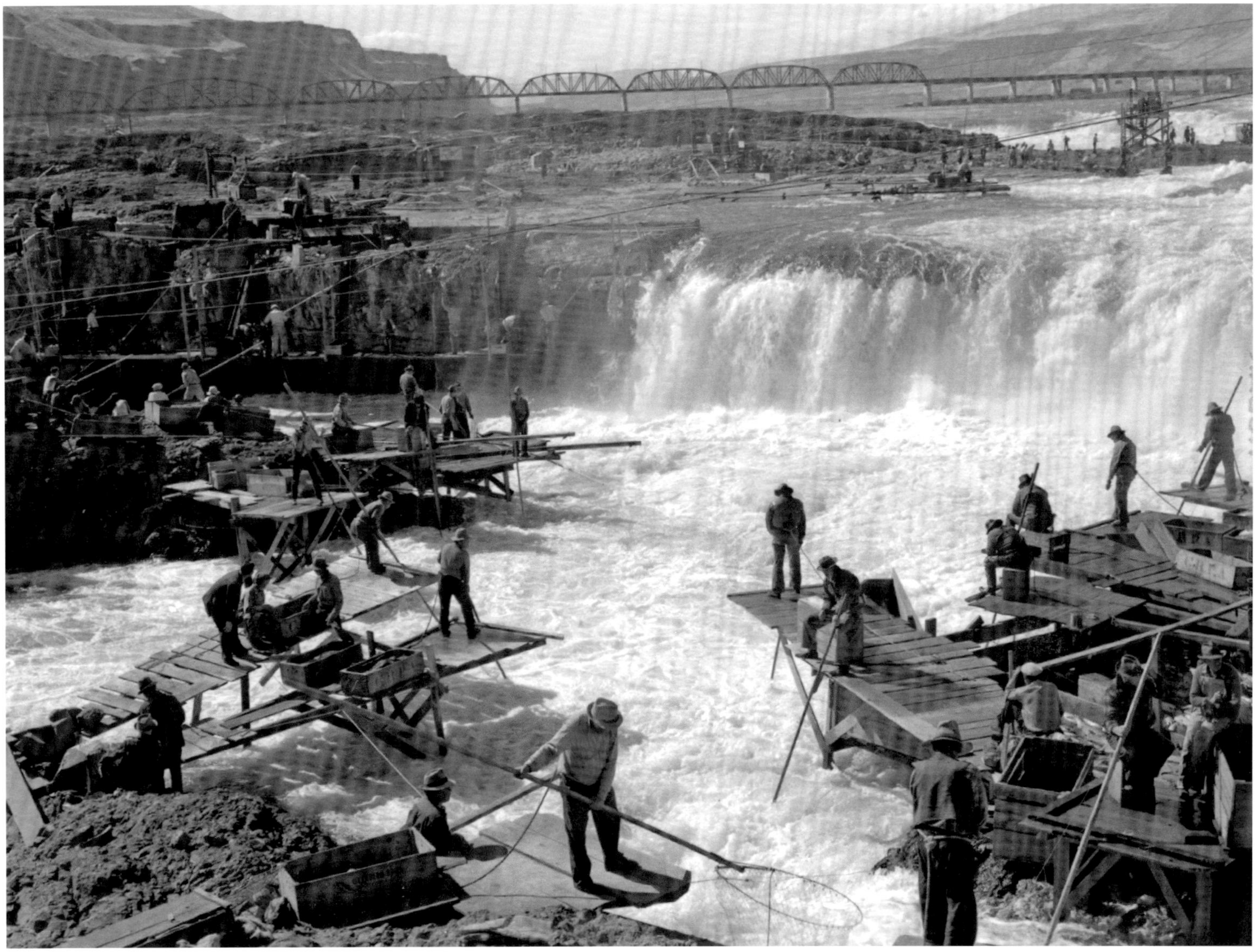

Indians are shown fishing for salmon at Celilo Falls in 1941. After The Dalles Dam flooded these fishing waters in 1957, Native Americans received $4 million in compensation to spend on timber and tourism. Salmon can still migrate upriver to spawn, using fish ladders installed alongside this dam and others on the Columbia River for this purpose.

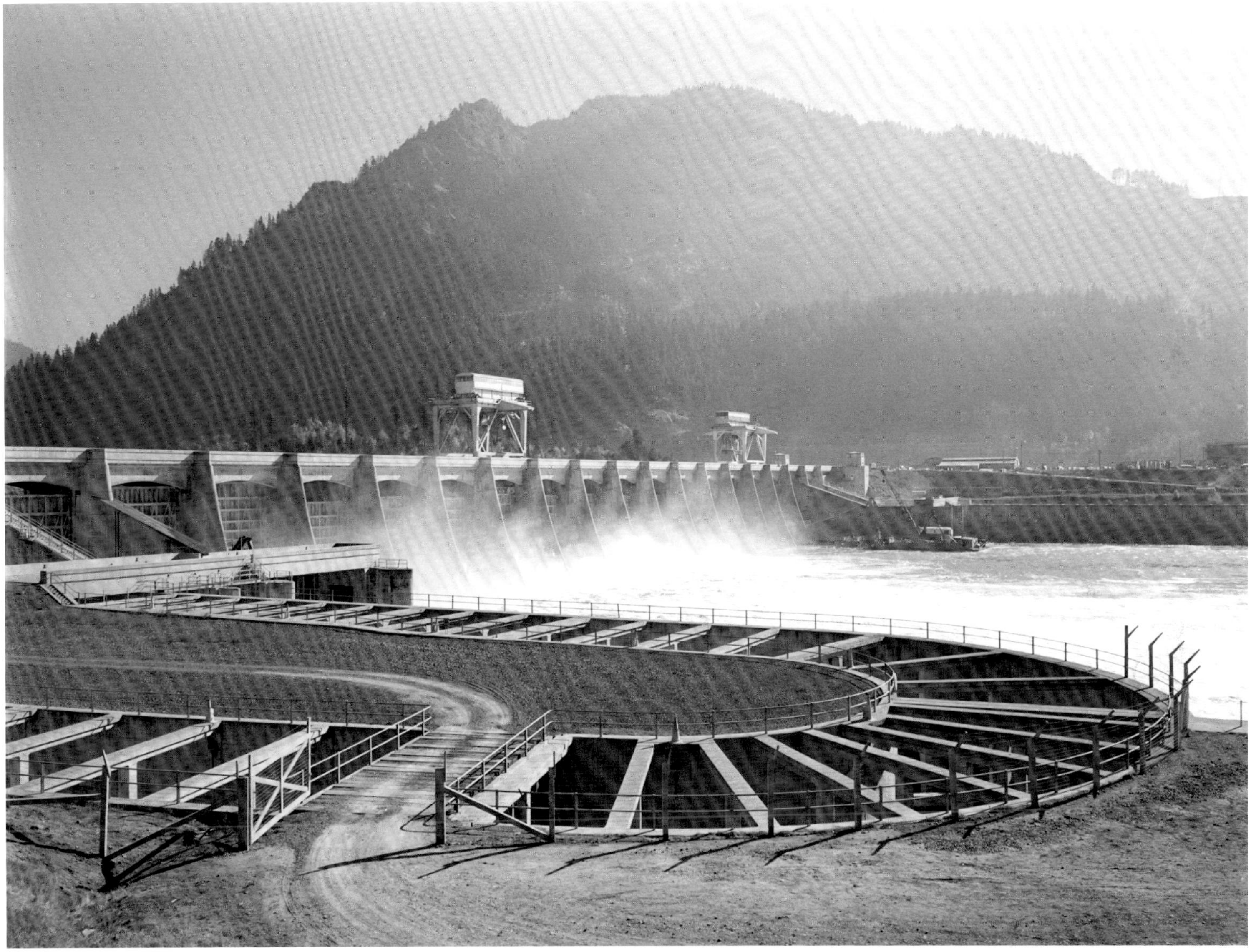

Bonneville Dam and its fish ladders on the Columbia River, as they appeared in 1941. Bonneville Dam is just west of The Dalles Dam and is the first dam circumnavigated by migrating salmon, which make use of the ladders to bypass the obstacle.

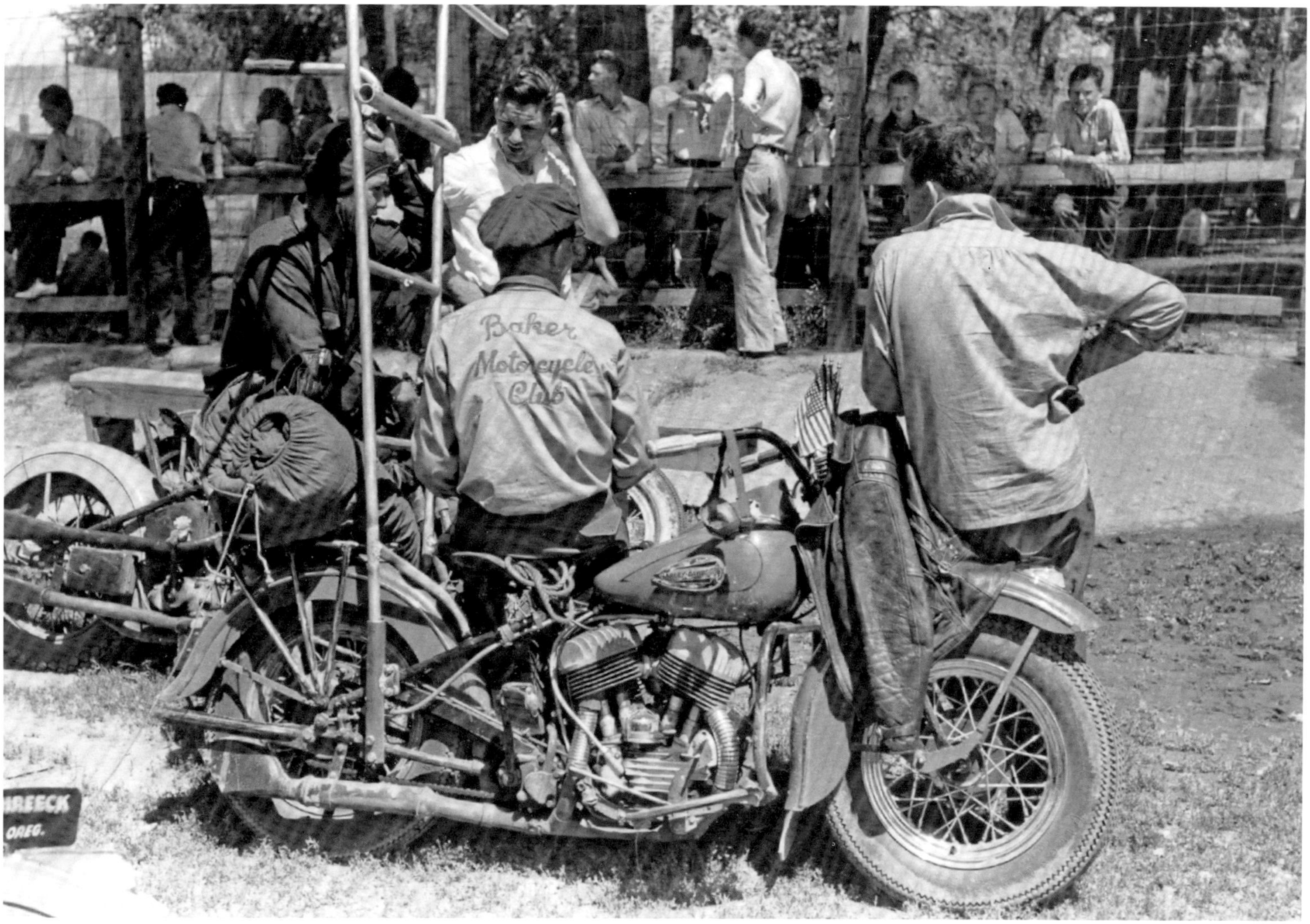

Oregon bikers of 1941. Then as now, Harley-Davidson was a popular brand.

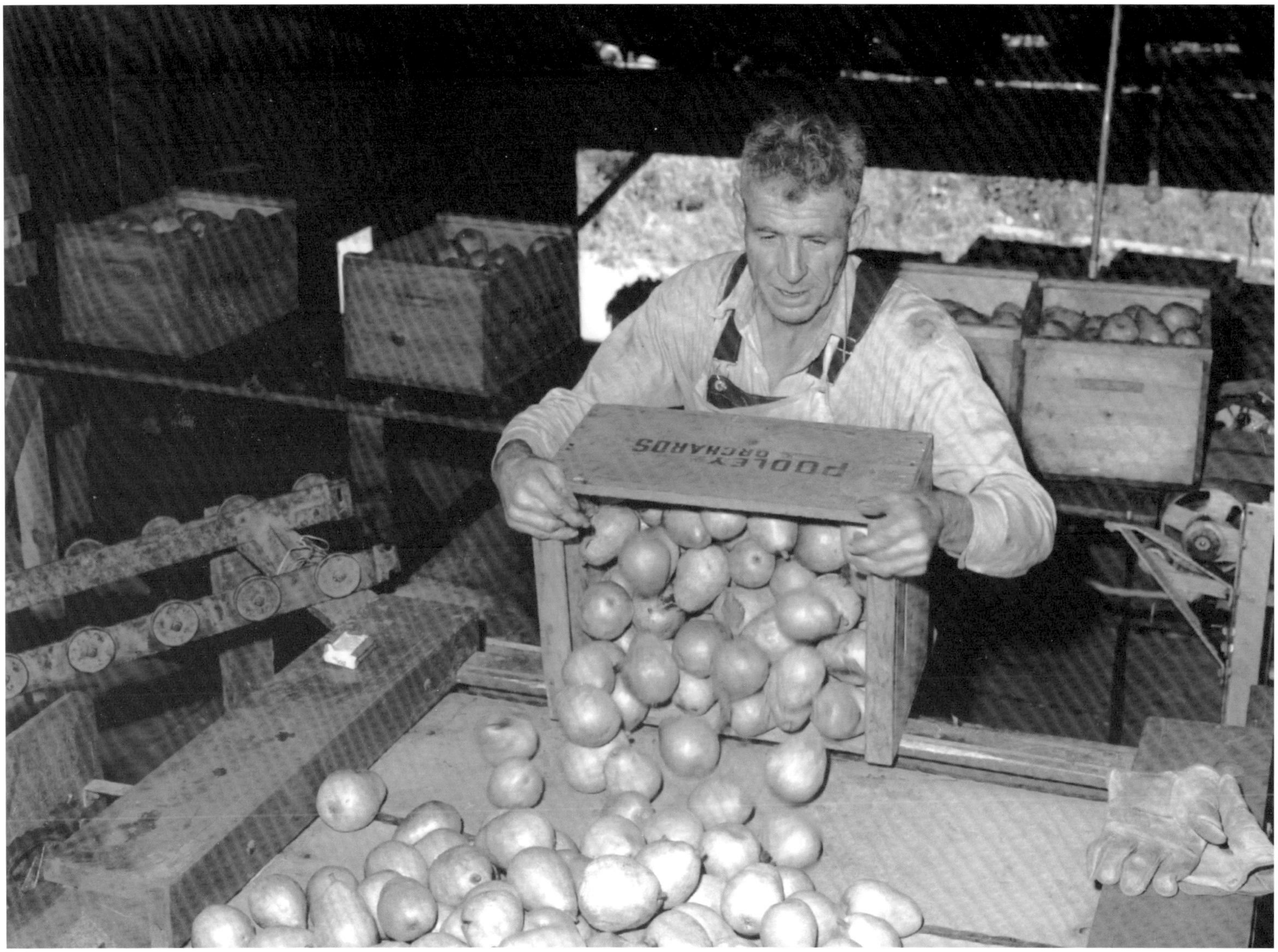

Freshly picked pears are dumped into a chute that leads to washing vats at this Hood River plant in September 1941. Hood River was settled in 1858 and grew as a lumber town and center for the fruit-growing industry. Since the 1980s, Hood River has been known as a recreational area for windsurfing on the Columbia River.

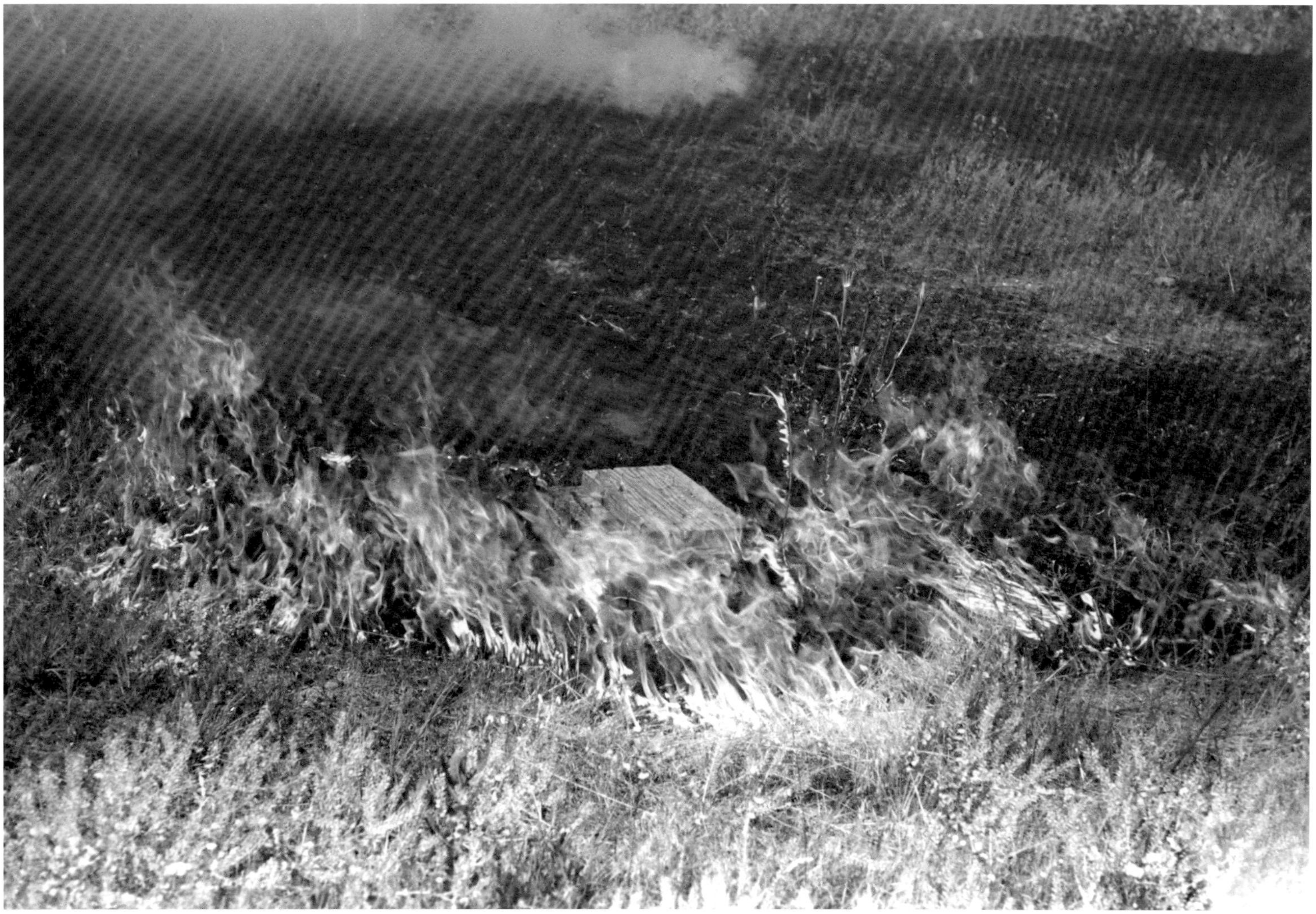

Dry conditions in eastern Oregon have often led to grass fires, like the one burning here in 1941.

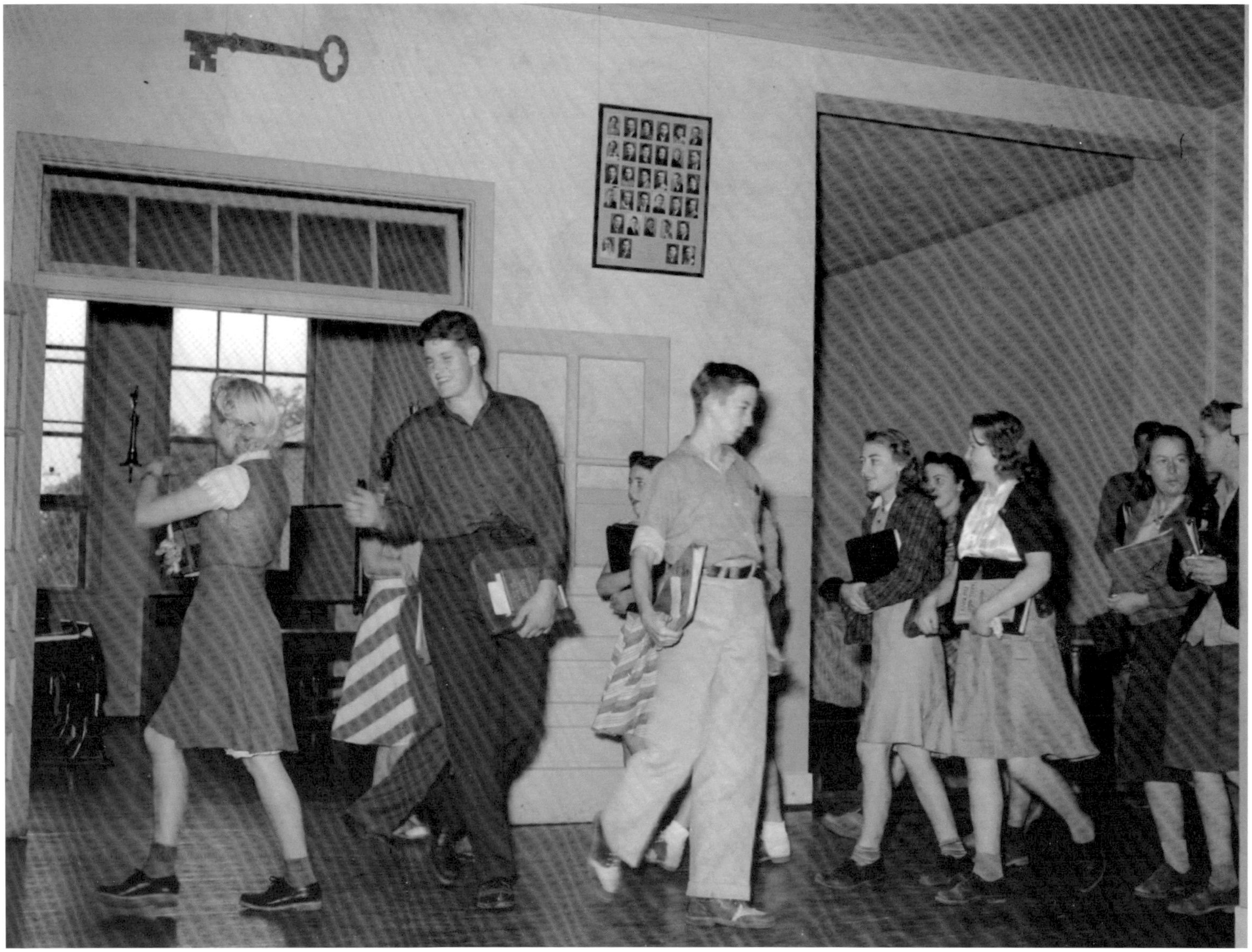

High school boys and girls walk between classes at their Hermiston school in 1941. During World War II, schools like this one would change their curricula to reflect the realities of the war and prepare students for potential military service.

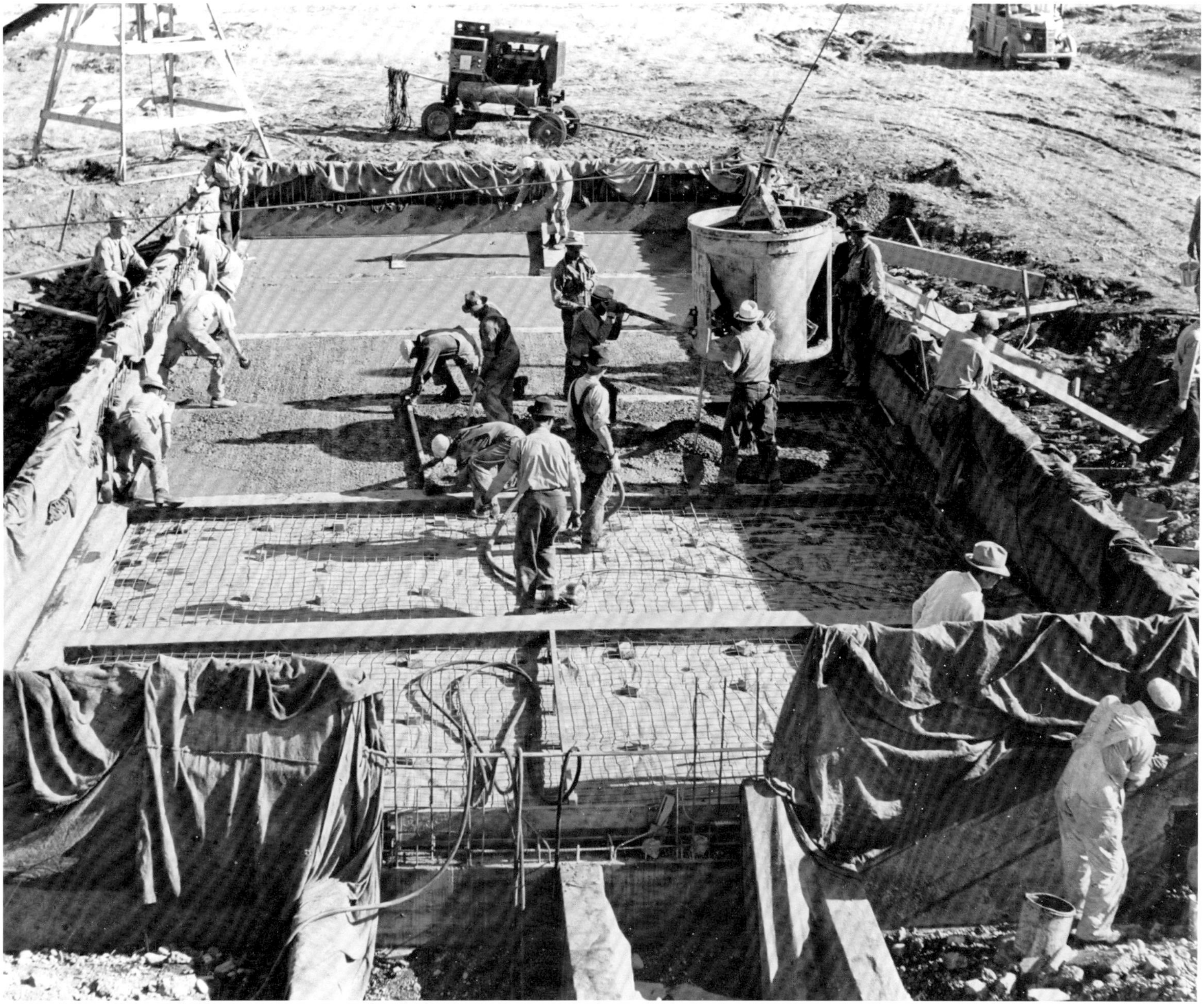

Workers pour concrete during construction of igloo number 5E34 at the Umatilla Ordnance Depot in 1941. The Umatilla Army Depot opened in 1941 as a storage facility for the nation's ordnance and chemical weapons. The facility is still in use today, for storage of chemical weapons.

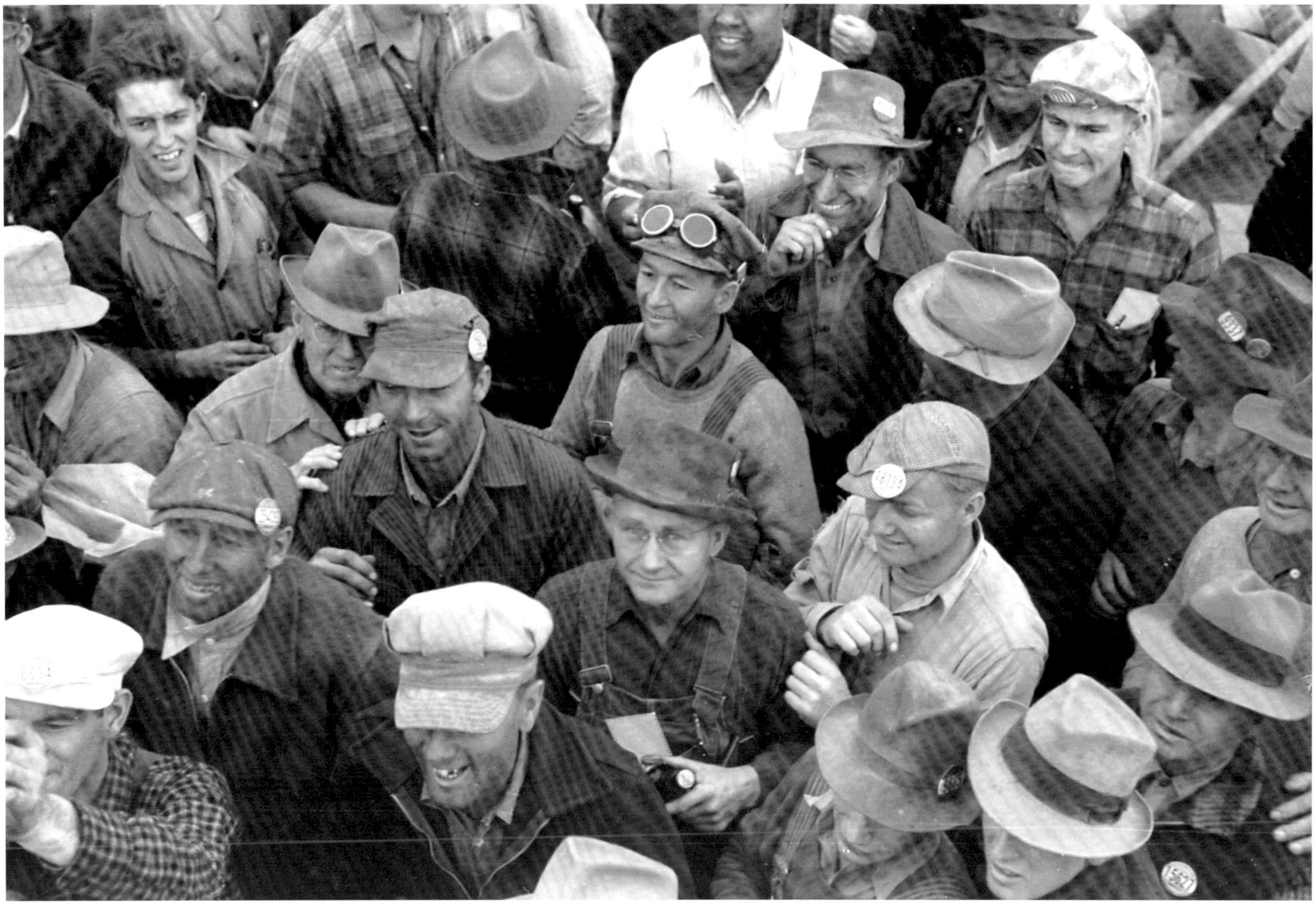

Employees at the Umatilla Ordnance Depot in Hermiston enjoy a beer party in September 1941, given by the contractor as thanks for the 24 chemical and ordnance storage facility igloos built in 24 hours by these men.

In the 1920s, the first migrant agricultural workers began to arrive in Oregon. During World War II, a shortage of labor in the fields on the West Coast led Congress to establish the Bracero Program with Mexico to ensure a continuous supply of agricultural workers to the United States. The program ran between 1942 and 1964. Many Americans who relied on agriculture for their living opposed the hiring of these workers.

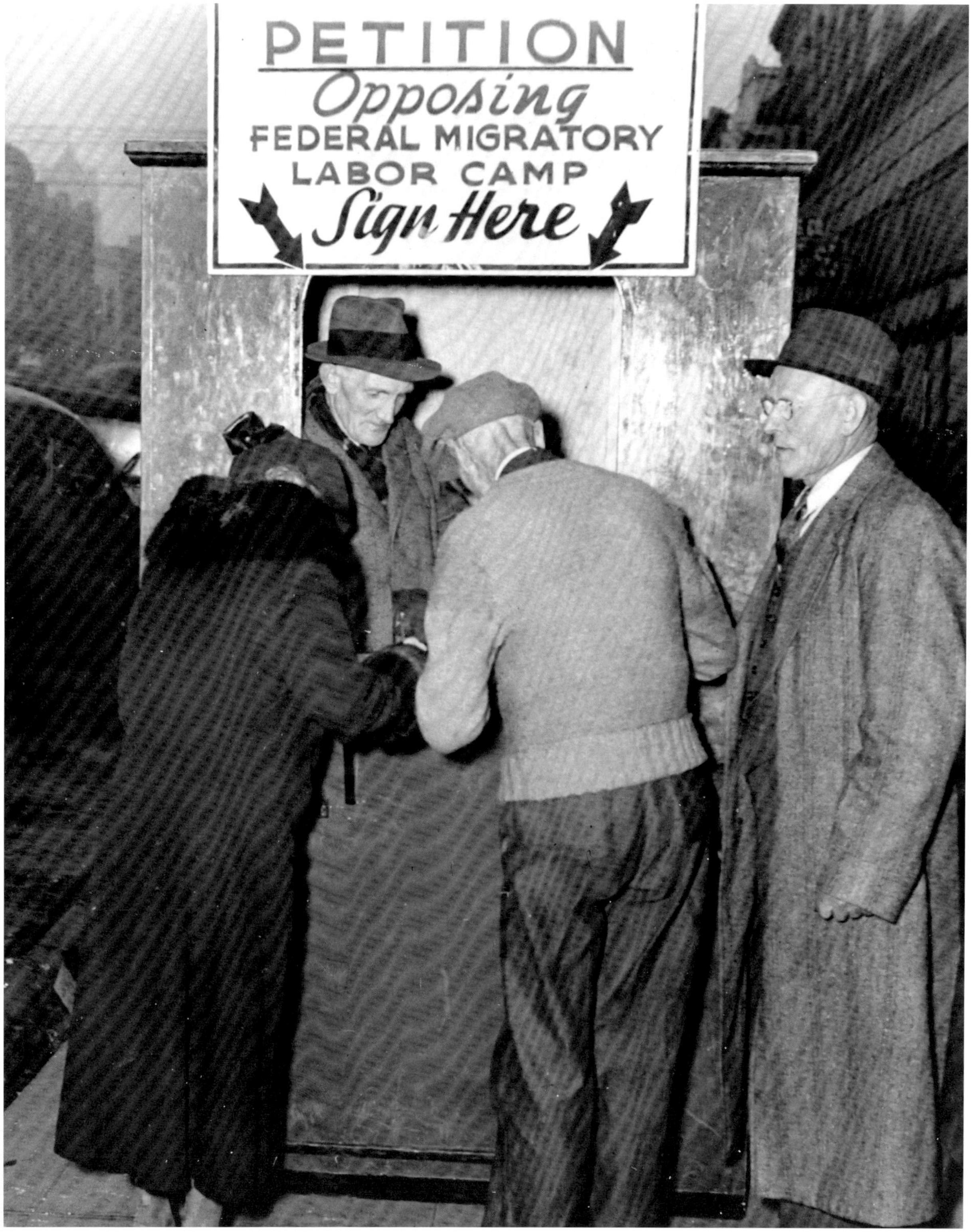

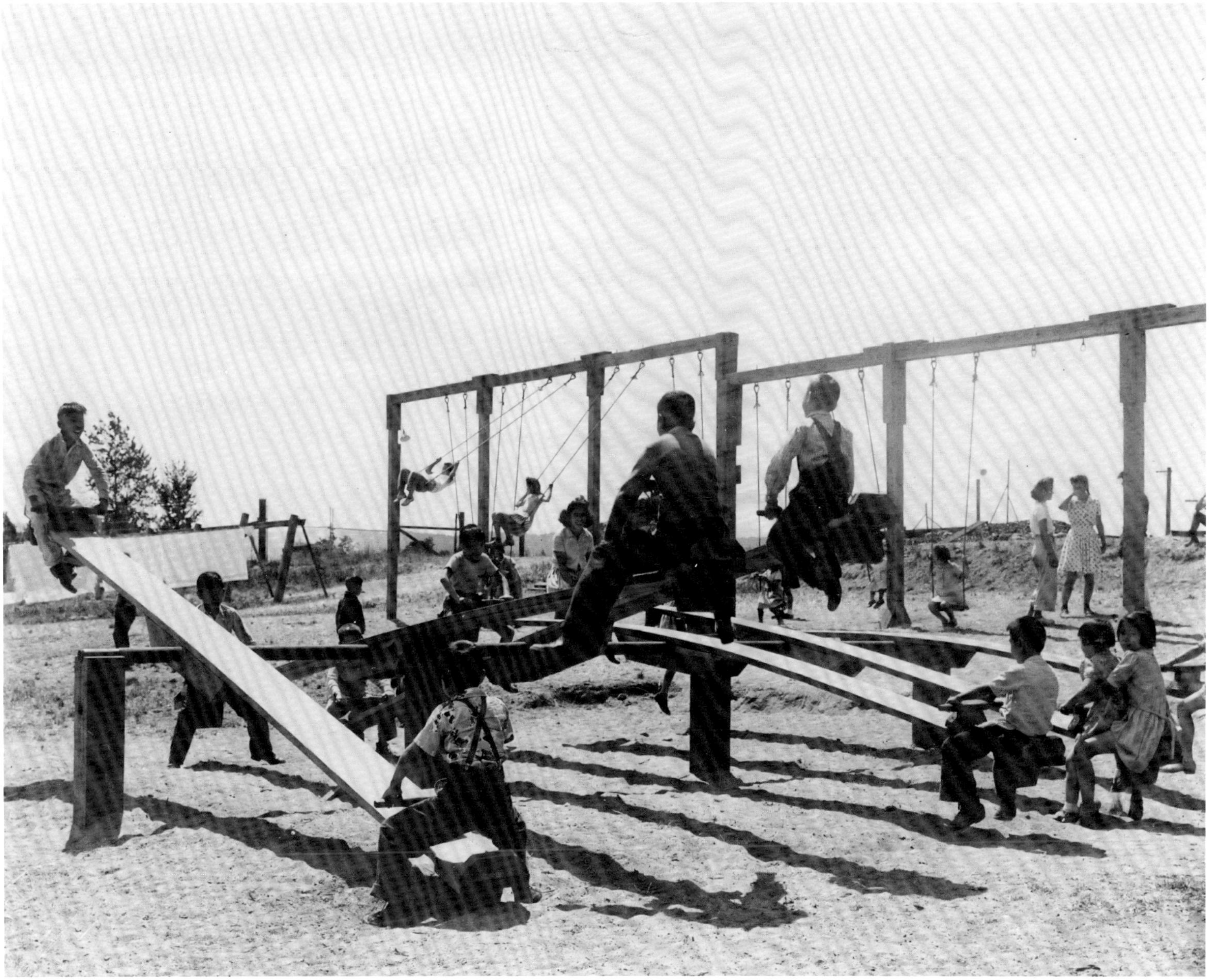

Children's playground in the recreation area of the North Portland Assembly Center, where Japanese-Americans awaited transfer to internment camps during World War II.

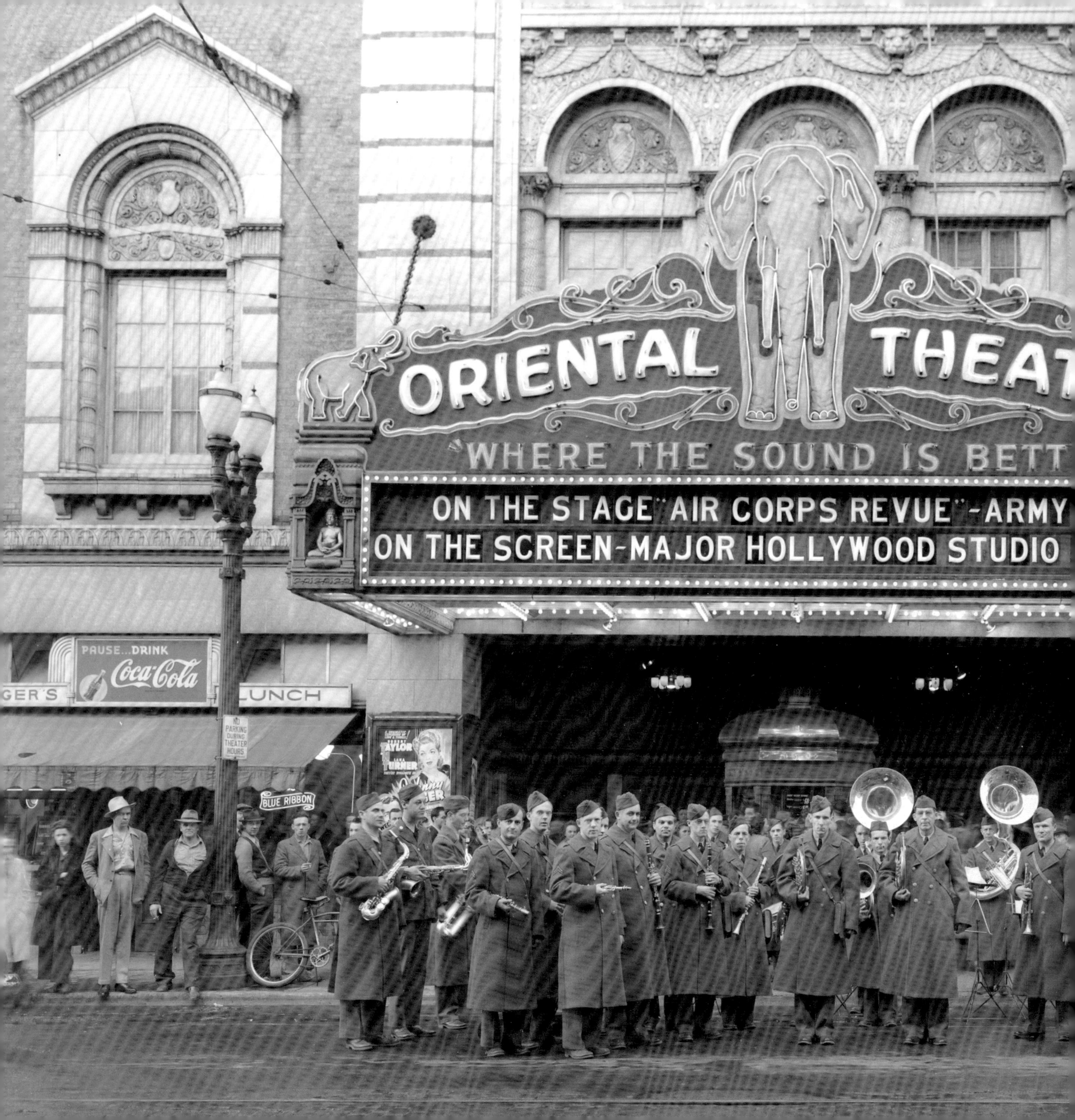
ORIENTAL THEAT
WHERE THE SOUND IS BETT
ON THE STAGE "AIR CORPS REVUE" - ARMY
ON THE SCREEN - MAJOR HOLLYWOOD STUDIO
PAUSE...DRINK
Coca-Cola
LUNCH
NO PARKING DURING THEATER HOURS
BLUE RIBBON

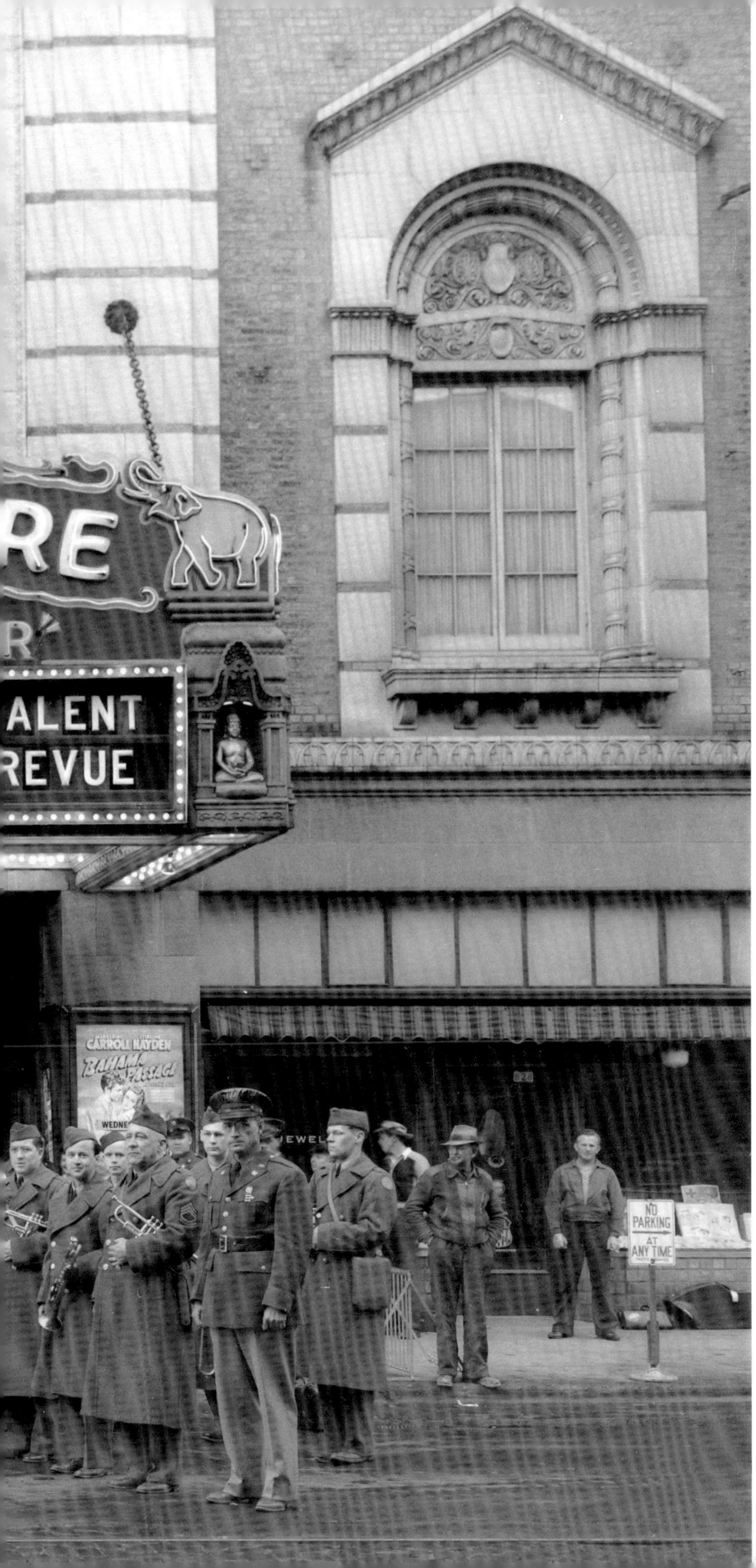

An air corps band poses for a group shot on Grand Avenue in front of the Oriental Theatre in Portland, around 1942. The Oriental Theatre was one of a series of movie palaces built in Portland during the early twentieth century.

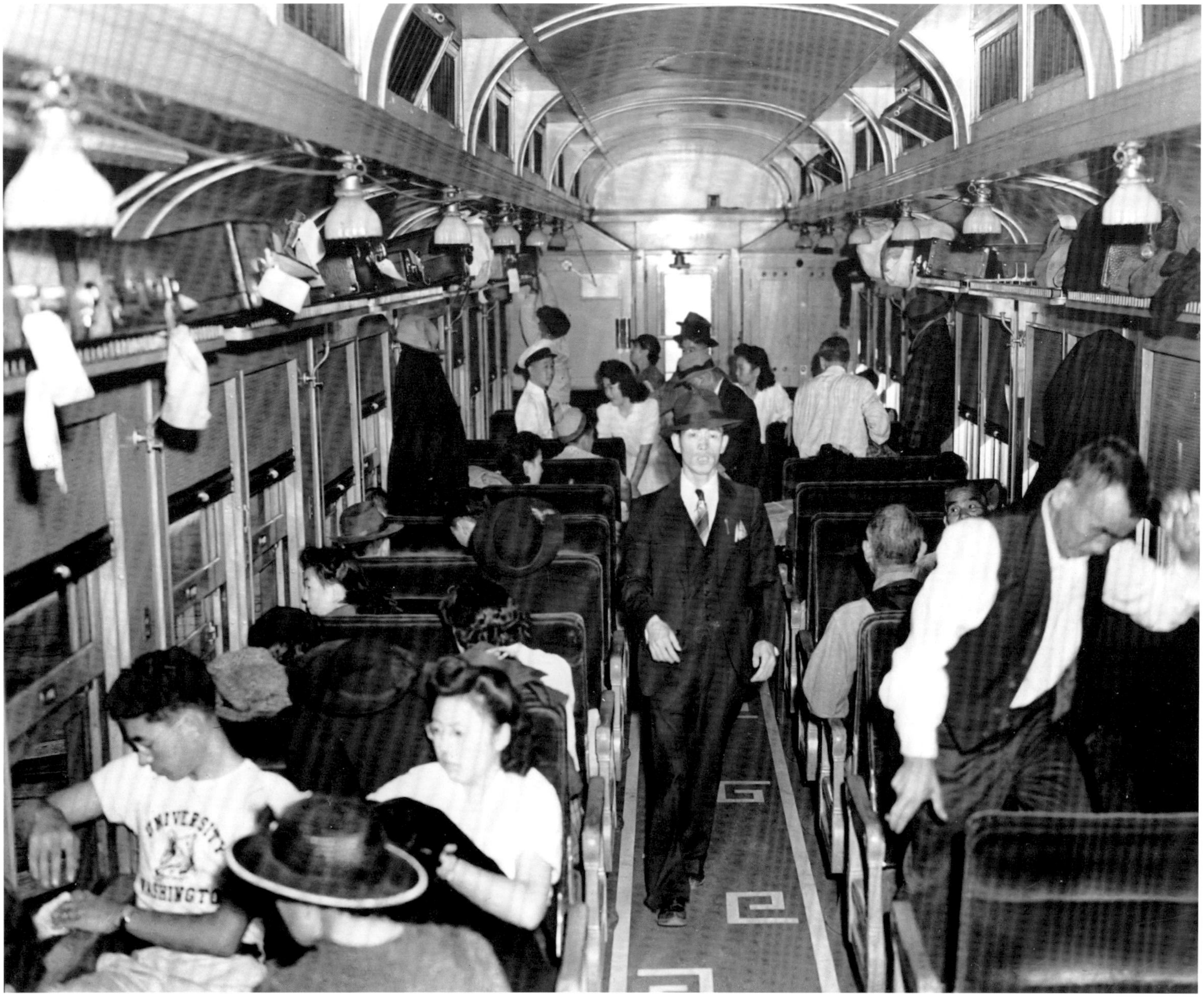

Japanese-Americans and resident aliens in Portland were evacuated from their homes in 1942 and taken by train to the North Portland Assembly Center. From there they were transferred to internment camps to await the outcome of World War II.

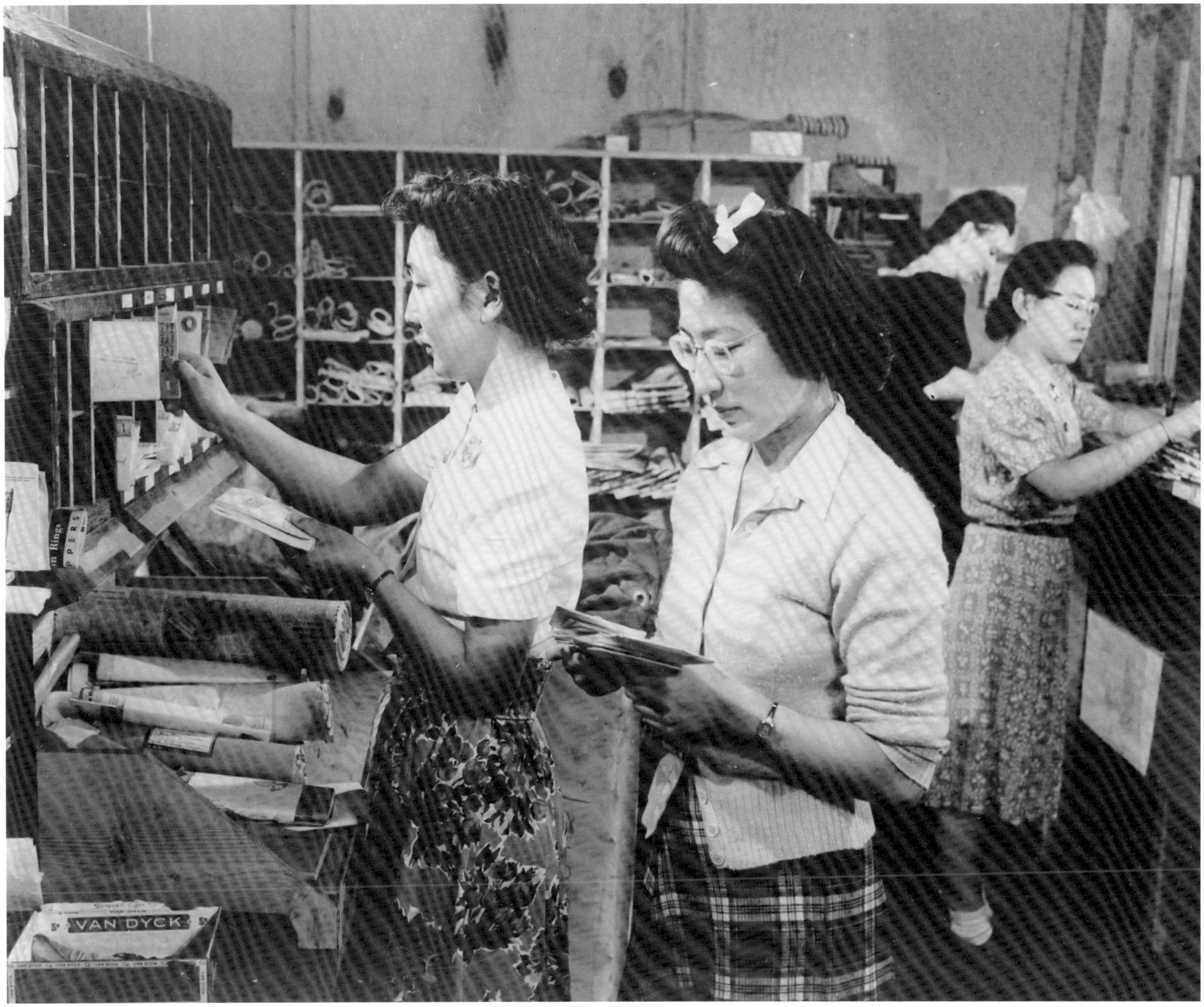

Scene at the post office at the North Portland Assembly Center, where evacuees were temporarily housed before being transferred to internment camps for the duration of the war.

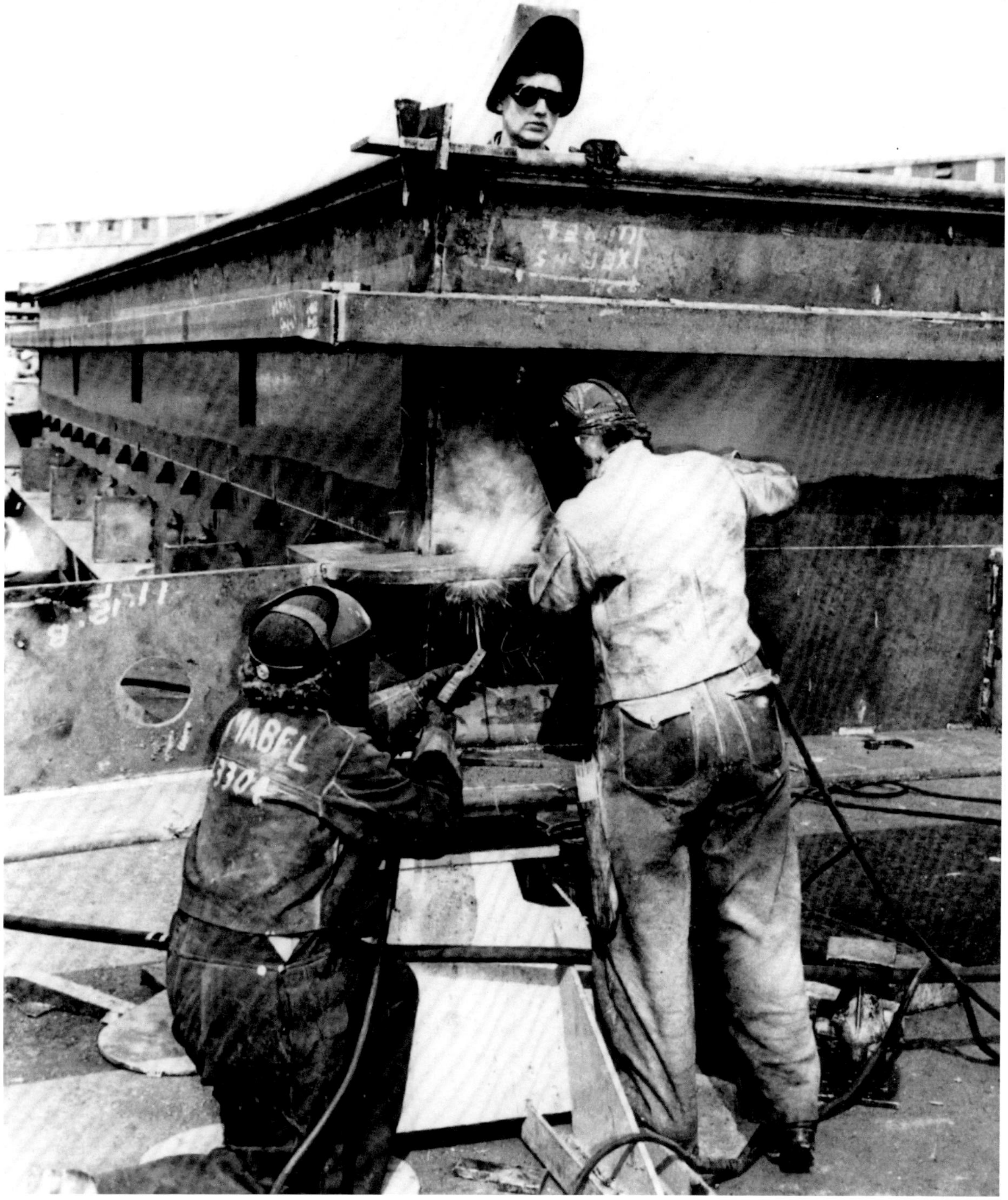

Three women work at welding a hatch to a ship, probably at the Kaiser Shipyards in Portland, during World War II. Women, minorities, and teenagers were eagerly sought after to work in the shipyards as Portland's war effort accelerated in 1943.

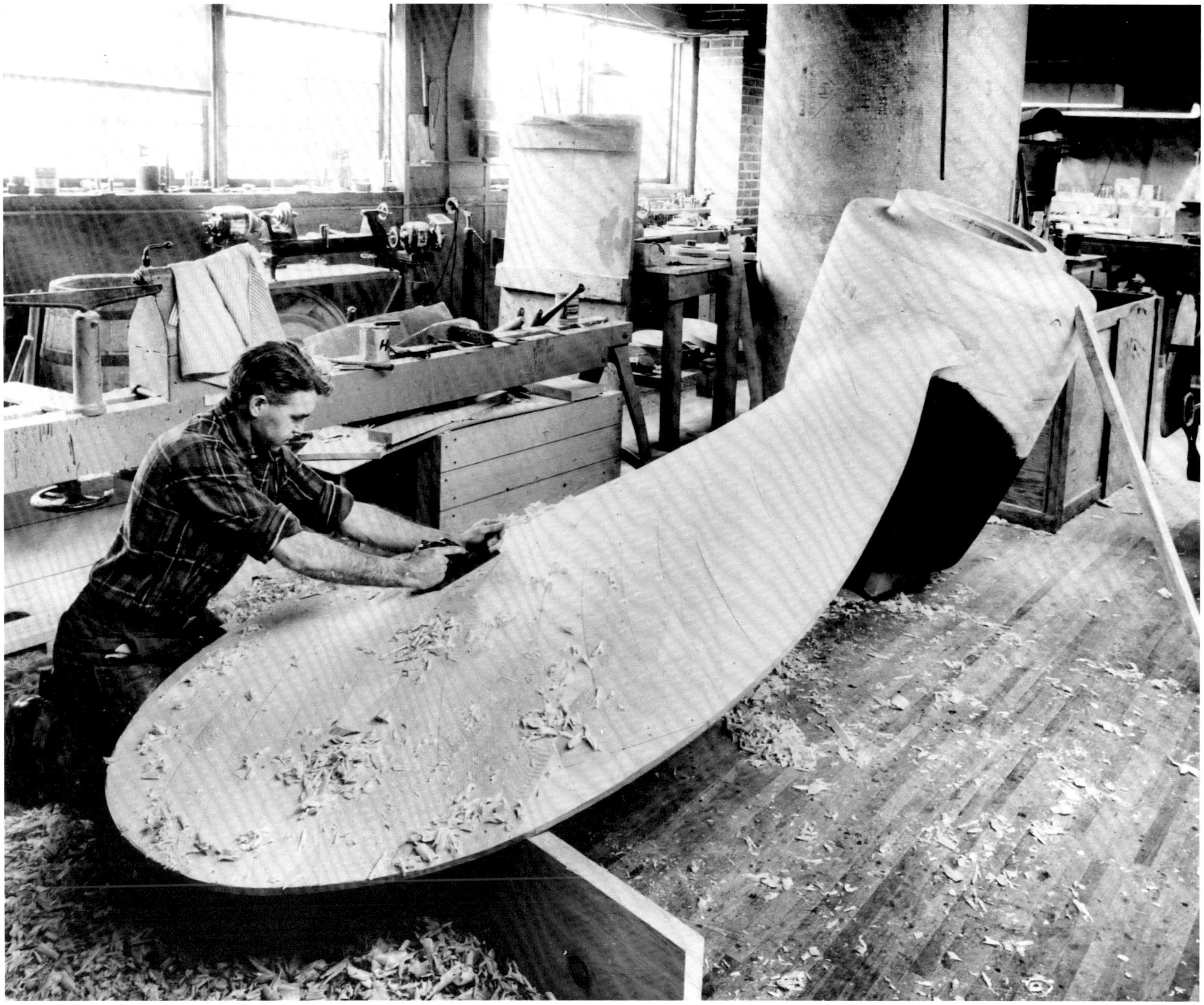

A Kaiser Shipyards employee makes a wood pattern for a cargo ship's metal propeller. The ship was bound for the Soviet Union, which was fighting on the Allied side during World War II.

Trucks carrying war materiel for Consolidated Freightways are halted in the mountains by a herd of sheep during World War II.

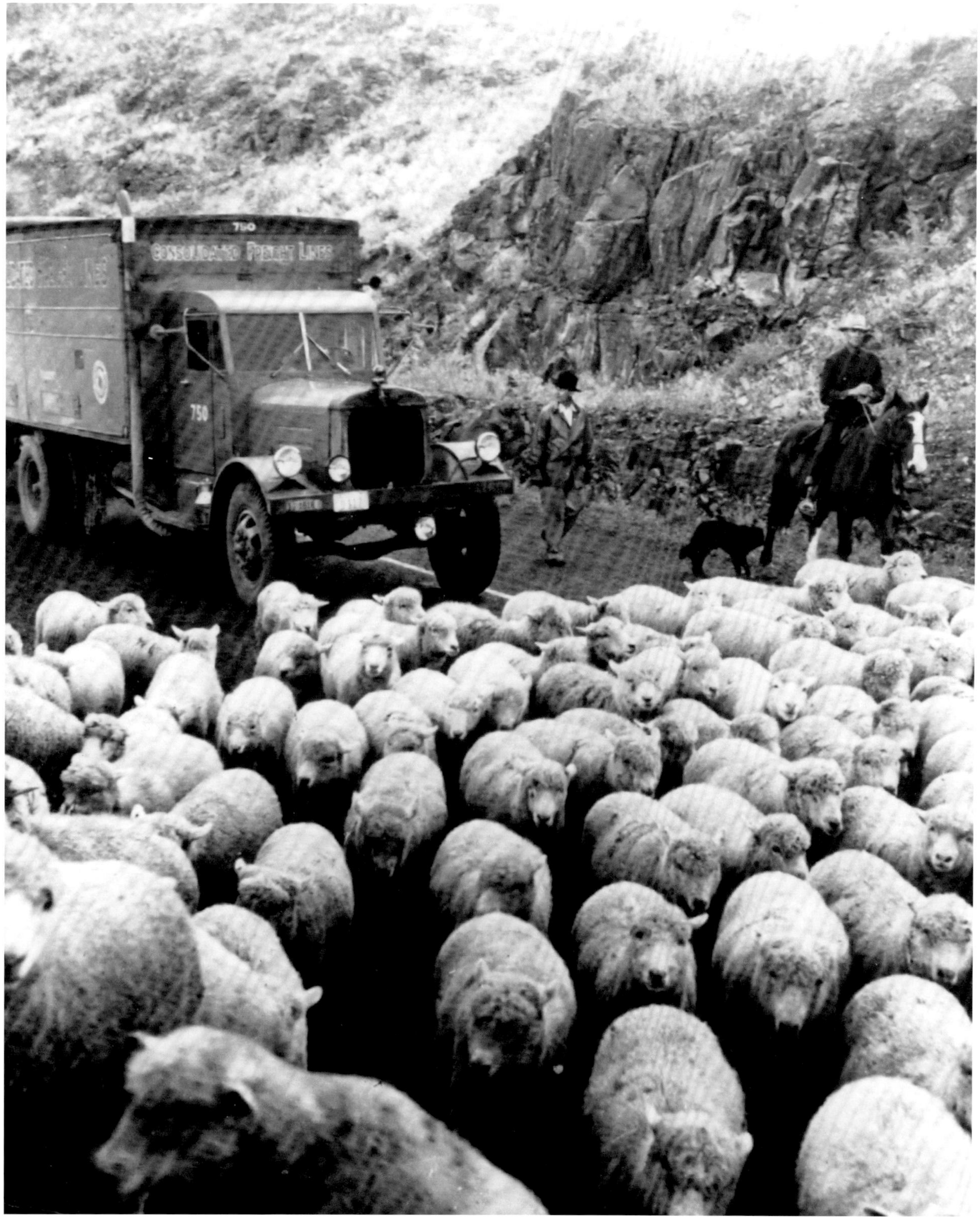

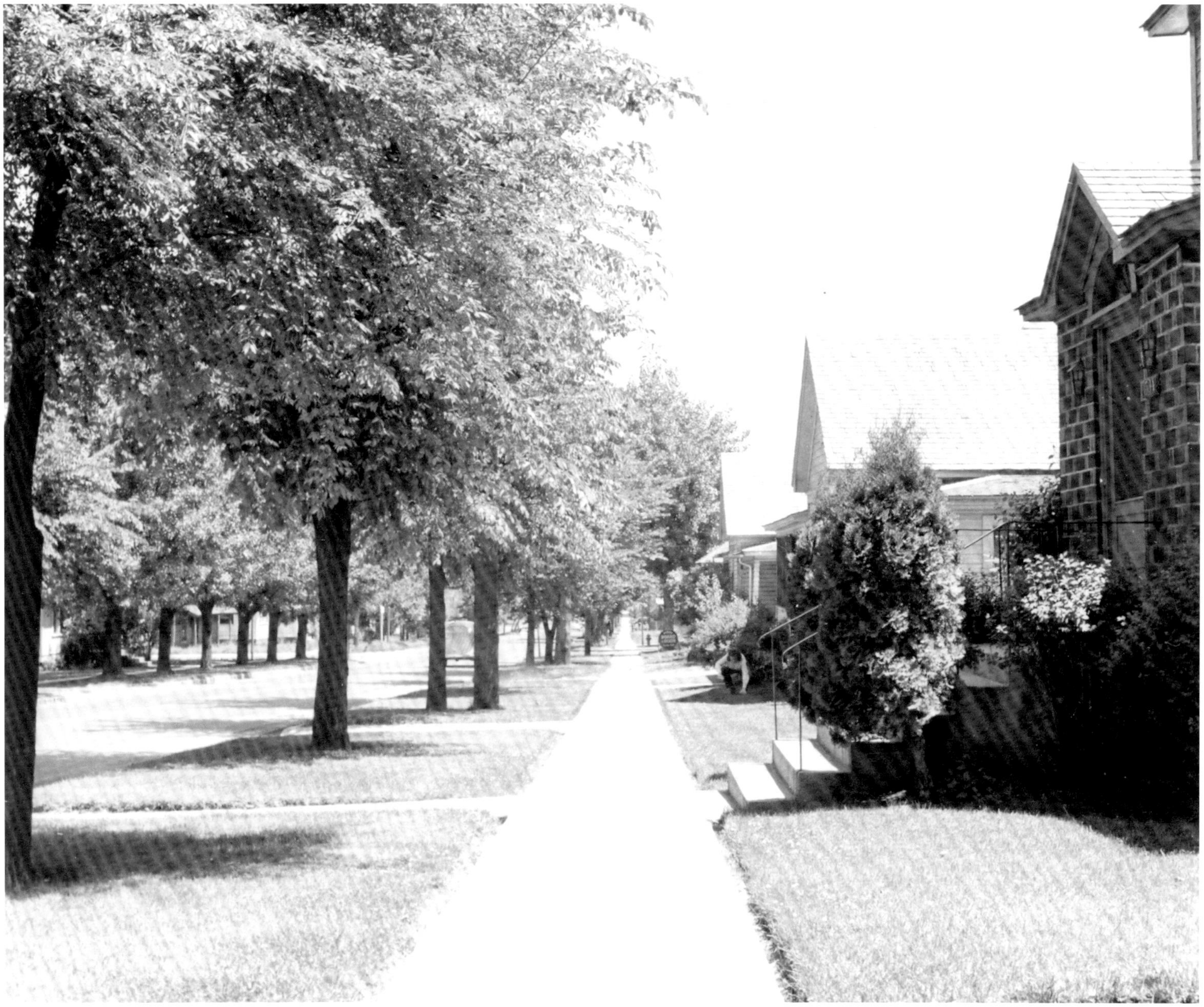

A residential neighborhood in Klamath Falls as it appeared during the war year 1942. Klamath Falls became a fairly prosperous town, owing to its timber industry and agriculture, which was aided by the Klamath Project. The project first brought irrigation to the dry lands of the area beginning in 1907, resulting in increased crop production. The 225,000 acres irrigated would yield harvests of barley, alfalfa, potatoes, wheat, and other crops.

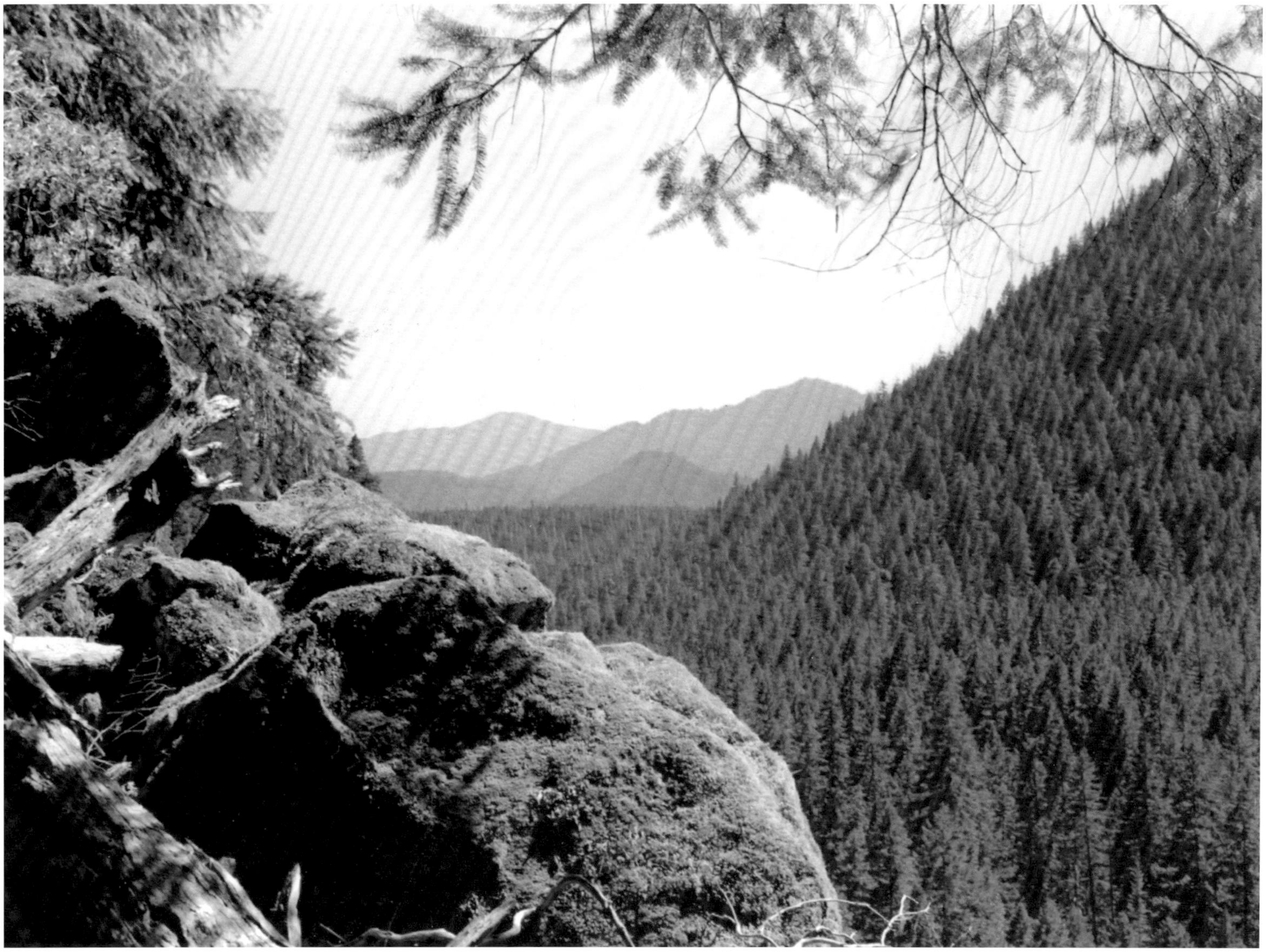

A view of the Willamette National Forest, in Linn County. Timber harvests in Oregon increased dramatically in the 1940s, but by the 1950s much of the old-growth forest in northwestern Oregon had been harvested.

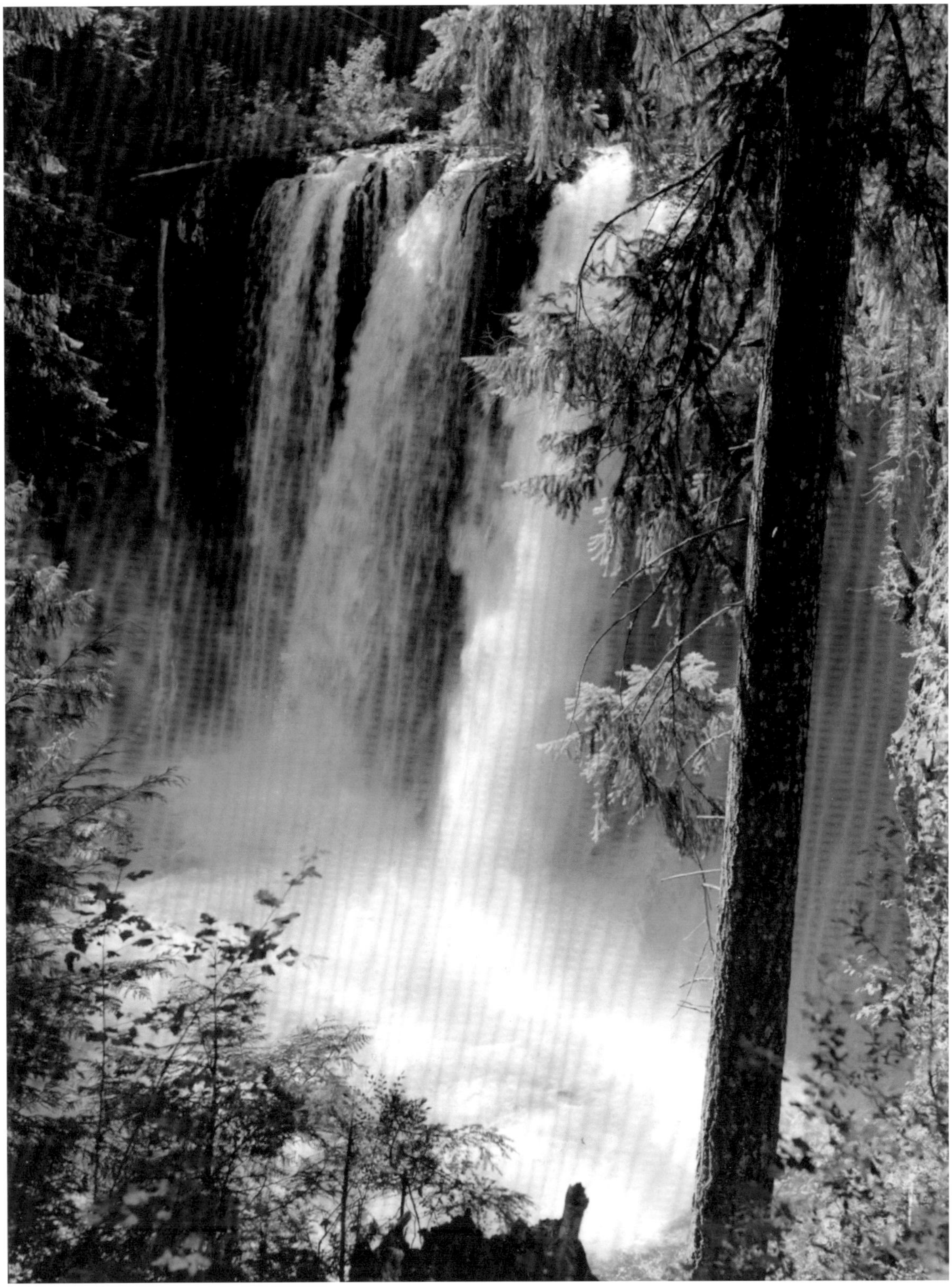

Tamolitsh Falls of the McKenzie River in the Willamette National Forest in Linn County, as it appeared in 1942. The McKenzie River is located in the Cascade Range in Lane County and joins the Willamette River near Eugene.

Logs are loaded onto trucks in Grant County in 1942. Settlers first came to the area in the 1860s to work in the gold mines. Other industries soon sprang up, including ranching and lumber mills.

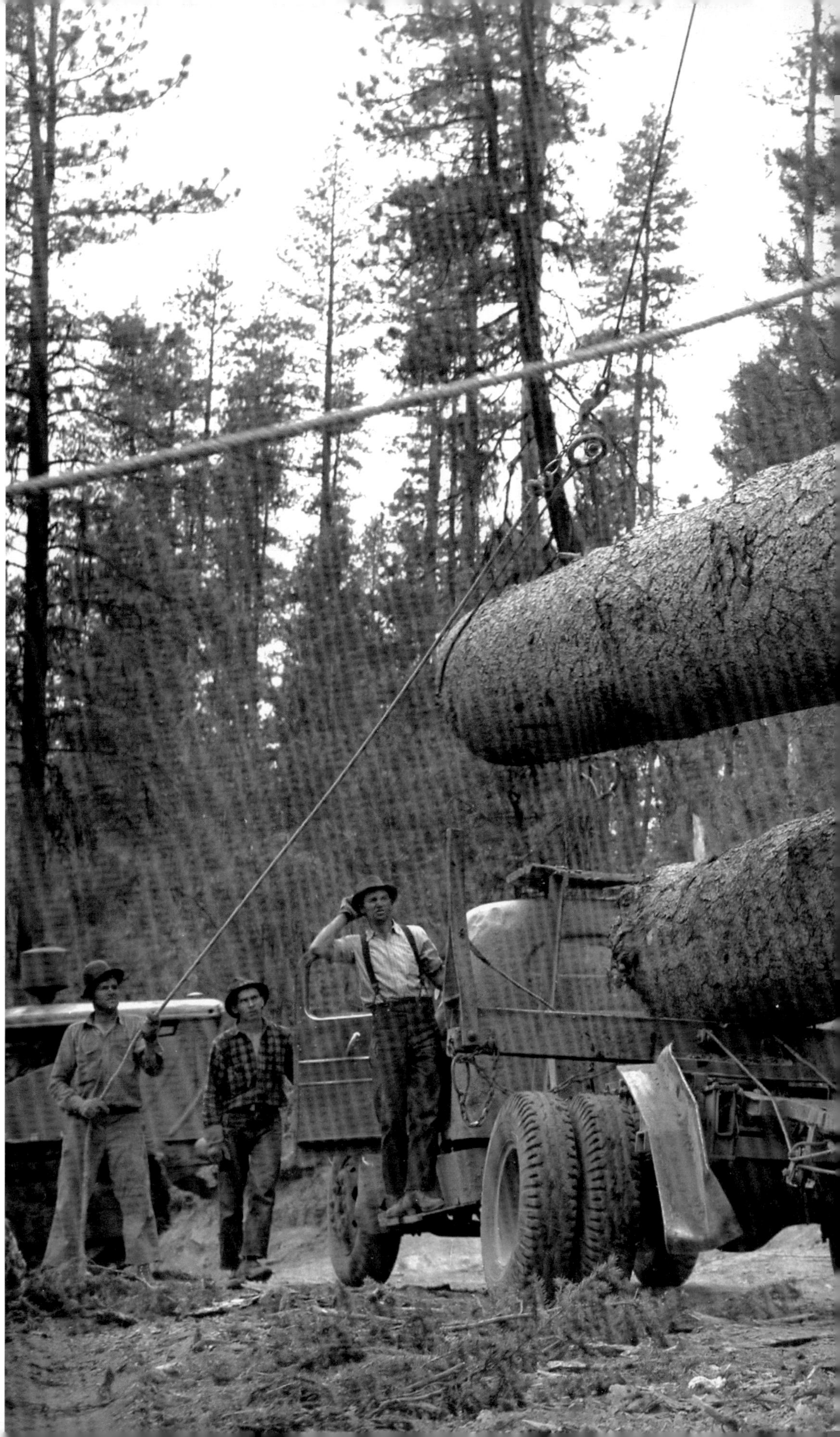

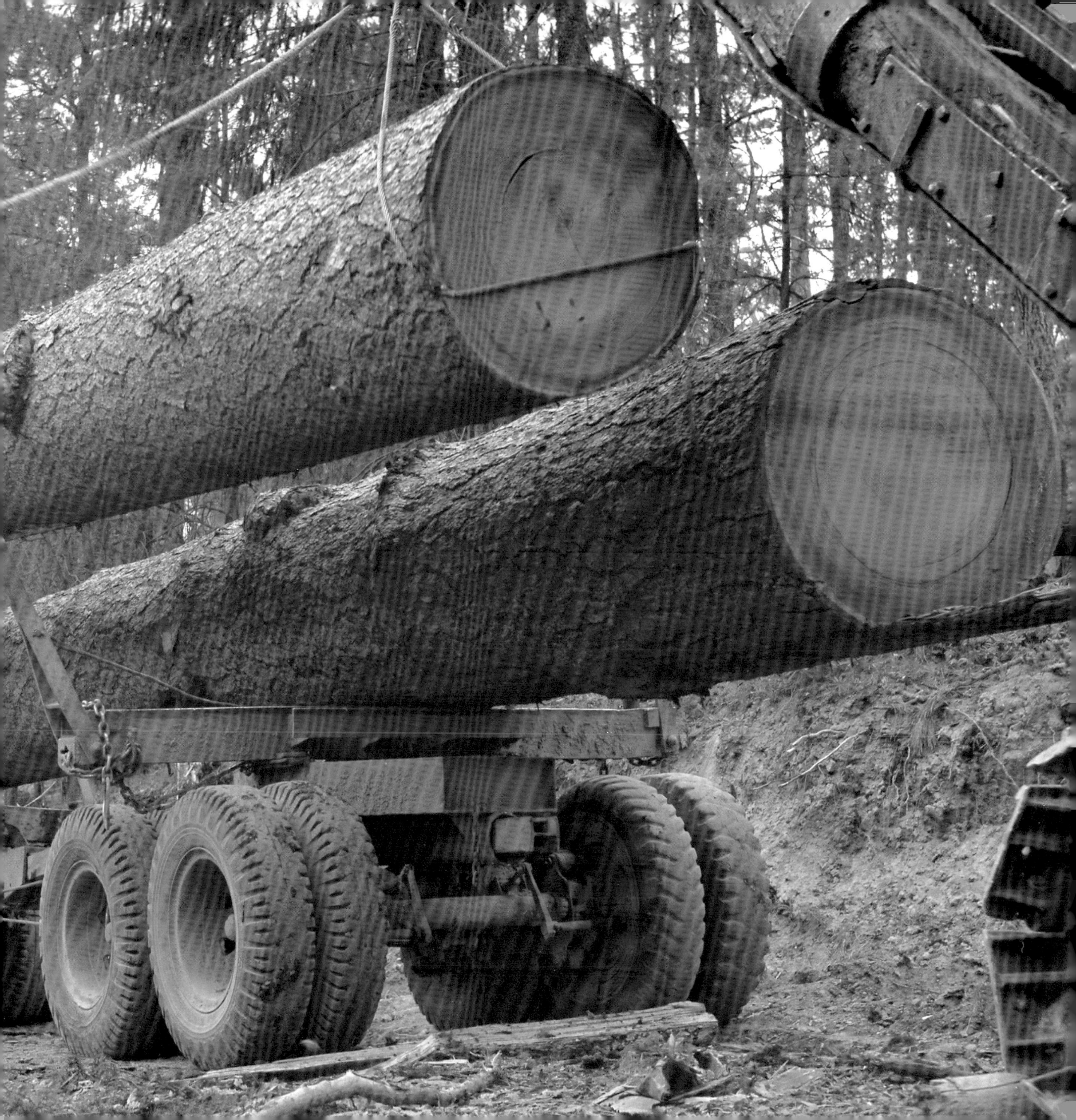

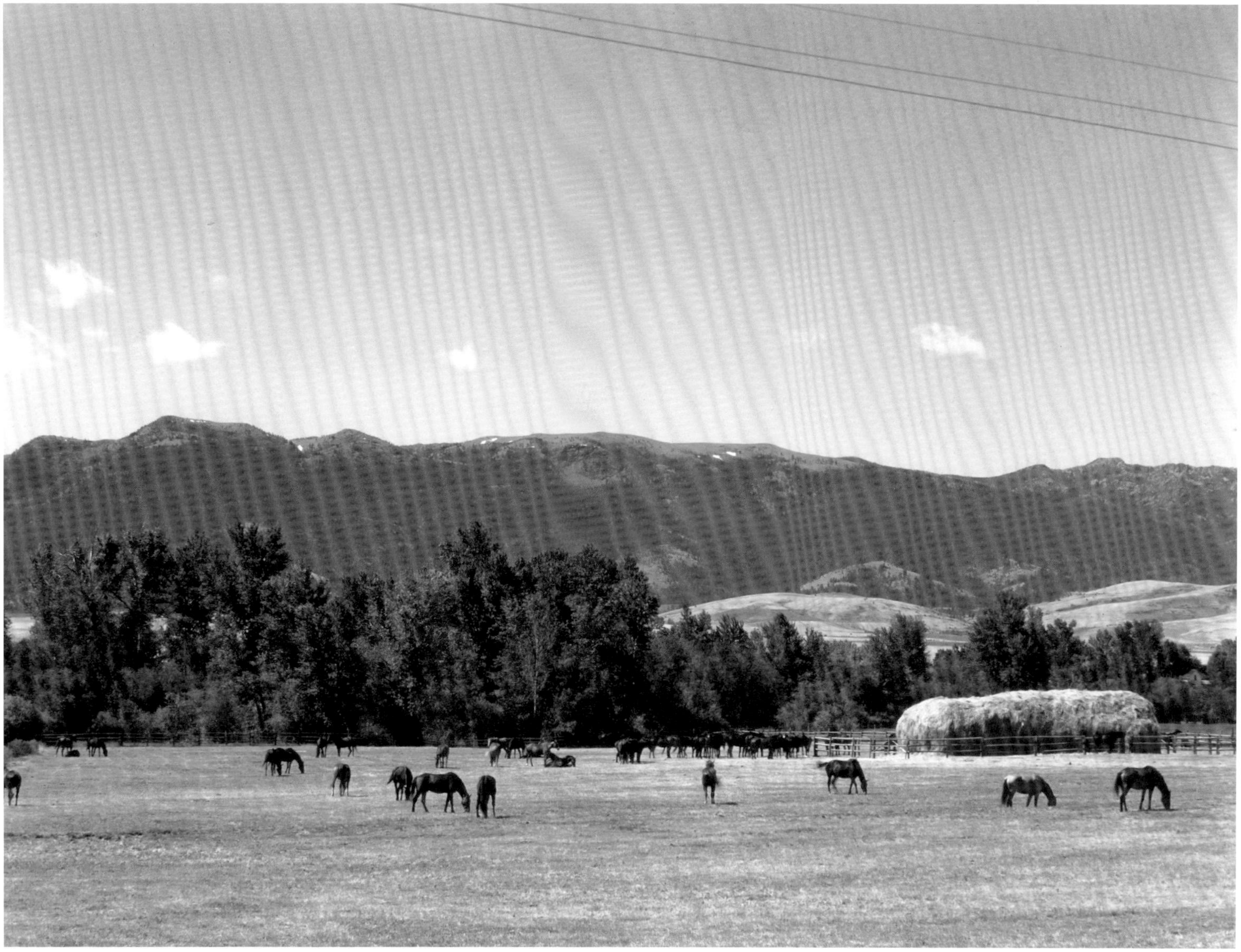

A horse-breeding ranch in Grant County. In the 1880s, many Chinese immigrants settled in the community of John Day and worked in the mining industry. Ing "Doc" Hay and Lung On founded a Chinese herbal remedy store (called the Kam Wah Chung Store), which treated residents of the area who worked in mines, lumber mills, and on farms and ranches, until 1948.

Vignettes of Modern Times

(1946–1971)

Oregon ended the Second World War prosperous and at peace, but industries like timber, fishing, and agriculture would begin to decline as the postwar era unfolded. Technological progress in the timber industry meant that fewer people were needed to harvest logs. Old-growth timber had been depleted, and replanted trees could not grow fast enough to satisfy the demand. To complicate matters, a record number of raw logs were being sent to Japan for processing. The fishing industry suffered from overfishing, which led to a decline in jobs. In the three decades following the war, small farms declined by more than 50 percent, usually giving way to large-scale corporate farms able to profit by operating large tracts of acreage. Retail giants like Safeway swept into Oregon after World War II, outcompeting hundreds of neighborhood and small-town grocery stores. Manufacturing jobs went into a decline in the late 1940s. By 1970, Oregon was experiencing a shift toward lower-paying jobs in the service-related industries, in the process eliminating even more jobs from other industries.

On the upside, new industries began in Oregon or moved to the state during the three decades after the war, which helped to diversify the economy. Among them were Tektronix, Intel, and Hewlett Packard in the field of high technology. In the early 1970s, Blue Ribbon Sports (now Nike), a sports shoe and apparel company, also set up shop. Tourism became a large industry in the state as many small towns throughout the state began attracting visitors eager to experience the state's natural beauty.

During the era, Oregon activists began to push for stronger social and environmental legislation. Oregon broke new ground in the passage of a series of employment, housing, and public accommodation laws in the 1940s and 1950s for minorities. In the 1960s and 1970s, the state was a national leader in enacting legislation regarding comprehensive land-use planning, recycling, and the banning of fluorocarbons. New laws to protect timberlands would eventually pose further challenges to Oregon's logging industry. Between 1982 and 1992, approximately 40,000 Oregon lumber workers would lose their jobs.

Oregon continues to attract visitors in search of the great outdoors today.

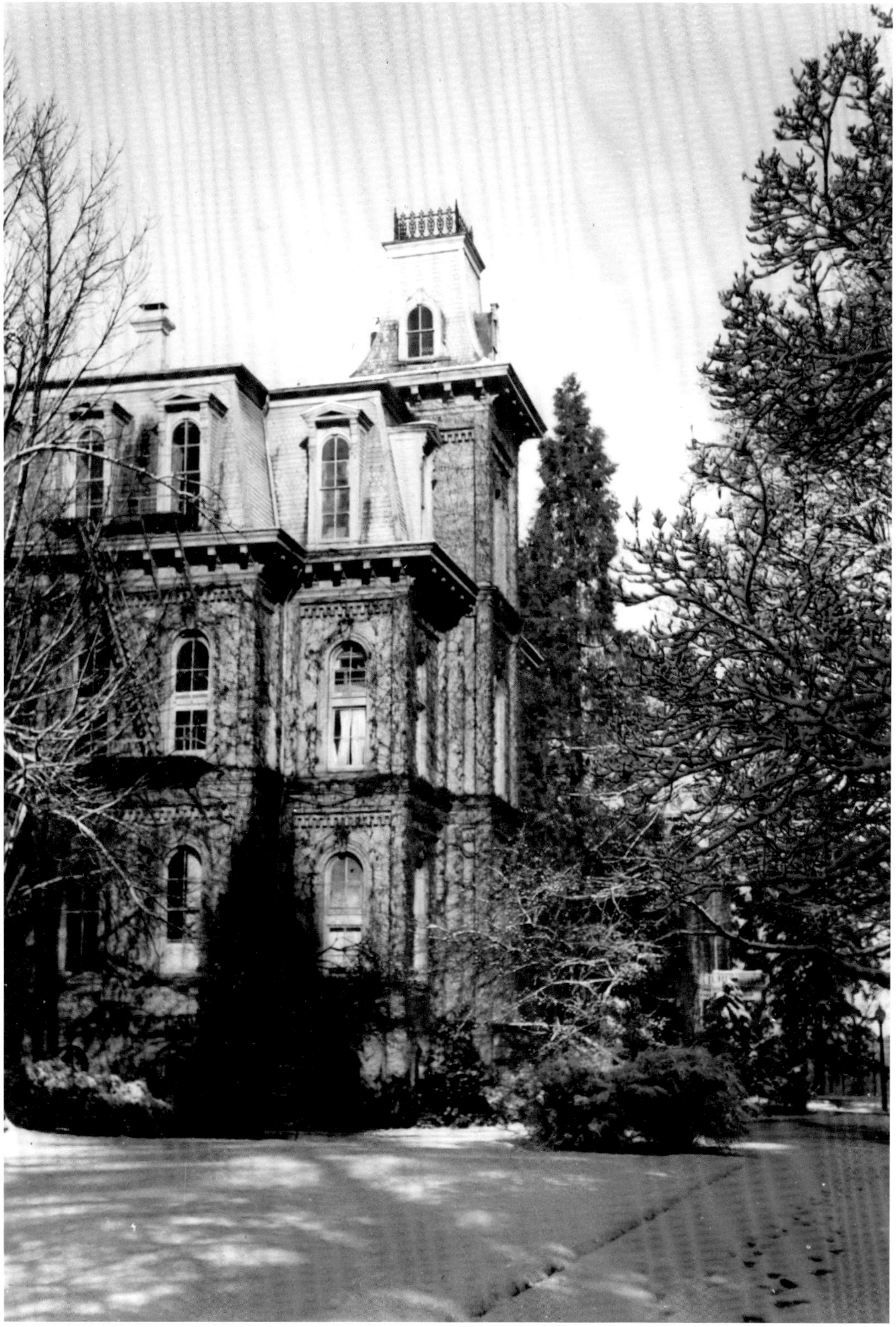

Deady Hall at the University of Oregon in Eugene was constructed in 1876 as the first building on campus. It was named for Matthew Deady, a judge during the days of the Oregon Territory and president of the board of regents for the University of Oregon from 1873 to 1893.

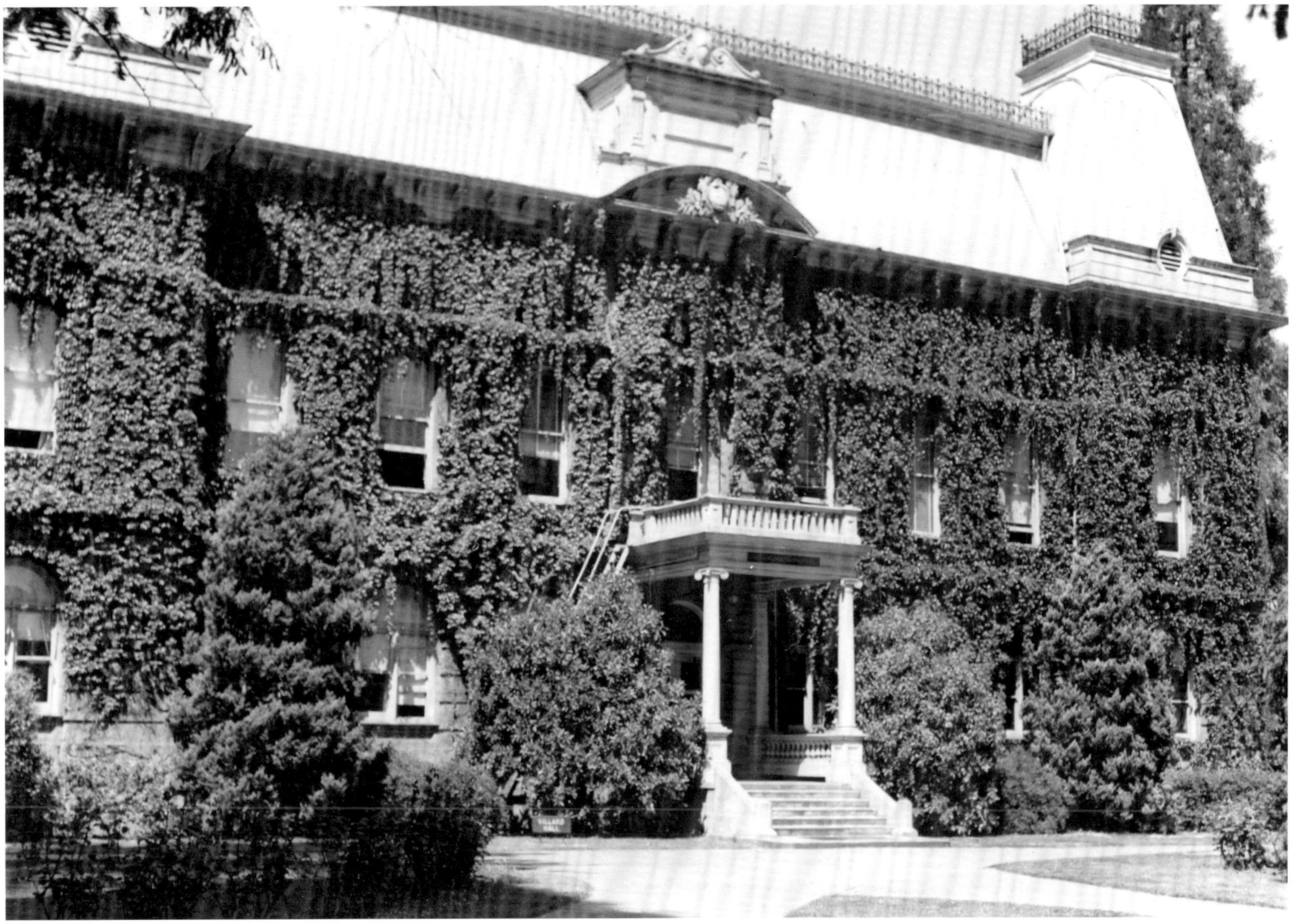

Villard Hall, at the University of Oregon in Eugene, was built in 1886 and named for the railroad magnate Henry Villard, who had made significant financial contributions to the university. Villard owned the Oregon Steam Navigation Company, the Oregon Railway and Navigation Company, and the Northern Pacific Railroad, and would become president of General Electric in 1893.

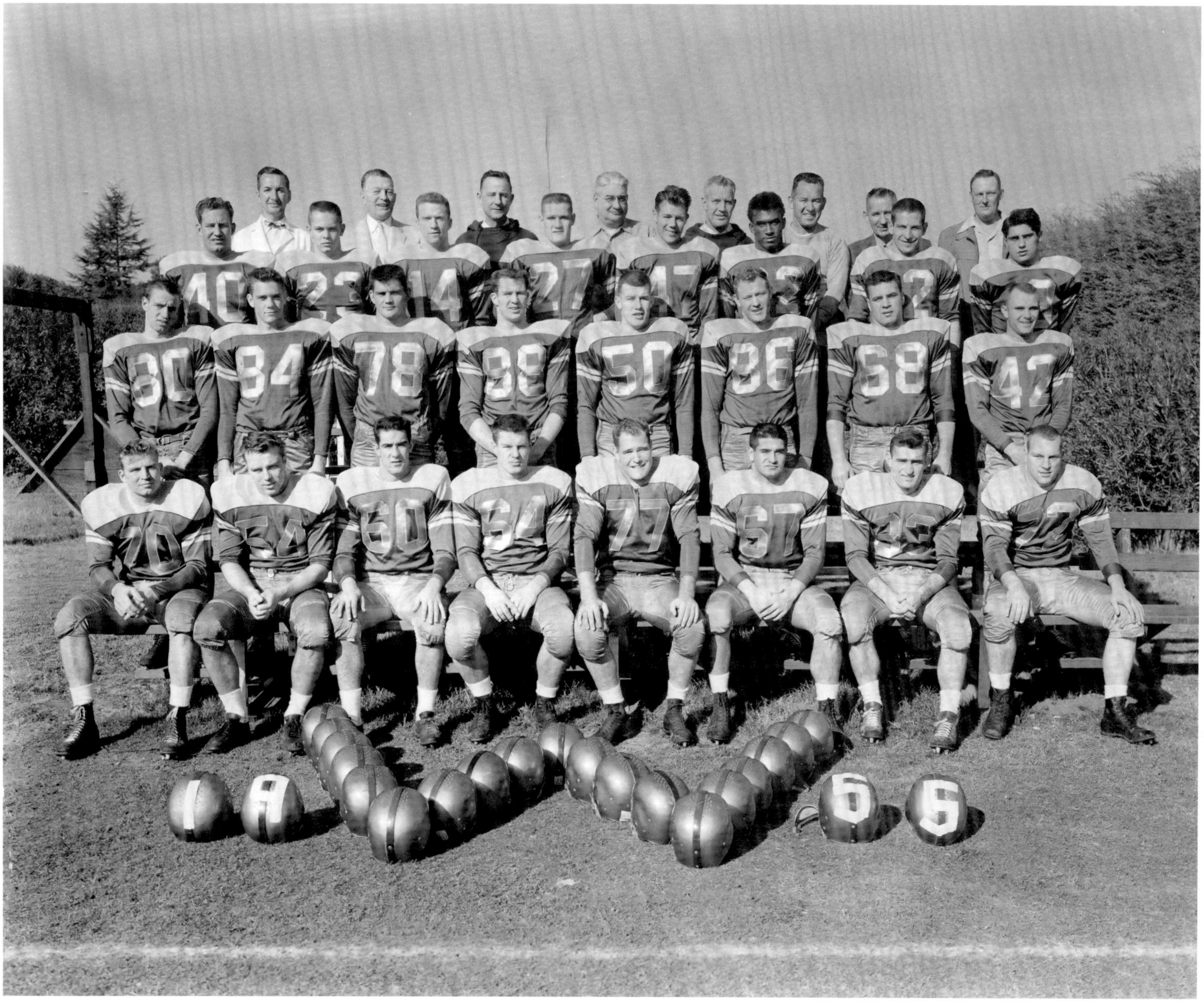

The University of Oregon was established in 1872 in Eugene and has built one of the strongest track and cross country programs in the United States, with many outstanding athletes. Track coach Bill Bowerman and one of his athletes, Philip Knight, founded a shoe company in 1964 that would devise innovative footwear for runners and other athletes, including football players like these fellows, ultimately becoming the corporation known today as Nike.

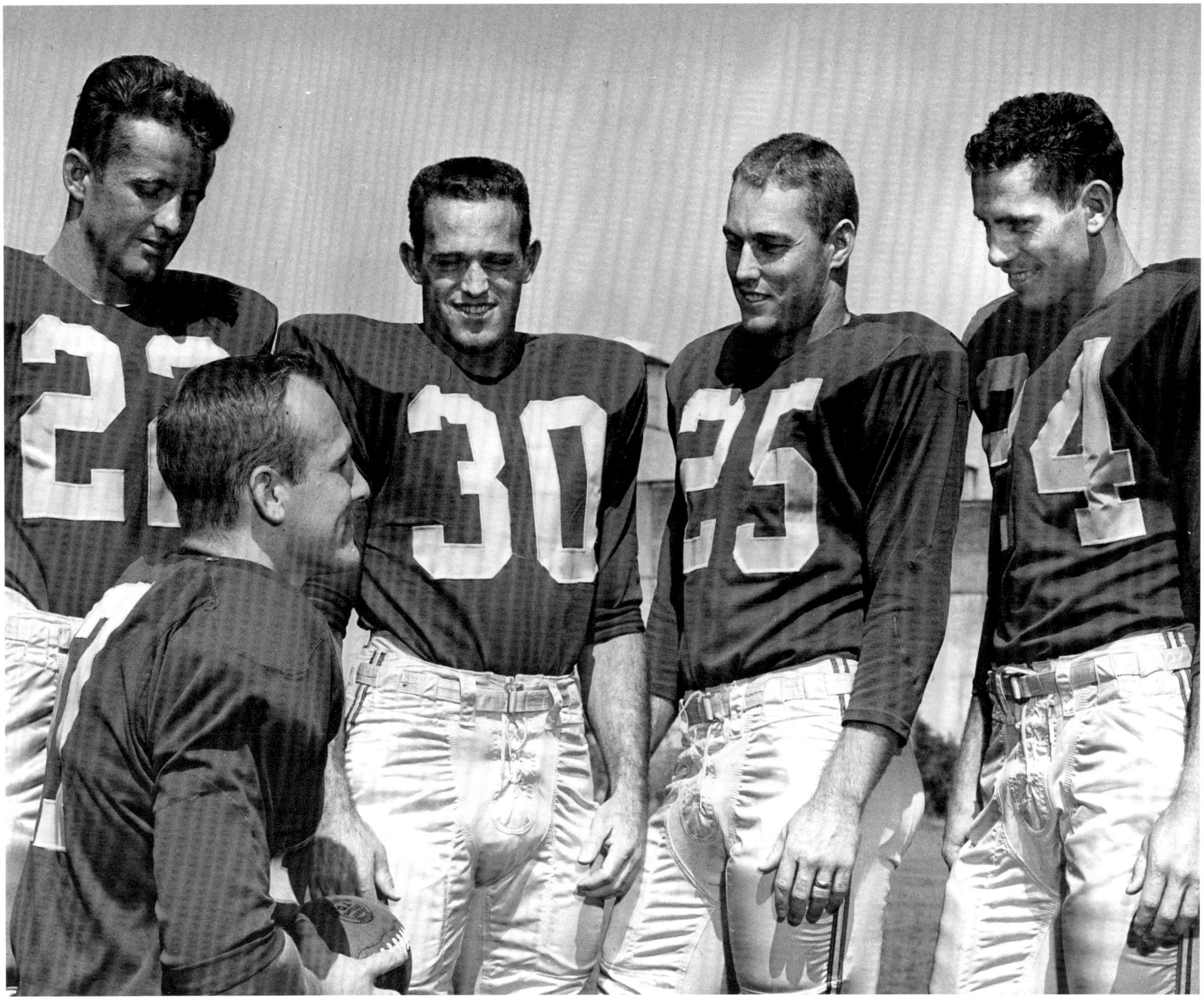

University of Oregon football players discuss strategy in 1957. From left to right are Leroy Phelps, Jim Shanley, Charley Tourville, and Len Read. Kneeling is quarterback Jack Crabtree. Voted Most Valuable Player at the 1958 Rose Bowl, Crabtree would go on to play professional football. In 1967, Autzen Stadium would open as the home of the University of Oregon football team.

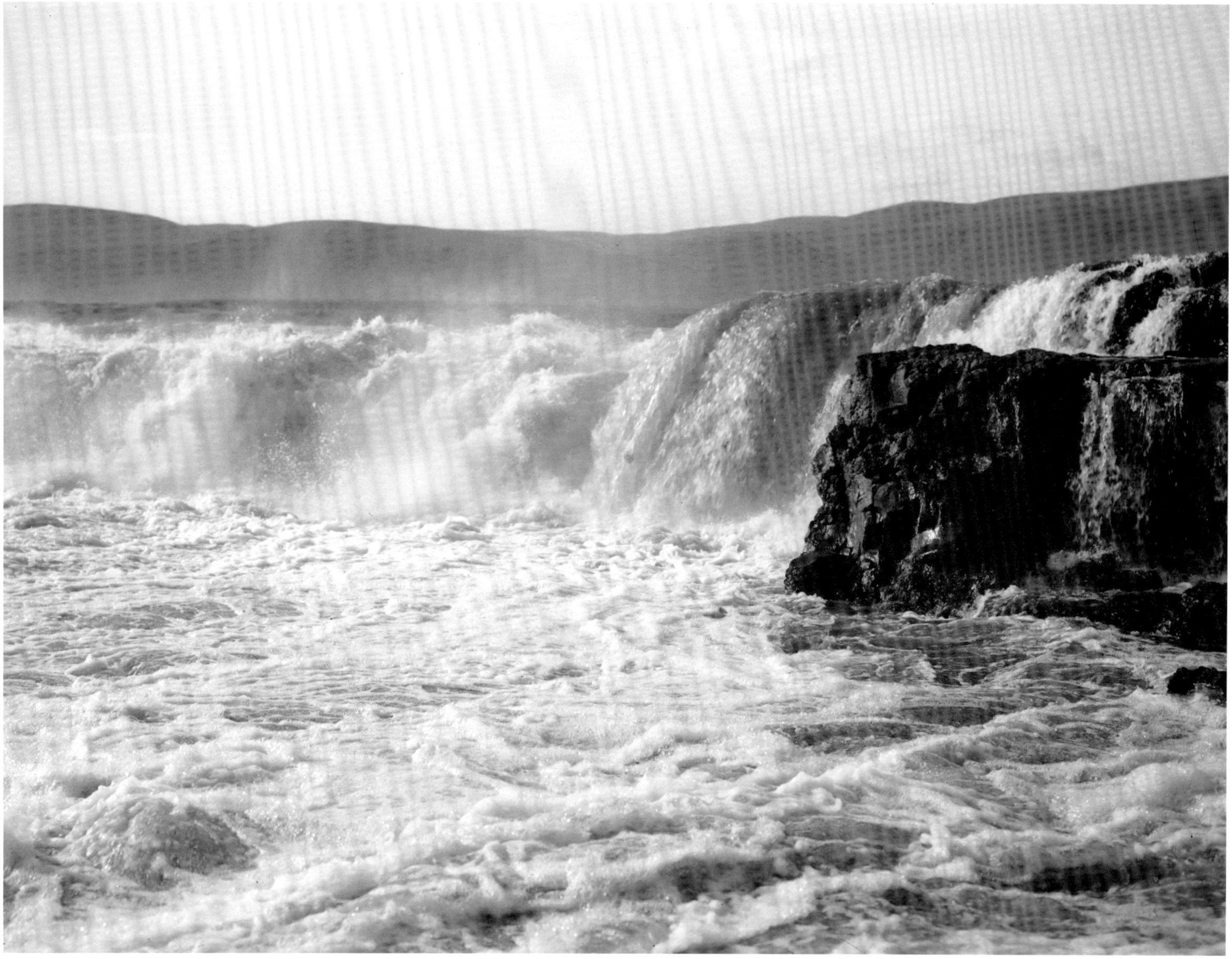

Celilo Falls on the Columbia River on the morning of March 10, 1957, as the massive steel and concrete gates of The Dalles Dam closed off the downstream surge of water and covered the ancient fishing and trading area. In six hours the falls were completely covered by the river's waters.

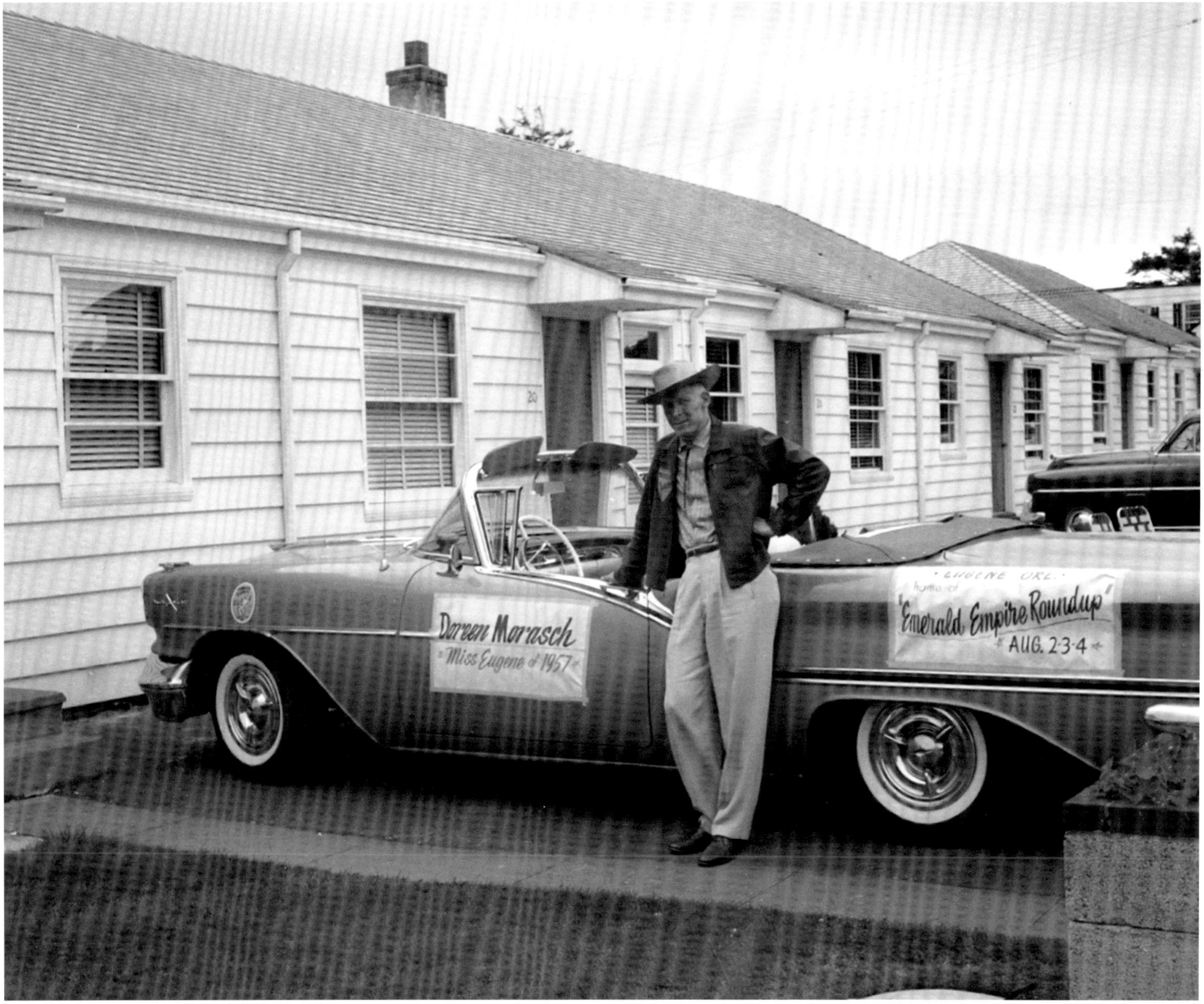

The Miss Oregon Contest for 1957 as advertised at Seaside. In the 1860s, the town of Seaside on the Oregon Coast became a weekend retreat for wealthy Portlanders. Beginning in 1898, the Spokane, Portland & Seattle Railway began service between Seaside and Portland. The completion of the Oregon Coast Highway in the 1930s and the Sunset Highway in 1947 gave automobile traffic access to the town, and increasing numbers of people began to live and retire in Seaside. By 2007 the population of the city was 6,400.

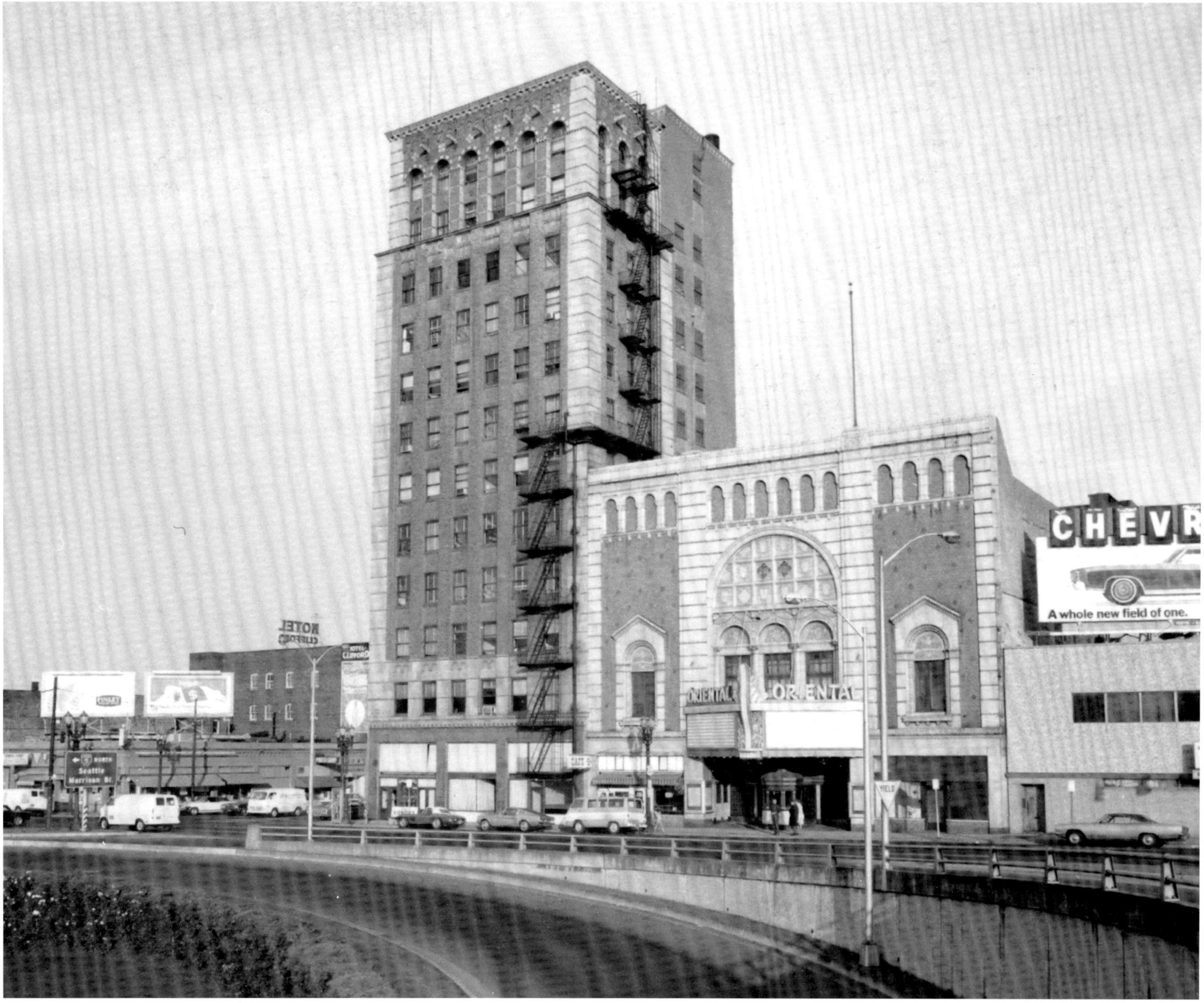

The Oriental Theatre, appointed in East Indian and Cambodian motifs, opened on January 5, 1928, at 148 NE Grand Avenue in Portland with seating for 2,040 patrons. This 1969 photograph shows the theater and the Weatherly Building from the Morrison Street Bridge. The theater was razed in 1970.

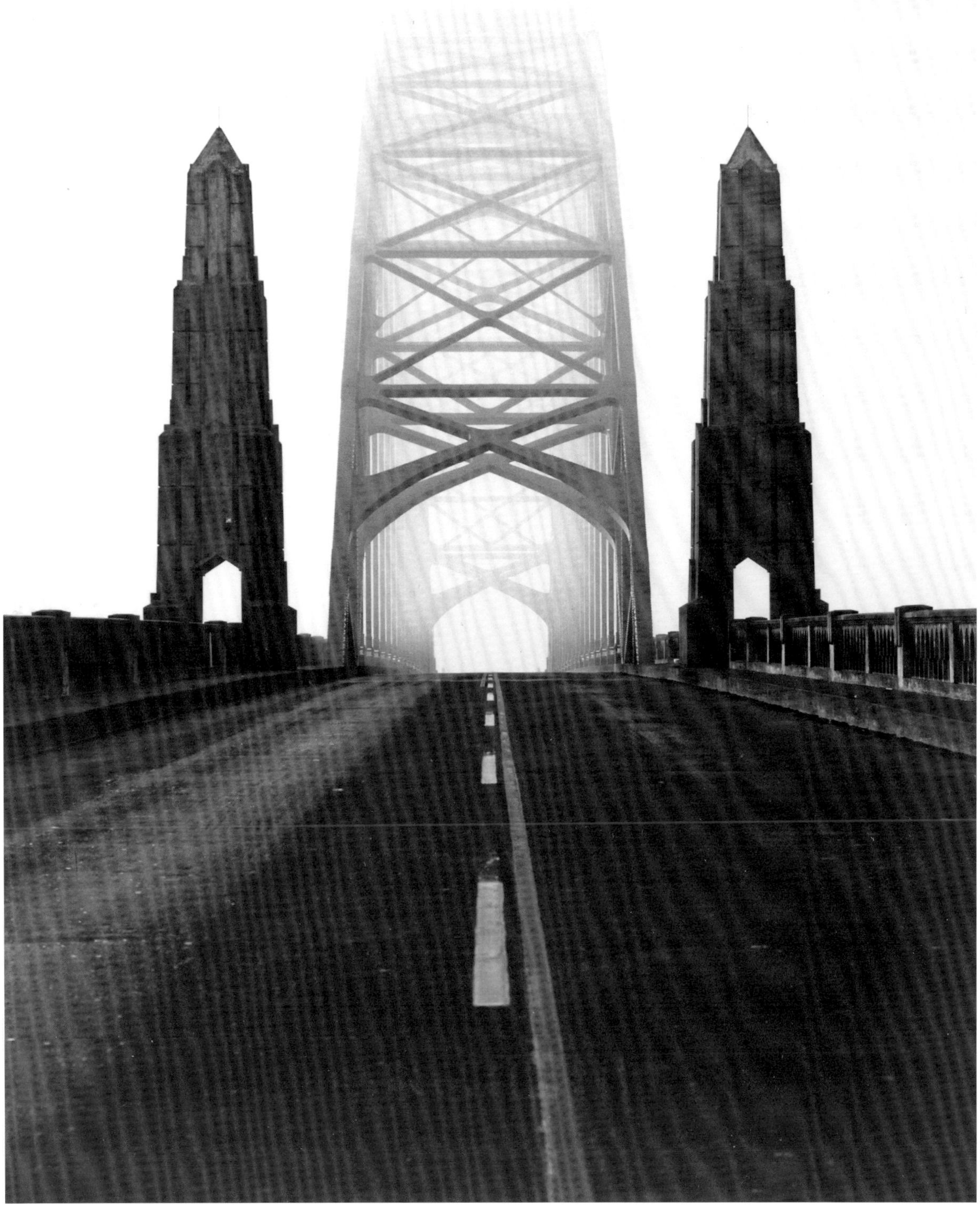

Yaquina Bay Bridge, a distinctive multi-span arch bridge in Newport, opened to traffic in 1936 and is shown here in 1968. Newport began as an undeveloped port on the Oregon Coast in 1865, becoming a financially viable resort, although difficult to reach, through the efforts of Colonel T. Edgenton Hogg and his railroad and steamship business, which was bringing tourists to Yaquina Bay by 1884. Newport was not easily reached by automobile until the opening of the Oregon Coast Highway in 1932, which gave tourists better access to the city.

Jacksonville, Oregon, as it appeared in 1971. The view is at California Street from Third Street facing west. Today Jacksonville welcomes tourists anytime of year, and particularly to the Peter Britt Music Festival in August.

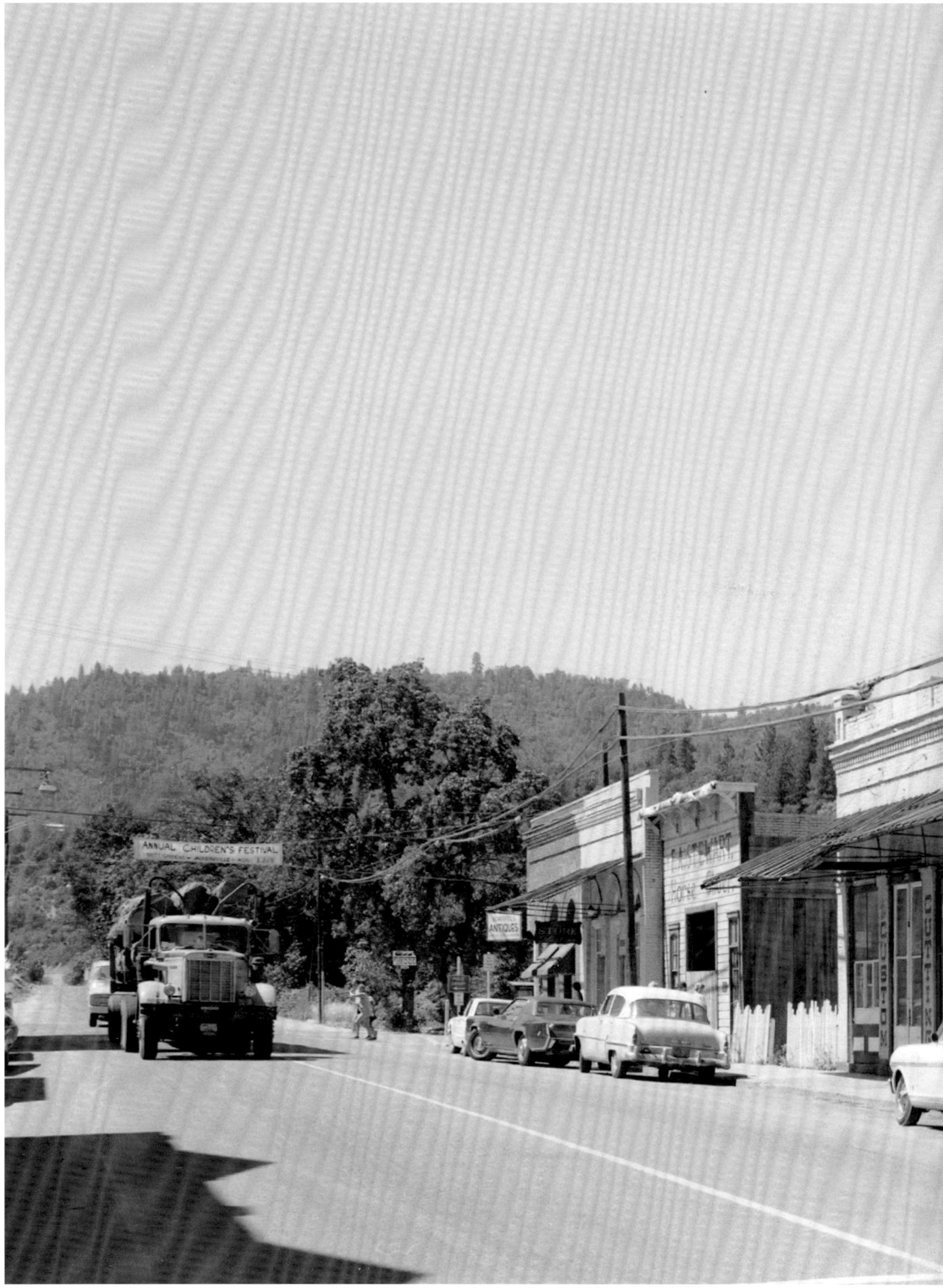

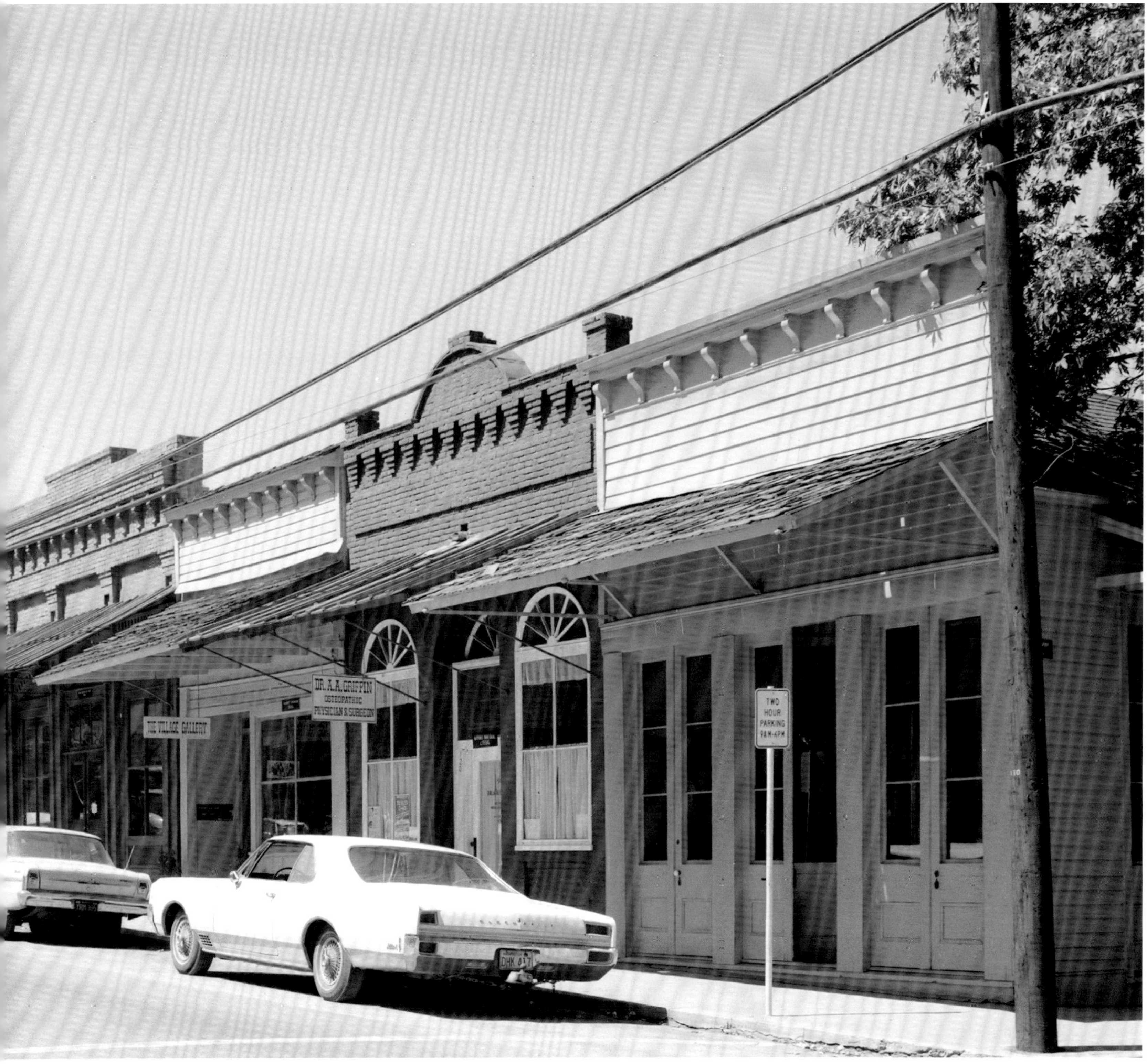
THE VILLAGE GALLERY
DR. A.A. GRIFFIN
OSTEOPATHIC
PHYSICIAN & SURGEON
TWO
HOUR
PARKING
9AM-6PM

St. Joseph Church, at Fourth and D streets in Jacksonville, was constructed in 1858. The discovery of gold in the southern Oregon locale around 1852 led to the founding of the town. When the gold ran out and the railroad bypassed the town, Jacksonville fell into a decline. Efforts to preserve the town proved successful many years later when Jacksonville was placed on the National Register of Historic Places in 1966.

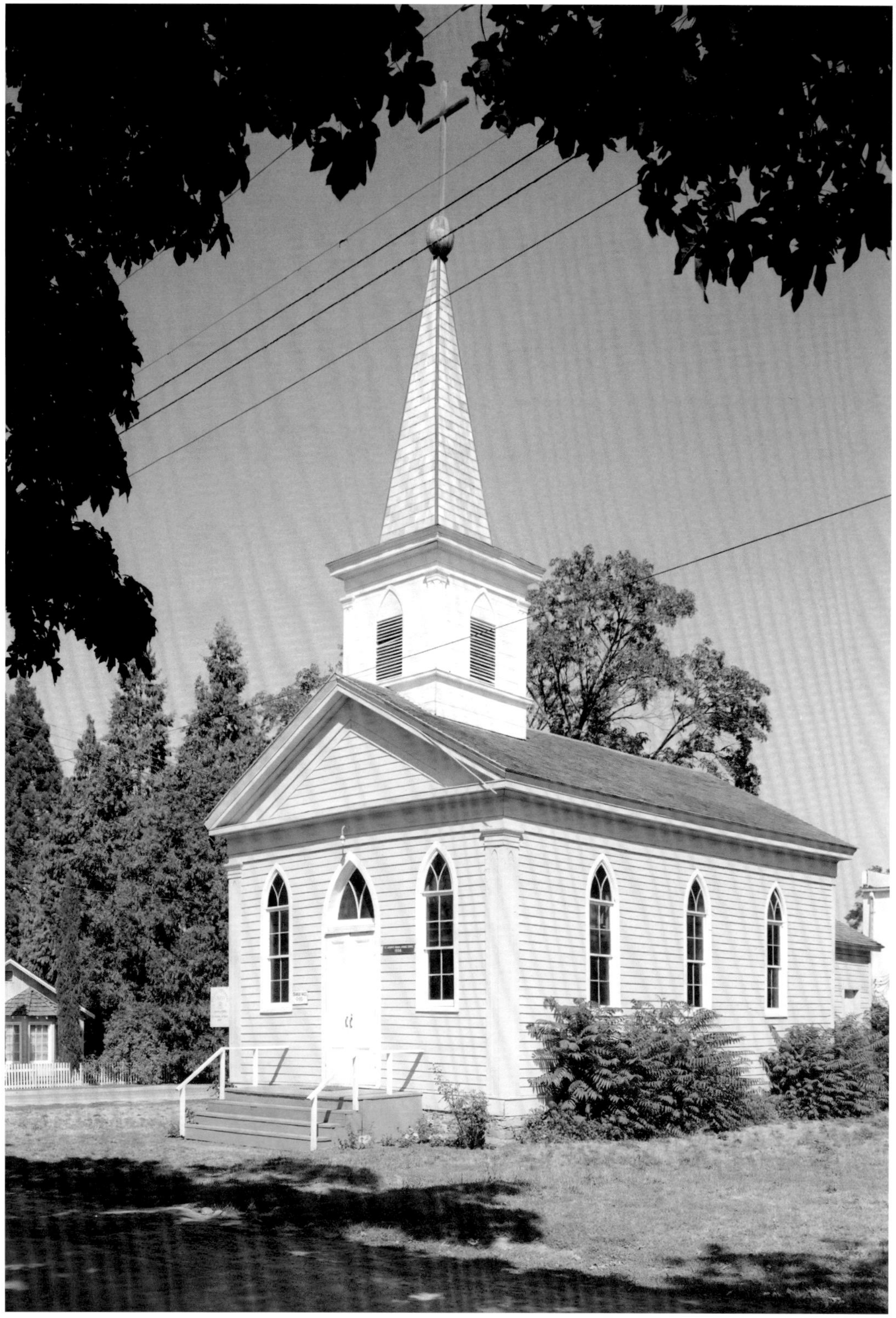

Notes on the Photographs

These notes, listed by page number, attempt to include all aspects known of the photographs. Each of the photographs is identified by the page number, photograph's title or description, photographer and collection, archive, and call or box number when applicable. Although every attempt was made to collect all data, in some cases complete data may have been unavailable due to the age and condition of some of the photographs and records.

ii **Panorama of Portland, 1923**
Library of Congress
6a19789u

vi **Streetcar for Fire Prevention**
Library of Congress
LC-H822-T1904-004

x **Railroad Surveying Crew**
Library of Congress
LC-USZ62-83479

2 **Native American Encampment, 1860**
Library of Congress
3g11416u

3 **Hunters and Quarry in Coast Range**
Library of Congress
3c05466u

4 **Family Encamped near Heppner**
University of Oregon Library
PH004_0315td

5 **Fisherman and His Catch**
University of Oregon Library
PH035_2073jc

6 **Indians as Blacksmiths and Farmers**
Library of Congress
3a53068u

7 **Umatilla Reservation Police Force**
University of Oregon Library
PH036_5090

8 **Early Oregon Classroom**
University of Oregon Library
PH004_0198td

9 **Marshfield from the Water**
Library of Congress
3c25013u

10 **Coos Bay Mining Operation**
Library of Congress
3c25011u

11 **Revolving Pile Driver**
Library of Congress
3c25008u

12 **Unloading Rock at Coos Bay**
Library of Congress
3c18811u

13 **Transporting Rock by Rail, 1890s**
Library of Congress
3c25018u

14 **Scene at Coos Bay Jetty**
Library of Congress
3c25015u

15 **Tillamook Rock Lighthouse**
Library of Congress
09063u

16 **Portland Library**
Library of Congress
15381u

17 **University of Oregon Library Football Team, 1896**
University of Oregon Library
A_ATHFBL1890s0003rb

18 **Picnic at Snoqualmie Falls**
Library of Congress
3b05292u

19 **Panorama of Portland**
Library of Congress
3c20205u

20 **Stagecoach En Route to Crater Lake**
Library of Congress
LC-USZ62-74433

21 **Opening the State's Interior to Commerce**
Library of Congress
LC-USZ62-64403

22 **Multnomah Athletic Club Football**
University of Oregon Library
A_ATHFBLND00 18rb

23 **Public Library at Medford**
Library of Congress
3b38867u

24 **Fishing Nets**
Library of Congress
3b34799u

25 **The Oregon Caves**
Library of Congress
3a42112u

26 **Scene on the Columbia River**
Library of Congress
3a00947u

27 **Oregon City Interurban**
University of Oregon Library
PH008_1058md

29 **An Urban Streetcar Line, 1890s**
University of Oregon Library
PH008_2965md

30 **Timber Industry Log Raft**
Library of Congress
3b03607u

32 **Panorama of Portland and Mount Hood, 1903**
Library of Congress
3c02715u

33 **Oregon Short Line Steam Engine**
Library of Congress
3b40615u

34 **Three Youngsters on Picnic**
Library of Congress
3b05273u

35 **East Side Railway Interurban**
University of Oregon Library
PH008_1159md

36 **Astoria Canning Operation**
Library of Congress
3a51749u

37 **Climbers at the Summit of Mount Hood**
Library of Congress
3b03609u

38 **Oceanside Lark**
University of Oregon Library
PH037_P3100td

40 **Catches of the Day**
Library of Congress
3b34798u

41 **Lewis and Clark Centennial Exposition Grounds**
Library of Congress
3c27725u

42 **Lewis and Clark Exposition Main Entrance Gates**
Library of Congress
3b29493u

43 **Lewis and Clark Exposition Crowd**
University of Oregon Library
PH037_0649td

44 **Clackamas County Exhibit**
University of Oregon Library
PH037_0920td

45 **City Park Monument Commemorating Sacajawea**
Library of Congress
3b46123u

46 **Forestry Building at Lewis and Clark Exposition**
Library of Congress
3b12013u

47 **Forestry Building at Lewis and Clark Exposition no. 2**
Library of Congress
3b05750u

48 **Balloon over Lewis and Clark Exposition**
Library of Congress
3b04466u

49 **Airship in Flight at Lewis and Clark Exposition**
Library of Congress
3a47435u

50 **Exposition Processional**
University of Oregon Library
PH037_0864td

51 **Middle Cascades Mountains**
Library of Congress
3c23513u

52 **STEAMERS IN THE CASCADE LOCKS**
Library of Congress
3b02638u

53 **ONTARIO, 1907**
Library of Congress
6a09036u

54 **ROSES ALONG PORTLAND STREET**
Library of Congress
3c17736u

55 **PANORAMA OF PORTLAND, 1908**
Library of Congress
6a14304u

56 **PASSENGER TRAIN AT PILLAR OF HERCULES**
Library of Congress
LC-USZ62-88930

57 **THE WILLAMETTE RIVER**
Library of Congress
6a14293u

58 **FORT ROCK**
Library of Congress
6a08913u

59 **SECOND STATE CAPITOL AT SALEM**
Library of Congress
3b07447u

60 **PENDLETON ROUND-UP PARTICIPANTS**
Library of Congress
6a28906u

61 **PENDLETON ROUND-UP, 1911**
Library of Congress
6a28929u

62 **HOPS HARVESTERS**
Library of Congress
LC-USZ62-42798

63 **CURTIS PORTRAIT OF CHINOOK ON THE COLUMBIA**
Library of Congress
3b45411u

64 **CURTIS PORTRAIT OF CAYUSE WOMAN**
Library of Congress
3c15021u

65 **CURTIS PORTRAIT OF UMATILLA GIRL**
Library of Congress
3c10503u

66 **PANORAMA OF THE DALLES**
Library of Congress
3c07042u

67 **HOOD RIVER VALLEY FROM VAN HORN BUTTE**
Library of Congress
6a08795u

68 **STEAMBOATS AT CASCADE LOCKS**
University of Oregon Library
PH023_0010jc

69 **HORSE-DRAWN THRESHING MACHINES**
Library of Congress
LC-USZ62-70223

70 **TEDDY ROOSEVELT AT EUGENE**
Library of Congress
3b21382u

71 **HOOD RIVER VALLEY, 1912**
Library of Congress
6a08787u

72 **ST. MARY'S CHURCH AT MT. ANGEL**
Library of Congress
LC-USZ62-85355

73 **PANORAMA OF ONTARIO, 1912**
Library of Congress
6a08894u

74 **BIRD'S-EYE VIEW OF ASTORIA**
Library of Congress
6a09019u

75 **BOATERS ON CRATER LAKE**
Library of Congress
3c36264u

76 **RANGER WITH COYOTE PELTS**
Library of Congress
3c01041u

77 **SUFFRAGETTES AT PROCLAMATION SIGNING**
Library of Congress
11271u

78 **SADDLE MOUNTAIN OF THE COAST RANGE**
Library of Congress
6a14338u

79 **SALMON CANNING OPERATION**
Library of Congress
3b41277u

80 **BUILDING THE HILL TERMINAL AT FLAVEL**
Library of Congress
6a08849u

82 **BOUNTY OF SALMON, 1913**
Library of Congress
3b41276u

83 **CAMP MURRAY AT GEARHART**
Library of Congress
6a32867u

84 **EARLY DELIVERY TRUCK**
University of Oregon Library
PH037_50352td

85 **YOUNGSTERS AT SKINNER'S BUTTE IN EUGENE**
University of Oregon Library
PH003_N580td

86 **On the Pier at Hotel Moore in Seaside**
Library of Congress
6a14314u

87 **Game of Polo in Progress**
Library of Congress
LC-USZ62-95492

88 **Scene at Great Northern Terminal at Flavel**
Library of Congress
6a08933u

90 **Tillamook County Fair, 1915**
Library of Congress
6a27099u

91 **Ships Loading at Marshfield**
Library of Congress
6a08859u

92 **Charles Evans Hughes in Portland**
Library of Congress
22565u

93 **Front Street in Portland, 1916**
University of Oregon Library
PH037_P610td

94 **Southwest Morrison Street in Portland**
University of Oregon Library
PH037_P1813td

95 **Interior of Pendleton Woolen Mill**
University of Oregon Library
PH004_0188td

96 **St. Mary's Academy at Medford**
Library of Congress
LC-USZ62-52054

97 **Second Capitol and Environs at Evening**
Library of Congress
3b33389u

98 **Columbia River Salmon Haul**
Library of Congress
3b04461u

99 **Scene at Jordan Valley**
Library of Congress
LC-USZ62-79366

100 **Crown Point and the Vista House**
Library of Congress
3c06673u

102 **Swimwear of Yesteryear**
University of Oregon Library
PH037_19503td

104 **Scene at Crater Lake National Park**
Library of Congress
3c00993u

105 **Bird's-eye Panorama of Columbia River**
Library of Congress
14563u

106 **Early Rappelers on Mount Hood**
University of Oregon Library
PH037_P1131td

107 **Rider at Davis Creek Canyon**
Library of Congress
3c01039u

109 **Early Aircraft at Portland, 1920**
Library of Congress
LC-USZ62-54137

110 **Routines at Multnomah Athletic Club**
University of Oregon Library
PH037_49285td

111 **Celilo Falls on the Columbia**
Library of Congress
3c07043u

113 **Panorama of Scappoose**
Library of Congress
6a08886u

114 **Curtis Portrait of Klamath Man, 1923**
Library of Congress
3c36575u

115 **Klamath at Crater Lake**
Library of Congress
3c03070u

117 **Curtis Portrait of Klamath Woman in Dugout Canoe**
Library of Congress
3c36573u

118 **Fire in Wallowa National Forest**
Library of Congress
3c00885u

119 **Charred Trees and Timber**
Library of Congress
3c00994u

120 **Vocational Instruction at Salem, 1925**
University of Oregon Library
PH037_45671td

121 **Children at Portland Cleanup Drive**
University of Oregon Library
PH037_AS33td

122 **Wolf Creek Tavern near Medford**
Library of Congress
129843pu

123 Portland's St. John's Bridge
University of Oregon Library
PH037_74512td

124 Bird's-eye View of the Oregon Coast Highway
Library of Congress
8c36714u

125 Interior View of Bonneville Dam Powerhouse
Library of Congress
17395u

127 Bonneville Dam Under Construction
Library of Congress
3c10887u

128 Melon Patch Open-air Market
Library of Congress
LC-USZ62-64441

129 Old College Hall at Pacific University
Library of Congress
131158pu

130 Clearing Growth at Abandoned Homestead
Library of Congress
8b27852u

131 Crater Lake National Park, 1936
Library of Congress
14579u

132 Clouds over the Columbia at Sunset
Library of Congress
LC-USF346-BN-004795-D

134 Two Farmers by Dorothea Lange
Library of Congress
8c36736u

135 Threshing Wheat West of Malin
Library of Congress
LC-USF34-020911-C

136 Migrant Camp in Marion County
Library of Congress
8b34456u

137 Guiding Logs to the Chute
Library of Congress
8b34539u

138 Migrant Camp at Klamath Potato Fields
Library of Congress
8b34875u

139 An Independence Grin
Library of Congress
8b34560u

140 Klamath Woman with Animal Hide
Library of Congress
8b35695u

141 Scene at Migrant Camp in Merrill
Library of Congress
8b35607u

142 Migrant Youth at Merrill
Library of Congress
8b35576u

143 Drawing Water from Willow Creek Pump
Library of Congress
8b35111u

144 Boys with Lessons at Lincoln Bench School
Library of Congress
8b35059u

145 Signs of the Times
Library of Congress
8b35603u

147 Quaker Congregation at Dead Ox Flat
Library of Congress
8b35186u

148 Sweet Potato Harvest at Irrigon, 1939
Library of Congress
8b34934u

149 Western Pacific at Irrigon by Dorothea Lange
Library of Congress
8b34939u

150 Umpqua River Bridge
Library of Congress
3d02341u

151 Malheur County Sheep Shearers
Library of Congress
LC-USF34-039040-D

152 Migrant Labor Camp at Stayton
Library of Congress
8e07338u

154 The New Oregon State Capitol
Library of Congress
3d02337u

156 Family Picnic at Vale, 1941
Library of Congress
8a30361u

157 Cooking Demonstration at 4-H Fair in Adrian
Library of Congress
LC-USF34-039109-D

158 Fourth of July at Vale
Library of Congress
LC-USF34-039609-D

159 Fourth of July at Vale no. 2
Library of Congress
LC-USF34-039608-D

160 Fourth of July at Vale no. 3
Library of Congress
8a30311u

161 Fourth of July at Vale no. 4
Library of Congress
8a30187u

162 Two Youth with Comic Book
Library of Congress
8a30302u

163 Men in Front of Barbershop
Library of Congress
LC-USF3301-013094-M1

164 Fishing at Celilo Falls, 1941
Library of Congress
LC-USF34-070154-D

165 Bonneville Dam and Fish Ladders
Library of Congress
8c22867u

166 Motorcycle Racers at Vale
Library of Congress
LC-USF3301-013098-M4

167 Processing Pears at Hood River Plant
Library of Congress
LC-USF34-070355-D

168 Eastern Oregon Grass Fire
Library of Congress
8a30313u

169 Between Classes at Hermiston School, 1941
Library of Congress
LC-USF34-070500-D

170 Construction of Umatilla Ordnance Depot
Library of Congress
8e01630u

171 Umatilla Depot Construction Workers
Library of Congress
8a30624u

172 Petition Opposing Migrant Workers
Library of Congress
8e04024u

173 Playground at Portland Assembly Center
Library of Congress
3c27897u

175 Air Corps Band at Oriental Theatre in Portland
University of Oregon Library
PH037_P679td

176 Japanese-Americans and Aliens En Route to War Housing
Library of Congress
3c20148u

177 Post Office Workers at Portland Assembly Center
Library of Congress
3c27889u

178 Welders at Kaiser Shipyards
Library of Congress
LC-USZ62-98367

179 Crafting a Propeller for the War Effort
Library of Congress
8e01610u

180 Sheepish Delay
Library of Congress
LC-USZ62-55616

181 Residential Street in Klamath Falls, 1942
Library of Congress
3e02210u

182 View of the Willamette National Forest
Library of Congress
LC-USF34-073130-D

183 Tamolitsh Falls of the McKenzie River
Library of Congress
LC-USF34-073194-D

184 A Load of Logs in Grant County
Library of Congress
8c32416u

186 Grant County Horse-breeding Ranch
Library of Congress
1a34229u

188 Deady Hall at University of Oregon Library in Eugene
Library of Congress
129854pu

189 Villard Hall at the University of Oregon Library
Library of Congress
129852pu

190 Sports Programs at the University
University of Oregon Library
UA_ATHFBL1950s_00010

191 Football Heroes
University of Oregon Library
UA_ATHFBL1950s_00013

192 Last Look at Celilo Falls, 1957
University of Oregon Library
PH037_0947td

193 Scene at Seaside
University of Oregon Library
PH021_beauty_promotertd

194 Last Days of the Oriental Theatre
Library of Congress
130797pu

195 Yaquina Bay Bridge at Newport, 1968
Library of Congress
09503u

196 Jacksonville, 1971
Library of Congress
129705pu

198 St. Joseph Church in Jacksonville
Library of Congress
129790pu